GCSE RELIGIOUS STUDIES FOR EDEXCEL A

Catholic Christianity

with Islam and Judaism

Cathy Hobday, Andy Lewis,
Paul Rowan and Cavan Wood

OXFORD
UNIVERSITY PRESS

OXFORD
UNIVERSITY PRESS

Great Clarendon Street, Oxford, OX2 6DP, United Kingdom

Oxford University Press is a department of the University of Oxford. It furthers the University's objective of excellence in research, scholarship, and education by publishing worldwide. Oxford is a registered trade mark of Oxford University Press in the UK and in certain other countries

British Library Cataloguing in Publication Data
Data available

978-0-19-837046-8

10 9 8 7 6 5 4 3

Paper used in the production of this book is a natural, recyclable product made from wood grown in sustainable forests. The manufacturing process conforms to the environmental regulations of the country of origin.

Printed in India by Multivista Global Pvt. Ltd

Index by Indexing Specialists (UK) Ltd.

Links to third party websites are provided by Oxford in good faith and for information only. Oxford disclaims any responsibility for the materials contained in any third party website referenced in this work.

endorsed for
edexcel

In order to ensure that this resource offers high-quality support for the associated Pearson qualification, it has been through a review process by the awarding body. This process confirms that this resource fully covers the teaching and learning content of the specification or part of a specification at which it is aimed. It also confirms that it demonstrates an appropriate balance between the development of subject skills, knowledge and understanding, in addition to preparation for assessment.

Endorsement does not cover any guidance on assessment activities or processes (e.g. practice questions or advice on how to answer assessment questions), included in the resource nor does it prescribe any particular approach to the teaching or delivery of a related course.

While the publishers have made every attempt to ensure that advice on the qualification and its assessment is accurate, the official specification and associated assessment guidance materials are the only authoritative source of information and should always be referred to for definitive guidance.

Pearson examiners have not contributed to any sections in this resource relevant to examination papers for which they have responsibility.

Examiners will not use endorsed resources as a source of material for any assessment set by Pearson.

Endorsement of a resource does not mean that the resource is required to achieve this Pearson qualification, nor does it mean that it is the only suitable material available to support the qualification, and any resource lists produced by the awarding body shall include this and other appropriate resources.

Nihil obstat: Philip Robinson, Censor Deputatus
Imprimatur + Bernard Longley, Archbishop of Birmingham
4th August 2016

The Nihil obstat and Imprimatur are a declaration from within the Catholic Church that the parts of this publication concerned with doctrine and morals are free from error. The Nihil obstat and Imprimatur apply to Chapters 1–4, 9 and 10. It is not implied that those who have granted the Nihil obstat and Imprimatur agree with the contents, opinions or statements expressed.

Thank you

The authors would like to offer the following thanks:

With all my love and thanks to my family – *Cathy Hobday*

Dedicated to Emily and Tommy. With huge thanks to the amazing RE community who helped with this project – *Andy Lewis*

With thanks to Mary, for the stable, and to Laura, for everything – *Paul Rowan*

For my wife Sarah, Matthew and Martha – *Cavan Wood*

The publisher would like to thank the following reviewers and advisers for their generous help:

Ann Angel; Sheikh Mohammad Saeed Bahmanpour; Andy McMillan, Creator of MrMcMillanREvis Videos; Rabbi Benjy Rickman, Head of RE, King David High School, Manchester; Philip H. Robinson, RE Adviser to the CES; Dr Anthony Towey, Aquinas Centre, St Mary's University.

Contents

You will study **either** Islam **or** Judaism

You will study **either** Philosophy and Ethics **or** Textual Studies

Introduction: *Edexcel GCSE Religious Studies*

This book covers all you'll need to study for your Edexcel GCSE in Religious Studies. Whether you're studying for the full course or the short course, this book will provide the knowledge you'll need, as well as plenty of opportunities to prepare for your GCSE examinations.

GCSE Religious Studies provides the opportunity to study a truly fascinating subject: it will help you to debate big moral issues, understand and analyse a diverse range of opinions, as well as to think for yourself about the meaning of life.

How is the specification covered?

The Edexcel 'A' full course specification is split into **four Areas of Study**:

- *Area of Study 1: Study of Religion*
- *Area of Study 2: Study of Second Religion*
- *Area of Study 3: Philosophy and Ethics*
- *Area of Study 4: Textual Studies*

This book has **four sections** which exactly match the above Areas of Study:

- For Area of Study 1, you will cover Catholic Christianity.
- For Area of Study 2, you will cover *either* Islam *or* Judaism.
- You will then study *either* Area of Study 3 (Philosophy and Ethics through Catholic Christianity) *or* Area of Study 4 (Textual Studies through St Mark's Gospel).

Your teacher will explain to you which Areas of Study you are going to cover in the exam.

How do I use this book?

So that you are fully prepared for your exams, you need to work through each chapter for your chosen Areas of Study. At the end of every topic there are exam-style questions which you should use to test your knowledge and practice your writing. Answering exam questions regularly, throughout your GCSE course, will really help you to be confident when exam term arrives.

In the main topics there are lots of features to guide you through the material; these are highlighted opposite.

Specification Focus provides you with the relevant description from the Edexcel specification, so that you can see exactly what the exam board expects you to know.

Catechism of the Catholic Church are useful Catechism quotations to help deepen your understanding.

Build Your Skills are activities that focus on developing the skills you'll need for your exams, and consolidating the knowledge you'll need too.

Key quotations will appear in boxes like this. Important, learnable phrases within a quote will often be made **bold**. Quotations from the key sources of wisdom and authority listed in the specification, which you will need to know, are highlighted in **magenta**.

Exam-style Questions gives two exam questions so that you can have a go at writing about the information you've studied in that topic. The letter in brackets at the start of each question tells you the question type (A, B, C, or D), and the number in brackets at the end tells you how many marks you are aiming for.

Useful Terms are made **orange** in the text and defined here. All of these key terms are also provided in an alphabetical **glossary** at the end of the book.

Summary provides a short, bullet-pointed list of key information for ease of reference.

At the end of every chapter there are two pages called 'Revision and Exam Practice'. These are designed to help you revise the information you have studied in that chapter, and coach you as you practice writing exam answers.

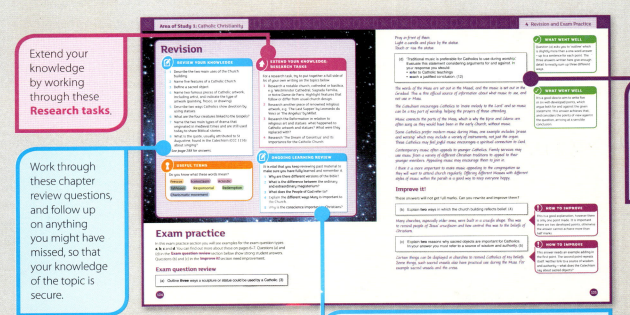

Extend your knowledge by working through these **Research tasks**.

Work through these chapter review questions, and follow up on anything you might have missed, so that your knowledge of the topic is secure.

Exam-style questions, along with sample answers and guidance, help you practice your writing skills.

The Ongoing Learning Review revises key parts of the previous chapter to encourage continual revision.

Know your exam questions!

In your exam, each question will be split into four parts: **a**, **b**, **c**, and **d**. Here they are, explained 'at a glance'.

Part (a)

REMEMBER

One mark is awarded for each correct point.
AO1 only

(a) **"Outline three…" (3)** *or*
   "State three…" (3)

Outline **three** events of the death of Jesus. (3)

Outline **three** ways humans are made in God's image (3)

Write THREE simple sentences
- Avoid anything that could be considered repetition.
- You *can* put multiple points in a sentence, but make sure you are clear enough to achieve all marks.

This is testing your knowledge.

Part (b)

REMEMBER

One mark is awarded for a simple point; two marks are awarded for a developed point .
AO1 only

(b) **"Explain two…" (4)** *or*
   "Describe two…" (4)

Explain **two** ways Catholics work for evangelisation. (4)

Describe **two** differences in the way Apostolic Succession is viewed by Catholics and the main religious tradition of Great Britain. (4)

Write TWO clearly developed points
- Setting out your writing like two paragraphs makes it clear that it is two developed points.
- Use connectives to signal a developed point; the word 'because' is always useful.

Both the 'Explain' and 'Describe' questions are testing your knowledge and understanding.

The 'Describe' question is also testing your ability to understand and contrast the differences between religious traditions.

Part (c)

REMEMBER

Up to 4 marks are awarded for knowledge and understanding and 1 mark is awarded for an appropriate source of wisdom and authority.

AO1

(c) **"Explain… In your answer you must refer to a source of wisdom and authority." (5)**

Explain **two** ways the Trinity is important to a Catholic's faith and understanding of God. In your answer you must refer to a source of wisdom and authority. (5)

Explain **two** difficulties that Jews faced in understanding Jesus as the Incarnation. In your answer you must refer to a source of wisdom and authority. (5)

Write TWO clearly developed points, supported by a source of wisdom and authority
- Setting out your writing like two paragraphs makes it clear that it is two developed points.
- You must make connections between relevant areas of study; for example linking Trinity (1.1) with the Marks of the Church (3.4).
- You are being asked to show understanding of the question topic beyond recalling factual information.
- You must include a source of wisdom or authority which clearly supports one of the points you have made.
- Sources can include quotations from religious texts such as the Bible, the Catechism of the Catholic Church, Papal documents, and theologians.

Part (d)

(d) "[statement]" **Evaluate** this statement considering arguments for and against. In your response you should:
- refer to Catholic teachings*
- refer to different Christian points of view*
- refer to non-religious points of view*
- refer to relevant ethical/philosophical arguments*
- reach a justified conclusion." **(12/15)**

The viewpoints you are required to consider will vary between questions and between Areas of Study.

"The accounts of Creation in Genesis 1–3 provide conflicting ideas about how God created the world." Evaluate this statement considering arguments for and against. In your response you should:
- refer to Catholic teachings
- refer to different Christian points of view
- reach a justified conclusion. **(15)**

"Only formal prayer is really important in worship". Evaluate this statement, considering arguments for and against. In your response you should:
- refer to Catholic teachings
- reach a justified conclusion. **(12)**

You should aim to write at least FIVE or SIX developed points to answer this question.

- Ensure you use a good standard of English and include key words that you have learned (particularly in Questions 1 and 3).
- You must break down the key ideas of the question topic.
- You must make connections between relevant topics.
- You are asked to make a judgment after showing understanding of the question.
- Try to have a 'chain of reasoning' in your answer; how do your ideas link together?
- There may be differing views, approaches or emphasis for different people. You must refer to views from **all** the groups listed in the bullet points.
- You need to reach a considered conclusion based on your reasoning.

USEFUL TERMS

Evaluate: Decide how important, useful, valuable or effective something is. Identify merits and limitations. Justify your decision and come to a conclusion.

HOW DO YOU ENSURE A POINT IS DEVELOPED?

- The PEE method: Point, Example, Explain
- Using a connective such as: because, therefore
- Including phrases such as: as a result, for example, this shows that, this means that

Example:
(b) Explain **two** ways Catholics work for evangelization. (4)

The Church calls Catholics to announce and spread the Gospel (1) <u>as a result</u> missionaries will often work in places such as Africa. (+1)

It is also about living the Gospel in daily lives (1) and <u>this means</u> performing acts of charity or kindness, setting an example to others about what it means to be Christian. (+1)

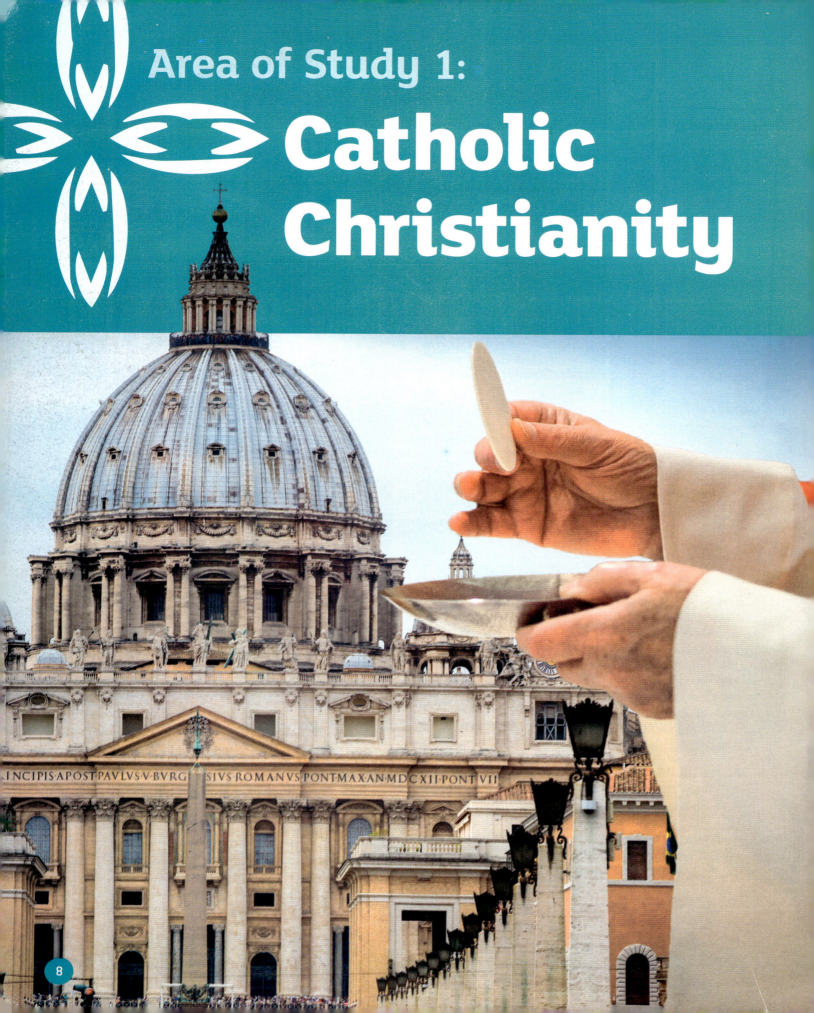

Area of Study 1:

Catholic Christianity

Chapter 1: Beliefs and Teachings

Chapter 2: Practices

Chapter 3: Sources of Wisdom and Authority

Chapter 4: Forms of Expression and Ways of Life

1.1 The Trinity

What is the Trinity?

The Catholic Church teaches that there is only one God who gradually reveals himself in history in three persons, called the Father, the Son, and the Holy Spirit. This 'one God in three persons' (CCC 253) is called the Trinity. This means:

- There is only one God.
- The Father is God; the Son is God; the Holy Spirit is God.
- The Father, the Son, and the Holy Spirit are not the same as each other.

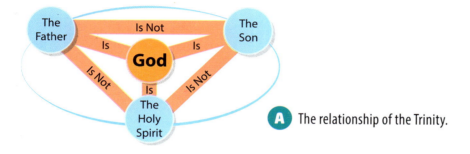

 A The relationship of the Trinity.

The Trinity in the Nicene Creed

- The **Nicene Creed** is the Christian declaration of faith, first drawn up in 381CE at Constantinople (see 1.2).
- Belief in the Trinity is an important part of this declaration, which is repeated by Catholics at every Sunday Mass and major Feast Day.
- The Nicene Creed is both an individual statement of what a Catholic believes, and a shared statement that unites Catholics as one body and Church.

> ❝I believe in one God, the Father almighty, maker of heaven and earth, [...]
> I believe in one Lord Jesus **Christ**, the Only Begotten Son of God, born of the Father before all ages, [...]
> I believe in the Holy Spirit, the Lord, the giver of life, who proceeds from the Father and the Son [...]❞
>
> *Extracts from the Nicene-Constantinopolitan Creed*

The oneness of God and the Father, Son, and Holy Spirit

Catholics believe the **Bible** teaches the nature of God as a Trinity:

- *God is one:* 'Hear, O Israel: the Lord our God is one Lord' (Deuteronomy 6:4). Catholics believe there is only one God.
- *The Father is God:* 'Pray then like this: "Our Father who art in heaven"' (Matthew 6:9). Catholics believe the Father is God.

SPECIFICATION FOCUS

The Trinity: the nature and significance of the Trinity as expressed in the Nicene Creed; the nature and significance of the oneness of God; the nature and significance of each of the Persons individually: God as the Father, Son and Holy Spirit; how this is reflected in worship and belief in the life of a Catholic today.

✝ CATECHISM OF THE CATHOLIC CHURCH

'The Trinity is One. We do not confess three Gods, but one God in three persons.'
CCC 253

USEFUL TERMS

Baptism: ceremony using water as a sign of the washing away of sin and new life in Christ

Bible: the Christian scriptures, consisting of the Old and New Testaments

Christ: means 'anointed one' in Greek, the same as the word 'Messiah' in Hebrew

Denominations: different groups or churches within Christianity

Doxology: expression of praise of God

Eucharist: the sacrament in which Catholics receive the bread and wine which has become the body and blood of Jesus. It is also the name given to the consecrated bread and wine which are received during this sacrament

- *The Son is God:* 'the Word was God […] The Word became flesh and dwelt among us' (John 1:1, 14). Catholics believe the Son is God. The Word made flesh is Jesus.
- *The Holy Spirit is God:* 'when Jesus was baptized […] he saw the Spirit of God descending like a dove' (Matthew 3:16). Catholics believe the Holy Spirit is God.

Catholics also believe that this is God's gradual **revelation** of himself:
- 'outside' them (as the Father and creator)
- 'beside' them, as 'one of them' (as the Son and saviour)
- 'inside' them (as the strengthening Holy Spirit).

The explanation of God as a Trinity is significant for Catholics because it reveals some of the mystery of God, as well as providing a way for them to understand how he connects to them in different ways. Most importantly, the relationships of love within the Trinity teach Catholics about love in their own lives. If human beings are made in God's image (see 1.4), that means they are also made to give and receive love.

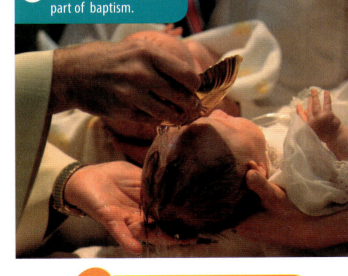
B The Trinity is an important part of baptism.

The Trinity in Catholic worship and belief today

The celebration of baptism

Baptism, which is the entry rite into the Catholic Church and most Christian churches and **denominations**, is performed 'In the name of the Father and of the Son and of the Holy Spirit', as instructed by Jesus in Matthew 28:19.

The celebration of the Eucharist

The most important act of worship for Catholics is the Mass – also called the **Eucharist** – in which people receive the **sacrament** of the Eucharist: Jesus' body and blood (see 2.1). The Mass is full of references to the Trinity. For example:
- It begins with the Sign of the Cross and the words 'In the name of the Father, and of the Son, and of the Holy Spirit'.
- The Eucharistic Prayer is an act of thanksgiving and praise to the Father, in which the Son becomes present in the consecrated bread and wine, through the coming down of the Holy Spirit.
- At the end of the Eucharistic Prayer, called the **doxology**, glory is given to the Father, through the Son, with the Son, and in the Son, in the unity of the Holy Spirit.

USEFUL TERMS

Nicene Creed: the Christian profession of faith

Revelation: truth or knowledge revealed by a deity; the way God makes himself known to believers

Sacrament: a religious ceremony; a visible sign of God's grace

BUILD YOUR SKILLS

1 a What are the three persons of God?
  b In pairs, discuss how each person of God is important in a different way.

2 a What is the Nicene Creed?
  b Why do you think the Trinity is included in the Nicene Creed?

EXAM-STYLE QUESTIONS

B Explain **two** ways the Trinity is reflected in Catholic worship. (4)
C Explain **two** ways the Trinity is important to understand God. In your answer you must refer to a source of wisdom and authority. (5)

SUMMARY

- Catholics believe that God is a Trinity of three persons.
- Catholics do not believe in three Gods, but in one God in three persons.
- The Nicene Creed professes the Christian belief in the Trinity.
- The Trinity is mentioned often during baptism and the Mass.

1.2 The Trinity in the Bible

SPECIFICATION FOCUS

Biblical understandings of God as a Trinity of Persons: the nature and significance of God as a Trinity of Persons, including reference to the baptism of Jesus (Matthew 3:13–17) and historical development of the doctrine of the Trinity, including reference to the First Council of Nicaea and the First Council of Constantinople.

What is a doctrine?

A doctrine is anything that one person teaches to another. It is usually an idea or belief which has support or agreement in a field of study and is passed on to others who wish to learn in that field.

A football coaching manual is as much a collection of doctrines as any document written by the Church. People who have studied and practised the game of football pass on their wisdom to someone learning about the sport. Their doctrines correct mistakes and poor advice about football and replace it with more accurate knowledge. So too, the Catholic Church passes on its doctrines to help people better understand God, themselves, and life. Many of the doctrines passed on by the Catholic Church in the early centuries of its history are shared by other Christians too.

What is a creed?

The Latin word *credo* means 'I believe'. So a creed is a formal expression of what the Catholic Church believes and teaches – a summary of some of its main doctrines. Each of the Catholic Church's creeds (for example the Nicene Creed) was written to correct a mistake (also known as a heresy) that was believed and being taught in the Church.

Historical development of the Trinity

Tradition and belief

Catholics today can interpret the Bible to see how God is revealed as a Trinity within it. However, the doctrine of the Trinity did not come from the Bible. The Bible as Catholics know it today was not compiled until the end of the fourth century.

Before this, over a period of roughly 350 years, the Church gradually came to understand that God was a Trinity by reflecting on the traditions and beliefs used over that time (called the **Apostolic Tradition**). There were many written individual **scriptures** but for the early Church the scriptures were never more important than Apostolic Tradition. The Church used this to work out how God could be one, and yet at the same time how Jesus could also talk about himself and the Holy Spirit as being God.

USEFUL TERMS

Apostolic Tradition: the wisdom inspired by the Holy Spirit which influences the words and practices of the Church

Doctrine: a belief held by the Church

Ecumenical council: a worldwide gathering of all the bishops of the world with the Pope, or his approval

Excommunicate: exclude someone from sacramental participation in the Church

Scripture: sacred writings, believed in Christianity to be the Word of God, set down in human writing under the inspiration of the Holy Spirit

 A Doctrine is a way of sharing wisdom just as a football coach shares his knowledge.

The baptism of Jesus

Some parts of scripture were of course discussed as the Church tried to come to a conclusion. The baptism of Jesus by John the Baptist is recorded in the Gospels of Matthew, Mark, and Luke.

> ❛And when Jesus was baptized, he went up immediately from the water, and behold, the heavens were opened and he saw **the Spirit of God descending like a dove, and alighting on him; and lo, a voice from heaven, saying, "This is my beloved Son**, with whom I am well pleased".❜
> *Matthew 3:16–17*

The baptism of Jesus is important because in that moment God revealed himself as the Trinity. This was used to help develop the **doctrine** of the Trinity (see 1.1).

Disagreements

In the early history of the Church, different followers of Jesus said different things about who he was and how he was related to God the Father. Because of the Jewish origins of Christianity, some members of the Church could not accept Jesus as anything other than a prophet (a spokesman) for God. They did not believe that Jesus was truly God himself, but that he was somehow lower than the Father. An Egyptian priest named Arius (250–366CE) was a key figure who believed this.

Alexander, the Bishop of Alexandria, and Athanasius (Alexander's successor) opposed this idea.

- Alexander **excommunicated** Arius from the Church in 321CE.
- The Roman Emperor Constantine was not happy that the Church was becoming divided and he commanded Alexander and Arius to sort out their differences.
- When this did not happen Constantine called the Council of Nicaea in 325CE.

B 'The Baptism of Christ' by Paolo Veronese (c.1580–1588).

C Alexander, the Bishop of Alexandria.

13

The First Council of Nicaea

This was the first of the Church's **ecumenical councils** (see 3.4). The bishops agreed with Alexander and produced a statement of their beliefs to clear up any doubts – not what is today called the 'Nicene Creed', but an early version of it called the Creed of Nicaea. The Creed of Nicaea contained the crucial word *homoousios*, affirming that the Son was 'consubstantial' (made of the same substance) with the Father. Both are truly eternal, having no beginning, both are truly God. Those who disagreed with the Council used another word, *homoiousios* (meaning 'of similar substance').

Arius and his supporters continued to argue. After much trouble Athanasius, who replaced Alexander as bishop in 328CE, eventually succeeded in persuading the majority that Jesus was *homoousios* with the Father.

The Holy Spirit and the First Council of Constantinople

In *c.* 360CE, the questions that had been raised about the Son being God were also being asked about the Holy Spirit. Was the Holy Spirit God or not? And how was he related to the Father and the Son?

- St Basil the Great, St Gregory of Nyssa, and St Gregory of Nazianzus were very influential in helping sort this problem out.
- Basil put forward the formula that God was one substance or reality in three persons: one God in the persons of the Father, the Son, and the Holy Spirit.
- Gregory of Nazianzus also taught that there were two natures of Christ, divine and human, in his one person.

In 381CE the First Council of Constantinople met to resolve the disputes. This council reaffirmed the Creed of Nicaea from 325CE, but expanded it to underline that the Holy Spirit was also fully God. This new, expanded creed is technically called the Nicene-Constantinopolitan Creed, but is often shortened to the Nicene Creed and it is the best expression of the doctrine of the Trinity.

D The First Council of Constantinople.

 SUMMARY

- A doctrine is a teaching passed on by the Catholic Church to help others know about God, themselves, and life.
- A creed is a formal statement of what the Catholic Church believes and teaches.
- The Council of Nicaea in 325CE produced the Creed of Nicaea, which said that Jesus was just as much God as the Father is God – they were consubstantial.
- In 381CE the First Council of Constantinople declared that the Holy Spirit was also consubstantial with the Father and the Son.

 BUILD YOUR SKILLS

1. a How was the Trinity present at the baptism of Jesus?
   b What were the arguments used by Arius for Jesus being *homoiousios*?
   c What were the arguments used by Alexander and Athanasius for Jesus being *homoousios*?

2. Write a paragraph comparing the arguments and explaining why each man believed they were right.

? EXAM-STYLE QUESTIONS

A Outline **three** Catholic beliefs found in the Nicene Creed. (3)
C Explain **two** effects of the Council of Nicaea to Catholic understanding of the Trinity. In your answer you must refer to a source of wisdom and authority. (5)

1.3 Creation

What is Creation?

The very first words of the Bible are, 'In the beginning God created the heavens and the earth' (Genesis 1:1). These words feature in the early creeds of the Church, which describe God as 'creator of heaven and earth' (Apostles Creed), 'of all that is, seen and unseen' (Nicene Creed).

For the Catholic Church, as for all Christians, there is a big difference between *creating* and *making*. To create means to give existence to a thing that does not exist. To make a thing is to give a new form to something which already exists. Only God creates, while human beings make. The Hebrew language did not talk of God making the universe, but of *creatio ex nihilo*: creation out of nothing.

Creation in Genesis 1–3

The main accounts of Creation are located in chapters 1–3 of Genesis. The first account in Genesis 1 is more of an overview – it describes how God created the various parts of the universe in six days, and then that he rested on the seventh day. Catholics believe the second account in Genesis 2 is a more detailed account of one of those days – when God created man, which according to Genesis 1 was the sixth day.

Genesis 1–2 shows that God is a benevolent Creator, placing human beings in a garden full of wonderful trees and plants. Another sign of God's goodness is that he creates human beings as free. Adam and Eve are told that the tree of the knowledge of good and evil is the only tree that human beings cannot eat from – but God leaves them free to do so. Genesis 3 then describes the first, or original, sin of Adam and Eve: eating the fruit from the tree, and introduces the idea that sin leads to suffering. If humans do not obey the teachings of God, things cannot work out right or happily.

In the Genesis accounts, Catholicism sees God present implicitly as the Trinity. He is the Father who creates everything: 'God said "Let there be light"; and there was light' (Genesis 1:3); but he creates with the help of the Holy Spirit: 'the Spirit of God was moving over the face of the waters' (Genesis 1:2).

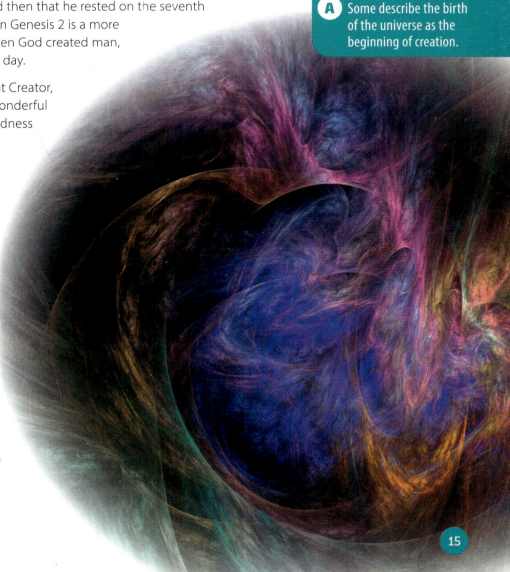

A Some describe the birth of the universe as the beginning of creation.

SPECIFICATION FOCUS

Creation: the nature and significance of the biblical account of Creation including Genesis 1–3; and how it may be understood in divergent ways in Christianity, including reference to literal and metaphorical interpretations; the significance of the Creation account for Catholics in understanding the nature and characteristics of God, especially as Creator, benevolent, omnipotent and eternal.

Creation in John 1

The Gospel of John also refers to the Creation, but focuses on how Jesus was present from the very beginning as God, and as 'the Word':

> ❛In the beginning was the Word, and the Word was with God, and the Word was God. **He was in the beginning with God; all things were made through him**, and without him was not anything made that was made.❜
> *John 1:1–3*

This claim of John is echoed in Colossians.

> ❛for in him [Christ] all things were created, in heaven and on earth, visible and invisible [...] He is before all things, and in him all things hold together.❜
> *Colossians 1:16–17*

John then describes how the Son, the Word within the Trinity, became **incarnate** as man: 'the Word became flesh and dwelt among us' (John 1:14) (see 1.5).

Divergent Christian understanding of Creation

These Creation accounts are understood in different ways by different Christians.

- Some Christians interpret them literally, as an exact retelling of what actually happened. They are often called Creationists.
- Other Christians interpret them as myths; sacred stories which are metaphorical or symbolic and are told to help humans understand that God brought all that exists (including human beings) into being. They believe all of reality has God as its First Cause or Creator (see 9.6).

Most Catholics belong to this latter group of Christians and use scientific theories to help them understand the origins of the universe (e.g. the Big Bang theory) and human beings (e.g. evolution). Indeed, the Big Bang theory was proposed by a Belgian cosmologist and Catholic priest, Father Georges Lemaître.

The Catholic Church would say that science explains *how* the universe and human beings came into being (the physical processes and scientific theories), whereas religion explains *why* they came into being (because God desired that the universe should exist).

The Catholic Church suggests that Genesis was never intended as a historical or scientific book, and that it uses block logic, rather than step logic, which means the truth is contained within it as a whole, not in a step-by-step literal way. Some Catholic scholars have suggested the story of Creation is like a meditation on the nature and purpose of the universe.

B Father Georges Lemaître, 'father of the Big Bang theory', with Albert Einstein.

USEFUL TERMS

Benevolence: the belief that God is loving and good

Catechism: a single authoritative book containing the doctrines of the Roman Catholic Church concerning faith and morals

Incarnate: made flesh

Omnipotence: the belief that God is all-powerful

Significance of the Creation account for Catholics

Catholics can understand something of the nature of God through the Bible, but the correct interpretation of the scriptures comes from the teaching of the magisterium, which is the authoritative and inspired teaching of the Pope and bishops. An example of such teaching is found in the **Catechism**.

When Catholics consider the Creation accounts in this light, they can see:

- God as Creator: 'God said, "Let there be light"; and there was light' (Genesis 1:3).
- God as **benevolent** (loving): 'God saw that the light was good' (Genesis 1:4).
- God as **omnipotent**: 'And God said, "Let the waters under the heavens be gathered together into one place, and let the dry land appear." And it was so' (Genesis 1:9).
- God as eternal: 'In the beginning was the Word, and the Word was with God, and the Word was God' (John 1:1).

In this way, the Creation accounts reveal the first indication of God's loving nature: the gift of the world to man (see CCC 288). God's love was to be revealed more fully later, especially in Jesus.

BUILD YOUR SKILLS

1 a What are the events of Creation as presented in Genesis 1 and 2?
   b What does Genesis 3 add to the account of Creation for Catholics?
   c What does John 1:1–5 add to the story of Creation?

2 In pairs, mind map the different characteristics of God revealed in the Creation accounts, together with the evidence that shows them.

SUMMARY

- There are two accounts of Creation in Genesis 1–3.
- John 1:1–5 provides an account of the Word's (the Son's) role in Creation.
- The Catholic Church interprets the Genesis accounts symbolically: as sacred stories which explain that God is the ultimate Creator of all that exists.
- The accounts of Creation implicitly show the Trinitarian nature of God as Father, Son, and Holy Spirit.
- Creation reveals God as Creator, benevolent, omnipotent, and eternal.

CATECHISM OF THE CATHOLIC CHURCH

'Of all the divine attributes, **only God's omnipotence is named in the Creed:** to confess this power has great bearing on our lives. We believe that his might is *universal*, for **God who created everything also rules everything and can do everything**. God's power is loving, for he is our Father, and *mysterious*, for only faith can discern it.'
CCC 268

C A modern stained glass window depicting creation.

EXAM-STYLE QUESTIONS

B Explain **two** characteristics of God revealed in the accounts of Creation. (4)

D 'The accounts of Creation in Genesis cannot be understood as literally true.' Evaluate this statement considering arguments for and against. In your response you should:
- refer to Catholic teachings
- refer to different Christian points of view
- reach a justified conclusion. (15)

1.4 Creation and the nature of humanity

What is humanity?

Humanity means 'the human race'. Genesis 1:26–31 describes the creation of humans and the power and responsibility God gives them. The Creation accounts are significant in understanding the nature of humanity because they set out God's intention for the human race.

> ❝Then God said, "**Let us make man in our image, after our likeness; and let them have dominion** over the fish of the sea, and over the birds of the air, and over the cattle, and over all the earth, and over every creeping thing that creeps upon the earth." So God created man in his own image, in the image of God he created them; male and female he created them.❞
> *Genesis 1:26–27*

Human beings created in the *imago Dei*

Imago Dei means image of God in Latin. Genesis 1:27 says 'God created man in his own image'. This is important for Catholics because they believe that although human beings are not divine, they possess a relationship with God, their Creator, which is different from that of other creatures. Catholics believe that being created in God's image gives humans dignity, or worthiness.

Here are five ways in which human beings are said to bear the image of God.

1. Human beings are rational

Humans have been given intelligence, and so by reflecting on things in the created world, they can find their way to the God who created them. As St Paul says, 'Ever since the creation of the world [God's] invisible nature, namely, his eternal power and deity, has been clearly perceived in the things that have been made' (Romans 1:20).

 SPECIFICATION FOCUS

The significance of the Creation account in understanding the nature of humanity: the nature and significance of the nature of humanity being created in the image of God, including reference to Genesis 1–3 and divergent understandings of humanity's relationship with Creation (dominion and stewardship); the implications of these beliefs for Catholics today.

 CATECHISM OF THE CATHOLIC CHURCH

'Of all visible creatures only man is able to know and love his Creator. He alone is called to share, by knowledge and love, in God's own life. It was for this end that he was created, and **this is the fundamental reason for his dignity**'.
CCC 356

CATECHISM OF THE CATHOLIC CHURCH

'By his reason, [the human person] is capable of understanding the order of things established by the Creator.'
CCC 1704

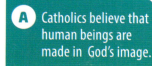
A Catholics believe that human beings are made in God's image.

B Genesis suggests that human beings are stewards of God's creation.

2. Human beings have free will and conscience

Human beings are meant to use their ability to choose in order to choose what is true, not false, and what is right, not wrong. In this way they imitate God. Genesis 3 illustrates the result of a misuse of free will, when Adam and Eve disobey God and are banished from the Garden of Eden.

Conscience is the voice of God within an individual, encouraging them to do good and not evil. These are moral obligations which come from an absolute moral authority, not from a mistaken human authority. 'His conscience is man's most secret core […] There he is alone with God whose voice echoes in his depths' (*Gaudium et Spes* 16). Everybody experiences the obligation to follow their conscience, even if they don't manage to do so.

Once they have sinned, life becomes much harder for Adam and Eve, as seen in the difficulties they face in the rest of Genesis 3. A good example of how sin complicates life can be seen in the example of lying: a liar must have a good memory about what they have said and to whom they have said it. After their sin, Adam and Eve lie and literally 'cover up': 'they knew that they were naked; and they sewed fig leaves together and made themselves aprons' (Genesis 3:7). They hide from God and when God finds them (as an omnipotent God always will), they try to rationalize and pass the buck for what they have done – Adam blames Eve for the sin, and Eve blames the serpent.

Catholics believe God loves humans and is a friend regardless of their sins. When he goes in search of them, Catholics believe the answer is not to hide or try offer excuses, but to repent and receive the grace of God to help make amends, and to turn back to God.

CATECHISM OF THE CATHOLIC CHURCH

'By free will, [the human person] is capable of directing himself towards his true good. He […] is endowed with freedom, an outstanding manifestation of the divine image.'
CCC 1704–1705

C Catholics believe they should listen to their conscience.

3. Human beings can relate to God

To be created in the image of God means that human beings also have the potential to enter into a relationship with the God who created them. Image here means that God has created human beings with a specific goal – to relate to God in this world and to enjoy eternal life with him beyond death.

Some Christian commentators describe the 'God-shaped hole': a longing within human beings which only God can fill.

- In the absence of God, humans experience a deep sense of longing or yearning – which is really a yearning for God.
- Human beings misunderstand this, accidentally or deliberately, as a longing for things within the world.
- Because humans are made by God for God alone, nothing and nobody else can ever satisfy, no matter how wonderful.
- Just as the reality of hunger points to the reality of food, Catholics believe the hunger for God points to the reality of God and heaven.

 Helping the homeless would be a way for Catholics to demonstrate God's love.

4. Human beings can give and receive love

God is a community of persons (Father, Son, and Holy Spirit) who give and receive love to one another and to Creation. If human beings are made in the image of God, this means that human beings are made to give and receive love. They can never fully be whom they are intended to be – whom they are created by God to be – until they too enter into the divine life of giving and receiving love. Human happiness can only come through love.

5. Human beings are answerable to God

The image of God can also be a reminder of the authority of God over human beings, as their Creator. In the ancient world, rulers would often put images of themselves before the people (e.g. paintings, statues, and images of their heads on coins) as a reminder of their authority and power over the people. In Genesis 2:17, God warns Adam that he will be punished if he eats from the tree of knowledge of good and evil: 'in the day that you eat of it you shall die'.

Therefore, to be created in the image of God could be interpreted as humans being accountable or answerable to God for their lives. Those who bear God's image must use their lives to serve him by giving and receiving love, as he does.

The meaning of dominion and stewardship

In the Genesis accounts of Creation (see 1.3), God created human beings last. They are the most important part of Creation, but they are still creatures, not the Creator, and therefore part of Creation. The rest of Creation is 'a garden' (Genesis 2:8) over which God grants humans 'dominion' (Genesis 1:26). 'Dominion' means authority to rule, but the nature of the world as a garden suggests God intended this to be expressed in loving cultivation and care. Human beings are meant to be stewards of Creation.

USEFUL TERMS

Atheist: a person who does not believe in the existence of God(s)

Grace: the blessing and mercy of God

Secular: concerned with the physical world alone, rather than the spiritual

This can create a dilemma for Catholics: the accounts of Creation suggest two apparently conflicting instructions. First to rule or dominate over the earth, but secondly to care for, or steward, it. Many Catholics believe God made human beings superior to the rest of Creation by giving them reason and free will. That is why God entrusts human beings with mastery over nature (Genesis 1:28–29), and expects them to rule with consideration and compassion.

Through the Mass, the sacraments, and the teachings of the Church, Catholicism tries to give to human beings the various spiritual **graces** required to achieve the mastery of self, which CCC 377 identifies as the core meaning of mastery.

Secular understanding of stewardship

Many secular groups have definite ideas about the nature of humanity, which are sometimes compatible in part with the ideas of Catholics even if they do not follow from a belief in God. Humanists do not believe that God granted humans stewardship over the earth, but they do believe humans have a moral responsibility to care for the planet, as this is in the best interests of humanity:

> ❛A humanist's moral reasoning would be based on a concern for the consequences for human welfare and happiness. Our welfare is highly dependent on the environment and the continued existence of many other species. Humanists also appreciate the happiness and inspiration that contact with nature and animals can bring.❜
> *A Humanist discussion of environmental issues*

SUMMARY

- Human beings alone are created in the image of God.
- Human beings bear the image of God in their rationality; free will and conscience; capacity to relate to God; ability to give and receive love; and in being answerable to God.
- Human beings are part of Creation, but superior through reason and free will which makes them stewards of Creation.
- The conflict between dominion and stewardship suggests humans should rule, but with consideration and compassion.

✚ **CATECHISM OF THE CATHOLIC CHURCH**

'The mastery over the world that God offered man from the beginning was realized above all within man himself: **mastery of self.**'
CCC 377

🖉 **BUILD YOUR SKILLS**

1 How would a Catholic explain the idea that humans are made in God's image?

2 In pairs, summarize the five ways in which Catholics believe humans bear resemblance to God, using bullet points and key quotations.

3 a What do Catholics understand by the idea of stewardship?
  b How does this conflict with the idea of dominion?

❓ **EXAM-STYLE QUESTIONS**

A Outline **three** ways Catholics are made in God's image. (3)

D 'The nature of humanity makes humans superior in Creation.' Evaluate this statement considering arguments for and against. In your response you should:
  - refer to Catholic teachings
  - reach a justified conclusion. (15)

E Catholics believe 'mastery' means responsibility to cultivate and care for the earth.

Jesus as incarnate Son

Incarnation means 'en-fleshment'. It refers to God becoming a human being in Jesus.

One of the most important things to understand about Catholicism is that it is not first and foremost a way of thinking, or a system of rules for behaviour, but a relationship to the mysterious person of Jesus Christ. Jesus Christ is the God-man: fully God and fully human at the same time.

In the Trinity, God is both one reality and three persons at the same time. The Gospel of John explains how, at a certain moment in history, the second person of the Trinity (the Word of God or the divine Word) became flesh (human).

> ❝ And **the Word became flesh and dwelt among us**, full of grace and truth; we have beheld his glory, glory as of the only Son from the Father. ❞
> *John 1:14*

When the power of the Holy Spirit came upon the Virgin Mary the Word became human: he was called Jesus of Nazareth, later to be called Jesus Christ (Luke 1:35).

Jesus is the second person of the Trinity, the Word or Son (who has always existed) made flesh: 'In the beginning was the Word, and the Word was with God, and the Word was God' (John 1:1). So he is both God and man at the same time, fully God and fully human. That is why Jesus frequently says and does things that only God can say and do.

Examples in scripture of Jesus' divinity

> ❝ Jesus said to them "Truly, truly, I say to you before Abraham was, I am" ❞
> *John 8:58*

Here Jesus is claiming for himself the name that God revealed to Moses – 'I am' (Exodus 3:14). He claims to have existed before Abraham (who lived possibly 2000 years before Jesus).

> ❝ Heaven and earth will pass away, but my words will not pass away ❞
> *Matthew 24:35*

Jesus is claiming that his words will last longer than Creation itself, because God is eternal and everlasting.

In the miracle when Jesus cured a paralysed man, Jesus said, '"Take heart, my son; your sins are forgiven." And behold some of the scribes said to themselves, "This man is blaspheming"' (Matthew 9:2–3). The scribes knew that only God could forgive all sins. A human being could only forgive sins done against him/herself.

SPECIFICATION FOCUS

The Incarnation: Jesus as incarnate Son, the divine Word including John 1, both fully God and fully human; the scriptural origins of this belief, including John 1:1–18 and its importance for Catholics today.

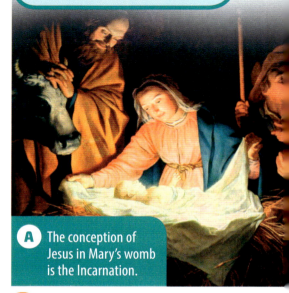

A The conception of Jesus in Mary's womb is the Incarnation.

USEFUL TERMS

Blasphemer: someone who claims the attributes of God or shows contempt or a lack of reverence for God

Blasphemy: saying something about a sacred being which is not permitted by a religion

Incarnation: enfleshment – God the Son taking human form as Jesus Christ

Sabbath: the holy day of Judaism, which begins at sunset on Friday and finishes when the stars appear on Saturday; also the name given to the holy day of rest for Christians which is now a Sunday

Sins: acts against the will of God

Son of Man: a title connected to the Messiah

That is why the scribes condemned Jesus as a **blasphemer**– they thought he was showing contempt for God by claiming to be God's equal in forgiving the **sins** of the paralysed man.

This anger towards Jesus is often seen because people think he is committing **blasphemy**. When Jesus claimed to have existed before Abraham, some people wanted to kill Jesus: 'So they took up stones to throw at him; but Jesus hid himself, and went out of the temple' (John 8:59).

Jesus is often seen not to keep the sacred command to rest on the **Sabbath** day in order to perform some act of compassion or love. He allows his disciples to pick grain when they are hungry on the Sabbath, which would have been a forbidden act of work for Jews. When the Pharisees object, Jesus claims that 'The **Son of man** is lord of the Sabbath' (Matthew 12:8). Jesus is saying that he himself is God and greater than the Sabbath and that nothing is more important than love in God's eyes.

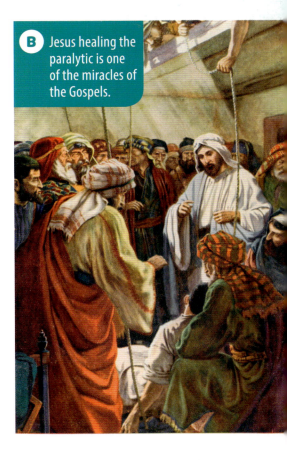

 B Jesus healing the paralytic is one of the miracles of the Gospels.

Why is the Incarnation important for Catholics today?

The **Incarnation**, the physical revelation of God as a man, is as important to Catholics today as it was on the day of Jesus' conception. Catholics believe the gospel – the good news – that Jesus was the divine Word made flesh; God become fully human. He was crucified by the Romans, died, and then resurrected before he ascended to heaven.

- Catholics believe that God became human in Jesus so that human beings might become divine by sharing in Jesus' life through the Church.
- In a certain sense the Catholic Church seeks to continue the Incarnation throughout history, by inviting human beings to share in the life of Christ, through the sacraments and the life of the Church.

C Picking grain on the Sabbath was regarded as working and therefore forbidden.

BUILD YOUR SKILLS

1 a What does Incarnation mean?
  b What was the purpose of the Incarnation?

2 Explain the relationship between the Incarnation and the Trinity.

SUMMARY

- Incarnation means en-fleshment.
- The second person of the Trinity, the Word of God, became human in Jesus of Nazareth.
- Jesus Christ is the God-man: fully God and fully human at the same time.
- Scripture references the Incarnation of Jesus.
- The Incarnation continues through the life of the Church.

EXAM-STYLE QUESTIONS

B Explain **two** examples from the Bible where Jesus claims equality with God. (4)

C Explain **two** difficulties that Jews faced in understanding Jesus as the Incarnation. In your answer you must refer to a source of wisdom and authority. (5)

1.6 The Paschal Mystery

The Paschal Mystery and salvation

The Catholic Church teaches that human beings are saved from sin by the whole work of Jesus Christ on earth, and especially by the Paschal Mystery: Jesus' **Passion**, death, **resurrection**, and **ascension**.

'Paschal' means 'Passover', which is the Jewish celebration of the Israelites' being led to freedom by Moses in Egypt. 'Mystery' means a religious truth with infinite meaning.

There are many similarities between the Old Testament account of Moses, and the New Testament accounts of Jesus. Both were saviours sent by God to lead their people from a state of oppression. The element of blood **sacrifice** in both accounts is also important: the blood of the Passover lambs and the blood of Jesus, the lamb of God. The difference is that Jesus completed **salvation** for humanity.

Catholics believe that salvation has been God's plan to bring people back to a relationship with him, after they turned away through sin. This 'original sin' is recorded in the story of Adam and Eve in Genesis 3 which created the need for salvation. Every human born since then has been carrying the same fracture in their relationship with God.

What is redemption?

Redemption is a metaphor used to explain how the Paschal Mystery 'effected' or 'brought about' the salvation of humanity.

- To redeem is to regain possession of something in return for payment.
- Romans 6:20 describes humans as 'slaves of sin'.
- Just as a slave can be set free – redeemed – by paying a sum of money to their slave-owner, humanity can regain its relationship with God through redemption: 'the Son of man came [...] to give his life as a ransom for many' (Matthew 20:28).
- Jesus' death redeemed humans, to make them 'slaves of God' instead (Romans 6:22).

SPECIFICATION FOCUS

The events in the Paschal Mystery: Catholic teachings about the life, death, resurrection and ascension of Jesus, including reference to Luke 24; the redemptive efficacy of these events and their significance for Catholics today.

CATECHISM OF THE CATHOLIC CHURCH

'[Jesus] accomplished this work principally by the Paschal mystery of his blessed Passion, Resurrection from the dead and glorious Ascension, whereby "**dying he destroyed our death, rising he restored our life**".'
CCC 1067

USEFUL TERMS

Ascension: the moment the resurrected Jesus is taken up to heaven

Passion: Jesus' arrest, trial, and suffering

Redemption: the forgiveness of sins through Jesus' sacrifice; redemption is part of salvation

Resurrection: in Christianity, Jesus' rising from the dead in a transformed body

Sacrifice: to make an offering of yourself or a gift at some cost

Salvation: the process of being saved from sin and returning to God through his grace

A An image from the 2004 film *The Passion of the Christ*. Catholics believe that Jesus suffered to save humanity.

What is justification?

Justification is another metaphor used to explain how the Paschal Mystery brought about salvation. It explains how humans are joined again in a relationship with God. The Catechism talks at length about justification.

- Only a just (righteous, holy, loving) person can be in relationship with God.
- As a man without sin, Jesus was able to pay the price of a sacrifice to God.
- Humans are then 'justified by his grace' (CCC 1992). They live by Jesus' grace.

What does the Catholic Church teach?

The life of Jesus

It is important to remember that, during his lifetime, most followers of Jesus did not understand that he was God. It was only after Jesus' death that the early Christians realized that he was God moving among his people: 'The Word was God [...] the Word became flesh' (John 1:1–14). The Church believes that Jesus' life reveals at least four reasons for his presence:

- 'The Word became flesh for us in order to save us' (CCC 457).
- 'The Word became flesh so that we might know God's love' (CCC 458).
- 'The Word became flesh to be our model of holiness' (CCC 459).
- 'The Word became flesh to make us partakers of the divine nature' (2 Peter 1:4). Jesus was sent to share the grace of God. Humans can live with God's life.

The death of Jesus

- The Gospels relate a spiritual battle between Jesus and the powers that oppose him. Jesus faces cowardice, betrayal, denial, lies, religious and institutional corruption, violence, cruelty, and injustice.
- Jesus did not behave in the same way but responded with forgiveness: 'Father, forgive them; for they know not what they do' (Luke 23:34).
- Catholics, like all Christians, believe that Jesus erased the sins of the world with God's mercy, because it was God himself, not a mere human being, who died on the cross.

The resurrection of Jesus

The Catholic Church teaches that Jesus rose again to life after three days, according to the scriptures:

> ❝the men said to them, "Why do you seek the living among the dead? He is not here, but has risen. Remember how he told you, while he was still in Galilee, that the Son of man must be delivered into the hands of sinful men, and be crucified, and on the third day rise."❞
> *Luke 24:5–7*

- Christian faith and the Catholic Church are founded on the fact of the resurrection of Jesus.
- The resurrection proves that Jesus is God – no one but God can conquer death.

✝ CATECHISM OF THE CATHOLIC CHURCH

'Justification detaches man from sin which contradicts the love of God and purifies his heart of sin. Justification follows upon God's merciful initiative of offering forgiveness. **It reconciles man with God.** It frees from the enslavement to sin, and it heals.'
CCC 1990

B The resurrection of Jesus.

- The resurrection is not a past event, but a present event. Jesus *is* risen, and that is an important distinction: "'I am with you always'" (Matthew 28:20).
- Christ had a transformed risen body, and so will humans after death.

The ascension of Jesus

The Catholic Church teaches that Jesus' ascension to heaven prepares the way for humans to follow him. Jesus does not die before he ascends; he retains his physical, risen body. The ascension does not undo the Incarnation.

> Then [Jesus] led [the disciples] out as far as Bethany, and lifting up his hands he blessed them. While he blessed them, he parted from them and was carried up into heaven.
> *Luke 24:50–51*

In the Incarnation, humanity was united with divinity in Jesus. When God raised Jesus from the dead and took him into heaven at the ascension, Jesus' risen human body and soul were taken up into God. The ascension was also the 'letting go' of Jesus, necessary so that the Holy Spirit could come at Pentecost and continue Jesus' work in the Church.

What is redemptive efficacy?

This is another way of asking: how does the Paschal Mystery bring about human salvation? The answer is that it saves humans from eternal death and separation from God. The passion and death of Jesus allowed the redemption of humanity.

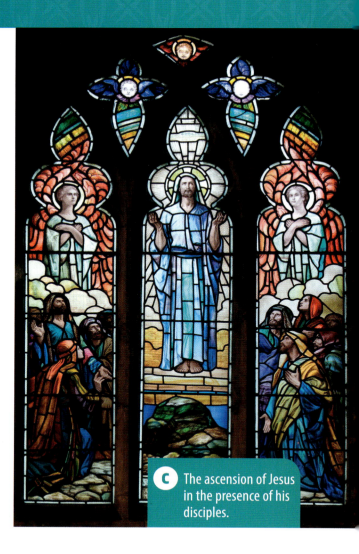

C The ascension of Jesus in the presence of his disciples.

SUMMARY

- Human beings are saved from sin by the work of Jesus Christ on earth but especially by the Paschal Mystery.
- The Paschal Mystery is the Passion, death, resurrection, and ascension of Jesus.
- Redemption is a metaphor used to explain how the Paschal Mystery 'brought about' salvation.
- Justification explains how the Paschal Mystery restores humans to a just relationship with God.
- Jesus' resurrection is the foundation of the Christian faith and the Catholic Church.
- The ascension prepares the way for humans to follow Jesus to heaven and for the Holy Spirit to continue the work of salvation within the Church.

BUILD YOUR SKILLS

1 a What does redemption mean for Catholics?
   b Why do Catholics believe redemption is necessary?

2 In pairs, discuss how each part of the Paschal Mystery shows redemption, justification, and salvation.

EXAM-STYLE QUESTIONS

B Explain **two** reasons why the Pascal Mystery is important for Catholics. (4)
C Explain **two** ways the resurrection is significant for Catholics today. In your answer you must refer to a source of wisdom and authority. (5)

1.7 The significance of the Paschal Mystery

The Holy Spirit as God's grace

At the ascension the apostles receive their **evangelizing** mission to proclaim and live out the Gospel: 'Go therefore and make disciples of all nations' (Matthew 28:19) (see 2.8). But Jesus also told them to wait in Jerusalem for the Holy Spirit to come to help them in that mission (Acts 1:1–5, 8).

- The apostles were empowered for their mission by the Holy Spirit at Pentecost (Acts 2).
- This is the event where the Holy Spirit came down from heaven and entered the apostles.
- It is regarded as the beginning of the Christian Church.

The Holy Spirit is both an expression of God's grace and the means by which it is experienced. The Holy Spirit helped Jesus' apostles and the members of the Church who have come after them down the centuries to understand and live out more fully the salvation that the Paschal Mystery brought.

Why is the Holy Spirit important?

Jesus told the disciples that the Holy Spirit would come in his place:

> ❛It is to your advantage that I go away, for if I do not go away, the Counsellor [the Holy Spirit] will not come to you; but if I go, I will send him to you.❜
>
> *John 16:7*

🔍 SPECIFICATION FOCUS

The significance of the life, death, resurrection and ascension of Jesus for Catholic beliefs about salvation and grace, including John 3:10–21 and Acts 4:8–12; the implications and significance of these events for Catholic practice today.

🔑 USEFUL TERM

Evangelizing: proclaiming and living out the Gospel or good news of Jesus

Westbu

A The dove is often used as a symbol of the Holy Spirit.

This suggests that the Holy Spirit had a particular role to play in the plan of salvation. This role began after Jesus ascended. The Spirit brings Christians into an ever more intimate relationship with the Father and with Jesus.

It is clear, for example, that Peter knew Jesus and his life, death, resurrection, and ascension better, more intimately and accurately, in the Acts of the Apostles than in the Gospels – after the Holy Spirit had come. St Theophilus of Antioch described the Holy Spirit as 'wisdom'. Sometimes it is the wisdom of hindsight that enables the true meaning of past events to be seen.

The Holy Spirit today

For Catholics, the Holy Spirit makes Jesus bodily present to all those who receive him in the Eucharist (see page 29) and the Holy Spirit. The historical, bodily Jesus is separated from Christians by 2,000 years and where he lived is over 2,000 miles from the UK. But the Holy Spirit makes Jesus known here as easily as Jesus made the Father known to the people of Jerusalem because the Holy Spirit is part of the Trinity:

- the Father is the transcendent God outside us;
- the Son is God beside us as one of us;
- the Spirit is God inside us.

The Spirit is the most intimate connection, the bond of intense love, between the Father and the Son.

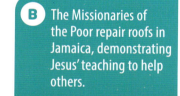

USEFUL TERM

Ordained: take holy orders as a priest, bishop or deacon

Repentance: saying sorry to God for sins

Choosing to accept salvation

Catholics believe that the events of the Paschal Mystery brought salvation for all:

> ❝For God sent the Son into the world, not to condemn the world, but that the world might be saved through him.❞
> *John 3:17*

However, it is important to realize that this does not mean everyone is automatically saved. The concept of free will means that God can only *offer* salvation: it is up to the individual to accept that offer.

Peter rebuked the Jewish elders who did not believe in Jesus, as having failed to accept his offer of salvation: 'This is the stone which was rejected by you' (Acts 4:11). If individuals accept the offer of salvation, this does not mean they have 'saved themselves'; they have accepted that Jesus has saved them from sin through his sacrifice.

B The Missionaries of the Poor repair roofs in Jamaica, demonstrating Jesus' teaching to help others.

> ❝And there is salvation in no one else, for there is no other name under heaven given among men by which we must be saved.❞
> *Acts 4:12*

There is then a 'price' to be paid by everyone – to live by and exemplify the teachings of Jesus: 'If any one serves me, he must follow me' (John 12:26). The implication is that salvation is an ongoing process, something to be lived out every day of a Christian life, and shared with others.

The significance of salvation and grace

For Catholics, the Mass (the Eucharist) and the sacramental life of the Church are the sources for experiencing salvation and receiving the grace necessary to continue Jesus' saving mission today (see 2.1, 2.2, and 2.8).

C Catholics receiving the body and blood of Christ in the Mass.

- In Baptism, humans are redeemed from slavery to sin, are justified (see 1.6), and are made adopted children of God in Jesus.
- In Confirmation, humans receive a fresh outpouring of God's grace through the Holy Spirit to strengthen them to continue Jesus' saving mission.
- In the Sacrament of Reconciliation, the **repentance** of sin forgiven by God's grace, frees humans again from slavery to personal sin.
- In the Sacraments of Matrimony and Holy Orders, the graces needed in the vocation of marriage and family life or as an **ordained** minister of the Church are received.
- In the Sacrament of the Sick, God's healing grace and strength unite the suffering of individuals with Christ's Passion.
- In the Mass, and especially in Holy Communion, the Sacrament of the Eucharist, Catholics receive Christ's body and blood, the same body and blood that were broken and poured out, and raised to new life at the resurrection, to redeem humanity.

The Eucharist is the Paschal Mystery made present again sacramentally. Catholics believe they receive, in the form of consecrated bread and wine, the same Christ who died, was raised from the dead, and is risen today. The Holy Spirit changes the bread and wine into the real presence of Christ.

- Participating in the Eucharist is a sign of acceptance of God's offer of salvation.
- It is also the bestowal of God's grace through the presence of Jesus in the sacrament, strengthening the individual in their life of faith and love.

 BUILD YOUR SKILLS

1 a Draw a diagram to explain the relationship of the Father, Son, and Holy Spirit.
   b How is the presence of the Holy Spirit different to the presence of Jesus?
   c Why is this important for Catholics?

2 Choose three of the sacraments and explain how they communicate salvation and grace for Catholics.

 EXAM-STYLE QUESTIONS

A Outline **three** ways the Holy Spirit works in the Church. (3)
B Explain **two** ways the Paschal Mystery brings salvation. (4)

SUMMARY

- The Holy Spirit helps the Church to understand, and live out more fully, salvation.
- Humans cannot save themselves, but can choose to accept salvation.
- Catholics participate in the Paschal Mystery through the life of the Church.
- God's grace gives Catholics strength to do this through the liturgy and the sacraments.
- The Eucharist is the most important expression of the Paschal Mystery in the Church today.

What is eschatology?

Ta eschata is Greek for 'the last things'. Eschatology is the study of Christian teaching about the last things for a human life and soul: death, judgment, heaven, hell, and **purgatory**.

Life after death

Before his death while he was still ministering, Jesus talked about resurrection and everlasting life:

> ❝Jesus said to her, "I am the resurrection and the life; he who believes in me, though he die, yet shall he live, and whoever lives and believes in me shall never die."❞
> *John 11: 25–26*

Based on Jesus' words as recorded in the Gospels, the Catholic Church teaches that life after death is not only caused by Jesus, but it is found *in* Jesus. Catholics believe they share in eternal life after death because they are part of the body of Christ through the Catholic Church (see 3.5).

There are many ideas in society and other religions about what happens after death, including reincarnation, becoming angels or ghosts, or even that death is the absolute end. These are not part of Catholic belief.

For Catholics, life after death is explained through the Paschal Mystery: the death and resurrection of Jesus. Catholics believe that after death, they will be resurrected. The resurrection of Jesus is proof that this will take place. However, unlike Jesus this does not take place immediately. The Catechism explains that humans do not receive their glorified bodies straight away. The soul of the individual is taken to a first judgment to determine whether individuals are able to enter heaven.

What is judgment?

St Paul suggests that judgment will be a reality for everyone because human beings are made in the image of God and are therefore answerable to God for what they have done with the gift of life:

> ❝For we must all appear before the judgment seat of Christ, so that each one may receive good or evil, according to what he has done in the body.❞
> *2 Corinthians 5:10*

Catholics believe that there are two types of judgment: Particular and General (Last).

SPECIFICATION FOCUS

Catholic beliefs about eschatology: life after death; the nature of resurrection, judgment, heaven, hell and purgatory, including reference to John 11:17–27 and 2 Corinthians 5:1–10; divergent Christian beliefs about life after death, with reference to purgatory and the nature of resurrection; why belief in life after death is important for Catholics today.

CATECHISM OF THE CATHOLIC CHURCH

'The Christian meaning of death is revealed in the light of the Paschal mystery of the death and resurrection of Christ in whom resides our only hope.'
CCC 1681

USEFUL TERM

Purgatory: a place or state of purposeful suffering where the souls of sinners are purified before going to heaven

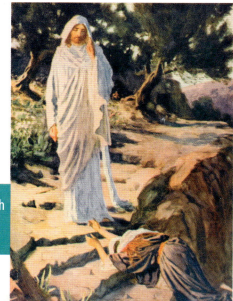

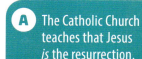 **A** The Catholic Church teaches that Jesus *is* the resurrection.

Particular judgment is the first judgment of an individual's life and asks whether the person has lived a life of love, has repented of their sins, and has tried to follow Jesus' example. As a result of this the person will:

- enter heaven immediately if they die in a state of perfection
- enter heaven after a state of purification called purgatory in which anything that is not love, e.g. hateful attitudes, is removed
- be sent to hell if they have demonstrated an unwillingness to love and are set in **unrepented sin**.

The Day of Judgment refers to the end of time when General or Last judgment will be made. Every person's earthly body will be resurrected and reunited with their soul, whether they are in heaven, purgatory or hell. In the **Parable** of the Sheep and Goats, Jesus explained how they would be judged by the Son of Man:

> ❝"Before him will be gathered all the nations, and he will separate them one from another as a shepherd separates the sheep from the goats, [...] Then the King will say to those at his right hand, 'Come, O blessed of my Father, **inherit the kingdom prepared for you** from the foundation of the world;[...] Then he will say to those at his left hand, 'Depart from me, you cursed, into the eternal fire prepared for the devil and his angels;[...] And they will go away into eternal punishment, but the righteous into eternal life."❞
> *Matthew 25:32, 34, 41, 46*

The Catholic Church teaches that General judgment is final, and eternal: 'the Last Judgment will reveal that God's justice triumphs over all the injustices committed by his creatures and that God's love is stronger than death' (CCC1040).

What is the nature of resurrection?

Not all Christians agree about the nature of resurrection and whether it is just the soul or their physical body that will be resurrected. The Catholic Church teaches that resurrection is when a person's soul is reunited with their 'glorified' (CCC 997) body. St Paul describes this glorified body as 'a building from God, a house not made with hands, eternal in the heavens' (2 Corinthians 5:1).

Although Jesus' body was raised from the tomb, 'he did not return to an earthly life' (CCC 999). There was something familiar but also unfamiliar about Jesus' resurrected body. At times his disciples did not always recognize him at first. For example in Luke 24:13–32, the disciples on the road to Emmaus think Jesus is a stranger on the road; and in John 20:11–16, Jesus has a conversation with Mary of Magdala who thinks he is a gardener.

The Church teaches human beings 'will rise again with their own bodies which they now bear, but Christ will change [their] lowly body to be like his glorious body' (CCC 999). The Church does not know how God will do this; not everything can be explained (CCC 268).

CATECHISM OF THE CATHOLIC CHURCH

'What is 'rising'? In death, the separation of the soul from the body, the human body decays and the soul goes to meet God, while awaiting its reunion with its glorified body. God, in his almighty power, will definitively grant incorruptible life to our bodies by reuniting them with our souls, through the power of Jesus' Resurrection.'
CCC 997

CATECHISM OF THE CATHOLIC CHURCH

'At the evening of life, we shall be judged on our love.'
St John of the Cross, Dichos, 64, cited in CCC 1022

USEFUL TERMS

Parables: earthly stories with a heavenly meaning, told by Jesus to illustrate his teaching

Unrepented sin: sins which have not been acknowledged/faced up to, and for which the individual may not feel sorry

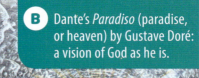
B Dante's *Paradiso* (paradise, or heaven) by Gustave Doré: a vision of God as he is.

31

What is heaven?

Eternal life with God in heaven is the goal of the Catholic faith. In 1 Corinthians 13:13, St Paul said that there are three things that last – faith, hope, and love – the greatest of which is love.

Heaven, therefore, is the 'place' or state of being in which everything that is not love passes away. It is the fulfilment of the deepest longing of the human heart.

It is impossible to describe the joy of heaven, because 'no eye has seen, nor ear heard, nor the heart of man conceived, what God has prepared for those who love him' (1 Corinthians 2:9), and so the Bible and the Church's teaching use many different images for heaven: 'life, light, peace, a wedding feast, wine of the Kingdom, the Father's house, the heavenly Jerusalem, paradise' (CCC 1027). All of these images are useful, but none of them captures adequately the wonder of living with God in heaven. Seeing God as he really is in heaven is called the beatific vision by the Church.

What is hell?

Hell is not a positive punishment created by God to make humans suffer. Hell is the absence of something – the absence of the life, love, generosity, fun, laughter, and community that are offered by God.

Some people wonder how an all-good, all-loving God can send someone to hell for all eternity. How can God be all-merciful and all-loving if there is eternal punishment? Catholics believe in free will (see 1.4): if they arrive in hell it is because of the choices they have freely made. They have refused to love, and rejected God's guidance towards love through their conscience.

The images the Bible uses for hell vary and include:

- 'the hell of fire' (Matthew 5:22)
- 'where their worm does not die, and the fire is not quenched' (Mark 9:48)
- 'the wine of God's wrath' (Revelation 14:10)
- 'the outer darkness' (Matthew 22:13).

What is purgatory?

To purge is to clean or remove. Catholics believe purgatory is therefore a stage of purification (also called purgation). The Catechism gives the reason for this purification as 'to achieve the holiness necessary to enter the joy of heaven' (CCC 1030). Although this teaching of the Catholic Church has few explicit verses to support it in the Bible, it is hinted at by one or two including 1 Corinthians 3:15: '[H]e himself will be saved, but only as through fire.'

In purgatory, Catholics believe they will see how much God loves them, and feel shame, embarrassment and pain when they realize how they have resisted that love in life, and settled for second best. That pain will purify them and strip away any remaining selfishness to make them totally loving, totally holy, and worthy of entry to heaven. It is therefore purposeful suffering.

COMPARE AND CONTRAST

In your exam you may be asked to compare and contrast Catholic beliefs about the afterlife and their significance with either Muslim or Jewish beliefs. Look at 5.8 and 7.8 for detail on these.

CATECHISM OF THE CATHOLIC CHURCH

'**The chief punishment of hell is eternal separation from God**, in whom alone man can possess the life and happiness for which he was created and for which he longs.' *CCC 1035*

C Fire is a common image associated with hell.

Most Protestant or Evangelical Christian groups do not agree with the Catholic idea of purgatory because they believe that purgatory is unnecessary. They believe that after death God will cover the imperfections of those who are saved with the perfection of Jesus. Catholics believe these imperfections will be removed through the process of purification that is purgatory.

Why are the last things important for Catholics today?

Christian writer G. K. Chesterton said that, 'The way to love anything is to realize that it may be lost.' He meant that nothing brings home the value of something or someone – be it a person's health, a parent, a pet dog, or life itself – until it is taken away, or at least threatened. The Catholic Church teaches that humans will probably not appreciate life in this world until they realize that it is a fragile gift that is one day going to end.

D Is it possible to appreciate life without loss?

Death, judgment, and resurrection are reminders for Catholics that they should live consciously as Catholics today, not put off an act of love or kindness until tomorrow. Every choice matters and adds up on the day of death and judgment.

Jesus said to Martha, 'Martha, you are anxious and troubled about many things; one thing is needful' (Luke 10:41). That one necessary thing is God. Only God is eternal. God alone remains, and so a Catholic's relationship to the eternal God, expressed in the love given to people in life, is for them the only ultimately important thing.

SUMMARY

- Eschatology is the study of Christian teaching about the last things in a human life: death, judgment, heaven, hell, and purgatory.
- Catholic views on eschatology are rooted in the Paschal Mystery.
- Since God alone is eternal, Catholics believe that their relationship with God is the only ultimately important thing in this world.
- Catholics connect to God by showing love to others.

CATECHISM OF THE CATHOLIC CHURCH

'Death lends urgency to our lives: remembering our mortality helps us realize that we have only a limited time in which to bring our lives to fulfillment.'
CCC 1007

BUILD YOUR SKILLS

1 a Explain how the Paschal Mystery influences Catholic belief in life after death.
   b Using bullet points, explain the stages Catholics believe they will go through once they die.
   c How is this different within other Christian denominations?

2 a In a group, discuss what St John of the Cross meant by 'At the evening of life, we shall be judged on our love.'
   b How is St John's comment important for Catholic life today?

EXAM-STYLE QUESTIONS

B Describe **two** differences in the teachings about life after death between Catholicism and the main religious tradition of Great Britain. (4)

D 'All Christians believe the same thing about life after death.' Evaluate this statement considering arguments for and against. In your response you should:
   - refer to Catholic teachings
   - refer to different Christian points of view
   - reach a justified conclusion. (15)

Revision

REVIEW YOUR KNOWLEDGE

1   Name the three persons of the Trinity.
2   Describe two ways of interpreting the Creation story.
3   Define the Incarnation.
4   What is blasphemy and what did that mean for Jesus?
5   What are the events of the Paschal Mystery?
6   Define atonement for Christians.
7   What does the Bible teach about eternal life in John 3:16?
8   Define two characteristics of God's nature.

* See page 288 for answers.

EXTEND YOUR KNOWLEDGE: RESEARCH TASKS

For a research task, try to put together a full side of A4 of your own writing on the topics below.

1   Research the details of the Councils of Nicaea and Constantinople.
2   Research the different ways Creation is understood by particular Christian groups, including the museums, theme parks, and events run by them.
3   Research Christian charities or organizations concerned with stewardship and dominion such as Earth Ministry, and consider how they reflect the ideas in the Creation story.
4   Research what the Church has said in response to instances of evil and suffering, such as terrorist attacks or natural disasters.

USEFUL TERMS

Do you know what these words mean?

Apostolic Tradition   Sacrament   Passion   Unrepented sin   Eucharist   Sacrifice

Nicene Creed   Incarnation   Repentance   Grace   Resurrection   Son of Man   Ascension

Omnipotence   Purgatory   Revelation   Baptism   Salvation   Benevolence   Redemption

Exam practice

In this exam practice section you will see examples for the exam question types: **a**, **b**, **c** and **d**. You can find out more about these on pages 6–7. Questions (a) and (d) in the **Exam question review** section below show strong student answers. Questions (b) and (c) in the **Improve it!** section need improvement.

Exam question review

(a)   Outline **three** reasons why the Holy Spirit is important to Catholics. (3)

He is spiritually active in the world today.
He helps Catholics to understand and worship God.
He equips and strengthens them.

> (d) 'All Christians believe the same thing about life after death.' Evaluate this statement considering arguments for and against. In your response you should:
> - refer to Catholic teachings
> - refer to different Christian points of view
> - reach a justified conclusion. (15)

Most Christians believe that everyone has an immortal soul that lives on after they die in either heaven or hell.

The Bible teaches that heaven is a reward for those who believe in Jesus, 'whoever believes in him shall not perish but have eternal life' John 3:16. As a result of this, some Christians believe that only the followers of Jesus will go to heaven and those who do not follow Jesus will otherwise go to hell.

However some Christians believe that Jesus died to forgive all sins and so everyone will live forever in heaven, not just Christians: this belief is called 'universalism'.

Catholics believe in purgatory, where dead souls can be purified before going to heaven. The Catechism of the Catholic Church says this is to 'achieve the holiness necessary to enter the joy of heaven'. Most Protestant churches do not believe in purgatory.

All Christians believe in the resurrection of Jesus and see this as the proof that they too will experience a resurrection after death. There is disagreement about whether it is a physical resurrection too, but they agree that there will be a spiritual resurrection as taught by Jesus in the Bible (and for Catholics in the Catechism).

As a result, I think that, although everyone will have a spiritual resurrection after death, the way they believe they will experience this varies. As a result, I conclude all Christians do not believe exactly the same thing about life after death.

Improve it!

These answers will not get full marks. Can you rewrite and improve them?

> (b) Explain **two** differences in how the accounts of Creation can be interpreted within Christianity. (4)

The Biblical account of the creation of the world is true.
The Biblical account of creation is a metaphor.

> (c) Explain **two** ways the Trinity is important to a Catholic's faith and understanding of God. In your answer you must refer to a source of wisdom and authority. (5)

Christians believe the Trinity displays God's loving nature and they focus their worship on this.
The Trinity helps Christians to understand more about their own lives.

WHAT WENT WELL
Question (a) asks you to 'outline' which is slightly more than a one-word answer – up to a sentence for each point. The three answers written here give enough detail to neatly sum up three different reasons.

WHAT WENT WELL
It's a good idea to aim to write five or six well-developed points, covering the different points of view listed in the question bullet points. This answer achieves that, and considers the points of view against the question, arriving at a justified conclusion.

HOW TO IMPROVE
These are two simple points which lack explanation. They need more development to explain the difference between them.

HOW TO IMPROVE
The second point is not developed; try to add examples to show full understanding of the question. The answer also lacks the required source of wisdom or authority.

2.1 The sacramental nature of reality

The sacramental nature of reality: Catholic teachings about how the whole of creation manifests the presence of God; the meaning and effects of each of the seven sacraments, including Catechism of the Catholic Church 1210–1211; the practice and symbolism of each sacrament; how sacraments communicate the grace of God; divergent Christian attitudes to sacraments, including reference to Orthodox and Protestant Christianity.

What is a sacrament?

A sacrament is a religious ritual performed in the life of the Church that makes people holier. The Catholic Church also teaches that a sacrament is:

Visible or accessible to the senses

The Catholic Church believes Christ introduced the seven sacraments.

'An outward sign of an inward gift, instituted by Christ, in order to give grace to a human being.'

God's life, presence, or holiness

The sacramental nature of reality

The sacramental nature of reality means finding the grace of God within the physical world. God is invisible, but Catholics believe he speaks to humans through everything he has created. Anything in creation – bread, wine, water, oil, words, hands upon the head, songs, gestures, movements, books, debates, buildings, music, work, love, sport – can be used by God to communicate with his people and draw them into a relationship with him.

Sacraments, symbolism, God's grace and presence

There are seven sacraments: Baptism, Confirmation, the Eucharist, Reconciliation, Anointing of the sick, Matrimony, and Holy Orders. Each marks an important point between life and death for Catholics and links an individual's physical life with their spiritual life. The Sacraments of Initiation are Baptism, Confirmation, and the Eucharist. Only when a person has received all three are they fully initiated members of the Catholic Church.

Baptism

God's grace: brings **sanctifying grace** to the soul, cleanses original sin, and links the soul to God's love.

Symbolism: water to wash away sin; oil as a sign of being chosen by God for a special task; a candle lit to represent the light of Jesus in their life and in the world.

God's presence: washing away sin is a sign of God's loving forgiveness, which makes God's loving forgiveness present for the one who is baptized; the symbols are signs that the person is chosen by Christ to be a believer, a person of light, truth, and love, and is made into a Christian, a member of Christ's body. The Church says that baptism leaves an indelible sign on a person's soul, as they are claimed for Christ.

CATECHISM OF THE CATHOLIC CHURCH

'The seven sacraments touch all the stages and all the important moments of Christian life: they give birth and increase, healing and mission to the Christian's life of faith. There is thus a certain resemblance between the stages of natural life and the stages of the spiritual life.'
CCC 1210

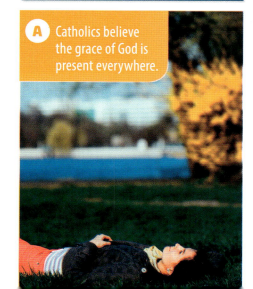
A Catholics believe the grace of God is present everywhere.

Confirmation

God's grace: increases sanctifying grace within an individual, strengthens their faith to become a mature, active Catholic Christian in the world.

Symbolism: reciting the baptismal promises is a symbol of the completion of baptism; oil with the words '[Name], be sealed with the Gift of the Holy Spirit' to symbolize the outpouring of the Holy Spirit, which is what happens at the moment the candidate is anointed and the bishop says the words of Confirmation.

God's presence: the reference to the Holy Spirit is a sign that God is present through the seven gifts of the Holy Spirit (wisdom, understanding, knowledge, fortitude/courage, counsel, piety, fear of the Lord). These equip the confirmed person for witness.

The Eucharist

God's grace: unites an individual to Christ into his presence is consumed within the consecrated bread and wine. It unites all Catholics who participate in the Eucharist. It is the sacrament above all others that increases spiritual strength.

Symbolism: bread and wine transformed as Christ's body and blood. Bread is the basic food of life and is a symbol of unity. Crushed grapes in wine represent how Christ was crushed for the salvation of the world.

God's presence: through the real presence of Christ in the consecrated bread and wine.

Reconciliation (Confession or Penance)

God's grace: removes the spiritual illness of sin, restoring or strengthening the sanctifying grace that can be lost or weakened through sin, and strengthens against the temptation to sin.

Symbolism: there is little symbolism associated with this sacrament. The important parts of the sacrament are the repentance of the sinner (shown through their act of contrition) and the forgiveness of God they receive (through the words of absolution spoken by the priest).

God's presence: through the offer of mercy, forgiveness, and advice given to the **penitent**.

Anointing of the sick

God's grace: gives strength in illness, comfort in suffering, and prepares the individual to meet death and eternity with confidence.

Symbolism: the laying of hands on the sick person, praying over them, anointing on the forehead and palms of the hands with oil blessed by the bishop on Maundy Thursday. Praying over them is calling down the Holy Spirit into their situation. Anointing them with oil is symbolic of the healing and cleansing this sacrament brings.

God's presence: these symbols show God's presence and love throughout a person's life, including illness, weakness, and even death. They show that God can be trusted at all times.

USEFUL TERMS

Penitent: the person acknowledging sorrow or sin

Sanctifying grace: a state in which God shares his life and love

CATECHISM OF THE CATHOLIC CHURCH

'the sacraments form an organic whole in which each particular sacrament has its own vital place. In this organic whole, **the Eucharist occupies a unique place as the "Sacrament of sacraments"**.'
CCC 1211

B Receiving the Eucharist when ill can give comfort to those who are suffering.

Matrimony

God's grace: in marriage, two people give their lives to one another exclusively for life. They have responsibility for one another and one another's souls. This sacrament provides them with grace, and strength.

Symbolism: the vows are solemn promises that are binding for their life together and a sign of the work of Christ who joins them together in the unbreakable bond of marriage. The couple gives the sacrament of marriage to each other, and the priest witnesses it and blesses it on behalf of the whole Church. Rings, circles without beginning or end, are also exchanged as a sign of God's unending love.

God's presence: God is present through the couple's lifelong love and commitment to each other.

Holy Orders

God's grace: in taking holy orders, a man receives serious responsibilities for the souls of people placed into his care. This sacrament gives him the grace to fulfil his role and carry out those responsibilities. It makes him the presence of Christ for his community.

Symbolism: laying on of hands and a special prayer of consecration. This calls down the Holy Spirit to make the man ready for ministry. Priests and deacons receive a stole as a sign of service. The priest also has his hands anointed, which is a sign that he can make people holy through the sacraments. The **chalice** and **paten** both signify the celebration of the Eucharist. The **mitre** is a sign of the bishops' office. A ring is a sign of the bishop's faithfulness to Christ and the Church. A pastoral staff is a sign of the bishop's role as shepherd of Christ's people.

God's presence: all of these are symbolic of God's loving presence to his people through the love and care of the ordained ministers of the Church.

Divergent attitudes to sacraments

Christian denominations have divergent beliefs regarding the seven sacraments recognized by the Catholic Church. Orthodox Christians recognize the same sacraments as Catholics. Most other Christians, including Protestant, Lutheran, Anglican, and Methodist recognize Baptism and the Eucharist as sacraments instituted by Christ. The other sacraments are often performed as rituals within the church, but are not given the same level of significance. Baptists do not use the word 'sacrament' but instead use 'ordinance' because they believe the rituals are expressions of faith, rather than a communication of God's grace.

C The laying on of hands is a symbolic part of ordination.

USEFUL TERMS

Chalice: cup for consecrated wine

Paten: plate for consecrated host

Mitre: pointed bishop's hat

BUILD YOUR SKILLS

1 a What does the sacramental nature of reality mean?
  b Why are the sacraments so important to Catholics?

2 a Summarize each of the seven sacraments in a table.
  b Add detail on how God's grace and presence are in each one.

EXAM-STYLE QUESTIONS

A Outline **three** sacraments. (3)
D 'Without the sacraments, Christians cannot be close to God.' Evaluate this statement considering arguments for and against. In your response you should:
  • refer to Catholic teachings
  • refer to different Christian points of view
  • reach a justified conclusion. (12)

SUMMARY

- The sacramental nature of reality means finding the grace of God in the physical world.
- Each sacrament brings Catholics closer to God in a different way, and communicates his love for them in varied but never-ending ways.
- The Sacraments of Initiation are Baptism, Confirmation, and the Eucharist.

2.2 Liturgical worship

What is liturgical worship?

Liturgical worship is the structured public service of worship followed in churches by Catholic Christians. Its content is set out by the Catholic Church and it brings God and Catholics together, to connect through Jesus.

The word 'liturgy' means the work of the people or an act of public service performed for the good of the people. The ceremonies in liturgical worship help redeem Catholics, save them from sin, and make them holy, more loving, more like God. Liturgy is not something that human beings do, but something that God does. Liturgical worship is how humans take part in the work of God.

In all of the public acts of worship in the Church, Catholics believe Christ is really present and acting on their souls to make them holy.

What is the Mass?

The Mass is the central act of worship for a Catholic. There are four main parts of the Mass.

The Introductory Rites: Gathering, Greeting, Penitential Rite, Gloria, and Collect

- The Mass begins with a gathering of the congregation to form the community around Christ.
- The sign of the cross is made, which shows that the people pray *in* God and not just *to* God. The priest greets the people in Christ's name and wears **vestments** that cover his ordinary clothes and, symbolically, his own identity. They show Catholics that he is the presence of Christ among them.
- In the Penitential Rite the priest then invites everyone, including himself, to think about their sins. For forgiveness to be received from God, there needs to be acknowledgement that there is something that needs forgiving.
- On a Sunday and on special feast days the Gloria is then said or sung to praise God.
- The Collect is a concluding prayer by the priest to draw together and offer all the prayers of the congregation to the Father. This prayer expresses the mood, theme, and focus of the Mass that day.

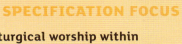

SPECIFICATION FOCUS

Liturgical worship within Catholic Christianity: the nature and significance of the Mass for Catholics, including its structure and the Eucharist as the 'source and summit of Christian life', with reference to *Lumen Gentium* paragraph 7; divergent Christian attitudes towards the practice and meaning of liturgical worship, including its significance for Catholics and the less structured worship in evangelical Christian denominations.

CATECHISM OF THE CATHOLIC CHURCH

'It is in the liturgy, especially in the divine sacrifice of the Eucharist, that the work of our redemption is accomplished.'
CCC 1068

USEFUL TERM

Vestments: long robe worn by priest over his clothes

A Women taking part in a Church procession at the start of liturgical worship.

The Liturgy of the Word

- This second part of the Mass contains readings from the Old and New Testaments and the Gospels. These readings are often linked to a common theme and to the time of the liturgical year, such as Advent, Christmas, Lent, Easter, or Ordinary Time (the rest of the year).
- The priest or deacon will usually give a **homily**.
- On Sundays and Feast days, the Nicene Creed (see 1.1) is then recited by the people, to show their faith.
- The Prayer of the Faithful (Bidding Prayers, **Intercessions**, or Universal Prayer) close the Liturgy of the Word as prayers are offered for the needs of the local community and the wider world.

The Liturgy of the Eucharist

- In the Liturgy of the Word Catholics listen to Jesus (in the Gospel) and in the response and prayers they speak back to him. In the Liturgy of the Eucharist they meet Christ.
- The bread and wine are brought to the altar, most often by members of the congregation, to prepare for offering of these during the Eucharistic prayer.
- The priest then says the Eucharistic Prayer of thanksgiving, which is the second of the two high points of the Mass, asking God to send down the Holy Spirit to make holy and transform the bread and wine into the body and blood of Christ. Catholics believe it is by these words that the bread and wine are changed into the body and blood of Christ, which is called transubstantiation. At the end of the Eucharistic Prayer Jesus, truly present under the forms of bread and wine, is offered to God the Father by the priest in the words, 'Through him, with him, and in him…'

The Communion Rite

- The priests and other ministers come down out of the sanctuary carrying Christ's body and blood and offer this as food and drink for the people. This is Holy Communion, sharing in and nourished by the life of Christ.

The concluding rites

- The priest greets, blesses, and then dismisses the people, so that they use the grace received in the Mass to build the kingdom of God's love in the world.

The place of the Eucharist

The sacrament of the Eucharist is described in CCC 1324 as 'the source and summit of the Christian life'. It is so important because it is a re-presentation of the saving events Jesus referred to in the last meal he had with his disciples before he died. Jesus celebrated the Last Supper with his disciples and, anticipating his death the next day, gave himself to the disciples and future Christians under the forms of bread and wine. He commanded them from that point on to celebrate this ritual of sharing bread and wine together: 'Do this in remembrance of me' (1 Corinthians 11:24).

Lumen Gentium is a Constitution; a document produced after the Second Ecumenical Council in 1964 which defined the nature and role of the Church in the modern

 B A priest praying the Eucharistic prayer.

◁▯▷ COMPARE AND CONTRAST

In your exam you may be asked to compare and contrast Catholic practices and worship with either Muslim or Jewish practices and worship. Look at 6.3 and 8.4 for detail on these.

 USEFUL TERMS

Homily: a commentary that follows a reading of scripture explaining and teaching the meaning of God's Word

Intercessions: prayers which request help or relief

 CATECHISM OF THE CATHOLIC CHURCH

'The celebration of the Eucharist is the heart of the Christian communion. In it the Church becomes Church.'
CCC 1325

world. In Chapter 1, 7:53–55 it explains how sharing the bread of the Eucharist (Christ's real body) brings Catholics together. Consuming it:

- makes individual Catholics part of Jesus' body, the Church
- makes Catholics part of one another
- creates the Church, the Body of Christ.

This uniting of Catholics to Christ and one another is called communion.

> ❝Really partaking of the body of the Lord in the breaking of the Eucharistic bread, we are taken up into communion with Him and with one another.❞
> *Lumen Gentium Ch1, 7:53*

C 'Behold the Lamb of God', part of the Communion Rite in Mass.

Members of the Catholic Church are not the Church because they live in the same neighbourhood or have similar ideas about things. They are the Church because in the Eucharist they share the body and blood of Christ. This is why the Mass is celebrated every day in the Catholic Church, except Good Friday and the Saturday before the Easter Vigil on Easter Sunday.

Divergent Christian attitudes to liturgical worship

Catholics believe that there is no higher good than God, therefore praising and thanking him for life is an important thing to do. They believe that doing this in community is significant because it brings individuals together as the Body of Christ within the church. The structured ceremonies contain signs and symbols which link back to Apostolic Tradition and the teachings of the Bible and magisterium; liturgical tradition is a key part of Catholicism.

Other Christian denominations such as evangelical Christians have much less structured worship because they believe formal liturgy can restrict or inhibit a Christian's connection to God. They believe connection with the Holy Spirit is important and therefore there is often spontaneous involvement from the congregation, either through actions such as arm waving, or vocal expressions of faith. Music, choirs, and instruments are often key parts of a service. However varied the style of worship among these Christian groups may be, of central importance to all of them is God's Word in the Bible and sharing that in community.

BUILD YOUR SKILLS

1 a What is liturgical worship?
  b Why is liturgical worship important?

2 a What are the four parts of the Mass?
  b How is each part important?

3 How does liturgical worship differ between different denominations?

EXAM-STYLE QUESTIONS

B Describe **two** differences in how the Eucharist is interpreted between Catholicism and the main religious tradition of Great Britain. (4)

C Explain **two** ways liturgical worship is important for Christians today. In your answer you must refer to a source of wisdom and authority. (5)

SUMMARY

- The liturgy is the work done by God, in Jesus Christ, for the good of all people.
- Liturgical worship is the participation of Catholics through the Church in God's work of making people holy.
- The Eucharist is both a remembrance and the making present again of Jesus' sacrifice. It is the source and summit of Christian life.
- Liturgical worship exists to help Catholics adore God and be given the grace to become more holy.
- Evangelical Christians have a less formal structure of worship to reflect their focus on the Holy Spirit and Word of God.

2.3 The funeral rite

A The funeral is a rite of the Church to accompany the deceased person at his/her journey's end.

SPECIFICATION FOCUS

The funeral rite as a liturgical celebration of the Church: practices associated with the funeral rite in the home, the church and the cemetery, including reference to 'Preparing my funeral' by Vincent Nichols, Archbishop of Westminster; the aims of the funeral rite, including communion with the deceased; the communion of the community and the proclamation of eternal life to the community and its significance for Catholics.

Liturgical celebration

The Nicene Creed states 'I look forward to the resurrection of the dead and the life of the world to come.' The death and resurrection of Jesus show the meaning of death for Catholics: that earthly life is a **pilgrimage**, a journey towards God. Death is not the end of life, but the entry into eternal life (see 1.8).

The funeral rite means the ceremonies carried out when a Catholic dies. They are liturgical because they are formal practices set out by the Catholic Church. A Catholic funeral, although sorrowful like any funeral, is also seen as a celebration because the individual has begun their journey to eternal life, hopefully in heaven. Participating in a funeral and being part of the Church's liturgical rite is a sign of love and respect for the deceased on the part of the Church.

The Church can be thought of as a mother handing one of her children back to the love of God the Father.

Practices in the home, church, and cemetery

Typically in the Catholic Church there are three types of funeral celebrations:
- the **Vigil** of the Deceased (which can be in the home or the church)
- the main funeral liturgy (in the church)
- the Rite of Committal and Commendation (in the cemetery or crematorium).

CATECHISM OF THE CATHOLIC CHURCH

'The Christian meaning of death is revealed in the light of the Paschal mystery of **the death and resurrection of Christ in whom resides our only hope**'.
CCC 1681

CATECHISM OF THE CATHOLIC CHURCH

'The Church […] accompanies him [the deceased person] at his journey's end, in order to surrender him into his Father's hands.'
CCC 1683

This can vary slightly according to local custom. For example, in Ireland a Vigil of Prayer at the house is often (though not always) wanted by the family, because that is part of that country's tradition. A Funeral or **Requiem** Mass in the parish church is encouraged by the Catholic Church but a Liturgy of the Word can be carried out instead. If the Catholic family is mostly non-practising, they may wish to go straight to the cemetery or crematorium.

The Cardinal Archbishop of Westminster, Vincent Nichols asked the Liturgy Commission of Westminster Diocese to prepare resources in order to help people with the difficult task of preparing for the celebration of a Catholic funeral. 'Preparing my funeral' is an A4 sheet which prompts Catholics to think about their own funeral in order that their relatives may better understand their wishes. They are asked to consider what they would like within the liturgy, such as particular scriptural readings and hymns, and whether they would wish a Vigil of the Deceased to take place before the funeral liturgy. A further leaflet explaining the detail of the funeral rites 'Preparing a funeral' was also written to give advice and support.

B A candle is lit at each corner of the coffin during the Mass.

The Vigil of the Deceased

The day before the funeral the deceased is often laid out in a coffin to be visited by friends and relatives. A service of prayers, songs, and a homily is conducted by the priest, including the greeting of the community, which brings everyone together in faith.

The funeral liturgy

This will either be the Mass (the Liturgy of the Word and the Liturgy of the Eucharist), or just the Liturgy of the Word. The priest will choose readings from the Bible which focus on the mystery of death and the deceased person's life of faith in Jesus.

A full Mass is encouraged because of the importance of the Paschal Mystery (Jesus' death and resurrection) within the Eucharist. Catholics regard the Church as the living body of Jesus: every Catholic is a part of that body and therefore part of the death and resurrection of Jesus.

The Farewell (or Commendation)

This is the final 'commendation to God by the Church'. There is a prayer of commendation in the main funeral liturgy in the church, but the final Rite of Committal and Commendation takes place in the cemetery or crematorium as the coffin is placed in its final resting place. During this final commendation, the people say their goodbyes in sorrow for the moment, but with hope in their hearts that they will meet again in eternal life.

Catholics believe that once you have become a Catholic, you remain part of the Church in life and death. That is why Catholics pray to saints for intercession – they believe they are still part of the Church in eternal life, and therefore capable of hearing prayers and interceding with God. When Catholics die, they believe they will be reunited with those who are in heaven.

> ✚ **CATECHISM OF THE CATHOLIC CHURCH**
>
> 'the Eucharist is the heart of the Paschal reality of Christian death. In the Eucharist, the Church expresses her efficacious communion with the departed.'
> *CCC 1689*

> 🔑 **USEFUL TERMS**
>
> **Pilgrimage:** a journey made for religious reasons
>
> **Requiem:** a Mass to remember someone who has died. Usually celebrated as part of the funeral but not always
>
> **Vigil:** time spent awake to keep watch or to pray

The aims of the funeral rite

The funeral rites are about connection as a Catholic family. The Church is the Body of Christ, and all Catholics are part of that. The funeral rites have three main aims:

1. Communion with the deceased – to support the deceased on their journey into the next life with **efficacious prayer**.
2. Communion of the community – to show how the people gathered are still connected to the deceased person in the Church, the Body of Christ.
3. Proclamation of eternal life to the community – to remind people that death is not the end of life, but the passage from this world to life with God.

Communion with the deceased

The Catholic Church believes that prayer for the deceased person, especially in the supreme prayer of the Eucharist, can support the deceased. Prayer for the deceased person is sometimes called suffrage. While the deceased has to make the journey of death alone, they can be supported by the prayer of the Church. Just as a child has to learn to swim alone, they can be encouraged by the presence of parents on the poolside. Catholics should also remember and celebrate the life of the deceased in prayer and try to forgive them for any wrongdoing.

Communion of the community

The funeral rites reassure Catholics that they can remain in connection with one another, especially by participating in the Eucharist of the Church to which they all belong, and by praying for one another, particularly during the Eucharist. Catholics can remain in connection with another Catholic through the Eucharist and prayer, whether that person is alive or dead.

Proclamation of eternal life

The funeral rites give hope to Catholics for the life after death that awaits them. The practices and rituals help reinforce belief and faith. The funeral is also an opportunity, as a potential moment of grace, to refocus on their own life and priorities.

 The funeral rite helps those who remain to support one another.

USEFUL TERM

Efficacious prayer: *efficax* is Latin for powerful and effective; in this context it is prayer to help and encourage the deceased person

BUILD YOUR SKILLS

1 a Why are Catholics encouraged to include the Eucharist in a funeral?
  b What is the purpose of the Committal and Commendation in the funeral rite?

2 a What are the three main aims of the funeral rite?
  b How do they connect Catholics as a family?

SUMMARY

- For the Catholic Church earthly life is a pilgrimage towards God. For all who try to live in Jesus, death is not the end, but the entry into eternal life.
- The funeral rite is a ritual in which the Catholic Church hands back a child to God the Father.
- The rites consist of: the Vigil, the funeral liturgy, and the Rite of Committal and Commendation.
- Communion with the deceased encourages Catholics to remember, celebrate, and pray for the deceased.
- Communion of the community brings Catholics together as part of the Catholic family.
- Proclamation of eternal life strengthens faith through the belief in life after death.

EXAM-STYLE QUESTIONS

A Outline **three** types of Catholic funeral celebration. (3)
C Explain **two** functions of the funeral rite in Catholic life. In your answer you must refer to a source of wisdom and authority. (5)

2.4 Prayer

What is prayer?

Prayer is communication with God. It is a form of worship which allows individuals to share life in conversation with God. Christians believe God is always there; prayer is the time to connect consciously with him. It can be done:

- privately or publicly
- alone or with others
- silently or with words
- speaking to God (active) or listening to God (receptive).

All the different forms are important. The Catechism describes prayer as 'the raising of one's mind and heart to God' (CCC 2559) which means focusing on God alone in both the mind and heart, and being open to hearing his answer. Humility before God and feeling genuinely sorry for any wrongdoing are also very important.

> ❝Prayer in my opinion is nothing else than a close sharing between friends; it means taking time frequently to be alone with him who we know loves us.❞
> *St Teresa of Avila (1515–1582)*

Different types of prayer and their importance

There are different stages of life, and many kinds of experience. These naturally require different types of prayer. CCC 2626–2643 lists the five types, themes, or purposes of prayer: adoration, thanksgiving, repentance, intercession, and petition.

Adoration

At certain moments Catholics simply want to acknowledge that God is God and they are his creatures, completely dependent on him for life and breath and everything else. At those moments Catholics adore (worship) him.

The '*Glory be*' prayer is an example of adoration:

> ❝Glory be to the Father, and to the Son and to the Holy Spirit, as it was in the beginning, is now, and ever shall be, world without end. Amen.❞

Thanksgiving

At other moments Catholics may simply wish to express love and gratitude to God for life itself, for family and friends, abilities and capacities, for Christ, salvation, and the Church, and for the little experiences of life and grace that come every day, and so they pray in thanksgiving.

Grace before meals is an example of thanksgiving.

Prayer as the 'raising of hearts and minds to God': the nature and significance of different types of prayer; the Lord's Prayer, including Matthew 6:5–14, set (formulaic) prayers and informal (extempore) prayer; when each type might be used and why; the importance of prayer and the importance for Catholics of having different types of worship.

A Prayer can be taking time to remember that all of life is lived in God's presence.

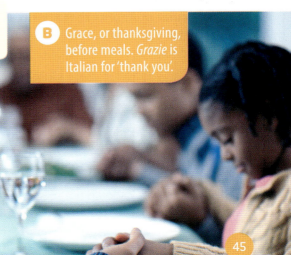

B Grace, or thanksgiving, before meals. *Grazie* is Italian for 'thank you'.

Repentance

At other moments Catholics feel the need to acknowledge sorrow for something they have done that they shouldn't have, or not done that they should have. This is a prayer of repentance. The *I Confess* at the Mass is an example of a prayer of repentance.

Intercession

Catholics may hear of people (close to them or strangers living elsewhere in the world) who are suffering or in some sort of need. Praying to God on behalf of someone else is intercessory prayer. Catholics may also ask the saints in heaven to pray for them.

At the Mass the Bidding Prayers/Intercessions/Prayer of the Faithful/Universal Prayer are examples of intercessory prayer, as is a private prayer 'for the intentions of the Pope'.

C Kneeling can be a sign of adoration as well as repentance.

Petition

Personal needs can be asked for in petitionary prayer, although this should not be a Catholic's first and only way of praying. Prayers of petition are when Catholics ask God for things. Intercession is a type of petitionary prayer, but Catholics can ask God for other things too: for themselves, for the grace to let God's will be done, or for the Kingdom to come.

An example of a prayer of petition is: 'Lord, please give me the desire, strength, and patience to study hard for my exams.'

The Catholic Church believes that the most important thing about prayer is not *how* people pray, but *that* people pray. Different types of worship and prayer allow communication with God which fits the purpose of the prayer. Variety in worship allows a much better connection between Catholics and God.

Catholics pray:

- **before important moments:** as the day begins, as they go to bed, when they eat, before exams, before sports events, before a performance, etc.
- **at all times:** St Paul says, 'Pray constantly' (1 Thessalonians 5:17). This does not mean constant, formal prayer, but being aware of God's constant presence and acknowledging this at different times, e.g. while walking, jogging, on public transport, driving, cooking, or working.
- **at particular moments that are set aside:** life requires structure, rhythms, and timetables, so Catholics should set aside certain times of the day to pray and remember where they are ultimately heading – towards the God in whose presence they live their lives at every moment.

✝ CATECHISM OF THE CATHOLIC CHURCH

'**The Lord's Prayer is the most perfect of prayers** [...] In it we ask, not only for all the things we can rightly desire, but also in the sequence that they should be desired.'
CCC 2763

D 'One of his disciples said to him, "Lord, teach us to pray."' *(Luke 11:1).*

Formal and extempore prayer

Prayer can be either formulaic/formal – using the formulas and words from the many centuries of the Church's tradition – or it can be extempore/informal, using a person's own words without planning or preparation.

Catholics believe they should not merely *say* their prayers but *pray* their prayers.

The Lord's Prayer (the *Our Father*)

When the disciples asked Jesus to teach them to pray, he taught them the Lord's Prayer. This is a very important set prayer for all Christians and can be used in many different settings and for many different purposes.

Our Father — Christians pray in the name of all God's people. Jesus introduced the idea of God as a father

who art in heaven, — Not meaning far away, but that God is beyond understanding

Hallowed be thy name. — God is holy and should come first

Thy kingdom come, — This refers to the final coming of Jesus and God's reign through him

Thy will be done, —

On earth as it is in heaven. — Christians should turn over their life and will to God and his will

The three petitions here are about God

Give us this day our daily bread; — This is asking God to give to the one praying whatever they truly need

And forgive us our debts, —

As we also have forgiven our debtors; — The person's own sins will not be forgiven if they do not forgive all those who have sinned against them

The four petitions here are about the person praying

And lead us not into temptation, — Do not allow the person praying to give in to trials or temptation

But deliver us from evil. — Keep them safe/free from evil

(Matthew 6:9–13)

Matthew 6:5–8 explains that prayer should not be done for show, or use empty words, but be heartfelt, sincere, and private communication which seeks a deeper relationship with God: 'go into your room and shut the door and pray to your Father who is in secret' (6:6).

BUILD YOUR SKILLS

1 a What does it mean to a Catholic to raise 'mind and heart' to God?
   b In pairs list the five different themes of prayer.
   c Discuss whether you think some of these are more important than others.

2 Why is the Lord's Prayer such an important prayer?

3 How is informal prayer used by Catholics?

SUMMARY

- Prayer is communication with God. It is being aware that life is always lived in God's presence.
- Catholics should pray regularly using both formal prayer and informal prayer depending on the purpose and setting.
- The five purposes of prayer are: adoration, thanksgiving, repentance, intercession, and petition.
- The Lord's Prayer is a key prayer for Catholics and Christians everywhere.
- There are different types of prayer because different stages of life and experiences require different responses.

EXAM-STYLE QUESTIONS

B Explain **two** examples of different types of prayer. (4)
D 'Only formal prayer is really important in worship.' Evaluate this statement considering arguments for and against. In your response you should:
   - refer to Catholic teachings
   - reach a justified conclusion. (12)

What is popular piety?

Popular piety (sometimes called **devotions** or non-liturgical worship) is celebration or worship of God which is not part of the official public liturgy of the Church. This means it does not follow a strict pattern or order of worship set out by the Church. However, there may be elements of public liturgy involved in the different forms. For example, when people pray the Rosary, they make the sign of the cross and pray the Lord's Prayer and the **Hail Mary**, which are also gestures and prayers used in the Mass.

Vatican II teaches that 'spiritual life […] is not limited solely to participation in the Liturgy' (*Sacrosanctum Concilium* 12). This means that the Catholic Church encourages Catholics to take part in other practices beyond church services that express spiritual life and offer worship to God. Examples of such devotions include:

- the Rosary
- Eucharistic adoration
- Stations of the Cross
- monthly **novenas**
- group prayer
- Bible-centred prayer
- pilgrimages
- veneration of sacred icons or **relics**.

Many of these forms of popular piety can be done in private, but are frequently done in public, in groups, and in a church, often led by a priest or deacon. However, they are never considered part of the official liturgical worship of the Church.

The Rosary

The Rosary is a form of prayer named after the Latin word *Rosarium*, meaning 'crown of roses'. This is because the string of prayer beads that help the person to count the prayers making up the devotion is in the shape of a circle/crown.

The nature and significance of the Rosary

The Rosary might be used in private prayer at home, in church, or walking to school; it might be used with others in church or elsewhere. It is sometimes said on the evening before a funeral Mass, when the coffin is brought into the church.

The prayers that comprise the Rosary are arranged in sets called decades. One decade is:

- one Lord's Prayer
- ten Hail Marys
- one Glory Be.

While praying each decade, the person tries to focus on a different **Mystery of the Rosary**, which is a particular event in the life of Jesus or Mary. Usually people pray five decades in one session. Additional prayers can be added before, between, and after the decades such as the Apostles' Creed and the Hail Holy Queen. The Rosary helps Catholics meditate on the grace of God. The focus on different mysteries allows them to think about the different elements of Jesus' life.

A Rosaries are often made of wood.

Catholicism encourages the praying of the Rosary as a way of giving honour to Mary. However, the Rosary is ultimately viewed by the Church as a way of going 'to Christ through Mary'.

The rosary is not widely used by other Christian denominations. Some Anglicans use the rosary as a private devotion, however not all the prayers are the same as many would not be comfortable praying to Mary. They would not use the Catholic mysteries of the rosary either.

Stations of the Cross

This is a series of prayers and meditations that honour the Passion (the suffering) and death of Christ. It is also known as the Way of the Cross, or the *Via Crucis* in Latin.

The 14 stations are often erected on the walls of a Catholic church.

- The station usually consists of a wooden cross and images representing the scene being recalled.
- At each station a reflection on the suffering of Christ at that scene is made, sometimes with a reading or vocal prayers.
- People then move to the next station.

The nature and significance of the Stations of the Cross

- They might be used in a Catholic church on Fridays (Jesus was crucified on a Friday), especially in Lent, and even more so on Good Friday.
- In the early Church people visited the scene of Christ's suffering and death in Jerusalem, and this practice was imitated throughout the Catholic Church by those who could not go to Jerusalem.
- Some Anglican, Methodist, and Lutheran churches also contain the stations of the cross. They can provide a particular focus during Holy week for Christians of all denominations.

Eucharistic adoration

Eucharistic adoration is where the **Blessed Sacrament** itself is adored and worshipped. Catholics do not simply believe the bread and wine represent Jesus, but that Christ is truly present within them when they have been consecrated. The consecrated host is placed in a **monstrance** and adored.

USEFUL TERMS

Devotions: practices which create a sense of devotion, love, and affection for God

Hail Mary: a prayer addressed to Jesus' mother, Mary. Catholics believe closeness to Mary is closeness to Christ

Mystery of the Rosary: the Joyful Mysteries, Sorrowful Mysteries, and Glorious Mysteries concentrate on joyful, sorrowful, and glorious moments in the life of Christ or Mary. In 2002 the Pope introduced five new mysteries, the Luminous Mysteries

Novena: nine days of public or private prayer for special occasions or intentions

Relics: an object connected with a saint such as physical remains, belongings, or something they used/touched

Vatican II: the Second Vatican Council – an ecumenical council held between 1962 and 1965

B Seven of the fourteen Stations of the Cross.

The nature and significance of Eucharistic adoration

Eucharistic adoration might be used as a way of focusing people in prayer in a parish, or on a retreat. It might be used as a way of praising and thanking God for something, or a way of praying in times of emergency, war, or disaster.

Vatican II recommends that Catholics **genuflect** on one knee before the Eucharist (although some genuflect on both knees when the Eucharist is on the altar).

Eucharistic adoration is not widely performed within other Christian denominations. However, in some Anglo-Catholic and Lutheran churches, Eucharistic adoration will take place during the church service.

 Displaying the host in a monstrance allows the whole congregation to see it.

Why is it important to have different types of worship?

It is important to have both liturgical and non-liturgical worship because they are different ways of doing the same thing: connecting Catholics to God through prayer. Liturgical worship helps Catholics pray in community, while the different forms of popular piety in non-liturgical worship help them to pray more individually (although they can be done with others).

The Catechism supports both types of worship, however it cautions that forms of piety 'extend the liturgical life of the Church, but do not replace it' (CCC 1675). Parish priests have a responsibility to guide Catholics and to: 'sustain and support popular piety and, if necessary, to purify and correct the religious sense which underlies these devotions' (CCC 1676).

✝ CATECHISM OF THE CATHOLIC CHURCH

'the religious sense of the Christian people has always found expression in various forms of piety […] the stations of the cross, religious dances, the rosary, medals, etc.'
CCC 1674

BUILD YOUR SKILLS

1   **a**   What is popular piety?
     b   Why are the forms of popular piety important?

2   **a**   What is the purpose of the Mysteries in the praying of the Rosary?
     b   Describe what is happening during Eucharistic adoration.
     c   How do different Christian denominations use forms of popular piety?

🔑 USEFUL TERMS

Blessed Sacrament: the real presence of Jesus in the consecrated bread and wine, either to be consumed or adored

Genuflect: to bend the knee or touch the ground (usually with one knee) as a gesture of respect

Monstrance: a decorative frame used to hold and display the consecrated host

SUMMARY

- Non-liturgical acts of worship are devotions which are not part of the official public liturgy of the Church.
- The Rosary is a string of beads to help focus a series of prayers.
- Eucharistic adoration is the worship of Christ as truly present in the Blessed Sacrament.
- The 14 Stations of the Cross depict moments of Christ's suffering and death.
- Liturgical worship helps Catholics pray in community, while non-liturgical worship helps Catholics pray more individually.

? EXAM-STYLE QUESTIONS

B   Explain **two** forms of popular piety. (4)

C   Explain **two** benefits of the forms of popular piety to Christians. In your answer you must refer to a source of wisdom and authority. (5)

2.6 Pilgrimage

> **Pilgrimage:** the nature, history and purpose of Catholic pilgrimage; the significance of the places people go on pilgrimage; divergent Christian understandings about whether pilgrimage is important for Christians today, with specific reference to Jerusalem, Lourdes, Rome, Walsingham and the Catechism of the Catholic Church 2691–2696.

The nature, history, and purpose of pilgrimage

Pilgrimages are defined as journeys made to religiously significant places with a spiritual purpose. Some of the earliest documents of the Church suggest that soon after Jesus' ascension, people began visiting places such as Bethlehem.

- By the fourth century, pilgrimage to Jerusalem and the **Holy Land** (where Jesus lived, taught, and performed miracles) had become more common with early churches being built at places that were significant in the Gospels.
- Later came pilgrimages to Rome to see the tombs of the early martyrs such as Peter and Paul, then to sites connected with the apostles and saints, as and where Christianity developed.
- The Reformation destroyed many places of pilgrimage connected to the saints in Europe. However, as transport improved in the nineteenth century, these grew again in popularity.

The purpose of pilgrimage varies. It may be to visit the origins of Christianity, and literally 'walk in the footsteps' of Jesus and the disciples. It may be an opportunity to pray or ask forgiveness from sin (in Church history, pilgrimages were sometimes made as a **penance** for sin, as a sign of a new beginning). For some it is an act of devotion, for others it refreshes and renews faith and shows commitment to God.

The significance of the places people visit on pilgrimage

The places Catholics may go on pilgrimage are significant for different reasons:

- Places connected to Jesus: the Holy Land offers the opportunity to visit sites connected to the birth, ministry, **crucifixion**, and resurrection of Jesus, e.g. the Church of the **Transfiguration** on Mount Tabor in Israel. It allows people to pray at the sites and better understand the Gospels.
- Places connected to Mary: these places are linked to Marian apparitions (places where Mary is believed to have appeared). Pilgrims feel a close connection to her at these sites, e.g. Lourdes in France, Fatima in Portugal, Knock in Ireland, and Guadalupe in Mexico.
- Places connected to the apostles: many of the early church leaders moved around the known world spreading the Gospel. Their relics were then taken further afield. St James' relics were taken as far as Santiago de Compostela in Spain. St Peter's Basilica in the Vatican City is an important destination because it is built over the tomb of the apostle Peter.

> ❝[Jesus] said to them, "Go into all the world and preach the gospel to the whole creation."❞
> *Mark 16:15*

Crucifixion: the death of Jesus on the cross

Holy Land: the original Land of Israel, which is now divided between modern Israel, Palestine, Lebanon, Jordan, and Syria

Penance: a punishment or act of reparation which shows repentance

Transfiguration: a change in appearance or form; the unveiling of Jesus as Messiah alongside the support of Moses and Elias

A The Church of the Nativity, Bethlehem. Originally built in 327ᴄᴇ then rebuilt in 565ᴄᴇ.

- Places connected to other saints: many sites have become places of pilgrimage due to their connection with the saints. The reasons that a pilgrim visits are often personal, but connected in some way to the life of the saint. Examples include Croagh Patrick, a mountain in Ireland connected to St Patrick, the patron saint of Ireland, and the **Basilica** of St Francis in Assisi, who formed several orders of brothers and sisters and is the patron saint of ecology.

- Places of ecumenical pilgrimage: these are places where Catholics go to spend time in prayer and communion with other Christians. Walsingham in Norfolk has both Catholic and Anglican shrines and hosts many ecumenical events. Taizé in France is an ecumenical community, focused on welcoming young people searching in their faith.

- Places of spiritual pilgrimage and retreat: some places of pilgrimage do not have the same connection to Jesus or the apostles. They may have historical importance in the growth of Christianity, or be simply set aside for retreat. Examples include Iona, which is a monastery dating from 563CE on a remote island of Scotland, and Buckfast Abbey in Devon.

Why pilgrimage is important for Christians today

In CCC 2696, the Catholic Church lists the most appropriate places for prayer, which includes places of pilgrimage. Regardless of denomination, pilgrimage gives Christians time and space for prayer. It allows connection with other Christians and can help a person feel closer to God. Pilgrimage can also be a response to the busy, commercialized, and increasingly secular modern world.

Jerusalem

As the place of Jesus' death and resurrection, Jerusalem remains an important place of pilgrimage. Visiting the place where their faith began is an intensely spiritual event for Catholics and Christians of other denominations.

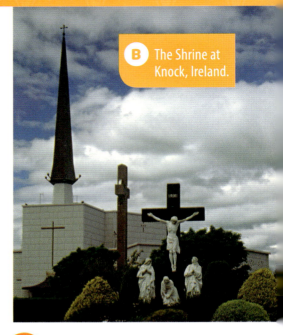

B The Shrine at Knock, Ireland.

USEFUL TERMS

Basilica: the name given to certain long, oblong churches granted special privileges by the Pope

CATECHISM OF THE CATHOLIC CHURCH

'Pilgrimages evoke our earthly journey toward heaven and are traditionally very **special occasions for renewal in prayer**. For pilgrims seeking living water, shrines are special places for living the forms of Christian prayer "in Church".'
CCC 2691

C The inside of St Peter's Basilica, Rome. Many claim it is the most beautiful and impressive Catholic church in the world.

Rome

The Vatican City in Rome remains the centre of the Catholic Church and the home of the Pope, the leader of the Catholic Church. Many Catholics like to greet and listen to the Pope in person and this is possible on a regular basis in Rome.

Christians who do not recognize the authority of the Pope in the same way Catholics do, such as Anglicans, Methodists, and Baptists may still wish to visit Rome as an important site in the history of their faith.

Visiting Rome also allows Catholics to incorporate traditional holiday sightseeing with aspects of pilgrimage. The Colosseum is not only interesting for its design, but also many early Christians were martyred there. The catacombs under the city are a series of man-made and natural caves where early Christians met, prayed in secret, celebrated the Mass, and were buried.

Lourdes

Lourdes is traditionally a place for the sick and injured to visit. The water which miraculously began to flow after the Virgin Mary appeared to a young girl called Bernadette Soubirous is said to have healing powers (see 9.2 and 9.3). Pilgrims pray, light candles, and bathe in the water. They can also take part in processions. Lourdes' significance is also as a place of communal pilgrimage to help others: groups such as HCPT take disabled and disadvantaged children on a pilgrimage holiday to Lourdes. Over 6 million pilgrims in total visit each year.

Walsingham

In 1061 a noblewoman received three visions of the house where Mary was visited by the angel Gabriel (see 9.2). She built a replica of this house at Walsingham. Her son then built a priory and it became a place of pilgrimage. For British Catholic pilgrims, Walsingham is an accessible place of pilgrimage, and they can spend time in prayer and communion with other Christians too, not just Catholics.

In 1922 an Anglican Shrine was created at Walsingham, widening its importance as a place of pilgrimage for many more Christians.

D Pilgrims join together on their way to Walsingham.

BUILD YOUR SKILLS

1 Explain the different benefits of pilgrimage to:
- Walsingham
- Lourdes
- St Peter's Basilica in Rome.

2 a In pairs, discuss how pilgrimage might be important in different ways for Christians.
 b Write a paragraph summarizing your discussion.

EXAM-STYLE QUESTIONS

A Outline three places Catholics might choose to go on pilgrimage. (3)

D 'Pilgrimage is a unique type of worship which every Christian should undertake.' Evaluate this statement considering arguments for and against. In your response you should:
- refer to Catholic teachings
- refer to different Christian points of view
- reach a justified conclusion. (12)

SUMMARY

- Pilgrimages are journeys to special places of religious significance.
- Places are often connected to the lives of Jesus, Mary, apostles, and saints.
- Lourdes has become a place of healing and new miracles continue to be reported.
- Rome has been an enormously important site in Church history since the earliest days of Christianity.
- Walsingham Priory is a place for Catholics to spend time in prayer with other Christians.
- Jerusalem is the place of where the Paschal Mystery took place. it is also the birthplace of the Church at Pentecost.

2.7 Catholic Social Teaching

🔍 **SPECIFICATION FOCUS**

Catholic Social Teaching: how Catholic Social Teaching reflects the teaching to show love of neighbour; Catholic teaching on justice, peace and reconciliation, *Evangelii Gaudium* paragraphs 182–237 – The inclusion of the poor in society; how these teachings might be reflected in the lives of individual Catholics including reference to Matthew 25: 31–46 (sheep and goats); the work of CAFOD, what it does and why.

Love of neighbour

In Mark 12:29–31 Jesus gave the two great commandments:

> ❝"Love the Lord your God with all your heart, with all your soul, with all your mind, and with all your strength." [...] "Love your neighbour as yourself." There is no commandment greater than these. ❞
> *Mark 12:29–31*

Catholics believe that everybody is a neighbour; that humanity should be a 'whole human family' *(Pope Paul VI, Gaudium et Spes)*. The parable of the Good Samaritan (Luke 10:25–37) is used by Jesus to explain the true meaning of neighbour. The selfless love demonstrated by the Good Samaritan informs the Catholic view that individuals should act without hesitation to help those in need.

> ❝Which of these three, do you think, proved neighbour to the man who fell among the robbers?" He said, "The one who showed mercy on him." And Jesus said to him, "Go and do likewise." ❞
> *Luke 10:36–37*

The Catholic Church gives seven themes to its Social Teaching:

SEVEN KEY THEMES OF CATHOLIC SOCIAL TEACHING

1. Sacredness of life and the dignity of the human person
2. Call to family, community, and participation
3. Human rights and the responsibility to protect them
4. Preferential option for the poor and vulnerable
5. Dignity of work and the rights of workers
6. Solidarity with all people as one global family
7. Stewardship and care for God's creation

The themes are broad and touch the lives of every Catholic around the world in some way, encouraging them to demonstrate their love of neighbour by taking action to help someone in need.

Justice, peace and reconciliation

Catholic Social Teaching then, is inspired by the two great commandments, the parables of Jesus, and his own example. It is personalistic: this means its focus is the dignity of the human person.

A The dignity of the human person is recognized by caring for the poor and vulnerable.

The Catholic Church, led by the Pope, promotes and explains its Social Teaching through different publications. Part of the papal document of *Evangelii Gaudium* explains the importance of the inclusion of the poor in society. It explains that every Christian is called by God to help the 'liberation and promotion of the poor' (Ch4: 187). It also expresses the importance of dignity (see Ch4: 190, right).

Catholic Social Teaching is concerned with how society should provide:

- Justice – promoting justice and eliminating or limiting injustice.
- Peace –encouraging harmony amongst all human beings; preventing or resolving war and conflict.
- Reconciliation – protecting the dignity and rights of the human person, wherever they may be.

These are not separate ideas, but must be considered in harmony by Catholics. One of the documents from the Second Vatican Council in 1965 explained:

> 'Peace is not merely the absence of war [...] it is rightly and appropriately called an enterprise of justice.'
> *Gaudiem et Spes Ch 5: 78*

> 'we must never forget that the planet belongs to all mankind and is meant for all mankind; the mere fact that some people are born in places with fewer resources or less development does not justify the fact that they are living with less dignity.'
> *Evangelii Gaudium, Ch4: 190*

Actions of individual Catholics

The Catholic Church has traditionally listed seven spiritual and seven corporal (bodily) works of mercy (pity or compassion). Catholics can show love of neighbour through any of these acts, such as forgiving offences, feeding the hungry, and visiting the sick.

These are influenced by the parable of the sheep and goats in Matthew 25: 31–46, where Jesus promises that those who perform such acts to those in need will be rewarded for having shown charity to Jesus himself. He meant that the image of God is present in every human being, therefore kindness to the person, is kindness to God.

Charitable giving (almsgiving) to relieve poverty and suffering is also a great way for individual Catholics to obey the commandment to love your neighbour.

- Jesus teaches that the 'poor in spirit' are blessed (Matthew 5:3), which means those whose spirit is detached from wealth, not addicted to or enslaved by it.
- Charitable giving therefore is a double blessing – one for the poor person who receives the money, and one for the person who gives.

CAFOD

The Catholic Church has several charitable organizations that carry out works of mercy wherever there is need across the world. CAFOD is based in England and Wales and is part of Caritas International, a group of over 160 Catholic agencies around the world.

B Pope Francis has made Social Teaching a special concern during his papacy.

CAFOD says, 'Inspired by Scripture and Catholic Social Teaching, and the experiences and hopes of people living in poverty, CAFOD works for a safe, sustainable, and peaceful world'. CAFOD describes its work under the following headings:

- **Global neighbours:** like the Good Samaritan, CAFOD believes that everyone in the world has the right to live with dignity. It fights injustice and poverty and looks to provide for the needs of people around the world, often reaching them through the local Catholic Church.

- **Rooted in the Catholic Community:** as the official aid agency of the Catholic Church in England and Wales, CAFOD works alongside those living in poverty, whatever their religion, belief, or culture.

- **Helping people help themselves:** CAFOD believes helping people to develop skills allows them to live with greater dignity, supporting their families through their own achievements. For example, helping farmers set up networks to share their seeds and local expertise.

- **Facing the toughest challenges:** such as war and conflict, climate change, inequality, HIV and AIDS.

- **There in a crisis:** whenever emergencies take place around the world CAFOD supports local organizations who can respond quickly with food, water and shelter, then offers long-term help for communities in crisis. Examples include the Ebola crisis in Sierra Leone and the refugee crisis in the countries around Syria and in Europe.

- **Raising awareness:** a percentage of CAFOD's funds goes toward educating the Catholic community in England and Wales about the need for emergency and long-term development aid and how they can help. This may be done through volunteers working in parishes and visiting schools, providing online and offline resources for parishes and schools, providing training for young leaders and for teachers, and through sharing stories about its partners' work in the media and on their website.

- **Working for social justice:** CAFOD believes that everyone has a part to play in working to ensure that global systems and agreements (for example in trade, business, politics and human rights) are fair for everyone. Through campaigning, ensuring communities influence decision makers, and living simply, people can help care for the world and bring about an end to poverty.

Source: Adapted from www.CAFOD.org.uk

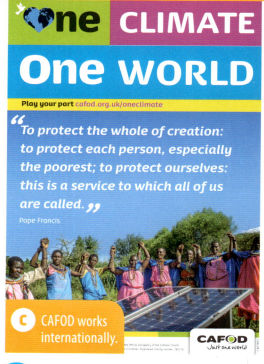

C CAFOD works internationally.

"To protect the whole of creation: to protect each person, especially the poorest; to protect ourselves: this is a service to which all of us are called."
Pope Francis

BUILD YOUR SKILLS

1 a From what principle does Catholic Social Teaching originate?
 b How did *Evangelii Gaudium* try to promote social justice?

2 a How do local Catholic agencies help people?
 b What differences can global agencies make to people's lives?
 c How does Catholic Social Teaching affect ordinary Catholics?

EXAM-STYLE QUESTIONS

B Explain **two** ways CAFOD demonstrates Catholic Social Teaching. (4)
D 'Catholic Social Teaching has the power to influence the whole world.' Evaluate this statement considering arguments for and against.
In your response you should:
- refer to Catholic teachings
- reach a justified conclusion. (12)

SUMMARY

- The Church works universally for the love of neighbour, following the commandments of Christ and his own example.
- Catholics follow the example of the Good Samaritan to respond to need.
- Catholic Social Teaching promotes justice, peace and reconciliation.
- Individuals can carry out acts of mercy and give charitable donations.
- CAFOD is a Catholic charity working in England, Wales, and internationally.

2.8 Catholic mission and evangelism

Mission and evangelism

The general idea of a mission is that of being sent to others in order to help them, or to bring them something that will benefit them. In Christianity, mission means being sent to others to bring them the gospel of Jesus. Christian mission reflects the Trinity.

- God sent the Word, the Son, from the Trinity, on a visible mission in order to save the world. The invisible Holy Spirit was sent into the world and the Church to help build the **kingdom of God**.

- Jesus sent the apostles into the world on a mission to 'make disciples of all nations, baptizing them in the name of the Father and of the Son and of the Holy Spirit' (Matthew 28:19–20). This is sometimes called the commission of Jesus. During the persecutions of the Church up to 313CE this often had to be done in secret.

- The apostles and their successors, the Catholic bishops, also later sent people to continue their work of announcing and living out the Gospel. This is called evangelism, or evangelization.

- Missionaries have travelled around the world to share the Gospel in new places. For example, in the fifth century, St Benedict laid the foundation for monks to bring the Gospel to the Western world. In the fifteenth and sixteenth centuries, the Spanish and Portuguese took Catholicism to South America when they colonized it.

- Every Catholic receives a mission from Jesus – they are sent by him, in his Church, empowered by the Holy Spirit, to share and build up the kingdom of God in love.

Evangelization is sometimes confused with proselytising. This is trying to convert individuals to a faith and often has a negative perception. Evangelization is about sharing and living out a message. After hearing that message, people may wish to learn more about Jesus, but that is a personal positive choice.

Evangelization was used as a term by Pope Paul VI in *Evangelii Nuntiandi* (1975) and Pope John Paul II in *Redemptoris Missio* (1990). Sometimes the Catholic Church uses the two words together and talks of the *evangelizing mission* of the Church, because the Church is sent by God to proclaim to and live out for others the Gospel.

SPECIFICATION FOCUS

Catholic mission and evangelism: the history and significance of mission and evangelism for Catholics; divergent ways this is put into practice by the Church and individual Catholics locally, nationally and globally, and how this fulfils the commission of Jesus and teachings of the Church, including *Evangelii Gaudium* Chapter 5.

CATECHISM OF THE CATHOLIC CHURCH

'The ultimate purpose of mission is none other than to make men share in the communion between the Father and the Son in their Spirit of love.'
CCC 850

USEFUL TERM

Kingdom of God: the rule of God over all creatures and things.

A For Catholics, sharing the gospel is a way of living the message of Jesus.

57

What is the 'new evangelization'?

Since *Evangelii Nuntiandi*, subsequent Popes have spoken of a new evangelization. The Church is no longer evangelizing so much in places that have not heard the Gospel before, but in the largely secular West, where many people have heard of the Gospel but are not particularly interested.

It is still important to reach out to people who may not know about the Gospel, and to existing Christians to help strengthen their faith; but reaching people who have lost a living sense of Catholic faith is seen as crucial to the new evangelization in the modern world. St John Paul II said that this new evangelization would need to be 'new in its ardor, new in its methods, new in its expressions' (Opening Address of CELAM).

How does the Church engage in the new evangelization?

In *Evangelii Gaudium* ('The Joy of the Gospel') Pope Francis says that a relationship with Jesus Christ in the Church is a cause of such joy that it causes people to go out on a mission to evangelize others.

Locally:

- This basic message of God's love is passed on by the Church through the whole life of the parish. Every part of parish life contains opportunity for discussion and proclamation: celebration of the Mass, sharing the sacraments, Bible study, charitable work, social events, parish retreats, outreach events, etc.
- The parish can engage with other Christian churches, faith communities, social workers, and agencies to show the Church's work for justice, social cohesion, and the common good: living out the Gospel message of love.
- Local diocesan newspapers such as the *Catholic Pic* in Liverpool help people learn more about their faith.

Nationally:

- The Bishops' Conference of a country helps Catholics to know and share the Gospel. There is a Department for Evangelization and Catechesis at the Bishops' Conference of England and Wales which supports evangelization.
- National initiatives such as 'Proclaim '15: building missionary parishes' can support and encourage parish evangelisation.
- National Catholic publications such as *The Catholic Times* and *The Tablet* are used by the Church to help evangelize people.

Globally:

- The Church proclaims the Gospel to the whole world through the Pope (e.g. on World Youth Day); TV (e.g. EWTN, Salt and Light), radio (e.g. Vatican Radio, *Word on Fire*), and other modern media (YouTube, the internet, *Word on Fire*.).
- The Church lives out the Gospel in the work of international charities such as CAFOD (see 2.7).

B Two key figures of the new evangelization: Bishop Robert Barron (above) and Pope Francis (below).

Individual Catholics

Pope Francis has talked about how individual Catholics can participate in evangelization. First by demonstrating the teaching of Jesus in their everyday lives: 'The primary reason for evangelizing is the love of Jesus which we have received [...] What kind of love would not feel the need to speak of the beloved, to point him out, to make him known?' (*Evangelii Gaudium*, Ch5: 264). Secondly, by sharing the love of Jesus with others: 'Jesus wants evangelizers who proclaim the good news not only with words, but above all by a life transfigured by God's presence' (*Evangelii Gaudium*, Ch5: 259).

Locally:

- Individual Catholics often evangelize by their choice of career – such as a doctor, teacher, carer, police officer, firefighter – which embodies the love of Christ for the world in a particular way.
- They spread the Gospel through local oral or written communication: being a catechist, a charity worker, or a lay missionary.
- Through the vocation of marriage and family life, Catholics live out the Gospel of Christ's love by loving each other faithfully and raising children to follow Christ.

Nationally:

- Individual Catholics may attend national events to share or learn about their faith.
- They may speak at or attend national events that connect their career with their faith, e.g. conferences on the vocation of the Catholic teacher.
- They may attend national workshops and conferences on **catechesis** and the new evangelization.

Globally:

- Individual Catholics may attend global gatherings to share and learn about their faith, e.g. the 2015 World Meeting of Families in Philadelphia, USA.
- They may write for or use new global media, e.g. blogs/websites that provide resources to help people take part in the Church's evangelizing mission.
- Some may live out their vocation in an international context, e.g. academics or pastoral workers who speak at international gatherings.

C The opening of the Catholic World Meeting of Families.

USEFUL TERM

Catechesis: teaching, usually in classes such as for confirmation or Holy Communion. Its focus is an increase in understanding of the faith for those who have already been baptized or accepted the faith

BUILD YOUR SKILLS

1 a What is evangelization?
  b Who takes part in evangelization in the Catholic Church?

2 a Why do Catholics believe evangelization is important?
  b How is new evangelization different to traditional evangelization?

SUMMARY

- Mission conveys the idea of a person being sent to others in order to help them, or to bring something that will benefit them.
- Evangelization and the Church's evangelizing mission is proclaiming to others and living out the Gospel of Jesus.
- Jesus was sent by the Father into the world on mission. The Spirit was sent by Father and Son.
- Jesus sent ('commissioned') the apostles to go into the world to proclaim and live out the Gospel.

EXAM-STYLE QUESTIONS

A Outline **three** ways an individual might participate in evangelization. (3)
C Explain **two** ways the 'new evangelization' is important for the Catholic Church today. In your answer you must refer to a source of wisdom and authority. (5)

Revision

REVIEW YOUR KNOWLEDGE

1. Name the three Sacraments of Initiation.
2. Describe why liturgical worship is important.
3. What are the parts of the funeral liturgy?
4. Describe efficacious prayer.
5. Describe the difference between formal and extempore prayer.
6. Define popular piety.
7. What is a pilgrimage?
8. Describe Jesus' two great commandments from Mark 12:29–31.

* See page 288 for answers.

USEFUL TERMS

Do you know what these words mean?

Sanctifying grace   Intercessions   Pilgrimage

Requiem   Vigil   Efficacious prayer   Devotions

Mystery of the rosary   Relics   Vatican II

Blessed sacrament   Genuflect   Monstrance

Penance   Crucifixion   Transfiguration

Kingdom of God   Catechesis

EXTEND YOUR KNOWLEDGE: RESEARCH TASKS

For a research task, try to put together a full side of A4 of your own writing on the topics below.

1. Research Taizé as a pilgrimage destination for Christians of different denominations.
2. Research the document 'Preparing my funeral' by Vincent Nichols, Archbishop of Westminster.
3. Research how forms of popular piety such as prayer beads or the Stations of the Cross might be used by non-Catholics.
4. Research examples of the work of the Catholic Church to fulfil Jesus' teaching of 'love thy neighbour', such as Caritas Anchor House, a homelessness charity.

ONGOING LEARNING REVIEW

It is vital that you keep reviewing past material to make sure you have fully learned and remember it.

1. What was the result of the First Council of Constantinople?
2. Explain three ways man is made in God's image.
3. How do Catholics understand redemption?
4. What is God's grace?
5. How do Catholics receive grace?

Exam practice

In this exam practice section you will see examples for the exam question types: **a**, **b**, **c** and **d**. You can find out more about these on pages 6–7. Questions (b) and (c) in the **Exam question review** section below show strong student answers. Questions (c) and (d) in the **Improve it!** section need improvement.

Exam question review

> (b) Describe **two** differences in how the Eucharist is interpreted between Catholicism and the main religious tradition of Great Britain. (4)

Catholics believe that the bread and wine is changed into the body and blood of Jesus Christ through transubstantiation. During Mass the Priest asks God to send down the Holy Spirit to make holy and transform the bread and wine.

Protestant Christians do not believe in transubstantiation. When they meet in church their focus is not on the liturgy of the Eucharist but on the liturgy of the Word. They believe that the bread and wine are symbolic of Jesus and their worship is centred on his teachings.

> (c) Explain **two** benefits of the different forms of popular piety to Christians. In your answer you must refer to a source of wisdom and authority. (5)

Popular piety is important because Vatican II teaches that 'spiritual life [...] is not limited solely to participation in the liturgy.' So this shows that the Catholic Church encourages Catholics to take part in devotions outside church services, for example by praying the rosary. The benefit of this is that praying the rosary can be done anywhere, at church, at home and often before funerals.

Another form of piety is Eucharistic Adoration; this is where the Eucharist is displayed in a monstrance for everyone to see. A benefit of this is that it is a good way of focusing people in prayer by praising or thanking God as they believe Christ is present among them, in the Eucharist.

Improve it!

These answers will not get full marks. Can you rewrite and improve them?

> (c) Explain **two** functions of the funeral rite in Catholic life. In your answer you must refer to a source of wisdom and authority. (5)

The funeral rite helps to support the deceased on their journey to the next life. The funeral rite also reminds the living that death is not the end of life but more eternal.

> (d) 'Catholic Social Teaching has the power to influence the whole world.' Evaluate this statement considering arguments for and against. In your response you should:
> • refer to Catholic teachings
> • reach a justified conclusion. (12)

I don't agree that Catholic Social Teaching has the power to influence the whole world because not everybody is a Catholic and so they won't listen to Christian teachings. Also, although Catholics believe everybody is their neighbour, it doesn't mean that everybody wants to be their neighbour, as wars show. There is lots of hatred in the world so it is difficult to solve this problem. Catholic Social Teaching does try to do this and thinks that if you start at home with your real neighbours, then that's a good place to start helping. The Pope tries to make every Catholic help poor people because they are the most in need. So if Catholics try really hard to follow what Jesus teaches, maybe they can change the world through loving their neighbour.

WHAT WENT WELL

There are two differences given here, each explaining a point with a good amount of detail, and contrasting the differences in belief.

WHAT WENT WELL

Question (c) requires the same level of explanation as a question (b), but with the support of a well-chosen source of wisdom or authority. The quotation used is from a Vatican II Constitution *Sacrosanctum Concilium* and appropriately shows how the Catholic Church supports popular piety as part of spiritual life.

HOW TO IMPROVE

These are statements rather than explanations where each point is developed; try to add examples to show full understanding of the question. The answer also lacks the required source of wisdom or authority.

HOW TO IMPROVE

This answer touches on several relevant ideas, but fails to develop the arguments in a meaningful and analytical way. Some of the suggestions, however, are inaccurate. There no balance and only a loose chain of reasoning – links between arguments. Using paragraphs is a good way to show development and separate points. Sources of wisdom and authority could be added, and the conclusion needs to be more focused to summarise the arguments made.

The origins, structure, and different literary forms of the Bible

The word 'Bible' comes from the Greek *biblia* meaning 'the books'. It is a collection of writings from approximately 40 authors, written across 1500 years, and was originally written in Hebrew, Aramaic, and Greek.

- What Christians call the Old Testament is what Jews call the Tenakh. The first Christians accepted the Jewish Scriptures because they were also Jewish.

- The New Testament was written by people who had access to the testimony of those who witnessed the life and work of Jesus first hand.

- By the third century there was an agreed collection of these writings which the Church believed to be genuine and accurate, revealing the true word of God; these then became approved or **canonical**.

- There are slightly different versions of the Bible. The version recognized by the Catholic Church has 73 books including the **deuterocanonical** books which are sometimes listed at the end of the Old Testament. These include Judith, Tobit, and the two books of the Maccabees. In other editions of the Bible the deutercanonical book are placed in the appropriate part of the Bible, depending on the type of writing they are. For example, Tobit comes after Nehemiah as one of the books of prophecy.

Catholics believe the different books of the Bible contain the revealed Word of God in different forms and with different purposes.

SPECIFICATION FOCUS

The Bible: the development and structure of the Bible as the revealed Word of God: the origins, structure and different literary forms of the Bible: Old Testament: law, history, prophets, writings; and New Testament: gospels, letters; including divergent Christian understandings about which books should be within the Bible with reference to the Council of Trent.

✝ **CATECHISM OF THE CATHOLIC CHURCH**

'The Old Testament is an indispensable part of Sacred Scripture. **Its books are divinely inspired and retain a permanent value**, for the Old Covenant has never been revoked.' *CCC 125*

Old Testament

Law: These books, written as commands from God, are called the Pentateuch or sometimes the Books of Moses. In Judaism they are known as the Torah. There are 613 laws in the Old Testament. Christians and Jews believe 'the Law' was revealed to Moses. The books are Genesis, Exodus, Leviticus, Numbers, and Deuteronomy.

History: These books document the history of the Jewish people from the time of the Judges through to the Persian Empire. These books include Joshua, Kings, and Chronicles.

Prophets: Messages from God, often about the future, are referred to as prophecy; the word 'prophet' literally means 'spokesperson'. Often they were warnings from God that exposed sin and called for repentance. They also contained many reminders of the covenant. These books include those from Isaiah to Malachi.

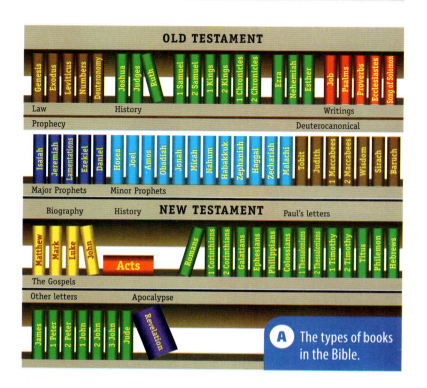

Ⓐ The types of books in the Bible.

Writings: The Poetic and Wisdom writings not only tried to tell stories, but to educate readers about the nature of God, reality, and virtue. These books are Job, Psalms, Proverbs, Ecclesiastes, and Song of Solomon.

New Testament

Gospels: The word 'gospel' literally means 'good news'. They were written approximately between 65 and 110CE. Each Gospel is distinctive and reflects the priorities of its author, but most of the key events in Jesus' life are described in all four Gospels. The Gospels are Matthew, Mark, Luke, and John.

> ❝But there are also many other things that Jesus did; if every one of them were written down, I suppose that the world itself could not contain the books that would be written.❞
> *John 21:25*

Letters: These are also called the 'Epistles', meaning a formal letter to an individual or group. The 21 personal letters were mainly, but not always written by the apostles to their churches. They were often challenges to the congregation and reminders to focus on the life and teaching of Jesus. They include all the books from Romans to Jude.

The Book of Revelation: This book is seen as apocalyptic, which means it describes the end of the world. It is quite different to the rest of the New Testament.

Divergent content of the Bible

The Catholic Bible includes seven Deuterocanonical books which are not present in the Protestant Bible because the Protestant Church deleted these from their Bible during the Reformation. Their inclusion in the Catholic Bible was affirmed at the Council of Trent in 1545, an important ecumenical council. Some Eastern Orthodox churches include additional scriptures in their Bible which are not recognized by the Catholic Church. The order of books in the Bible within denominations can also vary.

USEFUL TERMS

Canonical: authoritative parts of the Bible approved by the Catholic Church

Deuterocanonical: belonging to the second canon, a later addition to the Bible

CATECHISM OF THE CATHOLIC CHURCH

'The Gospels are the heart of all the Scriptures.'
CCC 125

CATECHISM OF THE CATHOLIC CHURCH

'The New Testament lies hidden in the Old and the Old Testament is unveiled in the New.'
CCC 129

B A fourth-century church basilica in Syria.

BUILD YOUR SKILLS

1. a How many types of book from the Bible can you write down?
   b Which two of these do you think are the most important for Catholics? Why?

2. a Explain why the Old Testament is important for Catholics.
   b Explain why some Christians would feel the New Testament is more important.

SUMMARY

- The Bible is not one book, but a collection of many books, by many authors.
- The Old Testament contains a wide variety of literary styles that includes laws, historical writings, prophecy, and poetry.
- The New Testament contains the accounts of Jesus' life (the Gospels) as well as the letters documenting the growth of the early Church.

EXAM-STYLE QUESTIONS

A Outline **three** types of book in the Bible. (3)
B Explain **two** ways the Bible is understood as the revealed Word of God. (4)

3.2 Interpretation of the Bible

Different interpretations of the Bible

Different denominations of Christians often form their own way or tradition of interpreting the text of the Bible. These different interpretive traditions can be grouped into different types, e.g. Liberal, Evangelical, Literal, Inspired.

> ‘All Scripture is inspired by God.’
> *2 Timothy 3:16*

SPECIFICATION FOCUS

Interpretation of the Bible: Catholic interpretation of the Bible and understanding of the meaning of inspiration; divergent interpretations of the authority of the Bible within Christianity: the literal Word of God, the revealed Word of God and as source of guidance and teaching, including 2 Timothy 3:16 and Catechism of the Catholic Church 105–108; the implications of this for Catholics today.

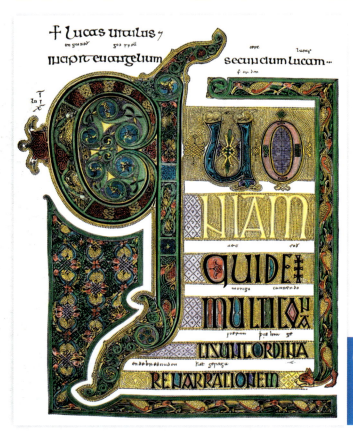

A page from the Lindisfarne Gospels; Catholics believe the Bible is the inspired word of God.

CATECHISM OF THE CATHOLIC CHURCH

‘**God inspired the human authors of the sacred books** […] it was as true authors that they consigned to writing whatever he wanted written, and no more.’
CCC 106

The inspired word of God

Catholics believe that the Bible is the inspired word of God, written down by human writers. This is sometimes regarded as the conservative Christian view. Catholics interpret the quotation above from 2 Timothy to mean that God is the primary author of the Bible and that through it he communicates the truth about himself and his loving plan of salvation. This means:

- The Bible is God's message in human words and as such is influenced by the human writer's personal beliefs and interests.
- There is truth in the message of the Bible. For example, God created the world, spoke through prophets, and took human form as Jesus.

 USEFUL TERMS

Inerrant: containing no errors

Lectionary: a book which contains the passages of scripture which are to be read at Mass, listed in the order of the liturgical year for each Sunday or weekday

- The Bible is not a science or history book. As a result, there is no problem in believing in evolution or the Big Bang theory and seeing the creation story in Genesis as a true poetic reflection on the significance of God as creator.

The literal word of God

Some Christians believe that the Bible is true, word for word. It is the word of God and must be taken literally in all ways, therefore it is called a literalist Christian view. This means:

- There are no mistakes and everything in the Bible is true; it is **inerrant**.
- If the Bible seems to contradict itself, there must be a reason for this.
- If the Bible seems to contradict science, scientists must be wrong.
- All moral guidance in the Bible is universal and applicable to today.

The liberal view

Some Christians believe that the Bible was written by humans inspired like any other writers. This is sometimes called the liberal view. This means:

- The Bible contains spiritual truths and not literal truths.
- The Bible helps people become closer to God by sharing human experience.
- There is much symbolism and poetry in the Bible which results in a range of beliefs. The miracles are an example of this.
- It means some parts of the Bible are outdated and irrelevant to modern life.

A source of guidance and teaching

The Bible, by its very diverse nature, can be used in many different ways. However, the Bible is meant to be read and understood as a whole text, so that no part of it is taken out of context. Reading it is also a prayerful activity, and different to reading other books or novels. The tradition and teaching of the Church should guide how a Catholic interprets what it says in the Bible.

- In Church, the **lectionary** provides the selection of approved readings from the Bible which are used for worship on a particular day or occasion.
- Catholics are encouraged to read the Bible for personal devotion and study outside of the Mass.
- There are many ways the Bible may be used at home: reading as a family after meals, as part of informal morning or evening family prayers (the Liturgy of the Hours is considered formal prayer), or in books written specially for children.
- The Bible can also be consulted in times of distress or confusion – Catholics can find advice to guide their behaviour, or comfort when times are hard.

The implications for Catholics today

- Catholics are not literalists and as a result can and do accept the teachings of science (the Big Bang, evolution) without rejecting the spiritual truths in Genesis.
- The Catechism teaches that God is the author of the Bible, which was written under the inspiration of the Holy Spirit (CCC 105). This is why when read in church the phrase 'The word of the Lord' is used.

'fundamentalist interpretation of this kind [...] tends to treat the biblical text as if it had been dictated word for word by the Spirit. It fails to recognize that **the word of God has been formulated in language and expression conditioned by various periods.**'
The Interpretation of the Bible in the Church, Pontifical Biblical Commission, 23 April 1993

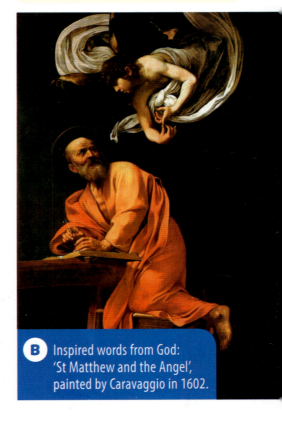

 **B** Inspired words from God: 'St Matthew and the Angel', painted by Caravaggio in 1602.

✝ **CATECHISM OF THE CATHOLIC CHURCH**

'The Church forcefully and specifically exhorts all the Christian faithful [...] to learn the surpassing knowledge of Jesus Christ, by frequent reading of the divine Scriptures. **Ignorance of the Scriptures is ignorance of Christ**.'
CCC 133

- Faith in Jesus is the most important thing. Faith in the Bible comes second. Even if someone can't read the Bible, they can still have faith in Jesus.

> ❛In the beginning was the Word, and **the Word was with God, and the Word was God** […] And the Word became flesh and lived among us, and we have seen his glory, the glory as of a father's only son, full of grace and truth.❜
> *John 1:1, 14*

 C The Bible is the most important source of wisdom for Christians.

- Catholics must consider the time and culture, literary genres, and ways of feeling, speaking, and narrating found in the Bible (CCC 110). This must be done with guidance of the Holy Spirit.

- The clergy use the magisterium to help the laity with interpretations of holy Scripture.

BUILD YOUR SKILLS

1 **a** In your own words outline the following terms:
- the inspired Word of God
- the literal Word of God
- a source of wisdom and guidance.

b Which of these do you think would be closest to the Catholic Church's understanding of the Bible? Why?

2 Write one PEE paragraph of an essay about the significance of the Word of God.

SUMMARY

- The Bible is interpreted in different ways by different Christians.

- This includes Christians who take it literally, those who believe it is inspired, and those who would interpret it more liberally.

- Catholics believe that God is the author of the Bible as a result of authors being inspired by the Holy Spirit. However, Catholicism is a living faith, not a 'religion of the book'.

- The Bible can only be understood by having a wide knowledge of its content and making sure it is interpreted properly, following the criteria laid down by the Church.

✝ CATECHISM OF THE CATHOLIC CHURCH

'The Sacred Scriptures contain the Word of God and, because they are inspired, they are truly the Word of God.'
CCC 135

? EXAM-STYLE QUESTIONS

C Explain **two** reasons why it is important to Catholics that the Bible is interpreted correctly. In your answer you must refer to a source of wisdom and authority. (5)

D 'The Bible should not be taken literally.' Evaluate this statement considering arguments for and against. In your response you should:
- refer to Catholic teachings
- refer to different Christian points of view
- reach a justified conclusion. (15)

3.3 The magisterium

Leaders and leadership in the Church

In the Catholic Church there is: one Pope, approximately 5,100 bishops, and over 400,000 priests *(2013 Pontifical Yearbook)*. Catholics who are not part of the clergy are called the laity. There are over 1.2 billion Catholics in the world.

- **Parish priests** are charged with the emotional and spiritual care of a particular area, called a parish. They lead the daily Mass as well as provide the sacraments for the parishioners.
- **Bishops** are each responsible for a diocese and all the priests, deacons, and the laity within it. Bishops also administer the sacrament of Holy Orders.
- **Archbishops** are more senior than bishops and are usually in charge of an archdiocese, which may have more than one bishop within it.
- **Cardinals** are a college of bishops, each of whom is nominated by the Pope, whose main role is to elect future popes. They may also serve as head of a department of the **Roman Curia**.
- **The Pope** or Pontiff is first and foremost the Bishop of Rome. He also exercises the magisterium (see page 68) and acts as a source of guidance and authority for Catholics. He appoints new bishops to care for the laity. The Pope leads the worldwide Church and is also the head of state of the Vatican City.

He is the successor of St Peter and therefore has the power and authority passed on from Jesus through the apostles, which is shared with other bishops. He teaches Catholics through his letters, addresses, and pastoral visits.

SPECIFICATION FOCUS

The magisterium of the Church: the meaning, function and importance of the magisterium both conciliar and pontifical with reference to Catechism of the Catholic Church 100; the magisterium as the living, teaching office of the Church and authentic interpreter of the affirmations of Scripture and Tradition, and why they are important for Catholics today.

USEFUL TERM

Roman Curia: a body of administrative groups and officials which carry out the official work of the Church

A Catholic bishops of England and Wales.

The magisterium of the Church

'Magisterium' comes from the Latin *magister* which means 'a master', and signifies authority to teach. This authority rests with the Pope and his bishops, and comes from the Holy Spirit, whom Jesus sent to guide the Church at Pentecost.

Jesus first gave the authority to preach and teach the truth of salvation to the apostles. This authority is now called the magisterium and it is exercised by the Pope and his bishops. The teachings that come from the Pope are called **pontifical** and can be ordinary or extraordinary. A second type of teaching called conciliar comes from an extraordinary gathering called an ecumenical council.

The ordinary magisterium

The ordinary magisterium means the everyday teaching of the Church which is to be found in the sayings and writings of bishops and Popes – in letters, homilies, exhortations, etc. The ordinary and universal magisterium is infallible and has complete authority for Catholics.

The extraordinary magisterium

This is the infallible teaching of the Church on a special matter which comes about in one of two ways:

1. **Conciliar**: Through an ecumenical council. This is when the Pope calls together all the bishops of the Church to settle a matter of dispute or to explore new questions facing the Church. There have only ever been 21 of these.

2. **Pontifical**: Through the ***ex cathedra*** declarations of the Pope. Under certain very particular and rare conditions the Pope can declare some teachings of the Church to be infallible:

   - Pope Pius IX, 1854, defined the Immaculate Conception of Mary.
   - Pope Pius XII, 1950, defined the **Assumption** of Mary.

When the extraordinary magisterium define a doctrine as infallible it is then called a **dogma**.

The living, teaching office of the Church today

Scripture means the Bible; Apostolic Tradition means the oral teachings of the apostles that were never written down. This Apostolic Tradition has been handed down to today's Church through **Apostolic Succession**, passed on by the Pope and bishops through centuries of repetition to form traditions within the Catholic Church. St Paul guides Christians to follow Apostolic Tradition:

> ❛So then, brethren, stand firm and hold to the traditions which you were taught by us, either by word of mouth or by letter. ❜
> *2 Thessalonians 2:15*

The role of the magisterium is to interpret the Bible and the Apostolic Tradition for the life of Catholics in the modern world. Examples of where this interpretation may be helpful are in helping Catholics to respond to new situations, such as

B Pope Francis is the 266th Pope.

USEFUL TERMS

Apostolic Succession: the belief that the tradition from the apostles has been handed down in the Church through the Pope and bishops and gives them authority

Assumption: the taking of Mary, body and soul, to heaven at the end of her life

Dogma: doctrines which have been infallibly defined by an ecumenical council or pope, which all Catholics must accept

Ex cathedra: means 'from the chair' and refers to the authority the pope has in inheriting the 'chair' of St Peter, as an heir would inherit a throne

Pontifical: relating to the Pope (the Pontiff)

CATECHISM OF THE CATHOLIC CHURCH

'The task of interpreting the Word of God authentically has been entrusted **solely to the Magisterium of the Church**, that is, to the Pope and to the bishops in communion with him.'
CCC 100

C A meeting of the Roman Curia.

advancements in technology and medicine like genetic engineering and IVF treatments.

- The magisterium is important as the supreme authority for Catholics, helping them to interpret scripture and tradition faithfully.
- As the magisterium addresses issues that did not exist in the time of Jesus or the apostles, Catholics cannot find the answers in the Bible.
- It ensures that teaching always addresses the needs of the current time, but in light of tradition.
- The magisterium's importance is in helping Catholics to continue to believe and live by the truth.

The Catechism of the Catholic Church (CCC)

The word Catechism originally meant 'to teach orally'. However it now means a doctrinal manual – a book of approved Catholic teachings. The Roman Catechism was first published in 1566 at the Council of Trent. It was only intended for use by priests and bishops. Pope Pius X published a Catechism for all Catholics in the early twentieth century. The current English edition is the Catechism of the Catholic Church (or CCC) which was written at the request of Pope John Paul II and promulgated by him in 1992. Ordinary Catholics can use the Catechism to help inform their faith and understanding.

CATECHISM OF THE CATHOLIC CHURCH

'The whole body of the faithful […] cannot err in matters of belief.'
CCC 92, Lumen Gentium 12

BUILD YOUR SKILLS

1 a Pick three examples of how the teachings of the ordinary magisterium are shared with Catholics.
  b Outline, in your own words, the two forms of the extraordinary magisterium.

2 Explain, in your own words, the role of the magisterium.

3 Write down three reasons the magisterium is still needed today.

SUMMARY

- The Pope is the head of the Catholic Church and the bishop of Rome.
- The teaching authority of the Church is called the magisterium.
- The authority to teach is held by the bishops of the Church in communion with the Pope.
- The magisterium is needed in all ages to interpret the signs and issues of the times and to see how these can be informed by the Bible and tradition.
- Apostolic Tradition is also used to guide the behaviour and actions of Catholics.

EXAM-STYLE QUESTIONS

B Explain **two** ways in which the magisterium contributes to the strength of the Catholic Church. (4)

C Explain **two** ways the magisterium communicates with Catholics. In your answer you must refer to a source of wisdom and authority. (5)

3.4 The Second Vatican Council

The nature, history, and importance of the Second Vatican Council

An ecumenical council is an assembly of bishops and other Catholic leaders who meet at the invitation of the Pope to discuss matters of faith and Church discipline.

The 21st ecumenical council of the Catholic Church is often known as *Vatican II*, the Second Vatican Council because it was the second to be held at St Peter's Basilica in the Vatican. It focused on relations between the Roman Catholic Church and the modern world.

The council was opened by Pope John XXIII on 11 October 1962 and closed under Pope Paul VI on 8 December, the Feast of the Immaculate Conception, in 1965. It published 16 documents:

- four Constitutions: the longest and most important documents of the council
- three Declarations and nine Decrees: these are shorter documents and give practical detail, dealing with specific questions.

Sacrosanctum Concilium (The Constitution on the Sacred Liturgy)

- This document focused on the reform of church services (liturgy) to ensure that there was more participation by the laity in them, particularly the Mass.
- Permission was given for the Mass to be celebrated in the local langauge, e.g. English, alongside Latin and the congregation were taught the words of the prayers, and responses, so they fully understood what was happening.

🔍 SPECIFICATION FOCUS

The Second Vatican Council: the nature, history and importance of the council; the nature and significance of the four key documents for the Church and for Catholic living: *Dei Verbum, Lumen Gentium, Sacrosanctum Concilium* and *Gaudium et Spes*.

🔑 USEFUL TERMS

Ecumenism: the idea that there should be one unified Christian Church

Non-theist: someone who is uncommitted towards a belief in God

> ❛The "Church earnestly desires that all the faithful should be led to [...] fully conscious, and active participation in liturgical celebrations. [...] **Such participation by the Christian people is their right and duty** by reason of their baptism."❜
> *Sacrosanctum Concilium 14*

A St Peter's Basilica in the Vatican.

- The congregation were permitted to receive the Eucharist in both forms for the first time.
- There was also a revision of the lectionary which means Catholics heard far more of the Bible than before the council.

Lumen Gentium (Dogmatic Constitution on the Church)

- This document focused on Catholic beliefs about the Church.
- The possibility of salvation for non-Christians and even **non-theists** was suggested. Previous teaching said anyone outside of the Catholic Church was not saved.
- The document also encouraged collegiality among the bishops – for them to work together as a group – which led to great responsibility for the magisterium in leading the Church.
- There were also reminders that all members of the Church are called to the *priesthood of the faithful*, as well as being part of the *universal call to holiness*. Both of these were reminders that everyone should participate in the sacraments and attend the Mass and confession. There was also an explanation of the important role of Mary.
- There was a greater emphasis on the importance of ordinary Catholics (the laity).

> ‘**It is the noble duty of pastors to recognize the services and charismatic gifts of the laity**. Pastors were not meant by Christ to shoulder alone the entire saving mission of the Church toward the world. ’
> *Lumen Gentium 30*

Dei Verbum (Dogmatic Constitution on Divine Revelation)

- This document focused on the relationship between tradition and the Bible. It considered the Word of God and how God's word is revealed to Catholics.
- It is important to understand that the Word of God is not a book but a person; God is revealed through Jesus.

> ‘To see Jesus is to see His Father (John 14:9). For this reason **Jesus perfected revelation by fulfilling it through his whole work of making Himself present and manifesting Himself**: through His words and deeds, His signs and wonders, but especially through His death and glorious resurrection from the dead and final sending of the Spirit of truth. ’
> *Dei Verbum 4*

B An ecumenical council.

- It made clear that both the Bible and tradition are equally important; the Catholic Church does not rely on the Bible alone.
- It clarified that the Bible is the Word of God, written by humans, inspired by the Holy Spirit.
- It highlighted the Gospels as being particularly important for Catholics because they contain direct revelation from Jesus, the Word of God made flesh (John 1).

Gaudium et Spes (Pastoral Constitution on the Church in the Modern World)

- This document considered humanity's relationship to society, including economics, poverty, social justice, culture, science, technology, and **ecumenism**.
- It highlighted the significant impact of modern science and technology, but explained the danger of losing the dignity of man in the modern world.
- It also reflected on the importance of talking with non-believers and other Christians.

> ❝ The joys and hopes, the grief and anguish of the people of our time, especially of those who are poor or afflicted, are the joys and hopes, the grief and anguish of the followers of Christ as well. ❞
> *Gaudium et Spes 1*

C *Gaudium et Spes* emphasized the importance of global society.

BUILD YOUR SKILLS

1 Explain, in your own words, what the Second Vatican Council was.

2 Choose two documents from the Council and explain the different reasons why each one is important:
- for the Church
- for ordinary Catholics.

EXAM-STYLE QUESTIONS

B Explain **two** significant changes to the Church after the Second Vatican Council. (4)

D 'The Second Vatican Council changed life dramatically for Catholics today.' Evaluate this statement considering arguments for and against. In your response you should:
- refer to Catholic teachings
- reach a justified conclusion. (15)

SUMMARY

- Vatican II was a large ecumenical council held in the Vatican to discuss Catholic Church teaching and beliefs in the modern world.
- Some of the major changes included the Mass being spoken in the local language rather than only Latin.
- Other changes included guidance on poverty and social justice in the world, as well as how to work with other Christians and non-believers.

Chapter 3 Sources of Wisdom and Authority

3.5 The Church as the Body of Christ

The Church as the People of God

When Catholics talk about being the People of God they mean that because they have come to Jesus in faith and through baptism, they are part of a 'chosen people […] a holy nation' (1 Peter 2:9) belonging to God.

Catholics believe that their shared unity is their strength as the Body of Christ.

The Church as the Body of Christ

The Church is described as the Body of Christ in the New Testament and the Catechism. It means that the Church is strong because its many individuals join together in community. The single 'body' that they create is the strength of the Church. Jesus has natural authority and leadership. As such, he is referred to as the head, controlling the direction of the body.

- Baptism makes Catholics members of the Body of Christ and unifies them with other members of the Christian community, and with Jesus:

> 'For by one Spirit we were all baptized into one body – Jews or Greeks, slaves or free – and all were made to drink of one Spirit.'
> *1 Corinthians 12:13*

- Catholics refer to the Catholic Church as the Body of Christ, while Protestants see the term as being more general and universal to all Christians.
- Christians continue the work of Christ on earth. They are his living body, spreading the Gospel in word and action after Jesus' ascension. This enables them to be Christ's presence on earth.

> 'For as in one body we have many members, and all the members do not have the same function, so **we, though many, are one body in Christ**, and individually members one of another.'
> *Romans 12:4–5*

The importance of this unity for Catholics today

Within the Body of Christ the People of God work in different ways to show their love for God and neighbour. The clergy lead the church; the religious brothers and sisters such as monks, nuns, and sisters devote themselves to a life of contemplative prayer and service; and most Catholics form the laity – engaging in society so that the kingdom of God grows in their part of the world.

SPECIFICATION FOCUS

The Church as the Body of Christ and the People of God: the nature and significance of the Church as the Body of Christ and the People of God, including Romans 12:4–6 and 1 Corinthians 12; why the Church as the Body of Christ and the People of God is important for Catholics today; divergent Christian attitudes towards these.

CATECHISM OF THE CATHOLIC CHURCH

'**The Church is the Body of Christ**. Through the Spirit and his action in the sacraments, above all the Eucharist, Christ, who once was dead and is now risen, establishes the community of believers as his own Body.'
CCC 805

A The Body of Christ unifies Christians worldwide.

The laity

This group includes all full (baptized and confirmed) members of the Church who are not the clergy. Lay people may live out their vocation to evangelize and follow Christ in different ways: by their choice of career; by working to spread the message of Jesus; through the vocation of marriage and family life.

The clergy

This group include deacons, priests, and bishops who administer the sacraments and help the Church work towards salvation and living Christ-like lives.

- By laying down their lives in service of others in the Church and world, they hope to bring God's love into the world.
- They try to build the kingdom of God by evangelizing and running parish communities.
- They lead the public worship of the Church, especially celebrating the sacraments, which bring spiritual nourishment and strength to God's people. At these moments they are acting *in persona Christi*, in the person of Christ.

The religious

This group includes monks, nuns, brothers and sisters who dedicate their lives in service and prayer to the Church.

- They live in separate communities and commit to living a life of poverty, chastity, and obedience. These are called the 'evangelical counsels'.
- Monks and nuns seek solitude to free them from distraction and self-absorption, allowing them to surrender to God more. They do this in a community of other monks/nuns.
- Religious brothers and sisters live, pray, and minister within the world. Their lives are often called active or apostolic, because they bring the Gospel to people in the world.

BUILD YOUR SKILLS

1. a Explain why Romans 12:4–6 is important for Catholics in understanding the Church as the Body of Christ.
   b How might this be interpreted differently by other Christians?

2. Describe how the following contribute to the Church as the Body of Christ:
   - The laity
   - The clergy
   - The religious.

SUMMARY

- The Body of Christ means the individuals who form the Christian family.
- The People of God means the group of people who have found faith in Jesus.
- References to the Body of Christ and the People of God are found in the New Testament and the Catechism.
- Each member of the Church has a responsibility to contribute to the Church in different ways.

CATECHISM OF THE CATHOLIC CHURCH

'By reason of their special vocation it belongs to the laity to seek the kingdom of God by engaging in temporal affairs and directing them according to God's will.'
CCC 898

B Solitude allows the religious to surrender to God.

CATECHISM OF THE CATHOLIC CHURCH

'In the consecrated life, Christ's faithful, moved by the Holy Spirit, propose to follow Christ more nearly [and pursue] the perfection of charity in the service of the Kingdom.'
CCC 916

EXAM-STYLE QUESTIONS

B Explain **two** ways the Church is understood as the Body of Christ. (4)

C Explain **two** ways referring to the Church as the Body of Christ helps Catholics understand their role in the Church better. In your answer you must refer to a source of wisdom and authority. (5)

3.6 The four marks of the Church

SPECIFICATION FOCUS

The meaning of the four marks of the Church: the nature of the Church as one, holy, catholic and apostolic including reference to the Nicene Creed and the First Council of Constantinople; how the marks may be understood in divergent ways within Christianity; why they are important for Catholics today.

The four marks of the Church

The Church is described as being *one, holy, catholic, and apostolic*. These are the 'four marks' of the Church and are found in the Nicene Creed which was confirmed at the First Council of Constantinople in 381CE (see 1.2).

- **One** means that there is one body and one Church; Christians are unified as one Church, even if this does not fit with Church structure on earth.
- **Holy** means set apart for a special purpose by, and for, God.
- **Catholic** means universal and refers to the fact that the Church spans the whole world and is united in the truth.
- **Apostolic** means the living tradition of the apostles, handed down over time.

The four marks of the Church are inseparable. As Jesus founded the Church, he marked it with these characteristics, which reflect its essential features and mission. The Church continues to fulfil these marks with the continued guidance of the Holy Spirit.

> ❝For just as the body is one and has many members, and all the members of the body, though many, are one body, so it is with Christ. **For in the one Spirit we were all baptized into one body.**❞
> *1 Corinthians 12:12–13*

One

The Church is one in three ways according to the Catechism:

- First in its source: the unity of the Trinity.
- Secondly due to the reconciliation of humanity made possible through the sacrifice of Jesus.
- Thirdly in its 'soul' that unites all the faithful (see CCC 813).

The sacraments further unite the Church, for example the service of the Mass is recognizable all around the world. The diversity of the Church and the vocations of Catholics are unified and bound in oneness.

Holy

Jesus is the source of all holiness: 'The one Christ is mediator and the way of salvation; he is present to us in His body which is the Church' (Dogmatic Constitution on the Church, No.14). Through its teaching, prayer, and worship the Church is a visible sign of holiness, while being a constant reminder to Catholics that they are called to a special purpose in their individual lives.

Catholic

St Ignatius of Antioch (*c*. 100) used the word catholic meaning 'universal' to describe the Church (Letter to the Smyrnaeans). The Church is indeed Catholic in that Jesus is universally present and that he has commissioned the Church to evangelize the world – 'Go therefore and make disciples of all nations' (Matthew 28:19). Protestants give a wider meaning to catholic, including the broader Christian community, not just the Catholic Church.

A St Ignatius introduced the idea of 'catholic'.

Apostolic

Jesus founded the Church and gave authority to his apostles, the first bishops. He entrusted a special task to St Peter, often referred to as the first Pope and Bishop of Rome, to act as his vicar (representative) on earth. This authority has been handed down through the Sacrament of Holy Orders in what is called Apostolic Succession from bishop to bishop, and then by extension to priests and deacons. Some Protestant denominations, such as Church of England believe connection to the apostles exists through commitment, beliefs, and mission rather than Apostolic Succession.

Why they are important for Catholics today

One

There are many differences within Christianity, with over 30,000 denominations. Other churches accept and profess the Nicene Creed, yet the Catholic Church believes that only they reflect the fullness of the marks. Ecumenism was an important part of the documents created by Vatican II (see 3.4). It places a duty on Catholics to work towards unity, including praying for and talking to non-Catholics.

B Jesus entrusted Peter with a special task, symbolized by the keys.

Holy

The Church provides a powerful way to Catholics to be holy, through regular prayer and the sacraments. Through these, the Church teaches Catholics to know, love, and serve God and to become more like him by working towards holiness and imitating Christ. Saints, those recognized by the Church to have lived a holy life worthy of honour, are also a good example for Catholics to follow.

Catholic

The history of the Catholic Church gives evidence of its strength, permanence, and unchanging nature. The Church, and Catholics today, suffered from persecution and various attacks, but remains universal. Catholics can take personal strength from the strength of the Church.

Apostolic

The magisterium has to guide Catholics today on issues such as nuclear war, euthanasia, and in vitro fertilization. They do this in light of the Bible and Apostolic Tradition. The duty to preserve, teach, defend, and pass on the faith therefore continues in the tradition of the apostles.

SUMMARY

- The 'four marks' of the Church are *one, holy, catholic, and apostolic*.
- The four marks are found in the Nicene Creed.
- The four marks remain important for Catholics today as they are part of their declaration of faith.
- The magisterium helps interpret the issues of the modern world in the light of Apostolic Tradition.

BUILD YOUR SKILLS

1 Explain why the four marks of the Church are considered inseparable.

2 a Pick one of the marks and explain what it means.
  b Pick a different mark and explain how it may be important in different ways for Christians today.

? EXAM-STYLE QUESTIONS

A Outline **three** of the marks of the Church. (3)

D 'The marks of the Church are less significant for Christians today.' Evaluate this statement considering arguments for and against. In your response you should:
  - refer to Catholic teachings
  - refer to different Christian points of view
  - reach a justified conclusion. (15)

3.7 Mary as a model of the Church

How is Mary a model of the Church?

Mary is a model of the Church because her life reflects the values, teaching, and beliefs of the Catholic faith. She is a role model, but this is separate to her importance as a model of the Church: the embodiment of what it means to be Catholic.

Joined with Jesus

All of Mary's religious significance comes from the unique status of Christ and the role she plays in his incarnation.

- Many of the doctrines surrounding Mary are also about Christ. This is true of the Immaculate Conception (she must be sinless in order to bear the sinless Jesus) and the Assumption (when Mary's body is raised to heaven by Jesus).
- Mary is called the mother of the Church since the Church is Christ's body and she is the Mother of Christ.

The Immaculate Conception is the Catholic belief that Mary herself was born free from Original Sin – that when she was conceived, God intervened and protected her soul from the stain of sin. It is *not* the same as the Virgin Birth of Jesus.

- The absence of sin was vital in order for her to bear Jesus, and therefore God.
- Due to God's omniscient (all-knowing) nature, Mary was destined to give birth to Jesus. However, she still needed to be open to God's will to accept this gift.

SPECIFICATION FOCUS

Mary as a model of the Church: the significance of Mary as a model of the Church – joined with Christ in the work of salvation, as a model of discipleship and as a model of faith and charity, including Luke 1:26–39 and Catechism of the Catholic Church 963–975; the implications of this teaching for Catholic life today.

CATECHISM OF THE CATHOLIC CHURCH

'Mary's role in the Church is inseparable from her union with Christ and flows directly from it.' CCC 964

 'The Madonna and Child' by Anna Maria von Oer.

Discipleship

Mary is sometimes called the first disciple because of her belief in Jesus from the first moment of his conception, as described in Luke 1:26–38 when Mary accepts the will of God that she should bear Jesus.

> ❛ And Mary said, "Behold, I am the handmaid of the Lord; let it be to me according to your word." ❜
> *Luke 1:38*

This is what contributes to her position as a model of the Church, not just a model of **discipleship** in general, because her sacrifice and role started before the birth of Jesus.

Faith and charity

Mary was a young unmarried woman who risked death by carrying Jesus. She demonstrated faith in God by:

- her acceptance that she would bear Jesus
- obeying the command in Joseph's dream to flee to Egypt to avoid Herod
- later returning to Nazareth.

In Luke 2:35 she is told by Simeon at the **Temple** that a 'sword of sorrow' would pierce her heart. Her continued trust in God makes her a model of the Church as she watched Jesus at the foot of the cross during his crucifixion. Catholics believe they should follow this example when faced with their own troubles – to keep faith and trust in God.

Her acts of faith and sacrifice are also acts of charity. She encouraged Jesus to solve the problem of the lack of wine at a wedding in Cana (John 2:1–11) and St Bonaventure (1221–1274CE) describes her ultimate act of charity: 'Mary so loved the world as to give her only-begotten Son'.

The implications of this teaching for Catholics today

As a result of her role as a model of the Church, Catholics pay special devotion to the Virgin Mary. She continues to provide inspiration and guidance.

- Most Catholic churches have a statue of Mary, sometimes in a special Lady Chapel.
- She has many titles including Theotokos (Mother of God), Blessed Mother, Virgin, Madonna, and Our Lady.
- The Church celebrates many Marian solemnities (the most important Feast Days) including:
  - December 8 – Feast of the Immaculate Conception
  - January 1 – Mary, Mother of God
  - March 25 – Feast of the **Annunciation**
  - August 15 – The Assumption of the Blessed Virgin Mary.

CATECHISM OF THE CATHOLIC CHURCH

'By her complete adherence to the Father's will, to his Son's redemptive work, and to every prompting of the Holy Spirit, the Virgin Mary is the Church's model of faith and charity.'
CCC 967

USEFUL TERMS

Annunciation: the announcement by the angel Gabriel that Mary would conceive Christ

Discipleship: following the teaching and the example of Jesus

Temple: the holiest building of Judaism, built on Temple Mount in Jerusalem and destroyed in 586BCE by the Babylonians, then again after rebuilding in 70CE by the Romans

CATECHISM OF THE CATHOLIC CHURCH

'**Mary is the perfect prayer, a figure of the Church** […] We can pray with and to her. The prayer of the Church is sustained by the prayer of Mary and united with it in hope.'
CCC 2679

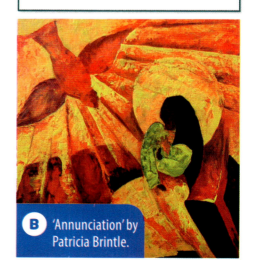

B 'Annunciation' by Patricia Brintle.

- There are many hymns, poems, and prayers dedicated to Mary. The most used prayer is the Hail Mary, based on the greeting of the angel Gabriel to the Virgin Mary in the Gospel of Luke (1:42). Other popular prayers include the Hail Holy Queen, the Magnificat, and the Angelus.

- Other ways of venerating Mary include use of the rosary, wearing a brown scapular, or maintaining a Mary Garden (a small sacred garden with a statue of Mary in it).

- There are religious orders and societies dedicated to Mary including the Marist Fathers and the Order of the Brothers of the Blessed Virgin Mary of Mount Carmel.

- Marian apparitions have resulted in many shrines and places of pilgrimage such as Lourdes, Guadalupe, Fatima, and Knock.

- These devotions reflect the importance and significance of Mary as a role model. She remains important in Catholic worship and as the Mother of God provides inspiration and guidance to Catholics today.

D The grotto in Lourdes where Mary appeared in 1858 to a young girl called Bernadette.

C A Mary Garden.

 BUILD YOUR SKILLS

1 a Explain why Catholics believe Mary is joined with Jesus in the work of salvation.
   b Explain why Catholics believe Mary is a model of faith and charity.

2 Explain fully how Catholics show devotion to Mary, giving specific examples.

3 Why is Luke 1:26–39 important in understanding the role of Mary?

 SUMMARY

- Mary is seen as a model for the Church because of her faith, unwavering trust, discipleship, and charity.

- She is a personal role model for Catholics: open to God and willing to accept his requests despite the difficulties she would face as the mother of Jesus.

- There are many feast days dedicated to Mary, special prayers such as the Hail Mary and the Rosary, and many places of pilgrimage connected to Marian apparitions.

? EXAM-STYLE QUESTIONS

B Explain **two** reasons why Mary is a model of discipleship. (4)

C Explain **two** reasons why it is important for Catholics to understand Mary as a model of the Church. In your answer you must refer to a source of wisdom and authority. (5)

3.8 Personal and ethical decision-making

Jesus as a source of authority for moral teaching

Christians who consider themselves 'morally good' are those who try to model themselves on God's ways. Jesus led by example, providing a way of living for Christians to follow. Morality is quite simply doing what is right and not doing what is wrong.

The Gospels give clear examples of what Jesus taught and how he acted in certain situations which can inspire Christians today.

A The Bible says that Jesus spent his time with those who were poor and destitute.

SPECIFICATION FOCUS

Sources of personal and ethical decision-making: the example and teaching of Jesus as the authoritative source for moral teaching; Jesus as fulfilment of the Law, including Matthew 5:17–24; divergent understandings of the place and authority of natural law; virtue and the primacy of conscience; the divergent implications of these sources of authority for Christians today.

CATECHISM OF THE CATHOLIC CHURCH

'Following Christ and united with him, Christians can strive to be "imitators of God as beloved children, and walk in love" **by conforming their thoughts, words and actions [...] and by following his example**.'
CCC 1694

Love for others

- Jesus set a perfect example of love in the Gospels. He showed his love for others by blessing and serving the poor, the sick, and the distressed. He also sometimes showed 'tough love' and challenged people's behaviour, e.g. in the story of the rich man (see 12.3)
- Jesus also instituted the Golden Rule often paraphrased as 'do to others as you would want them to do to you'. This is seen as a summary of The Sermon on the Mount. Jesus also made it clear that showing love for others would be a key way of recognizing Christians.

> ❛So in everything, do to others what you would have them do to you, for this sums up the Law and the Prophets. ❜
> *Matthew 7:12*

- Jesus also challenged his followers to display a self-sacrificial love, which is more important than the Golden Rule:

> **A new command I give you: love one another.** As I have loved you, so you must love one another. By this everyone will know that you are my disciples.
>
> *John 13:34–35*

Forgiveness

Forgiveness is a key theme in the Gospels: Jesus acts in word and by action. He was even able to forgive those who crucified him (Luke 23:33–35). Jesus encouraged people to forgive one another and, as a result, they would be forgiven by God. He made it clear that forgiveness was not limited and by forgiving, people would achieve salvation.

> For if you forgive other people when they sin against you, your heavenly Father will also forgive you.
>
> *Matthew 6:14*

B The Apostleship of the Sea are an organization who administer the sacraments, such as the Eucharist to seafarers far from home.

Servanthood

'The Servant King' is a title sometimes given to Jesus. He managed to lay aside his royal power to serve others. John 13:4 -5 describes how, at the Last Supper, he showed the disciples how to love one another, by being servants to one another. The ultimate act of servanthood was laying down his life at the crucifixion.

Social justice

Throughout the Gospels, Jesus addresses people's physical as well as spiritual needs. He makes it clear that this is part of his mission by declaring he will bring good news to the poor, free prisoners, give sight to the blind, and free the oppressed (Luke 4:18–19). In the Parable of the Sheep and the Goats he sets out the responsibility of Christians to help those in need.

> He got up from the meal, took off his outer clothing, and wrapped a towel around his waist. After that, he poured water into a basin and began to wash his disciples' feet, drying them with the towel that was wrapped around him.
>
> *John 13:4–5*

> Then the righteous will answer him, "Lord, when did we see you hungry and feed you, or thirsty and give you something to drink? When did we see you a stranger and invite you in, or needing clothes and clothe you? When did we see you sick or in prison and go to visit you?"
>
> 'The King will reply, "Truly I tell you, **whatever you did for one of the least of these brothers and sisters of mine, you did for me**."
>
> *Matthew 25:37–40 – The Parable of the Sheep and the Goats*

Jesus as fulfilment of the Law

Jesus is a source of authority in moral and ethical decision-making as he came to fulfil God's law (see Matthew 5:17–20). This means he helped people to understand what God wanted of them in respect to their beliefs, words, and actions. It is important to remember that Jesus learnt and obeyed the Law as a faithful Jew;

however, when he fulfilled it, he was helping people to understand the Law as God meant it. Jesus' fulfilment meant that those who followed him would be saved.

> ❛Do not think that I have come to abolish the Law or the Prophets; I have not come to abolish them but to fulfil them.❜
> *Matthew 5:17*

CATECHISM OF THE CATHOLIC CHURCH

'A human being must always obey the certain judgment of his conscience.'
CCC 1800

Sources of personal and ethical decision-making for Catholics

Catholics do not simply refer to one source when making personal and ethical decisions. They use:

- their conscience
- informed by scripture and tradition
- under the authority of the magisterium.

These are used together to establish an informed conscience and to make decisions based on the action itself and the motive.

The moral teaching and example that are found in the Bible, particularly in the Gospels, are authoritative for Catholics working out what decisions to make. It does not always have clear answers to personal and ethical dilemmas, but love for others, servanthood, and fighting for social justice may inform decisions.

> ❛[Conscience] is a messenger of him, who, both in nature and in grace, speaks to us behind a veil, and teaches and rules us by his representatives. Conscience is the aboriginal Vicar of Christ.❜
> *John Henry Newman, quoted in CCC 1778*

USEFUL TERM

Virtue ethics: considering the moral character of a person to help analyse their ethical decisions

CATECHISM OF THE CATHOLIC CHURCH

'For man has in his heart a law inscribed by God. […] **His conscience is man's most secret core and his sanctuary**. There he is alone with God whose voice echoes in his depths.'
CCC 1776

Natural law

Natural law is the belief that there is a discoverable moral law which never changes and applies to all human beings. It is based on the rational discovery of what leads to human flourishing, which is the same for all human beings. The Catholic Church follows the teaching on natural laws of St Thomas Aquinas' (1225–1274) in *Summa Theologica* that suggests that the most basic element of natural moral law is that human beings should do good and avoid evil. This is worked out by understanding what our purposes are as human beings.

1. To preserve human life.
2. To procreate.
3. To educate and to seek truth.
4. To live in society.
5. To worship God.

From these all other moral codes and the laws of states should flow.

> ❛Good is to be sought, evil avoided.❜
> *St Thomas Aquinas in* Summa Theologica

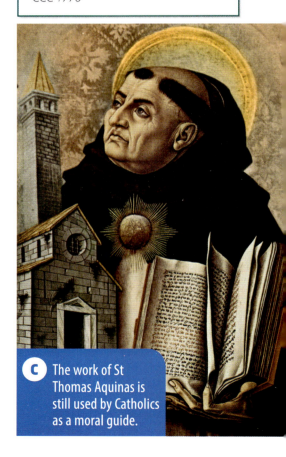

C The work of St Thomas Aquinas is still used by Catholics as a moral guide.

Virtue

St Thomas Aquinas was a Catholic priest and friar; a theologian and philosopher. He said that humans can establish right from wrong by using their conscience. They must make a rational decision so that both the action and motive are good. Aquinas referred to:

- cardinal virtues: prudence, justice, temperance, and fortitude
- theological virtues: faith, hope, and charity.

A virtue is a moral excellence. **Virtue ethics** are focused on the role of the individual's character and their virtues. They are used to evaluate particular actions. For example, instead of just believing that to lie is wrong, it should be considered what a decision to tell a lie or not tell a lie would say about someone's character and moral behaviour.

D A fully developed conscience helps Catholics to pick the right path.

The primacy of conscience

> ' [...] the will which disobeys the reason, whether true or mistaken, is always in the wrong. '
> *St Thomas Aquinas*

- Catholics have a sacred obligation to follow their own informed conscience.
- They must ensure that their conscience is informed by the Bible and tradition as interpreted by the magisterium. It is possible that a conscience can be wrong; sins can only be intentional thoughts and actions. However, if Catholics are making decisions to the best of their knowledge, knowing Christ and the Gospels, they must follow their conscience.

Divergent implications

The basic element of natural law to do good and avoid evil is something which resonates with all Christians, however it is a wide and unspecific law. The place and authority of natural law in relation to Christian belief can lead to divergent interpretation, particularly around issues which provoke strong emotional responses such as abortion, fertility treatment, or contraception. Some Christians believe natural law can be more widely interpreted than Aquinas suggests; others, such as Baptists, concentrate on the importance of 'freedom of conscience', as informed by the Bible, when making difficult decisions.

 BUILD YOUR SKILLS

1 Give an example of Jesus teaching morally or ethically.

2 How do you think Catholics could use Jesus' teaching to help them make decisions in their own lives?

3 a Outline the two features of natural law: virtue and primacy of conscience.
   b Why is each important?

? EXAM-STYLE QUESTIONS

B Explain **two** moral or ethical teachings of Jesus. (4)

D 'Jesus is the best role model for Christians when making decisions.' Evaluate this statement considering arguments for and against. In your response you should:
- refer to Catholic teachings
- refer to different Christian points of view
- refer to relevant ethical arguments
- reach a justified conclusion. (15)

 SUMMARY

- Jesus is seen as a role model for Christians when making moral decisions.
- Jesus gave clear examples of how Christians are expected to forgive, be servant-like, and fight for social justice.
- Natural law and virtue ethics can help to build an informed conscience and allow Christians to make the right decisions.
- Catholics have a sacred obligation to follow their conscience, but that it must be an informed conscience knowing Christ and the Gospels.

Revision

REVIEW YOUR KNOWLEDGE

1   Name three types of book in the Bible.
2   Describe two ways of interpreting the Bible.
3   Define the 'magisterium'.
4   Name the ecumenical council that took place from 1962 to 1965.
5   What was the description of the Church provided in Romans 12:5?
6   Name the four marks of the Church.
7   Define the Immaculate Conception.
8   What did Jesus say he was going to do to the Law in Matthew 5:17?

* See page 288 for answers.

EXTEND YOUR KNOWLEDGE: RESEARCH TASKS

For a research task, try to put together a full side of A4 of your own writing on the topics below.

1   Research the Council of Trent.
2   Research the response of the Church to stem cell research or IVF.
3   Research a Marian shrine besides Lourdes.
4   Research an organisation that works for social justice in the UK or abroad, e.g. SVP or Apostleship of the Sea.

USEFUL TERMS

Do you know what these words mean?

Canonical   Deuterocanonical   Inerrant

Lectionary   The Religious   Roman Curia

Assumption   Apostolic Succession

Doctrine   Dogma   *Ex cathedra*   Pontifical

Ecumenism   Annunciation   Discipleship

Virtue ethics

ONGOING LEARNING REVIEW

It is vital that you keep reviewing past material to make sure you have fully learned and remember it.

1   Why are sacraments important to Catholics?
2   How do different Christians interpret the sacraments?
3   How is prayer used by Catholics?
4   Why is Rome a place of pilgrimage for all Christians?
5   What does Catholic Social Teaching say about 'love of neighbour'?

Exam practice

In this exam practice section you will see examples for the exam question types: **a**, **b**, **c** and **d**. You can find out more about these on pages 6–7. Questions (b) and (d) in the **Exam question review** section below show strong student answers. Questions (a) and (c) in the **Improve it!** section need improvement.

Exam question review

(b)   Explain **two** significant changes to the Church after the Second Vatican Council. (4)

The Mass was no longer always in Latin. The Church encouraged Mass in the local language.

The Church no longer taught that heaven was only for Catholics, and suggested that non-Catholics may be able to achieve salvation. Before Vatican II the Church taught that non-Catholics could not be saved.

> (d) 'The Bible is the only source of wisdom for Christians.' Evaluate this statement considering arguments for and against. In your response you should:
> • refer to Catholic teachings
> • refer to different Christian points of view
> • reach a justified conclusion. (15)

Catholics believe that the Bible is the inspired word of God. This means it is from God, but written by humans.

Catholics believe that Bible is true as it was revealed by God to its human writers: 2 Timothy 3:16 says 'All scripture is inspired by God'.

However Catholics also have tradition and the magisterium as a source of wisdom. This includes the teaching from the bishops and the Pope, as well as the Catechism. Catholics use this additional guidance to help them better understand the Bible, and how to live a faithful life.

Some Christians take the Bible literally and believe every bit is true word for word. They may consider themselves Creationists, believing that God actually created the world in 6 days.

Other Christians may take a liberal approach and feel it needs reinterpreting by humans for today's world. They may use scientific and philosophical ideas to help them understand the wisdom within the Bible.

I believe that the Bible cannot be the only source of wisdom for Christians as many modern issues are not covered in the Bible, such as contraception and abortion. This is why Christians need more than just the Bible to make decisions about how to live their lives.

Improve it!

These answers will not get full marks. Can you rewrite and improve them?

> (a) Outline **three** types of book in the Bible. (3)

Rules, Parables and Gospels.

> (c) Explain **two** ways referring to the Church as the Body of Christ helps Catholics understand the Church better. In your answer you must refer to a source of wisdom and authority. (5)

The analogy of the body is an easy one for Catholics to understand.

The Body of Christ includes different people like the laity, the clergy and the religious who all do different things.

 ✓ WHAT WENT WELL

There are two significant changes given here, each explaining a different point with a good amount of detail.

 ✓ WHAT WENT WELL

It's a good idea to aim to write five or six well-developed points, covering the different points of view listed in the question bullet points. This answer achieves that, and considers the points of view against the question, arriving at a justified conclusion.

 ! HOW TO IMPROVE

Only one of these is correct, and as one-word answers none of them fulfil the requirement to 'outline', which requires a little more detail, up to about a sentence.

 ! HOW TO IMPROVE

These are relevant points to make, but they lack the development explaining exactly how and why they are useful for Catholics. Try to add examples to show full understanding of the question. The answer also lacks the required source of wisdom or authority.

The role of church buildings

The word church comes from the Greek *Kyriakós oíkos* which means 'house of the Lord'. The earliest surviving house churches are dated to between 233 and 256CE. Before this, the 'church' was simply the gathered people, and this meaning is still its main meaning today.

During the eleventh to the fourteenth centuries, numerous churches and cathedrals were built across Western Europe. Many of these are still used today and reflect a wide range of different architectural influences.

Churches are naturally a very important place for Catholics. They are the place of worship where communities regularly gather to celebrate their faith. As such, their architecture, design, and decoration are very important because they help Catholic Christians to worship. It is important to remember, however, that the Mass can take place outside of the church: 'worship [...] is not tied exclusively to any one place. The whole earth is sacred and entrusted to the children of men' (*CCC* 1179).

Churches vary according to the style of architecture in each time and place. Most Catholic churches in the UK have been built since 1829 (when it became legal for Catholics to worship again after the Reformation) and so many reflect more modern styles of architecture. Those that are older have been bought or gifted back to the Catholic Church. Whatever their design, the church building is an important symbol of God, a sign of the living Church (CCC 1180).

How church design reflects belief

- Where possible, churches are built facing east, pointing to the belief that Jesus rose from the dead and brought new life, just as the sun rises from the east. The Mass is a reminder of how Catholics share in the resurrection of Jesus.
- Many churches are cruciform, which means shaped like a cross. This reflects the cross as a symbol of the Church.

SPECIFICATION FOCUS

The common and divergent forms of architecture, design and decoration of Catholic churches: how they reflect belief, are used in, and contribute to, worship, including reference to the Catechism of the Catholic Church 1179–1181.

CATECHISM OF THE CATHOLIC CHURCH

'A church, "a house of prayer in which the Eucharist is celebrated and reserved, where the faithful assemble, [...] ought to be in good taste and a worthy place for prayer and sacred ceremonial".'
CCC 1181

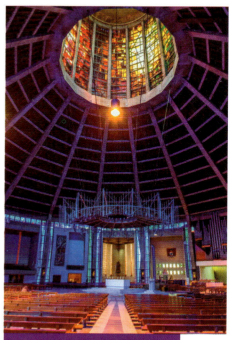

B Modern church design, such as Liverpool's Metropolitan Cathedral still reflects Catholic belief.

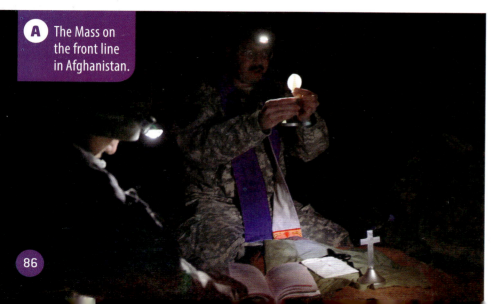

A The Mass on the front line in Afghanistan.

- Round churches are said by some to represent eternity and octagonal churches to reflect a star bringing light to the world. The Church of the Holy Sepulchre in Jerusalem is round and the Church of the Nativity in Bethlehem is octagonal. Their influence on later church design is a legacy of the **crusades**.

- Churches are often vaulted inside, creating an open space pointing upwards which suggests a connection with heaven. The great cathedrals were built as high as possible to get closer to God. The majority of churches have a spire for this reason.

- Stained-glass windows tell stories from the Bible, and were useful in times when many Catholics could not read.

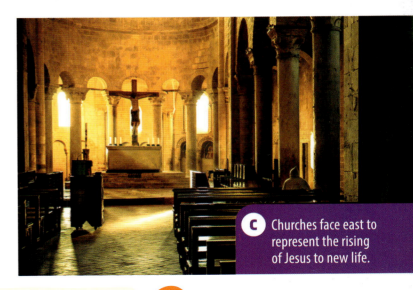

C Churches face east to represent the rising of Jesus to new life.

> ❛You learn your faith through the [church] building; they're sermons in stone, and that's why they're so important. ❜
> *Duncan Stroik, Catholic architect*

USEFUL TERMS

Crusades: religious military campaigns to the Holy Land

Votive: a vow, wish, or desire

How churches are used

Worship

The main service of the Catholic Church is the Mass. This can be celebrated every day by individual churches, but must be celebrated at least every Sunday. The Mass is the sacrament of the Eucharist, but can include other sacraments when necessary. For example, a Nuptial Mass includes the sacrament of matrimony. When a priest is to be ordained, the sacrament of Holy Orders is celebrated within the Mass.

Other uses

Most Catholic churches are open throughout the day (not just at times of the Mass) for people to offer their own private prayers. Catholics may use **votive** candles for personal prayer use. These are small candles placed before a statue of Jesus or Mary, which represent a private prayer the individual wishes to make. Most churches also contain the Blessed Sacrament in the tabernacle; some people will visit to feel a physical closeness to Jesus.

BUILD YOUR SKILLS

1. **a** Explain the significance of two elements of church design.
   b Which do you think is the most significant for Catholics? Justify your choice to a partner.

2. Explain the purpose of the church building, finding a quotation to support your explanation.

SUMMARY

- The Church is known as the 'House of God'.
- It is an important place for Catholics to pray and worship together.
- Church design often reflects symbolism in Catholicism: facing east, the shape of the cross, and connection with heaven through a raised ceiling or spire.

EXAM-STYLE QUESTIONS

A Outline **three** uses for the church in Catholic worship. (3)
B Explain **two** ways in which the church building reflects belief. (4)

4.2 Catholic church features

Why do internal features matter?

The internal features of a church help maintain it as the 'House of God' (CCC 2691). The prominent altar and lectern are used in liturgy while private prayer is encouraged through contemplation at statues and the Stations of the Cross.

The different features and their purpose

There are a number of common features which can be found in the majority of Catholic churches and which are referred to in the Catechism because of their significance.

The lectern

This is a book stand from which the readings are proclaimed (CCC 1184).

- It is important because Scripture is a key part of the Mass and other liturgy.
- Priests, deacons, and lectors (readers) use it to share the Bible, homily, and other prayers.
- Catholics believe the Bible is the Word of God, where he communicates his plan of salvation. The lectern represents this communication.

The altar

This is the focus of attention during the second half of the Mass as it is where the priest consecrates the Eucharist. It is positioned so that the congregation have a clear view of it.

- It represents the table at the Last Supper as well as serving as a reminder of the Altar of Sacrifice in the Temple in Jerusalem (CCC 1182).
- Altars will either be made out of stone, or contain a piece of stone called the altar stone (which usually contains relics of a saint). God told Moses to build an altar from stone (Exodus 20:25) and the New Testament repeats the idea of a strong foundation of stone: 'on this rock I will build my church' (Matthew 16:18).
- The sacrifice of Jesus offers Catholics redemption from sin and reminds them of the possibility of salvation (CCC 1186).

The crucifix

A cross with the crucified figure of Jesus (called a corpus) is found near the altar. It is a powerful reminder of Jesus' sacrifice made to redeem the human race.

- Catholics look at the crucifix during prayer to strengthen feelings of love, hope, and trust as they remember Jesus' sacrifice.
- Rather than an empty cross, the figure of Jesus is included to remind Catholics of his suffering sacrifice for them.
- The crucifix is used during the Mass procession, and during Holy Week services a life-sized crucifix may be used.

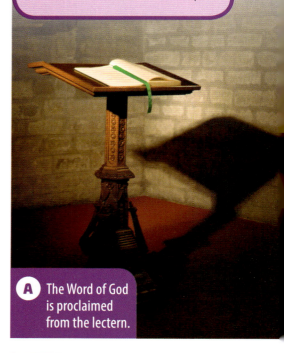

A The Word of God is proclaimed from the lectern.

B An altar and crucifix in a rural church.

The tabernacle

This is a box close to the altar where the consecrated host, or Eucharist, is kept (CCC 1183).

- As Catholics believe that Jesus is truly present in the Blessed Sacrament, they genuflect to the tabernacle (outside of the Mass) as they enter and leave the church.
- A sanctuary lamp is usually nearby, which reminds churchgoers of the presence of Christ in the tabernacle.
- Moses kept the Ten Commandments in the Tabernacle, reminding Catholics of the link between the old and new covenants (the agreements with God).

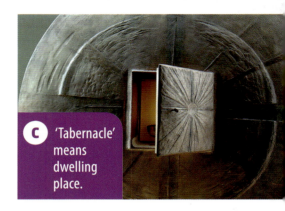

C 'Tabernacle' means dwelling place.

The baptismal font

Traditionally, the font was found at the back of the church so that babies could be baptized as soon as they entered the church for the first time. In many churches they are now found at the front so the congregation can witness the baptism. Some churches have a baptismal pool for adult baptisms (CCC 1185).

- It is important because baptism is the first Sacrament of Initiation (see 2.1).
- In the font, holy water washes away original sin and brings sanctifying grace to the individual's soul.

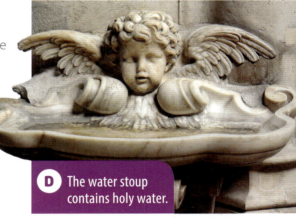

D The water stoup contains holy water.

Other features

- **The confessional:** this is a small room dedicated for private conversation during the sacrament of reconciliation (penance).
- **The Stations of the Cross:** images from the story of the Passion of Christ are another reminder of Jesus' death and suffering. Often they end at the tabernacle.
- **Statues:** these vary from church to church; however, there is usually one of Mary. They are visual aids to assist worship and reminders of Catholic beliefs about the saints.
- **Water stoup:** at the entrance to the church is a bowl of holy water. It is used to make the sign of the cross when entering and leaving the church to remind the congregation of their baptism and belief in the Trinity.

USEFUL TERM

Atonement: to make up for; in Christianity the restoration of the relationship between God and humans which was mended by Christ's sacrifice

BUILD YOUR SKILLS

1 a   Pick three examples of internal church features.
   b   Which of these would be most important for worship? Justify your choice to a partner.

SUMMARY

- The internal features of a Catholic church have clear and distinct purposes.
- These features help Catholics in their worship and prayer life.
- The lectern, altar, crucifix, and tabernacle particularly reflect Jesus' sacrifice, **atonement**, and reconciliation with God.

EXAM-STYLE QUESTIONS

C   Explain the importance of **two** internal features of churches for Catholics. In your answer you must refer to a source of wisdom and authority. (5)

D   'The church building, both in its design and internal features, brings Catholics closer to God.' Evaluate this statement considering arguments for and against. In your response you should:
   - refer to Catholic teachings
   - reach a justified conclusion. (12)

4.3 Sacred objects

What are sacred objects?

Sacred objects are items used during the liturgy and include sacred vessels. Other objects such as relics, rosary beads, candles, and holy water can also be classed as sacred and are called 'objects of devotion'. Many devotional objects are also found within the church, but not all, because non-liturgical worship frequently takes place elsewhere. Many Catholics may have a small altar or crucifix at home before which they pray, and these objects help them focus their mind and belief.

What does the church say about sacred objects?

The Catechism gives guidance on what kinds of holy images are acceptable to use on sacred objects and in decoration within church. CCC 1161 states that the cross, images of Jesus, Mary, angels, and saints 'are to be exhibited in the holy churches of God, on sacred vessels'. CCC 1162 explains the place of sacred objects as an important part of the whole Mass: 'the contemplation of sacred icons […] enters into the harmony of the signs of celebration.'

Sacred vessels

During the Mass a variety of different objects are used as part of the liturgy. The sacred vessels include:

- the chalice (cup) for the wine
- the paten (plate) which usually holds the larger host held up by the priest during the consecration
- the ciborium (covered dish) which contains the hosts before and after the consecration. The sacred host is stored in the ciborium when placed in the tabernacle after the Mass.

Other items are also used during the Mass but are not considered sacred vessels:

- *Cloths*: such as the corporal (a linen square for the chalice and host to rest on while on the altar), the purificator (a cloth for wiping the chalice between individuals drinking from it), and the pall (a stiffened piece of linen to cover the chalice).
- *Books*: these include the lectionary, which dictates the readings for the Mass, or other books such as the Gospels and Altar Missal (instructions for the different Mass services throughout the year).
- *Other objects*: these include the incense thurible (a metal incense burner on chains which can be swung) and the monstrance (a frame) which is used for exposition (showing) of the Blessed Sacrament.
- *Sacred vestments*: these include the chasuble (outer robe) and stole (scarf) that the priest wears.

The sacred vessels are an important part of the sacramental ritual of the Eucharist. Although Catholics worship only the body and blood, the sacred vessels help

SPECIFICATION FOCUS

The meaning and significance of sacred objects including **sacred vessels, sarcophagi, and hunger cloths within Catholicism:** the way these are used to express belief, including Catechism of the Catholic Church 1161, and the divergent ways in which they may be used in church and other settings.

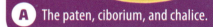

A The paten, ciborium, and chalice.

B The incense thurible is part of the liturgical ritual.

focus their devotion. They are recognizable symbols. You cannot necessarily see the actual wine and bread from within the congregation, but the sacred vessel which contains them will be visible.

Sarcophagi

- A sarcophagus is a box-like container for a corpse, usually carved in stone, and displayed above ground, though it may also be buried.
- Early Christians buried their dead in cemeteries (or 'sleeping places'). Tombs were found with inscriptions indicating the belief that these bodies were 'resting in peace' awaiting resurrection.
- Increasingly Christians began to be buried in sarcophagi, often with scenes of Jesus raising Jairus' daughter (Mark 5:21–43), the son of the widow of Nain (Luke 7:11–17), or Lazarus (John 11:38–44), which encouraged hope for families facing death.
- Sarcophagi are still occasionally used today. Most of the popes buried in St Peter's Basilica are in sarcophagi.
- Sarcophagi are used as objects of devotion as they are a physical reminder of the occupant. Catholics can focus their prayers on the individual and ask for their intercession if they are saints.

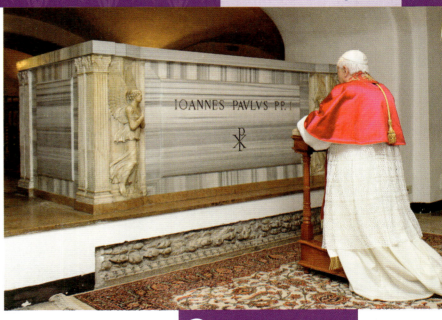

 Pope Benedict XVI praying at the sarcophagus of Pope St John Paul II.

Hunger cloths

- Hunger cloths were used during the Middle Ages to cover the altar during Lent. These cloths were covered in images and stories from the Bible to help people (who were often unable to read) learn about God.
- More recently, they have been created for use in developing countries. The cloths visually signify to people that God is with them in their lives, wherever they might be, and cares for every individual whatever their struggles.

BUILD YOUR SKILLS

1 Explain what a 'sacred vessel' means.

2 a Choose another item of devotion and explain how it is used.
 b Write a PEE paragraph giving a reason why it may help express belief to a Catholic.

SUMMARY

- Sacred objects help Catholics to focus during their worship, whether in church or elsewhere.
- Sacred vessels are used by the priest during the Mass, including those for the consecration of the bread and wine into the body and blood of Christ.
- Sarcophagi are still used today and help focus Catholics' prayers on an individual.
- Hunger cloths tell stories of God helping people in the Bible and are still used as a reminder of these in developing countries.

EXAM-STYLE QUESTIONS

B Explain the purpose of **two** sacred objects used by Catholics. (4)

C Explain **two** reasons why sacred objects are important for Catholics. In your answer you must refer to a source of wisdom and authority. (5)

4.4 Artwork in Catholicism

Meaning and significance

Artwork is a visual expression of faith and helps to illustrate, supplement, and portray the teachings of the Church. Often it tries to capture an image or story from the Bible, at other times it is simply an expression of the particular beliefs of the artist. It includes a wide range of art forms including paintings, mosaic, **frescoes**, and drawings.

Catholic art has played an important role in the history and development of Western art from the earliest Christian times. Artwork varies according to the popular or dominant style of the time and place.

Use of icons

Paintings which showed Jesus, Mary, saints, or angels were common in Catholic art up until the seventh century. Some branches of Christianity believed such art disobeyed the fourth Commandment: 'You shall not make for yourself a graven image, or any likeness of anything that is in heaven above' (Exodus 20:4).

Many such images were destroyed in the **Iconoclasm** in the eight and ninth centuries by Christians who believed they were blasphemy. At the Second Council of Nicaea in 787CE the Church condemned the iconoclasts and encouraged the use of icons. During the Reformation, the new Protestant groups tore down Catholic imagery, branding it idol worship, a claim again rejected by the Church at the Council of Trent (see 4.5).

Renaissance art

From 1300 to 1700CE Renaissance art often focused on religious themes or stories from the Bible, such as Leonardo da Vinci's 'The Last Supper'.

Modern Christian art

In the twentieth century, art by Father Sieger Koder, Sister Mary Stephens, or the Sisters of Turvey Abbey has been celebrated.

Artwork was originally important in the Church when many ordinary Catholics could not read or write. It was through Church artwork that they were able to access or experience their faith. Artwork was used as a way of remembering and revisiting stories from the Bible. Artworks were also often able to express the stories in a more relatable and understandable way that Catholics could study and reflect upon over time.

- The purpose of much Catholic art is to express belief and love and glory of God.
- Art can also be used by Catholics to influence or enhance their belief.
- Sometimes artwork challenges Catholics, and spurs discussion about an artist's interpretation.

SPECIFICATION FOCUS

The meaning and significance of paintings, fresco and drawings within Catholicism with reference to two specific pieces and Catechism of the Catholic Church 2502–2503: the divergent ways these are used to express belief by the artist and those who observe the art, and the divergent ways in which paintings, frescos and drawings may be used in church and other settings.

USEFUL TERMS

Frescoes: murals painted on fresh plaster

Iconoclasm: the destruction of religious icons and other images for religious or political motives

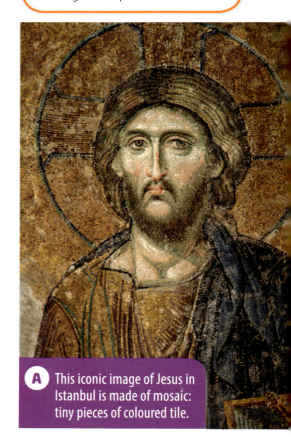

A This iconic image of Jesus in Istanbul is made of mosaic: tiny pieces of coloured tile.

Examples of Catholic art

The Sistine Chapel

The famous ceiling of the Sistine Chapel in the Vatican was painted by Michelangelo between 1508 and 1512. The chapel itself was built between 1477 and 1480 and named after Pope Sixtus IV.

It is the location for papal conclaves when cardinals vote for a new pope.

B 'The Lord's Supper' by Sister Mary Stephens.

C The Sistine Chapel.

One of the most famous parts of the chapel is 'The Creation of Adam', one of nine scenes from Genesis on the ceiling. The hands of God and Adam are outstretched to one another. Michelangelo was an intensely religious man, and it is believed he consulted the Old Testament regularly to take inspiration directly from the words of the scriptures. He was commissioned by Pope Julius II who demanded iconic paintings with many layers of meaning. Michelangelo's paintings were more than beautiful decoration to the glory of God, they were intended to serve as prompts for theological discussion.

D 'The Creation of Adam', on the ceiling of the Sistine Chapel.

The Return of the Prodigal Son

'The Return of the Prodigal Son' is an oil painting by Rembrandt. It is among the Dutch master's final pieces of artwork and was completed in about 1667. The painting is now found in the Hermitage Museum, Saint Petersburg, Russia. Copies are often found in Catholic churches and schools as a reminder of the story of the prodigal son (Luke 15:11–32).

Catholic priest Henri Nouwen (1922–1996) suggested that Rembrandt's painting was a way of helping ordinary Christians explore some of the meaning in the original parable. There are key themes to be explored within the painting such as the difference in the hands, the state of the son's sandals, and the role of the older brother. This is an important part of Catholic art – artists can say things without words, hint at the emotions of the characters through their expression and gesture, but also include symbolism. These are objects which carry a second meaning. There is much to read and learn in an apparently straightforward painting.

The use of art in church and other settings

The Catechism instructs that artistic images should be shown both within churches and beyond (CCC 1161). It also sets out requirements for the purpose of the art (CCC 2502) and states that it is the responsibility of bishops to promote sacred art and also to remove anything from places of worship which does not meet the Church's standards (CCC 2503).

Catholic art is not restricted to religious settings. The Rembrandt painting is displayed in a museum, and many modern Catholic artworks can be bought for display in homes. Displaying such a painting is a way of bringing Catholicism more vividly into the home, a daily visual reminder of an event or feeling, and also a focus for devotion or private prayer.

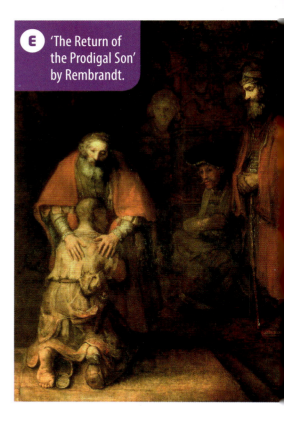

E 'The Return of the Prodigal Son' by Rembrandt.

 CATECHISM OF THE CATHOLIC CHURCH

'Sacred art is true and beautiful when [...] evoking and glorifying, in faith and adoration, the transcendent mystery of God.'
CCC 2502

 BUILD YOUR SKILLS

1 a Explain why artwork is important to some Catholics.
   b How is artwork used in church buildings?

2 Give an example of a specific piece of artwork.
   • Describe it in as much detail as possible.
   • Explain why it is considered significant by some Catholics.

 SUMMARY

• Art is a visual expression of faith that can help Catholics learn and remember stories from the Bible.

• Catholic art has played an important role in the development of Western art and two classic examples are the Sistine Chapel by Michelangelo and 'The Return of the Prodigal Son' by Rembrandt.

• Art can be used as a focus for theological discussion.

• Artwork can be used as a focus for prayer and meditation.

 **EXAM-STYLE QUESTIONS**

A Outline **three** examples of artwork used within Catholicism. (3)

B Explain **two** ways that artwork can help Catholics understand their faith better. (4)

Meaning and significance

Catholics today are guided by the Catechism's teaching on artistic works that they reflect a human being's inner riches. 'Arising from talent given by the Creator and from man's own effort, art is a form of practical wisdom, uniting knowledge and skill' (CCC 2501).

Catholics use sculpture and statues to recall the person or thing being depicted. They can also be used as a teaching tool, which was useful in the early Church when many were illiterate.

- During the Reformation, when the Protestant Church of England was formed, many statues were destroyed by Protestant denominations including Calvanists and Zwinglianists, as they were seen as idols.
- Catholics do not worship statues; they are simply an aid to prayer.
- Statues are treated as sacred objects and therefore dedicated to God. They must not be thrown away or sold but are either buried or burned when they have reached the end of their useful life or are no longer needed.
- In the Old Testament there are occasions when God directed the construction of statues (for example, cherubs in Exodus 25:18–20).

Christian disagreement about statues

The Council of Trent was held between 1545 and 1563 to discuss calls for reform within the Catholic Church. One of the things discussed was the use of statues in the Catholic faith. The Church confirmed use of statues was not idol worship, but honour shown to the individuals the statues represented.

Expressions of belief

Sculpture allows artists the chance to create more physical works of art. The 3D nature of sculpture can make a connection with a piece feel more real; they can also be handled, unlike other artwork. However, the Council of Trent also gave guidance that the creation of art should be moderate: 'figures shall not be painted or adorned with a beauty exciting to lust […] nothing that is profane, nothing indecorous' (Twenty-fifth session).

Sculptures placed in church have to be approved by the local bishop, who makes sure that sculptors have expressed the Bible faithfully and moderately in their work.

These statues help in prayer and meditation, helping to connect believers with Jesus Christ, or with the saints whose lives they look up to. Catholics can show devotion to statues in a number of ways:

- kneeling before them
- touching or kissing them
- lighting candles before them
- praying before them.

SPECIFICATION FOCUS

The meaning and significance of sculpture and statues with reference to Catechism of the Catholic Church 2501: the way these are used to express belief by the artist and those who observe the art, the way these are used to express belief, and the divergent ways in which sculptures and statues may be used in church and other settings.

A 'Christ the Redeemer' in Rio.

Use in church and other settings

- Most Catholic churches will contain a number of statues. There is usually at least one of Mary, which may be on a separate altar or in a Lady Chapel.

- It is very common to have a set of statues depicting the Nativity at Christmas time. Many families will have these at home, and they will also be displayed in church.

- At the Good Friday liturgy, Veneration of the Cross takes place where Catholics kiss the feet of Jesus on the cross. This adoration is an expression of honour and thanksgiving for Jesus' sacrifice.

- Many Catholics also decorate their homes with religious statues, reminding them to incorporate their spiritual values into their daily activities.

- Some Catholics will use statues during private prayer. This may be linked to a sacrament or pilgrimage. For example, a statue of St Francis may be a reminder of a pilgrimage to Assisi, where he was born.

B The foot of St Peter, in St Peter's Basilica at the Vatican, worn down by pilgrims touching and kissing his feet.

BUILD YOUR SKILLS

1 **a** Explain why sculptures and statues are important for some Catholics.
   b Outline an example of how they might be used by a Catholic.

2 In three paragraphs, explain why sculptures and statues are used to express belief and/or as a focus for devotion.

SUMMARY

- Statues and sculptures are a way of remembering individuals, stories, and teaching from the Bible, and the saints.

- They are used by Catholics in the home and church as a focus of prayer and reminder of their faith in their daily lives.

- Most Catholic churches will have statues in them. They may have separate altars or chapels dedicated to Mary or the saints, including a statue.

EXAM-STYLE QUESTIONS

A Outline **three** ways a sculpture or statue could be used by a Catholic. (3)
D 'Art and sculpture contribute greatly to Catholic life today.' Evaluate this statement, considering arguments for and against. In your response:
   - refer to Catholic teachings
   - reach a justified conclusion. (12)

C A Lady Altar with a statue of Mary holding Jesus.

How symbolism and imagery are used

Symbolism is where an object is used to mean something else. Christianity was not a legal religion until 313CE in the Roman Empire, so the earliest Christians used images which contained symbolism in order to avoid detection.

- Early imagery was deliberately subtle and indirect, so it would only be recognized by those who were Christians.
- Unlike Judaism, Christianity did not use symbols to avoid images of God.
- As Christianity grew and became more widespread, symbolism and imagery remained an important part of worship and art.

The cross and crucifix

The cross has been used commonly since the fourth century but was linked to Christianity from as early as the second century. It was a clear reminder of Jesus' death and subsequent resurrection. The crucifix – a cross which includes the figure of Jesus – did not appear in use until the fifth century.

- The cross or crucifix is found in all churches and often used as a focus for prayer. Some Catholics have them within their homes. They are often also worn by Christians today to show their faith.

The fish

The fish or 'ichthus' was of more importance for the first Christians than the cross as a secret symbol. Many claim this is because of its meaning in the **acrostic**. In Greek, 'Jesus Christ, Son of God, Saviour' is **Ἰησοῦς Χριστὸς Θεοῦ Υἱὸς Σωτήρ**. The five Greek letters **ΙΧΘΥΣ** form the Greek word for fish (ichthus).

It was also an obvious choice for a secret symbol because of its connection to the apostles – 'I will make you fishers of men' (Matthew 4:19) – and events in the life of Jesus (feeding the five thousand with five loaves of bread and two fish, for example).

- This fish is often used as a symbol in modern life to give a clear indication of Christian belief, for example as a bumper sticker, or as part of a business logo.

The Chi Rho

This is a symbol made from the first two letters of the Greek word for Christ: **ΧΡΙΣΤΟΣ**. The letters X (chi) and P (rho) are combined to represent Jesus as Christ.

- This symbol was used by Christians before being adopted by the Roman Empire once Christianity was accepted as its religion.

SPECIFICATION FOCUS

The purpose and use of symbolism and imagery in religious art: the cross, crucifix, fish, ChiRho, dove, including Catechism of the Catholic Church 701, Eagle, Alpha and Omega, symbols of the four evangelists; the way this symbolism is used to express belief, and the divergent ways in which they may be used in church and other settings.

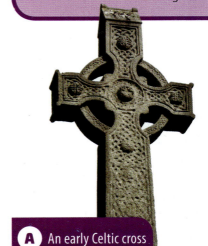

A An early Celtic cross

B Many Christians, particularly in the US use fish as a bumper sticker.

USEFUL TERM

Acrostic: where the first letter of each word in a sentence together make a separate word with particular meaning

- The Roman emperor Constantine (272–337ᴄᴇ) put the symbol on his shields before going into battle against Maxentius at Milvian Bridge. His victory signalled the start of the Roman Empire's gradual conversion to Christianity.
- The Chi Rho appeared on helmets, shields, and even on coins.

The dove

The dove is a symbol of both the Holy Spirit and baptism. The Holy Spirit appeared 'like' a dove at the baptism of Jesus (Luke 3:22), and a dove brought hope of renewed life to Noah when returning with a leaf from an olive tree after the flood (Genesis 8:11). The Catechism explains that the flood for which Noah built his ark symbolizes baptism.

- A dove is frequently used today as a symbol of peace, by both Christians and non-Christians.
- The phrase 'extending an olive branch' comes from Genesis 8:11 and means to offer peace.

The eagle

The eagle is a symbol of Jesus' divine nature. In Isaiah 40:31, those who wait patiently for God will be rewarded 'with wings like eagles'.

- The eagle is also a symbol of the evangelist John.

Alpha and Omega

These are the first and last letters of the Greek alphabet. In Revelation 22:13 Jesus says 'I am the Alpha and the Omega, the first and the last, the beginning and the end.' Together these letters form a symbol of Christ.

- These symbols continue to be used today by the Church to represent the eternity of Christ as part of the Trinity.
- They are found on the Paschal Candle and can be used in other church decoration, such as on the altar.

The evangelists

The evangelists or the four Gospel writers have been linked to the four living creatures said since early Christian times to have surrounded God's throne.

C A Paschal candle featuring the Chi Rho.

> ✝ **CATECHISM OF THE CATHOLIC CHURCH**
>
> 'The Spirit comes down and remains in the purified hearts of the baptized. […] Christian iconography traditionally uses a dove to suggest the Spirit.'
> *CCC 701*

> ❝The first living creature [was] like a lion, the second living creature like an ox, the third living creature with the face of a man, and the fourth living creature like a flying eagle. ❞
> *Revelation 4:7 (also found in Ezekiel 1:1–14, Ezekiel 10:1–22, and Daniel 7:1–8)*

D The Alpha and Omega are often found on parts of Church buildings.

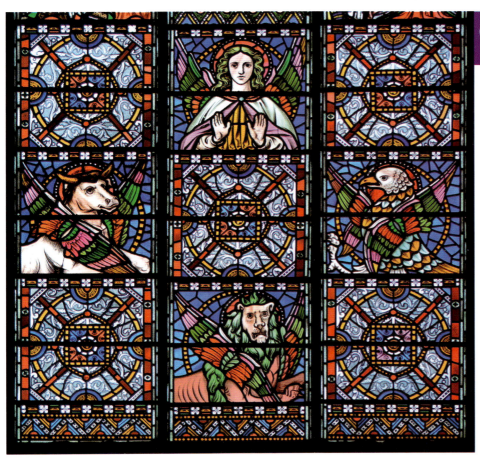

E The four evangelists represented by different creatures.

- The most commonly accepted ordering is that of St Jerome (347–420ᴄᴇ):
  - Matthew = Human/Angel
  - Mark = Lion
  - Luke = Ox
  - John = Eagle
- Within a church or cathedral there will often be symbols of the evangelists on the lectern or in other decoration around the altar or in stained-glass windows.
- They are found in the **baptisteries** of Italian cathedrals such as the Duomos in Florence and Padua.

USEFUL TERM

Baptisteries: special separate buildings containing the font or baptismal pool, popular in Italy

BUILD YOUR SKILLS

1 a Explain in your own words why early Christians used symbols.
   b Why are symbols still important to Catholics?

2 a How has the Chi Rho been used in divergent ways?
   b Explain the symbolism of the Alpha and Omega.

SUMMARY

- Christians have used symbols from the very beginning of their faith. At first it was to avoid detection.
- Many symbols including the cross, the fish, and those of the evangelists have remained in use and form part of the decoration of many churches.
- Christian symbols are used by Catholics today to express belief and faith.

EXAM-STYLE QUESTIONS

A Outline **three** symbols used by early Christians. (3)
B Explain **two** reasons why a fish is used as a Christian symbol. (4)

4.7 Drama

Meaning and significance

Drama – that is, an exciting or emotional event – is something that engages and captivates human beings. There are many dramatic moments and stories within the Bible, and it is unsurprising that these found their way out of the Church to become part of secular society. The Catechism itself describes the relationship between God and humanity as 'a covenant drama' which 'engages the heart' (CCC 2567).

Drama in the meaning of a play or **tableaux** was a popular form of entertainment from the Middle Ages onwards and although not part of Church worship, was often religious in nature, using the stories of the Bible as its basis. Many Catholics were illiterate and didn't understand Latin, so visual acts helped them to understand the stories, as well as providing entertainment.

USEFUL TERM

Tableaux: freeze-frame scenes, sometimes accompanied by music

Mystery plays

- Mystery plays, sometimes called miracle plays, were amongst the earliest forms of drama in medieval Europe. They focused on performing Bible stories, sometimes using the form of tableaux.

- Mystery plays were sometimes performed in Church grounds, but Pope Innocent III banned clergy from being involved in the plays in 1210.

- Increasingly they were often put on by guilds who moved from town to town, performing. Different guilds took responsibility for different bits of the Bible.

- Mystery plays were completely banned in England in 1534 as part of the Reformation. However, they continued to grow across Europe into more elaborate and professional performances.

- Since the 1950s there has been a revival of the mystery plays in England, particularly in places like York and Chester.

A A scene from a modern version of the mystery plays in York.

Passion plays

B A scene from a Passion play in York Minster Cathedral.

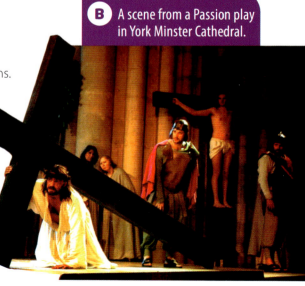

Passion plays, sometimes called Easter pageants, give a dramatic presentation depicting the Passion of Jesus Christ. They often include the story from his trial, suffering, and death. It is a traditional part of Lent in several Christian denominations.

- The Passion play became popular in medieval times, originally in Latin and then in the local language. Eventually more music and further characters were added, often so that more people could take part.

- Like mystery plays, Passion plays were banned in many places as part of the Reformation. However, in some parts of Europe they became popular again in the nineteenth century as they were performed in Catholic schools.

- They are now commonly performed at Easter and often take place in public spaces such as city centres and town squares as free, community-led performances. Often they are ecumenical projects, with different Christian churches working and performing together.

- There have been high-profile and televised Passion plays including Michael Sheen's version in Port Talbot in 2011.
- Oberammergau in Germany hosts one of the most famous Passion plays in Europe. The Wintershall Estate hosts one of the most well known in the UK.

Expressing belief using drama

- Drama is used to bring a realism to the stories of the Bible. People can express their beliefs by acting out parts of Scripture which helps them both understand and remember them.
- Those participating in the plays (acting and supporting) can see it as an act of worship, whilst those observing can also see it as a focus for their own prayer and devotion.
- A dramatic reconstruction may have a more powerful impact than simply reading/hearing the text on its own.
- The local Christian community often work together to stage drama, sharing their beliefs and joining together across denominational divides.
- Many of these dramas attempt to recast the story in contemporary terms, which helps to make the Gospel story relevant to modern experience.

The use of drama in church and other settings

- Mystery or Passion plays do not take place within the Church as part of worship.
- However, today the church may be used as a performance space for the plays.
- More often these plays take place in public areas, involving Catholics, other denominations, and non-Christians.

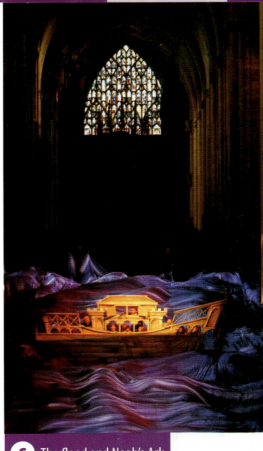

C The flood and Noah's Ark during a Mystery play in York Minster Cathedral.

BUILD YOUR SKILLS

1 a In pairs, mind map all the benefits of drama to Catholics in the Middle Ages.
   b How many of those benefits are relevant to Catholics today?
   c Are there any new benefits of drama for Catholics today?

2 Outline the history of one type of drama.

SUMMARY

- Drama became a popular way of sharing Bible stories during the Middle Ages as part of secular entertainment.
- Mystery plays helped people learn and remember Bible stories.
- Passion plays focused on the story of Jesus' death and resurrection.
- Drama can be used by individuals as a way of expressing their faith.
- Today these plays often help the local community share their beliefs and work together to put on the plays.

EXAM-STYLE QUESTIONS

A Outline **three** reasons Passion plays are still performed today. (3)
B Explain **two** reasons why some Catholics consider drama a secular activity and not worship. (4)

4.8 Music in worship

Traditional music in worship

Just as the words spoken during the Mass are set out in the Roman Missal, there is an official source of music called the Roman Gradual. The Catechism encourages Catholics to 'mak[e] melody to the Lord with all your heart' (CCC 2641). The Church's musical tradition is an important part of worship; but it is important to understand that the music connects to the order of the liturgy. Many parts of the Mass such as the Kyrie and the Gloria are sung or chanted following early church tradition, but hymns and worship songs usually include instruments.

A The choir will often provide the musical element of worship.

Hymns

A hymn is a religious song, written specifically for the purpose of praise, adoration, or prayer. It comes from the Greek word *hymnos* meaning a 'song of praise'.

- Some of the earliest hymns are the Psalms, found in the Old Testament.
- Hymns are not always sung in Catholic services, and when they are they might only be sung at certain times, for example at the entrance of the Mass procession, at the offertory, after communion, and during the recessional.
- They may link to the readings or theme of the Mass, or Church season. They may be led by a choir or music group, but are more often full congregational, with all joining in.

Plainchant

This is chanting: singing without any musical accompaniment, by one or more people. It was originally the only type of music allowed in Church.

- Gregorian chant is a collection of chants compiled by Pope Gregory the Great and often sung in Catholic churches and monasteries.

SPECIFICATION FOCUS

The nature and use of traditional and contemporary styles of music in worship: hymns, plainchant, psalms and worship songs including reference to Catechism of the Catholic Church 2641; the way different music is used to express belief and the divergent ways in which it may be used in church (including the Mass) and other settings.

CATECHISM OF THE CATHOLIC CHURCH

'The musical tradition of the universal Church is a treasure of inestimable value, greater even than that of any other art […] **"He who sings prays twice"**.' *CCC 1156*

USEFUL TERMS

Charismatic movement: an active style of Christian worship may include dancing and lively music (also sometimes called full body worship)

Responsorial: a chant recited in parts which includes a response by the congregation between each part

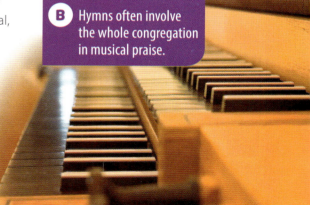

B Hymns often involve the whole congregation in musical praise.

Psalms

These songs are in both the Jewish Tenakh and Christian Bible. They have been attributed to a number of authors including King David and King Solomon, while others are 'orphans' with no clear authors.

- They were written over a period of around 500 years and were first used in the Temple in Jerusalem.
- They are still sung daily by religious orders around the world and all 150 will be sung over the course of a year.
- The second reading in the Mass is usually a **responsorial** psalm, which may be spoken or sung. Some hymns are based on the Psalms, such as 'The Lord's my shepherd' based on Psalm 23.

Contemporary music in worship

Worship songs are often referred to as contemporary worship music or 'Praise and Worship'. These have been developed since the 1950s in many different Christian churches with a more folk- or pop-based musical style. This style is often linked to the **charismatic movement**. The songs are often informal and familiar in their lyrics.

- These are used in some Catholic parishes or for some specific Masses such as those for Catholic youth groups.
- Worship songs are thought to appeal to younger Christians.
- Within charismatic Christian settings, music is seen as a way of allowing/accompanying an experience of the Holy Spirit. It may also be emotive and invite an involvement that words alone do not generate.

How music expresses belief

- Music and any form of hymn or song can allow a whole congregation to express their beliefs together. The words of the songs can help Catholics understand and remember Church teaching.
- Plainchant, hymns, and psalms are traditional forms of worship and praise to God, which have existed throughout Jewish and Christian history.
- Many of the core teachings of Christianity can be found within the words of Christian hymns, psalms, chants, and songs, e.g. 'Make me a channel of your peace', 'Here I am Lord', 'All Things Bright and Beautiful', 'How Great Thou Art', and 'This is my body, broken for you'.

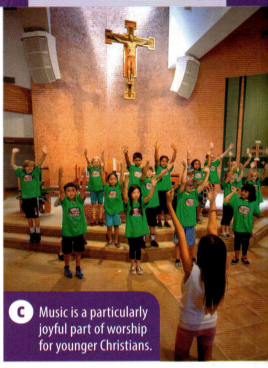

C Music is a particularly joyful part of worship for younger Christians.

BUILD YOUR SKILLS

1   a   Give three ways music is used during worship.
    b   Explain why Catholics might find music helpful as part of worship.
    c   Why might some Catholics see it as a distraction?

2   Are some types of music more appropriate for worship than others? Discuss this in pairs and note down your reasons.

EXAM-STYLE QUESTIONS

C   Explain **two** ways music is a part of worship for Catholics. In your answer you must refer to a source of wisdom and authority. (5)
D   'Traditional music is preferable for Catholics to use during worship.' Evaluate this statement considering arguments for and against. In your response you should:
    - refer to Catholic teachings
    - reach a justified conclusion. (12)

SUMMARY

- Plainchant, hymns, psalms, and worship songs allow Catholics to join together and pray together through the words and music of the songs.
- They help Catholics understand and remember Church teaching.
- They are used in the Mass and other services.

Revision

REVIEW YOUR KNOWLEDGE

1 Describe the two main uses of the Church building.
2 Name five features of a Catholic Church.
3 Define a sacred object.
4 Name two famous pieces of Catholic artwork, including artist, and indicate the type of artwork (painting, fresco, or drawing).
5 Describe two ways Catholics show devotion by using statues.
6 What are the four creatures linked to the Gospels?
7 Name the two main types of drama that originated in medieval times and are still used today to share Biblical stories.
8 What is the quote, usually attributed to St Augustine, found in the Catechism (CCC 1156) about singing?

* See page 288 for answers.

USEFUL TERMS

Do you know what these words mean?

Frescos   Iconoclasm   Acrostic

Tableaux   Responsorial   Redemption

Charismatic movement

EXTEND YOUR KNOWLEDGE: RESEARCH TASKS

For a research task, try to put together a full side of A4 of your own writing on the topics below.

1 Research a notable church, cathedral or basilica, e.g. Westminster Cathedral, Sagrada Familia, or Notre Dame de Paris. Highlight features that follow or differ from usual church design.
2 Research another piece of renowned religious artwork, e.g. 'The Last Supper' by Leonardo da Vinci or 'The Angelus' by Millet.
3 Research the Reformation in relation to religious art and statues: what happened to Catholic artwork and statues? What were they replaced with?
4 Research 'The Dream of Gerontius' and its importance for the Catholic Church.

ONGOING LEARNING REVIEW

It is vital that you keep reviewing past material to make sure you have fully learned and remember it.

1 Why are there different versions of the Bible?
2 What is the difference between the ordinary and extraordinary magisterium?
3 What does the People of God refer to?
4 Explain the different ways Mary is important to the Church.
5 Why is the conscience important to Christians?

Exam practice

In this exam practice section you will see examples for the exam question types: **a**, **b**, **c** and **d**. You can find out more about these on pages 6–7. Questions (a) and (d) in the **Exam question review** section below show strong student answers. Questions (b) and (c) in the **Improve it!** section need improvement.

Exam question review

(a) Outline **three** ways a sculpture or statue could be used by a Catholic. (3)

Pray in front of them.
Light a candle and place by the statue.
Touch or kiss the statue.

(d) 'Traditional music is preferable for Catholics to use during worship.' Evaluate this statement considering arguments for and against. In your response you should:
- refer to Catholic teachings
- reach a justified conclusion. (12)

The words of the Mass are set out in the Missal, and the music is set out in the Gradual. This is the official source of information about what music to use, and not use in Mass.

The Catechism encourages Catholics to 'make melody to the Lord' and so music can be a key part of worship, helping the prayers of those attending.

Music connects the parts of the Mass, which is why the Kyrie and Gloria are often sung as they would have been in the early Church, without music.

Some Catholics prefer modern music during Mass, one example includes 'praise and worship' which may include a variety of instruments, not just the organ. These Catholics may feel joyful music encourages a spiritual connection to God.

Contemporary music often appeals to younger Catholics. Family services may use music from a variety of different Christian traditions to appeal to their younger members. Appealing music may encourage them to join in.

I think it is more important to make music appealing to the congregation so they will want to attend church regularly. Offering different Masses with different styles of music within the parish is a good way to keep everyone happy.

Improve it!

These answers will not get full marks. Can you rewrite and improve them?

(b) Explain **two** ways in which the church building reflects belief. (4)

Many churches, especially older ones, were built in a crucifix shape. This was to remind people of Jesus' crucifixion and how central this was to the beliefs of Christians.

(c) Explain **two** reasons why sacred objects are important for Catholics. In your answer you must refer to a source of wisdom and authority. (5)

Certain things can be displayed in churches to remind Catholics of key beliefs. Some things, such sacred vessels also have practical use during the Mass. For example sacred vessels and the cross.

 WHAT WENT WELL

Question (a) asks you to 'outline' which is slightly more than a one-word answer – up to a sentence for each point. The three answers written here give enough detail to neatly sum up three different ways.

 WHAT WENT WELL

It's a good idea to aim to write five or six well-developed points, which argue both for and against the given statement. This answer achieves that, and considers the points of view against the question, arriving at a sensible conclusion.

 HOW TO IMPROVE

This is a good explanation, however there is only one point made. It is important there are two developed points, otherwise the answer cannot achieve more than half marks.

 HOW TO IMPROVE

This answer needs an example adding in the first point. The second point repeats itself. Neither link to a source of wisdom and authority – what does the Catechism say about sacred objects?

Area of Study 2:
Islam

Study choice
You will study **either** Islam **or** Judaism (Chapters 7 and 8) as your second religion.

Chapter 5: Beliefs and Teachings

Chapter 6: Practices

Belief in Islam

Islam means surrender, obedience or submission. It can also be translated as peace. These qualities:

- are reflected throughout the religion of Islam
- influence the way Muslims express their beliefs
- influence the way Muslims live their lives.

Beliefs are expressions of things you think are true. You must have faith to believe, but in Islam this is **iman**, or 'reasoned faith'. Muslims are expected to think about what they believe and then actively live out their faith with 'a knowledge in the heart, a voicing with the tongue, and an activity with the limbs' (Hadith).

Muslims believe Islam is the final religion, revealed by **Allah** to the Last Prophet, Muhammad. After Muhammad died, there were disagreements about who should succeed him as leader. As a result of this Islam divided into two main branches: Sunni and Shi'a. These branches share many of the same beliefs, but they have often expressed them in slightly different ways. Sunni tradition formulated the six Beliefs, and Shi'a the five roots of 'Usul ad-Din (see 5.2).

Sunni tradition

Sunni tradition is a branch of Islam which believes the Prophet Muhammad's first successor or **Khalifah** was his father-in-law Abu-Bakr. Sunnis believed their leader should be elected. Roughly 85 per cent of the world's Muslims are Sunni, and it is sometimes called '**Orthodox** Islam'.

Shi'a tradition

Shi'a tradition is a branch of Islam which believes the Prophet Muhammad's first successor or **Imam** was his son-in-law and cousin Ali ibn Abi Talib. Shi'a Muslims believe the true leader should be identified by Allah and be a descendant of Muhammad.

History of the six Beliefs

The six articles of faith (iman) are based on the **Qur'an** and the **hadith** of Muhammad. **Kitab al-iman**, translated as the 'Book of Faith', is found within Sahih Muslim, a book of hadith, and states:

> 'Iman is that you believe in God and His Angels and His Books and His Messengers and the Hereafter and the good and evil fate [ordained by your God].'
> *Hadith, Sahih Muslim*

SPECIFICATION FOCUS

The six Beliefs of Islam: their nature, history and purpose, including Kitab al-iman 1:4; how they are understood and expressed in Sunni and Shi'a Muslim communities today; the importance of these principles for Muslims.

USEFUL TERMS

Allah: the Islamic name for God

Hadith: sayings of the Prophet Muhammad. An important source of Islamic law

Imam: 1) Sunni leader of communal prayer; 2) Shi'a religious and political leader, the successor of the Prophet

Iman: faith arrived at by knowledge and understanding

Khalifah: (sometimes Caliph) an elected religious and political leader

Kitab al-iman: Book of Faith

Orthodox: traditional beliefs of religion

Qur'an: the Holy Book of Islam, as revealed to the Prophet Muhammad by God through the angel Jibril

A The mosque is a Muslim place of worship.

The six Beliefs

1. The unity of Allah (Tawhid)

Tawhid is that there is one God: this is the most fundamental belief of Islam. The profession of this faith in the **Shahadah** declares 'There is no god except Allah' and differentiates a Muslim from a kafir, or 'unbeliever'. This is very important as it expresses the unity of Allah and that nothing and no one is equal to Allah. The word kafir is not meant to be derogatory towards non-Muslims.

> ❛Say, 'He is God, the One, God the eternal. He begot no one nor was He begotten. No one is comparable to Him.'❜
> *Surah 112:1–4*

2. Belief in angels

Faith in the existence of angels is important as angels communicate Allah's messages:

> ❛He sends down angels with inspiration at His command❜
> *Surah 16:2*

Angels are created by Allah to carry out commands and reveal Allah's message to the prophets.

3. Books of Allah

This is belief in Allah's guidance to humans in the form of written guidance, or scriptures. These scriptures were sent to humans through the prophets. The Qur'an is the actual 'Word of Allah' as brought to Muhammad by the angel Jibril (Gabriel) and is the culmination of all previous sacred writings. The scriptures, in particular the Qur'an, provide guidance for life and help Muslims to achieve physical and spiritual fulfillment.

4. Faith in the prophets

Muslims must have faith in the prophets, particularly in Muhammad as the 'Seal' or last prophet. Allah has sent prophets throughout history, the first of which was Adam and the last being Muhammad. The prophets were appointed as messengers to communicate the message of Islam to humans. Muhammad is the most important because he was sent the 'Word of Allah' in the Qur'an. Anyone who does not believe in the finality of the prophethood of Muhammad is not accepted as a Muslim by Islam and Muslims.

5. Belief in the Day of Judgment and life after death

Muslims believe that one day Allah will end the world, then in a day of **resurrection** and judgment, every human being will stand before Allah to be judged. Allah will judge each individual deed and will reward or punish accordingly. After death all humans live on in the **Akhirah**. Those who are rewarded go to paradise (heaven), while those who are to be punished go to hell. The emphasis on individuals being responsible for each and every one of their deeds is an important part of Islam.

🔑 **USEFUL TERMS**

Akhirah: everlasting life after death, spent in either paradise or hell

Resurrection: in Islam, raising from the dead

Shahadah: the Islamic creed or profession of faith. The first pillar of Islam

Tawhid: the oneness and unity of Allah

B One of the names of Allah: Al-Wahid 'The One, The Unique'.

6. Belief in Allah's decree and predestination

The sixth and final belief is in Allah's divine decree, and destiny determined by Allah. This is known as **al-Qadr** or the 'measure' of what Allah decides. Muslims believe the plan of creation is under the direction of Allah and governed by Allah. Happiness and misery come from Allah and nothing can happen without Allah's will. 'No misfortune can happen, either in the earth or in yourselves, that was not set down in writing before We brought it into being' (Surah 57:22). This does not mean there is no free will. Individuals must make their choices, but their destiny is predetermined.

USEFUL TERM

Al-Qadr: predestination, a future already decided by Allah

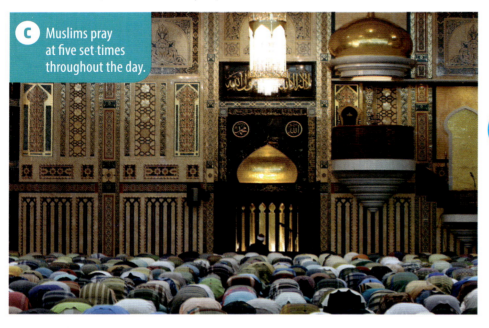

C Muslims pray at five set times throughout the day.

The importance of these principles for Muslims today

A core meaning of 'Islam' is obedience to Allah. Obedience requires iman; a faith arising out of knowledge, understanding, and conviction. The six Beliefs are the expression of faith in Sunni tradition and are important to Sunni communities today because:

- they continue to lead Muslims to Allah, and to each other
- faith leads humans to submission to Allah, following Islam, which is a way of life
- the six Beliefs guide Muslims in worship and daily life as a community.

BUILD YOUR SKILLS

1 a Summarize the six Beliefs for Sunni Muslims.
   b How do these differ in Shi'a tradition?
   c Which of these do you think is the most important for Muslims? Why?

2 a In pairs, think about how Muslims might use the six Beliefs to guide their everyday lives.
   b Which belief might be the most challenging one for Muslims to follow?

EXAM-STYLE QUESTIONS

B Explain **two** ways the six Beliefs might be used by Muslims in everyday life. (4)
D 'The differences between Sunni and Shi'a understanding of the six Beliefs are small but significant.' Evaluate this statement considering arguments for and against. In your response you should:
- refer to Muslim teachings
- refer to different Muslim points of view
- reach a justified conclusion. (15)

SUMMARY

- The six Beliefs are belief in: oneness of Allah, angels, books of Allah, prophets, the Day of Judgment, and predestination.
- The Beliefs are set out in books of hadith, e.g. Kitab al-iman in Sahih Muslim.
- The six Beliefs are the foundation of the whole Sunni tradition of Islam.
- They are important because belief in them leads Muslims to Allah.
- They continue to bring together Muslim communities in faith and belief.

5.2 The five roots of 'Usul ad-Din

What are the nature and history of the five roots?

Shi'a Muslim beliefs are summarized as 'Usul ad-Din. Usul can mean 'root' or 'principle', so these are often called the five principles, or the five roots. These beliefs are often compared to the roots of a tree since they form the foundation of a person's religion and nourish thoughts and actions. Just as the roots of a tree are vital for growth, life, and vitality, 'Usul ad-Din are fundamental to life as a Shi'a Muslim.

History of the five roots

The core beliefs of Sunni tradition are drawn together in books of hadith. Shi'a tradition also formalized their beliefs during the eighth and ninth centuries, and over time the five roots of 'Usul ad-Din evolved. Some of the roots are naturally similar in nature to the Sunni six Beliefs, but not all.

The five roots of Shi'a tradition

1. Tawhid (Oneness)

This is the belief in the oneness of Allah, shared with Sunni Muslims (see 5.1). It is the most important principle and comes from Surah 112, which Muhammad described as equal to one third of the Qur'an, despite its short length of two lines: 'Say, "He is God, the One, God the eternal"' (112:1–2).

2. 'Adl (Divine Justice)

'Adl is that Allah is fair and just. All Muslims believe that God is just, however, the Shi'a added this concept as a principle of faith because they argued that human action cannot be determined by God, otherwise it would be unjust to reward some and punish others for what all are predestined to do (see 5.7).

3. Nubuwwah (Prophethood)

Allah has sent prophets throughout history to guide human beings. The last of the prophets is the Prophet Muhammad, known as 'The Seal of the Prophets'.

4. Imamah (Successors to Muhammad)

The belief that after the Prophet Muhammad there are no more prophets, and no more divine scriptures. Instead Allah appointed twelve Imams to continue to guide human beings.

5. Mi'ad (Day of Judgment and Resurrection)

The belief in life after death, resurrection, and accountability after death for the life led on earth. On the Day of Judgment Allah will judge each individual deed, good and bad, and will reward or punish accordingly.

Formulation of these five principles does not mean that the Shi'a do not believe in other aspects of faith, such as angels and the revealed books of God. Rather they represent the most important aspects of faith from the Shi'a perspective.

SPECIFICATION FOCUS

The five roots of 'Usul ad-Din in Shi'a Islam (Tawhid (oneness of Allah); 'Adl (Divine Justice); Nubuwwah (Prophethood); Imamah (Successors to Muhammad) and Mi'ad (The Day of Judgment and the Resurrection): the nature, history and purpose of the five roots with reference to their Qur'anic basis, including Surah 112 (the oneness of Allah); the importance of these principles for different Shi'a communities today including Sevener and Twelver.

USEFUL TERM

'Adl: (sometimes Adalat) belief in Allah's justice and fairness

A Shi'a Muslims believe their five principles or roots nourish their faith.

History of Shi'a tradition

After Muhammad died in 632CE there was a difference of opinion between two groups about how his successor should be chosen. One group believed Muhammad had named his cousin and son-in-law, Ali, to be the leader (see Id-ul-Ghadeer in 6.8). They became known as Shiites, now Shi'a. Shi'a Muslims believe their leader, the Imam, must be a descendant of the Prophet Muhammad and must be appointed as such by Allah either through the Prophet or by the previous Imam. This is called the doctrine of nass which literally means 'annunciation'. Nass is the evidence that a living Imam has validated the next successor.

The Imam can commit no sin and is an intermediary between humans and Allah just as the Prophet Muhammad was. The Imam explains the Qur'an and the **Shari'ah** to guide people.

> ❝Who so ever knows not the Imam of his age dies the death of a heathen❞
> *Hadith in Shi'a traditions*

There is some dialogue and debate among Shi'a tradition as to how many Imams there have been. The majority of Shi'a believe there are twelve Imams, and the largest denomination is therefore called the Twelvers. There are also Fivers and Seveners: these are groups which broke away at the time of the fifth and seventh Imams respectively and therefore each group believes each one was the last true Imam.

The importance of 'Usul ad-Din for Shi'a communities today

Obedience to Allah is important to every Muslim, Sunni or Shi'a, just as every Muslim must come to faith with knowledge and understanding. 'Usul ad-Din are the expressions of faith in Shi'a tradition and are important to Shi'a communities today because:

- they continue to lead Muslims to Allah, and to each other
- faith leads humans to submission to Allah, following Islam, which is a way of life
- emphasising the justice of God places the responsibility on humans for what they say and do
- 'Usul ad-Din guide Muslims in worship and daily life as a community.

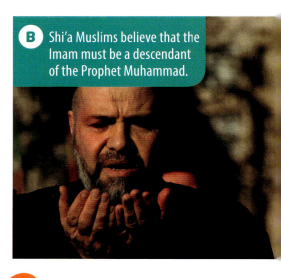

B Shi'a Muslims believe that the Imam must be a descendant of the Prophet Muhammad.

USEFUL TERMS

'Ibadah: loving obedience, submission, and devotion to Allah

Shari'ah: the moral and religious law which Muslims must obey, based directly on the Qur'an and sunnah

BUILD YOUR SKILLS

1 a Summarize each of the five roots.
   b How are they similar to or different from the six Beliefs?

2 Explain why 'Usul ad-Din are called the 'roots' of Islam.

3 How is the Imam important in Shi'a tradition?

SUMMARY

- The five roots of 'Usul ad-Din are oneness, justice, prophethood, leadership, and the Day of Judgment.
- Most Shi'as believe the Prophet Muhammad appointed Imam Ali as his successor and eleven Imams followed him who are divinely appointed.
- The five roots underpin the beliefs of Shi'a Muslims and are important today to continue to guide them in their faith.

EXAM-STYLE QUESTIONS

A Outline **three** roots of 'Usul ad-Din. (3)

C Explain **two** reasons why 'Usul ad-Din are the most important beliefs for Shi'a Muslims. In your answer you must refer to a source of wisdom and authority. (5)

The characteristics of Allah

The Qur'an mentions more than 130 names for God but Muslims believe God's names are infinite. The 99 names mentioned in narrations are said to have a particular effect for whoever knows them, and are not meant to restrict the names.

These names describe attributes of Allah and indicate love, mercy, majesty, power, compassion, and peace. Each name describes something about the nature of Allah, although they can never fully describe the wonder of Allah. The most repeated are: 'al-Rahman' (most kind) and 'al-Rahim' (most merciful).

Muslims believe that they need to link their belief to actions and demonstrate belief in Allah in everything they do. The word **'Ibadah** means loving obedience and submission to Allah. It used for both worship and action to show that worship and belief are inextricably linked. Before important actions, Muslims frequently recite the key characteristics of Allah in the sentence 'In the name of Allah, most kind, most merciful'.

Love of Allah is the starting point for everything a Muslim does and says and they will think first about what Allah expects when making moral decisions. Understanding the characteristics of Allah is therefore crucial to inform a Muslim's behaviour.

The most important of these characteristics are Tawhid and 'Adl.

SPECIFICATION FOCUS

The nature of Allah: how the characteristics of Allah are shown in the Qur'an and why they are important: Tawhid (oneness), including Surah 16:35–36, immanence, transcendence, omnipotence, beneficence, mercy, fairness and justice, Adalat in Shi'a Islam.

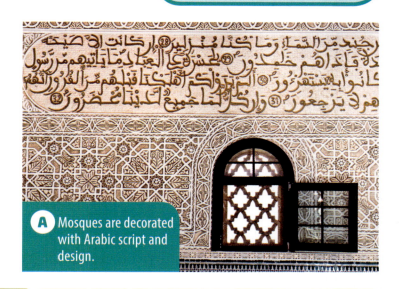

A Mosques are decorated with Arabic script and design.

Tawhid – Allah is one: the unique and only God. This is the heart of Islamic belief, reflected in the Shahadah.

Immanence – Allah is present within the world. This does not mean as part of creation, for he is the creator.

Transcendence – Allah is beyond the physical world as the creator, all-knowing and all-powerful.

Omnipotence – Allah has limitless and unimaginable power.

> ❛He is God, the One, God the eternal. He begot no one nor was He begotten. No one is comparable to Him.❜
> *Surah 112:1–4*

Beneficence – Allah acts with good intentions for the benefit of others.

Mercy – Allah shows compassion or forgiveness to those he could punish.

Fairness – Allah treats humans reasonably and with equality.

Justice/'Adl – Allah will punish and reward in a way that is right and fair.

> ❛no vision can take Him in, but He takes in all vision. He is the All Subtle, the All Aware.❜
> *Surah 6:103*

> ❛He is most forgiving, most merciful.❜
> *Surah 25:70*

Tawhid

At the heart of Islam lies the belief in Allah's oneness called Tawhid and so Islam teaches absolute **monotheism**.

> ❛Worship God and shun false Gods.❜
> *Surah 16:36*

Allah has no plural in Arabic and so the name itself means there is only one God.

In addition to the belief of the Oneness of Allah, Muslims also believe that Allah is unique and consequently cannot be drawn, illustrated, or represented. To regard anything as being equal to Allah is absolutely forbidden and is described as **shirk**. Anyone who commits shirk can no longer be considered a Muslim, such is the severity of the sin.

Geometrical designs, popular in Islamic culture, can reflect some of the unity and the beauty of Allah and are often used as decoration in mosques.

'Adl

Muslims believe that Allah rules with justice. 'Adl is the belief that Allah is completely just and fair. This means that Allah does not perform any action that would contradict this justice and fairness, as Allah is perfect. This does not mean Allah does not punish individuals, but that Allah will act justly towards those who have done wrong.

> ❛your Lord will not be unjust to anyone❜
> *Surah 18:49*

B Geometrical design is used to reflect the unity of Allah.

USEFUL TERMS

Monotheism: the belief in one God

Revelation: in Islam, the communication of the words of Allah

Shirk: believing in things other than Allah or as equals to Allah

---

 BUILD YOUR SKILLS

1. **a** Choose 5–10 names for Allah from the Qur'an and explain in a sentence what they reveal about the nature of Allah.
   b How might a Muslim be influenced by, or feel after reflecting on, these names?

2. Explain in 100 words how the idea of submission to Allah might affect how a teenage Muslim lives their life. Refer to the characteristics of Allah in your answer.

SUMMARY

- Allah is beyond human understanding and is within everything yet greater than everything.
- The 99 beautiful names for Allah in the Qur'an and hadith help Muslims understand something of the nature of Allah.
- Tawhid is the belief in the oneness of Allah.
- 'Adl is the belief that Allah is just.

EXAM-STYLE QUESTIONS

B Explain **two** strengths of 'Adl for Muslims. (4)

C Explain **two** names of Allah which influence the way Muslims try to live their lives. In your answer you must refer to a source of wisdom and authority. (5)

5.4 RiSalah

SPECIFICATION FOCUS

RiSalah: the nature and importance of prophethood for Muslims, including Surah 2:136; what the roles of prophets teach Muslims, exemplified in the lives of Adam, Ibrahim, Isma'il, Musa, Dawud, Isa, Muhammad.

What is the nature of prophethood for Muslims?

RiSalah means 'divine message' and is also used to mean prophethood or the channel of communication with Allah. Nubuwwah is also used to refer to the general office of prophethood.

Muslims believe that prophets are human beings appointed by Allah and sent to all nations to speak Allah's divine message. The prophets have been granted the gift of being infallible (unable to make mistakes).

What the roles of prophets teach Muslims

Twenty-five prophets are named in the Qur'an, although Muslim tradition says that there have been approximately 124,000 prophets sent by Allah. The prophets received their messages from an angel but their words became ignored, distorted, or overlooked and so Allah sent Muhammad as the final prophet.

All the prophets preached a message of the need for repentance, obedience to Allah, and choosing good over evil. They lived by example, and Muslims look to the behaviour and actions of prophets in order to improve the way they live their lives in obedience to Allah. It is believed the prophets were sinless and that every nation was sent a prophet, until Muhammad.

The Qur'an directs Muslims to be obedient to the teachings of the prophets:

> ❛So [you believers], say, "We believe in God and in what was sent down to us and what was sent down to Abraham, Ishmael, Isaac, Jacob, and the Tribes, and what was given to Moses, Jesus, and all the prophets by their Lord. We make no distinction between any of them, and we devote ourselves to Him."❜
> *Surah 2:136*

A The prophets demonstrated obedience to Allah.

Muhammad

B Muhammad was originally a trader.

Muslims believe that Muhammad was the last and greatest prophet of them all. He lived between 570 and 632CE. In around 610CE Muslims believe that Muhammad began to receive **revelations** from Allah through the angel Jibril (Gabriel). Over a period of 23 years these revelations were recorded to form the Qur'an. Muslims do not believe that Muhammad brought a new faith, but that he was the last of a long line of prophets sent by Allah to guide people back to the true faith, called Islam.

Stories about his life and work, together with quotations of what he said, are recorded in the hadiths. Accounts of practices and things he did have been passed down

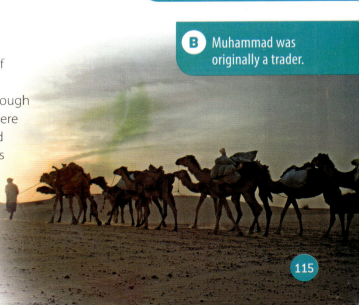

through generations and recorded as the **sunnah**. The greatest miracle of the Prophet Muhammad was receiving and sharing the message of the Qur'an: the final revelation of Allah. The Qur'an was given to Muhammad in Arabic and immediately written down in Arabic so the word of Allah would not be distorted. Subsequently it was compiled together in a single book form.

> 'Muhammad [...] is God's Messenger and the seal of the prophets'
> *Surah 33:40*

Muslims often follow the Prophet's name with the words 'peace be upon him' or 'pbuh' as a mark of respect. Muhammad is worthy of respect but not worship (Surahs 18:110 and 33:56). He called for social justice and preached against the idol worship of multiple gods (polytheism). In doing so Muhammad created harmony, uniting warring tribes into one religious community. He laid the foundation to establish the rule of Allah in the world.

Adam

Adam is regarded as the first Muslim and so Islam began with Adam. Adam is not divine but was an ordinary human being called by Allah to deliver his message and show human beings how they should live. Adam lived in a beautiful garden but fell from grace by giving in to the temptations of the devil. As a result Adam was expelled from the Garden of Eden, but after accepting his mistake he was forgiven and became the first prophet. Allah appointed Adam as a vicegerent and all human beings are now Allah's vicegerents on earth. This means humans have to be responsible and accountable for caring for the earth and doing Allah's will.

Ibrahim

Ibrahim (Abraham) is a highly regarded prophet who was gifted the sacred texts known as Sahifah Ibrahim (Scrolls of Abraham). He is seen as a father figure because he led many people away from their worship of idols. He faced many tests of faith, including being asked to sacrifice his beloved son. Allah saved him from the fire and prevented Ibrahim from completing the sacrifice. Muslims still celebrate Ibrahim's obedience to Allah by sacrificing an animal in his honour on Id ul-Adha (see 6.8). Ibrahim rebuilt a sanctuary called the **Ka'bah**, which became the location for the pilgrimage of **Hajj** (see 6.6).

He is celebrated in the Qur'an:

> '"Peace be upon Abraham!" This is how We reward those who do good: truly he was one of Our faithful servants.'
> *Surah 37:109–111*

USEFUL TERMS

Hajj: the annual pilgrimage to Makkah, which all Muslims must undertake at least once if possible

Jihad: to struggle or strive. This could be a spiritual or physical struggle

Ka'bah: a building in the centre of Islam's most sacred mosque in Makkah, regarded as the house of Allah

Sunnah: the teachings and deeds of Muhammad

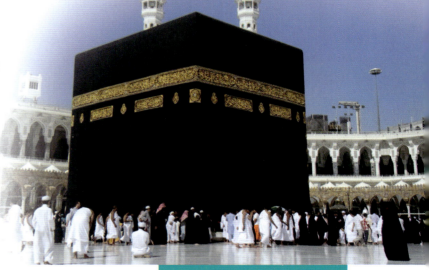

C Muslim tradition says that Ibrahim rebuilt the Ka'bah; an ancient site of pilgrimage.

Isma'il

Isma'il is the son Ibrahim was told to sacrifice in a dream. When Ibrahim told Isma'il of his dream he replied, 'Father, do as you are commanded and, God willing, you will find me steadfast' (Sura 37:102). For this reason Isma'il is seen as a model of obedience for Muslims. Isma'il was entrusted with care of the Ka'bah and to teach about Hajj. Muhammad is a descendant of Isma'il.

Musa

Musa (Moses) was a prophet who led the Jews out of slavery in Egypt and into the Promised Land. Musa was given the word of Allah in the Tawrat (Torah):

> 'To Moses God spoke directly'
> *Surah 4:164*

The Tawrat is regarded as one of the true revealed scriptures by Muslims, but people often ignored, rejected, or distorted the message. Musa is highly regarded as a prophet and as an example of obedient behaviour for Muslims.

Dawud

As well as being a prophet, Dawud (David) is acknowledged as an influential Muslim leader – king of the Kingdom of Israel. He came from lowly origins and played the harp for King Saul, but after he defeated the giant warrior Goliath in battle with a slingshot and prayers, he married Saul's daughter. He was gifted the sacred book of Zabur (the Psalms) after he became king. He was also granted skill in making armour, but only to be used in **jihad** (war to defend Islam).

D Muslims believe that Moses led the Jews out of Egypt.

Isa

Isa, or Jesus, was gifted with another revealed scripture: Injil (the Gospel). Muslims believe in the immaculate conception of both Isa and his mother Maryam (Mary), and that Isa was uniquely granted the gift of performing miracles. Muslims do not believe that Isa was crucified on the cross, but that he was taken by Allah to heaven and will return before the end of the world and gather all Muslims together. Isa is considered to be a Muslim who was sent to help humans find the path to Allah.

> ❛When Jesus came with clear signs he said, "I have brought you wisdom; I have come to clear up some of your differences for you. Be mindful of God and obey me."❜
> *Surah 43:63*

 E Muslims believe that Isa was sent to help people find the path to Allah.

BUILD YOUR SKILLS

1 a In pairs, discuss: do we need to be guided in life? Who do you turn to for guidance?
  b How does the Qur'an guide the life of a Muslim?

2 a Name three prophets mentioned in the Qur'an and write three sentences about each of them.
  b What can Muslims learn about them from the way they lived their lives?
  c Explain what Islam teaches about the prophets of Allah. How do Muslims show their respect for the prophets?

SUMMARY

- RiSalah means message or prophethood.
- Allah sent many prophets with the same message: repentance and obedience. Over time Allah's word was either ignored, or distorted.
- The prophets were role models for Muslims of how to be obedient to Allah.
- The first prophet was Adam and the last, and most important prophet was Muhammad.
- Musa is also important as Allah revealed the Tawrat through him, which guided Muslims before the Qur'an, but then became distorted.

? EXAM-STYLE QUESTIONS

B Explain **two** reasons why Muhammad is so important to Muslims. (4)

D 'Muhammad lived over 1,400 years ago. His example is no longer relevant for Muslims today.' Evaluate this statement considering arguments for and against. In your response you should:
- refer to Muslim teachings
- refer to different Muslim points of view
- reach a justified conclusion. (15)

5.5 Muslim holy books

What are the nature and history of Muslim holy books?

Muslims believe that Allah has spoken to human beings from the beginning of time through the angels and prophets. These messages, or revelations, were gathered together by each prophet in holy books which are referred to within the Qur'an:

- Tawrat (Torah) by Musa (Moses) (see Surah 5:43–48)
- Zabur (Psalms) by Dawud (David) (see Surah 4:163–171)
- Injil (Gospels) by Isa (Jesus) (see Surah 5:46–47)
- Sahifah (Scrolls) by Ibrahim (Abraham) (see Surah 53:36 and 87:18–19).

According to Islam, there are several written books of the word of Allah. Unfortunately, these books were vulnerable to distortion and despite the teachings of the prophets, people kept forgetting what Allah was like. Therefore, Allah called Muhammad to be his final prophet and gave him the Qur'an so that people would not forget his teachings.

Muslims respect all revealed holy books, but they believe that the words of the Qur'an are the actual words of Allah, which were revealed to the Prophet through the angel Jibril (Gabriel). The word Qur'an means 'recitation' and Muslims believe that the words existed in Al-Lawh Al-Mahfuz (the Sacred Tablet) from the beginning of time, to be revealed to Muhammad and recorded in the exact way that he received them.

> 'The Qur'an is nothing less than a revelation that is sent to him.'
> *Surah 53:4*
>
> '[The Prophet's] own heart did not distort what he saw.'
> *Surah 53:11*

The Qur'an was written in Arabic, the language in which it was revealed to Muhammad, and it is divided into chapters called suwar (singular: surah). There are 114 suwar and each is subdivided further into verses. Some suwar are short

USEFUL TERMS

Ramadan: the ninth month of the Islamic calendar in which the Qur'an was revealed to Muhammad

Wudu': ritual cleansing or ablution with water

A Dictated and recorded in Arabic, the Qur'an is said to be the final revelation of Allah to humanity and his undistorted Word.

melodious passages and others contain guidance on all aspects of a Muslim's faith and behaviour. For Muslims, the Qur'an is unique because it is the actual 'Word of Allah', and Muslims believe Allah is unique and incomparable.

The Qur'an was written in three stages. In the course of many revelations, the angel Jibril disclosed the will of Allah to Muhammad. For many years afterwards, Muhammad was followed by a group of disciples who made note of everything he said. After Muhammad's death, his friends collated the material into a permanent record. The third Khalifah (spiritual leader) 'Uthman had copies of the Qur'an made and sent it to cities with Muslim converts to spread the word.

The importance of the holy books for Muslims today

The Qur'an is given the position of supreme authority by Muslims and it is the guidance for their life: 'This is a clear lesson to people, and guidance and teaching' (Surah 3:138). As it is the last revelation of Allah, it is protected from corruption: 'falsehood cannot touch from any angle' (Surah 41:42).

B Muslims treat the Qur'an respectfully.

Some Muslims might study earlier holy books to consider their teachings in the light of the Qur'an, but the Qur'an remains the authoritative text for all Muslims.

Muslims treat the Qur'an with the greatest possible respect. It is usually wrapped in a cloth and kept on a high shelf when not in use.

- Before reading the Qur'an, a Muslim should perform **wudu'**.
- When it is being read or recited, everyone must remain silent and may not eat or drink.
- The most important way of showing respect for Allah is to memorize the whole Qur'an, so as to be able to recite it regularly in Arabic. Muslims who achieve this are recognized by the title 'Hafiz', attached as an addition to their name.

Muslims believe that the entire Qur'an in its essential form was revealed to the first heaven in one blessed night in the month of **Ramadan** called Laylat al-Qadr (The Night of Power). From there on it was brought down by Jibril, a few verses at a time, to Muhammad over a period of 23 years.

> ❝We sent it down on the Night of Glory [Power].❞
> *Surah 97:1*

BUILD YOUR SKILLS

1 a What holy books do Muslims acknowledge came before the Qur'an?
  b Why were these replaced by the Qur'an?

2 a Why do Muslims treat the Qur'an with particular care?
  b Explain how Muslims prepare to read the Qur'an.

SUMMARY

- Muslims respect all revealed holy books: Tawrat, Zabur, Injil, Sahifah, Qur'an.
- Muslims regard the Qur'an as the actual Word of Allah, as revealed to Muhammad.
- Muslims hold the Qur'an in the position of supreme authority and treat it with great respect.
- The Qur'an provides guidance for faith, behaviour, and life.

EXAM-STYLE QUESTIONS

A Outline **three** ways holy books are important for Muslims. (3)

C Explain **two** reasons why Muslims believe the Qur'an is the most important holy book. In your answer you must refer to a source of wisdom and authority. (5)

5.6 Malaikah

What is the nature of angels?

Muslims believe in the existence of malaikah, or angels who perform various duties entrusted to them by Allah. For Sunni Muslims, belief in angels is the second of their six core beliefs. This belief is important for Muslims because angels provide a link between Allah and their prophets.

> 'if anyone is an enemy of God, His angels and His messengers, of Gabriel and Michael, then God is certainly the enemy of such disbelievers.'
> *Surah 2:98*

- Angels are the messengers of Allah, revealing his message to generations through the prophets.
- According to the Qur'an angels were Allah's first creation.
- Angels are created by Allah out of light and are not physical beings, although they can take a form when required. They have no gender.
- Angels do not commit sins or have free will; they are incorruptible and immortal.

How are Jibril, Izra'il, Mika'il, and Israfil shown in the Qur'an?

The Qur'an does not name all the individual angels; Israfil is named in a hadith and Izra'il is only referred to as Malak al-Mawt (Angel of Death). Jibril, Izra'il, Mika'il, and Israfil are the most important, or 'archangels', for Muslims.

- Jibril (Gabriel) – angel of revelation: Jibril gives Allah's messages to the prophets, including communicating the Qur'an to Muhammad.

> 'Gabriel – who by God's leave brought down the Qur'an to your heart'
> *Surah 2:97*

- Izra'il (Azrael) – angel of death: Izra'il is responsible for taking the last breath from humans and all living creatures when they die.

> 'The Angel of Death put in charge of you will reclaim you, and then you will be brought back to your Lord.'
> *Surah 32:11*

- Mika'il (Michael) – angel of mercy: Mika'il is responsible for nourishment; he brings the rain and wind and is in charge of the weather.
- Israfil (Raphael) – trumpeter: Israfil is responsible for the Day of Judgment and will sound the Last Trumpet.

SPECIFICATION FOCUS

Malaikah: the nature and importance of angels for Muslims; how angels Jibril, Izra'il and Mika'il are shown in the Qur'an including Surah 19, 32:11, and 2:97–98, and their significance for Muslims today.

A Muslims believe that angels were created from light.

B Mika'il, the angel of mercy, brings nourishment to the land and humanity.

What is the importance of angels?

Angels act as servants of Allah and obey him, showing the utmost regard and respect. They are always in service, bowing or standing before Allah and are not scornful of worshipping him, nor do they tire and get bored: 'they glorify Him tirelessly night and day' (Surah 21:20).

This teaches Muslims the importance of humility before Allah: they can look to the behaviour of angels as an example of the selfless worship they should show Allah.

- Ordinary people cannot see angels unless they take on a visible form; the prophets can see angels in their natural form. Some companions of Muhammad saw angels who came to help them during a battle.
- Angels can deliver good news such as the news that the prophet Ibrahim would have a child and the message from Jibril to Maryam the mother of Isa (Jesus) that she would miraculously give birth.
- The most famous stories in Islam of messages delivered by angels are to do with the revelation of the Qur'an to the Prophet Muhammad in the cave of Hira on Mount Nur.

In additional to the archangels, other angels have specific jobs which would influence the life of a Muslim. Hafaza angels keep watch day and night over every human being; al-kiraman al-katibin are honourable scribes who record every good and bad deed a person does for the book they receive on the Last Day.

Muslim tradition has added to what the Qur'an says, but it is based on the Qur'an. One hadith teaches Muslims to strive to the standard of the angels, to be guided by their minds rather than their physical desires as the Qur'an teaches them.

The significance of angels for Muslims today

Angels teach Muslims the importance of obedience and submission to Allah's will. The archangels are particularly important for Muslims because they hold important roles which directly affect the lives of Muslims – Jibril brought the word of Allah to Muhammad, Mika'il will sustain them during life, Izra'il will take their last breath, and Israfil will summon them to the Day of Judgment. Belief in them is key, because they represent important parts of Muslim faith.

C The cave of Hira, Mount Nur, Makkah in Saudi Arabia.

 God created angels from intellect without sensuality, the beasts from sensuality without intellect and mankind from both intellect and sensuality. **So when a person's intellect overcomes his sensuality he is better than the angels**, but when his sensuality overcomes his intellect he is worse than the beasts. *Hadith*

 BUILD YOUR SKILLS

1   In groups, discuss the purpose of angels within Islam.

2   How does the Qur'an describe angels? Use direct quotations to support your answer.

3   a   Complete a mind map with the different ways angels affect the daily lives of Muslims.
    b   Which do you think is the most important effect?

SUMMARY

- Allah created angels from light to carry out his commands.
- Angels cannot sin or disobey Allah.
- The angels reveal Allah's message to the prophets.
- Jibril, Mika'il, Izra'il, and Israfil are assigned special roles which affect different parts of Muslim life.
- Muslims today try to follow the example of all angels in their obedience and submission to Allah.

EXAM-STYLE QUESTIONS

A   Outline **three** qualities of angels. (3)

C   Explain **two** ways belief in angels affects the lives of Muslims today. In your answer you must refer to a source of wisdom and authority. (5)

5.7 Al-Qadr

What are the nature and importance of predestination for Muslims?

Al-Qadr is the belief of predestination – that the universe follows the divine master plan of Allah: 'The overall scheme belongs to God' (Surah 13:42).

Belief in the oneness of Allah (tawhid) leads to the belief of al-Qadr that Allah has a master plan for the universe that he has created. Allah:

- is all-powerful (omnipotent)
- knows everything past, present, and future (omniscient)
- has a plan for the world and the power to make that plan happen.

Sahih Al-Bukhari 78:685 is a hadith which supports the idea that a person's destiny is set by Allah:

> ❝The Prophet said, "Allah says, 'The vow, does not bring about for the son of Adam anything I have not decreed for him, but his vow may coincide with what has been decided for him'."❞
> *Sahih Al-Bukhari 78:685*

Some Muslims believe the master plan is written by Allah in Al-Lawh al-Mahfuz (The Preserved Tablet). However, within this plan human beings do have choice and the will to make their own decisions. This is important because everyone is held accountable on the Day of Judgment for the choices they have made. Allah does not force people to follow a path, but his **omniscience** means he knows the choices people will make.

Sunni and Shi'a Muslims disagree about how much free will an individual has. Shi'as believe Surah 13:11 in the Qur'an allows the possibility that Allah can change their destiny, according to the actions they take. Sunni Muslims believe they have choices on the way towards this destiny. However, their choice is already known to God before they even make it, so in one sense their destiny is set.

> ❝God does not change the condition of a people **unless they change** what is in themselves❞
> *Surah 13:11*

Al-Qadr, human freedom, and the Day of Judgment

The Day of Judgment is the day on which Muslims believe Allah will destroy the present order of the world and create a new order, then resurrect the dead to judge them individually. They will proceed to either paradise or hell depending on his judgment.

🔍 **SPECIFICATION FOCUS**

Al-Qadr: the nature and importance of Predestination for Muslims; how al-Qadr and human freedom relates to the Day of Judgment, including reference Sahih Al-Bukhari 78:685; divergent understandings of predestination in Sunni and Shi'a Islam; the implications of belief in al-Qadr for Muslims today.

A Muslims must follow Allah's laws. They have free will and are responsible for their own decisions and actions.

🔑 **USEFUL TERM**

Omniscience: complete knowledge of all human actions, past, present, and future

The belief in the afterlife and personal accountability encourages Muslims to do good things. Muslims believe that:

● after death, all humans live on in the Akhirah or everlasting life

● life on earth is preparation for the Akhirah, and this is where they can perform actions that will lead to reward or punishment

● as Allah will judge people on the basis of their actions, they must behave well to secure their position in the next life.

It follows, therefore, that human beings have free will since it would be illogical to punish someone if they were not accountable or responsible for their actions.

The eighth-century Muslim theologian, Al-Ashari, explained how free will is linked to al-Qadr by asserting that Allah knows what people will do before they do it, but that humans have the freedom to make the decision to do, or not do what Allah wants.

B Muslims helping their community after devastating floods in Carlisle.

The implications of al-Qadr today

The Qur'an reassures Muslims that they should continue to do good deeds to work towards their destiny because it will make their life easier.

> ❛There is the one who gives, who is mindful of God, who testifies to goodness – We shall smooth his way towards ease. ❜
> *Surah 92:5–7*

Belief in al-Qadr:

● helps guide Muslims to be better people through their actions

● can support faith during difficult times. Predestination includes both success and failure in life, but remembering that all this is Allah's plan for them can give Muslims strength

● can also help a Muslim to move forward and not look back on actions with regret – as the result is as Allah intended.

 BUILD YOUR SKILLS

1 a Explain in your own words what Sunni Muslims believe predestination to mean.
  b Explain in your own words what Shi'a Muslims believes predestination to mean.

2 a What is the belief of free will for Muslims?
  b How does this connect with Al-Qadr?

3 Why do Muslims believe they must continue to carry out good deeds?

? EXAM-STYLE QUESTIONS

B Explain **two** reasons why free will is important within the belief of al-Qadr. (4)

D 'Every person makes their own destiny.' Evaluate this statement considering arguments for and against. In your response you should:
  ● refer to Muslim teachings
  ● refer to different Muslim points of view
  ● reach a justified conclusion. (15)

SUMMARY

● Al-Qadr is the belief that everything follows a divine master plan.

● Muslims believe that Allah is all-powerful (omnipotent) and all-knowing (omniscient).

● Muslims believe that human beings have the freedom to choose their actions and are responsible for the consequences, whether they are good or bad.

● Shi'a Muslims believe their actions can change their destiny, if Allah agrees.

● On the Day of Judgment every Muslim is held accountable for their actions.

SPECIFICATION FOCUS

Akhirah: Muslim teachings about life after death; the nature of judgment, paradise and hell; how they are shown in the Qur'an including Surah 17:49–72; divergent ways in which Muslims teachings about life after death affect the life of a Muslim today.

What do Muslims teach about life after death?

Akhirah is the belief in life after death. The Qur'an teaches death is not the end, but the beginning of the life to come.

- Life is a test from Allah and only makes sense if there is life after death.
- Muslims believe they should live their lives as best they can because their behaviour will lead to either reward or punishment.
- The Day of Judgment is when Allah will raise the dead and judge all people justly according to their beliefs and actions.

> ❛God created the heavens and earth for a true purpose: to reward each soul according to its deeds.❜
> *Surah 45:22*

What is the nature of judgment?

According to Islam, Allah has given the Qur'an to guide Muslims to live their lives in a way which is pleasing to Allah. Surah 17:49–72 describes the resurrection and judgment of individuals that will take place and is influenced by their behaviour during life. Muslims should live being aware that their thoughts, words, and actions are being noted.

> ❛Your Lord has the most knowledge about all of you: if He pleases He will have mercy on you, and if He pleases He will punish you.❜
> *Surah 17:54*

- If Muslims fail to follow the Qur'an, they are responsible for the punishment that follows.
- The Qur'an teaches that the last day will be heralded by the sound of a trumpet and everything will stop. The world will be destroyed and there will be a resurrection (raising) of the dead to the plain of judgment.

> ❛When we are turned to bones and dust, shall we really be raised up in a new act of creation?❜
> *Surah 17:49*

- Each person will receive the book of their life which has been recorded and kept by the angels. Those who are given the book in their right hand will go to paradise, and those given it in their left will be sent to hell.
- The period between individual death and judgment is known as **Barzakh** and there are different beliefs about its nature. This is where the souls of the dead await the Day of Judgment. A person's place in Barzakh is linked with their words and

COMPARE AND CONTRAST

In your exam you may be asked to compare and contrast Muslim beliefs about the afterlife and their significance with Catholic beliefs. Look back at 1.8 for detail on these.

USEFUL TERM

Barzakh: meaning 'barrier'; it is the state between death and the Day of Judgment

actions on earth. For a good person Bazakh will be a foretaste of paradise. Muslims believe their souls will be questioned and tested after they are buried in the grave.

- It is entirely up to Allah whether a person remains in paradise or hell for eternity: 'your Lord carries out whatever He wills' (Surah 11:107). Some Muslims believe Allah will intercede as the 'merciful and compassionate', as will Muhammad and some categories of Muslims such as the Hafiz (see 5.5).

What is the nature of paradise?

Paradise is a higher stage of life compared to this world, just as life in the world is a higher stage of existence compared to when humans are growing in the womb. The Qur'an says that the real life comes in Akhirah (Surah 29:64); the life of this world prepares us for it. As such it is not possible to perceive the reality of life after death. The Qur'an describes paradise as a place of perfect happiness and nearness to Allah; a heaven. There are descriptions in the Qur'an of paradise as 'al-Jannah' (the Garden).

Paradise is beautiful, there is no fear or pain or unhappiness. Muslims are reunited with those they love who have gained entrance, and are indulged in food and non-intoxicating pure wine. There are eight gates in paradise, giving entry to eight increasingly wonderful levels depending on how good your life has been.

What is the nature of hell?

Hell is called Jahannam and is the punishment of eternal separation from Allah. Those sent here face the horrors of torments of fire and eternal punishment including boiling and being chained up.

'We shall send those who reject Our revelations to the Fire. When their skins have been burned away, We shall replace them with new ones so that they may continue to feel the pain.'
Surah 4:56

'As for those who believe and do good deeds, We shall admit them into Gardens graced with flowing streams and there they will remain forever.'
Surah 4:57

A Many Muslims believe that paradise is unimaginably beautiful.

To be placed in hell is the punishment for those who have done wrong in their lives. There are seven gates and levels of hell, each successively worse, and there are many names in the Qur'an for the different types of fire within it, including 'jaheem' (blazing fire) and 'id-hutama' (that which breaks to pieces).

There is also Zaqqum, 'the cursed tree' (Surah 17:60) with poisonous fruit that boils the inside of those who eat it.

How these affect the life of a Muslim

The Muslim teachings about life after death detail the joy of paradise and the torment of hell graphically. This is a strong motivation for Muslims to observe the teaching of the Qur'an and to make the decisions Allah wishes them to make in their daily life. It also reassures Muslims that their efforts will be rewarded and can give them a sense of purpose. Ultimately, the teachings remind Muslims that every part of this life is a test for the life to come after: Akhirah.

> 'But if anyone desires the life to come and strives towards it as he should, as a true believer, his striving will be thanked.'
> *Surah 17:19*

SUMMARY

- Akhirah is a belief in life after death. Muslims believe that life on earth is a test.
- After death there will be a life in the grave called Barzakh, followed eventually by the Day of Judgment.
- Allah will resurrect and judge, holding everyone accountable for their beliefs and actions.
- After judgment people will be sent to paradise or hell, which provides all Muslims with a strong motivation to live their life in the way Allah has commanded them to.

BUILD YOUR SKILLS

1 Summarize what Muslims believe happens after death.

2 **a** In pairs, discuss: How do you behave if your parents:
   - offer you a reward
   - threaten a punishment?
   b What might a Muslim see as the benefit of a detailed description of paradise and hell in the Qur'an?
   c What disadvantages might they see?
   d How might these influence the behaviour of Muslims?

EXAM-STYLE QUESTIONS

B Describe **two** differences in the belief of life after death between Islam and the main religious tradition of Great Britain. (4)

D 'Belief in life after death allows Muslims to live a better life.' Evaluate this statement considering arguments for and against. In your response you should:
   - refer to Muslim teachings
   - refer to different Muslim points of view
   - reach a justified conclusion. (15)

Revision

 REVIEW YOUR KNOWLEDGE

1 Name four meanings of Islam.
2 List the six Beliefs.
3 Recall the five roots of 'Usal ad-Din.
4 Describe what the roles of the prophets teach Muslims.
5 Describe why the Qur'an is important.
6 Describe the significance of angels for Muslims today.
7 Define al-Qadr.
8 What do Muslims believe happens after death?

* See page 288 for answers.

 EXTEND YOUR KNOWLEDGE: RESEARCH TASKS

For a research task, try to put together a full side of A4 of your own writing on the topics below.

1 Research the development of the Sunni and Shi'a traditions within Islam.
2 Research how their beliefs affect and influence the lives of British Muslim teenagers today.
3 Research news stories of actions by Muslims which could be regarded as good deeds to contribute to a good and faithful Muslim life.
4 Research how the hadith are important to Muslims in the way they live their lives.

 USEFUL TERMS

Do you know what these words mean?

Allah Hadith Imam Iman Khalifah Kitab al-iman Qur'an Al-Qadr Tawhid
'Adl Shari'ah 'Ibadah Shirk Hajj Ka'bah Sunnah Ramadan Wudu' Barzakh

Exam practice

In this exam practice section you will see examples for the exam question types: **a**, **b**, **c** and **d**. You can find out more about these on pages 6–7. Questions (a) and (d) in the **Exam question review** section below show strong student answers. Questions (b) and (c) in the **Improve it!** section need improvement.

Exam question review

> (a) Outline **three** roots of 'Usul ad-Din. (3)

The Oneness of Allah (Tawhid).

Allah has sent prophets to guide humans (Nubuwwah).

After the Prophet Muhammad there are no more prophets or scriptures (Imamah).

 WHAT WENT WELL

Three roots, correctly identified with their Arabic name and neatly outlined.

(d) 'Every person makes their own destiny.' Evaluate this statement considering arguments for and against. In your response you should:
- refer to Muslim teachings
- refer to different Muslim points of view
- reach a justified conclusion. (15)

I agree that in Islam, every person makes their own destiny as Muslims believe they have free will.

They believe life on earth is preparation for Akhirah and their actions will determine whether they will be punished or rewarded, so because of this they control their own destiny.

However Muslims believe in al-Qadr, that the universe follows the divine master plan of Allah who is omnipotent, omniscient and has a plan for the world. Therefore, it could be argued that their destiny is already known and some Muslims believe this plan is written by Allah in Al-Lawh al-Mahfuz (The Preserved Tablet).

Sunni Muslims believe they can make their own choices on the journey due to their free will but their destiny is already set by Allah. Consequently even though they are in control of their actions, their choice is already known by Allah before they make it, so you could argue that their destiny is already set.

Shi'a Muslims believe Surah 13:11 means that Allah can change a person's destiny based on their actions: 'God does not change the condition of a people unless they change what is in themselves'. This suggests that they are truly in control of their own destiny.

To conclude I believe that Islam suggests every person does make their own destiny. Although Muslims believe Allah is omnipotent and omniscient and some may argue that their destiny is already set, they have to make their choices without knowing their ultimate destiny. Therefore every person controls their own destiny.

WHAT WENT WELL

This answer contains a series of detailed points which evaluate the statement thoroughly. Relevant sources of wisdom and authority are quoted. Different Muslims points of view are discussed and considered before arriving at a justified conclusion.

Improve it!

These answers will not get full marks. Can you rewrite and improve them?

(b) Describe **two** differences in the belief of life after death between Islam and the main religious tradition of Great Britain. (4)

Muslims believe their souls will be questioned in the grave in Barzakh.

Christians believe humans have complete free will so can determine whether they go to heaven or hell.

(c) Explain **two** reasons why Muslims believe the Qur'an is the most important holy book. In your answer you must refer to a source of wisdom and authority. (5)

The Qur'an is the actual words of Allah.

The Qur'an is a guide for Muslim life and it has never been corrupted.

HOW TO IMPROVE

These points each deal with one belief of Islam or Christianity, but there is no comparison or reference to the opposing view for each point.

HOW TO IMPROVE

These are relevant points to make, but they lack the development explaining exactly how and why they make the Qur'an so important. Try to add examples to show full understanding of the question. The answer also lacks the required source of wisdom or authority.

The Ten Obligatory Acts

Diversity within Islam

There is more diversity in Islam than language, culture, and geography. Although many of their beliefs and traditions are the same, there is some difference in how Sunni and Shi'a Muslims summarize their beliefs: six beliefs for Sunnis and 'Usul ad-Din for Shi'as. There are also important differences in the practices they carry out.

Sunni tradition follows the Five Pillars of Islam – five basic acts which form the foundation of Muslim life and belief. These acts are also part of Shi'a tradition; however, they have a different name and there are more of them.

Ten Obligatory Acts of Shi'a tradition

Shi'a tradition holds there are ten key practices which every Muslim should carry out during their life. Most of these are everyday acts, but some like Hajj may only be once-in-a-lifetime events. These practices are summarized as Furu ad-Din: the Ten Obligatory Acts. Furu literally mean branches and is used in contrast to Usul which mean roots and principles. In a sense these Acts are branches of 'Usul ad-Din and subsidiary to them.

1. Salah: the five obligatory daily prayers

Allah ordered Muslims to pray five times a day (see 6.3). They pray to Allah using set prayers and movements, often in a mosque, but sometimes wherever they are at prayer times. **Salah** is also a pillar in Sunni tradition.

2. Sawm: fasting during the month of Ramadan

Muslims are not permitted to eat or drink between dawn and sunset during Ramadan (see 6.4). Muslims believe **sawm** helps towards their spiritual development as it helps them gain better self-control, appreciate Allah's gifts, and understand the needs of the poor. Also a pillar in Sunni tradition.

3. Hajj: the annual pilgrimage to Makkah

All Muslims must undertake this at least once in their lives if they find it physically and financially possible (see 6.6). Also a pillar in Sunni tradition.

4. Zakah: giving to the poor

Zakah is sometimes described as charitable giving and sometimes as a religious tax. Actually it is neither as it is an obligatory payment of 2.5 per cent which a Muslim has to make to the poor based on his or her wealth at the end of each lunar year. The payment is seen as a way of purifying income. Also a pillar in Sunni tradition.

5. Khums: the payment of 20 per cent of an individual's surplus income

Historically **khums** required the Muslim army to pay one fifth of the 'spoils of war' such as treasure and seized goods. In modern times this is applied to ordinary Muslims and is often drawn from the profit from a business (see 6.5).

A The Obligatory Acts are like branches which flourish from the strong roots of 'Usul ad-Din.

6. Jihad: striving or struggling for Allah

This means striving to maintain the Muslim religion in Allah's name (see 6.7). There are many interpretations of what this struggle should involve. Greater jihad is an internal spiritual struggle to be a better Muslim and lesser jihad is a physical struggle with any enemies of Islam.

7. Amr bil-Ma'ruf: encouraging others to do good

8. Nahy anil-Munkar: discouraging others from doing bad

Shi'a Muslims believe the Qur'an orders them to encourage good and right behaviour and to speak against wrong (Surah 3:104). In doing so, they will help their progress towards paradise in the afterlife.

9. Tawalla: expressing love for Allah or good

Shi'as believe this love extends to friends of Allah, such as the prophets, the righteous, and those who seek truth. They should only associate with just and good people, although they should treat everyone justly.

10. Tabarra: expressing disdain for the enemies of Allah or evil

Shi'as believe they shouldn't associate or ally with anyone who is an enemy of Allah or his prophets, and anyone who oppresses or who commits evil acts.

> 'The believers, both men and women, support each other; they order what is right and forbid what is wrong; they keep up the prayer and pay the prescribed alms; they obey God and His Messenger. God will give His mercy to such people: God is almighty and wise.'
> *Surah 9:71*

The importance for Shi'a Muslims today

Shi'a Muslims describe the Ten Obligatory Acts as being like the branches of a tree which flourish and grow from strong roots. The core beliefs roots of Shi'a tradition are called the five roots (see 5.2). Shi'a Muslims believe that carrying out the Ten Obligatory Acts strengthens their belief, but also that a strong belief supports them in their actions. Like the branches, leaves, and roots of a real tree work together to flourish, so too do belief and practice in Shi'a tradition.

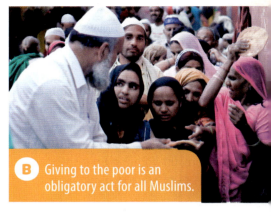

B Giving to the poor is an obligatory act for all Muslims.

C Muslims should encourage others to do good.

BUILD YOUR SKILLS

1 a Summarize each of the Ten Obligatory Acts in a sentence.
     b Add another sentence to each summarizing their purpose.

2 How do Sunni Muslims understand these principles?

3 How do the Ten Obligatory Acts link to the five roots of 'Usul ad-Din?

SUMMARY

- There are Ten Obligatory Acts or practices in Shi'a tradition.
- These Acts guide how Shi'a Muslims should behave in everyday life.
- Some of these are the same as the Five Pillars of Sunni tradition.
- Shi'a Muslims demonstrate and strengthen their belief by performing the Ten Acts.

EXAM-STYLE QUESTIONS

A Outline **three** Obligatory Acts for Shi'a Muslims. (3)

C Explain **two** ways Muslims are encouraged to perform Obligatory Acts. In your answer you must refer to a source of wisdom and authority. (5)

6.2

Shahadah

The Five Pillars

A pillar is a support, something that holds up a structure. A pillar needs a firm foundation beneath it. Sunni Muslims believe that if the structure is the religion of Islam, the foundation is the Qur'an and the five pillars are the five fundamental practices of Islam on which everything else depends.

Sunni Muslims believe the Five Pillars are the non-negotiable practices of Islam because they are established in the Qur'an. They are:

- Shahadah (witness)
- Salah (prayer)
- Sawm (fasting)
- Zakah (charity)
- Hajj (pilgrimage).

SPECIFICATION FOCUS

Shahadah as one of the Five Pillars: the nature, role and significance of Shahadah for Sunni and Shi'a Muslims, including reference to Surah 3:17–21; why reciting Shahadah is important for Muslims, and its place in Muslim practice today.

USEFUL TERMS

Minaret: the spire of the mosque from where the call to prayer is broadcast

Mu'adhdhin: the person who leads and recites a mosque's call to prayer

A Sunni Muslims believe the Five Pillars support the structure of Islam.

A Muslim is someone who has submitted to the will of Allah as revealed in the Holy Qur'an to the Prophet Muhammad. The Five Pillars are practical signs of this submission.

Shi'a Muslims adhere to the Five Pillars of Islam within their larger set of practices called the Ten Obligatory Acts. They are also guided by the Five Roots of 'Usul ad-Din (see 5.2). Sunni Muslims follow the Five Pillars as well as the rest of the Ten Obligatory Acts although they may not list them among their formal set of practices.

B The Shahadah in Arabic.

The Shahadah

The Shahadah is the declaration of faith for all Muslims and is based on the teaching of the Qur'an in Surah 3:17–21:

> ❝God bears witness that there is no God but him, as do the angels and those who have knowledge. He upholds justice. There is no god but Him, the Almighty, the All Wise.❞
> *Surah 3:18*

It is the central pillar and provides a summary of Islamic belief.

1. I bear witness that there is no God but Allah.
2. I bear witness that Muhammad is the Messenger of Allah.

Some Shi'a Muslims will also add a third phrase to the Shahadah:

3. Ali is the friend of God.

This connects to the Shi'a belief that Ali, the son-in-law and cousin of Muhammad was the Prophet's first successor (see 5.1).

C The call to prayer is made from the minaret of the mosque.

The importance of Shahadah

Reciting the words of Shahadah is very important for Muslims because they sum up the core Muslim beliefs. They are the belief in the oneness of Allah (Tawhid) and of the prophethood of Muhammad. The Shahadah is an act of acceptance of the Qur'an as the word of Allah. If someone wants to convert to Islam they must repeat the Shahadah in front of witnesses to be recognized as a Muslim. They must recite this creed with sincerity; it is not enough just to say the words.

The words of the Shahadah are recited by the **mu'adhdhin** in the call to prayer from the **minaret** of the mosque. Muslim fathers are expected to whisper the words into the ear of their newborn child so they are the first words the baby hears.

Muslims try to say the Shahadah at the time of their death to reconfirm their faith before leaving this world. The words will be repeated by those around them then, and again during their funeral.

Muslim practice today

Shahadah is Arabic for 'to bear witness'. By bearing witness to the Prophet Muhammad, Muslims are acknowledging belief in Risalah (prophets and scriptures) and Akhirah (afterlife) and showing a commitment to submitting to the will of Allah in everyday life. It is a central part of Muslim practice and links Muslims in their belief, wherever they may live.

 BUILD YOUR SKILLS

1. a What are the two parts of the Shahadah?
   b In pairs, discuss why each part is important.
2. a When do Muslims recite the Shahadah?
   b What are the benefits for Muslims of reciting the Shahadah?

 EXAM-STYLE QUESTIONS

A Outline **three** ways the Shahadah is said in everyday life. (3)

B Describe **two** differences in public declarations of faith between Islam and the main religious tradition of Great Britain. (4)

SUMMARY

- Shahadah is the First and central pillar of Sunni tradition.
- It summarizes belief in Tawhid: the oneness of Allah.
- It expresses belief in the Prophet Muhammad as Allah's messenger.
- A person must recite the Shahadah to become a Muslim.

What is Salah?

Salah is worship of Allah through regular prayer. It does not mean an individual's private prayer or request to Allah, but prayers of Muslims together, or at the same time: Salah is a physical, spiritual, and mental act following prescribed words and actions. It is the Second Pillar of Islam for Sunni Muslims and the First Obligatory Act for Shi'a Muslims.

The Prophet Muhammad called Salah the centre pole of Islam. The Qur'an commands performance of Salah more than any other activity, and for many reasons.

Salah is a pillar that displays the relationship in Islam between the Qur'an and the sunnah. The sunnah is a record of what the Prophet Muhammad said and did.

The Qur'an commands Muslims to pray at fixed times but it does not state what the fixed times are. Muslims therefore follow the example of how the Prophet Muhammad prayed, as recorded in the sunnah. So Salah is a mixture of what the Qur'an says and how Muhammad performed the ritual.

There are five obligatory times for prayer:

- *Fajr*: dawn, before sunrise
- *Zuhr*: midday, after the sun passes its highest point
- *Asr*: the late part of the afternoon
- *Maghrib*: just after sunset
- *Isha*: between sunset and midnight in the Shi'a tradition.

Sunni Muslims are required to pray at these five set times. Shi'a Muslims combine the midday and afternoon prayers, and the sunset and night prayers, so they pray three times a day.

Most mosques have a board showing the times of prayers for that week plus the time of **Jummah**. Times of prayer vary from week to week everywhere because of the changing times of sunrise and sunset.

For Muslims the main purpose of Salah is that it puts them into contact with Allah five times a day. They submit themselves to Allah's will in public and are united with other Muslims seeking brotherhood, sisterhood, and love as they pray in lines using the same actions and words. Together they acknowledge the oneness, power, and holiness of Allah and hope that their sins will be forgiven. As one hadith says 'the five prayers remove sins as water removes dirt'.

> 'keep up the prayer: prayer restrains outrageous and unacceptable behaviour. Remembering God is greater: God knows everything you are doing.'
> *Surah 29:45*

SPECIFICATION FOCUS

Salah as one of the Five Pillars including reference to Surah 15:98–99 and 29:45: the nature, history, significance and purpose of Salah for Sunni and Shi'a Muslims, including different ways of understanding them; how Salah is performed, including ablution, times, directions, movements and recitations, in the home and mosque and Jummah prayer.

> 'Celebrate the glory of your Lord and be among those who bow down to Him: worship your Lord until what is certain comes to you.'
> *Surah 15:98–99*

A A prayer board guides Muslims to the exact times of prayer.

Prayer is obligatory for everyone except children, menstruating women, and women who have just had a baby.

How Salah is performed

Wudu'

Salah is performed in a mosque or in the home only after careful preparation. Muslims perform wudu' (see 5.5) prior to Salah because Allah commanded this in the Qur'an.

> 'You who believe, when you are about to pray, wash your faces and your hands and arms up to the elbows, wipe your heads, wash your feet up to the ankles...'
> *Surah 5:6*

The method of wudu' includes the intention to perform wudu' and there are recommended acts such as washing the hands, gargling, and washing the nose in addition to the obligatory acts listed in Surah 5:6.

As prayer is so sacred, cleanliness is vital. Wherever Muslims pray, the floor must be clean so the prayer mat will never have been trodden on by anything unclean. Many Muslims have a special room in their house which will not be entered while wearing outdoor shoes so it is clean for Salah. Anyone visiting a mosque will have to remove their shoes before entering the prayer hall so that it is clean.

Directions, movements, recitations

How Salah is performed is vital for Muslims. They have to face the **qiblah** direction which is towards the Ka'bah in **Makkah**, Saudi Arabia when they say prayers.

In a mosque this is shown by the mihrab (an alcove in the wall). Many prayer mats have a compass to find the direction of Makkah.

In a mosque the time for prayer may be announced by the mu'adhdhin who calls out the **Adhan**. The Adhan states that Allah is great, that there is no God but Allah, and that the Prophet Muhammad is his messenger and calls people to join the prayer.

Movements and recitations

Muslims carry out a set of prayer rituals and each unit of prayer is called a **rak'ah**. There are different numbers of rak'ah for each prayer time. There is a set of actions and words performed during Salah and all the prayers are said in Arabic using the same actions and facing the same direction, thus showing unity among Muslims:

- Muslims silently make their intention known to Allah, including how many rak'ahs they will do and for what purpose.
- Raise the hands to the ears and recite.
- Place the right hand over the left on the navel and focus where they stand and recite (some schools of thought say the arms are left at sides).
- Bend over to the position of ruku (bent at waist, hands on knees) and recite.
- Stand back up, with the arms by the sides and recite.

B A Muslim woman prepares for Salah by performing wudu'.

USEFUL TERMS

Adhan: the words of the call to prayer

Jummah: Friday prayer

Makkah: the most holy city of Islam, the city where Prophet Muhammad was born

Qiblah: the direction of the sacred shrine of the Ka'bah in Makkah

Rak'ah: a sequence of ritual prayer movements

- Kneel down and place the palms and head on the floor in the sajdah position and recite.
- Rise from the sajdah and sit back.
- Go back to sajdah and recite.
- Stand up and recite.

This completes one rak'ah.

At the end of the last rak'ah, Sunni Muslims look to the right shoulder and recite, then to the left shoulder and recite. Shi'a Muslims raise their hands three times and recite.

Muslims may also make their own personal prayer to Allah called Dua at any time, although these prayers are often performed after the Salah.

Jummah prayer

> ❝Believers! When the call to prayer is made on the day of congregation [Friday], hurry towards the reminder of God and leave off your trading – that is better for you, if only you knew.❞
> *Surah 62:9*

Jummah means Friday prayer. This weekly worship brings Muslims together in unity, giving them the opportunity to learn from the Imam. The service will have a sermon led by the Imam on how to behave as a Muslim in the local and global community.

Surah 62:9 in the Qur'an advised Muslims to gather in this way, recognizing the priority of this community prayer over other business at this time.

SUMMARY

- Salah is the obligatory five daily prayers commanded in the Qur'an and in the sunnah.
- It is the Second Pillar (Sunni) and the First Obligatory Act (Shi'a).
- Muslims must prepare for Salah by performing wudu' and facing the qiblah towards Makkah.
- Muslims perform a set number of rak'ahs: particular movements and prayers in Arabic.
- Salah is important because it is a divine command from Allah in the Qur'an and helps Muslims remember the greatness of Allah.

C Many Muslims feel a sense of oneness with Allah and their fellow Muslims during Salah.

COMPARE AND CONTRAST

In your exam you may be asked to compare and contrast Muslim practices and worship with Catholic practices and worship. Look back at 2.2 for detail on these.

BUILD YOUR SKILLS

1 a What are the five times of obligatory prayer for Muslims?
   b Why are Muslims encouraged to pray so frequently?

2 a What is a rak'ah?
   b Why do Muslims perform set movements during prayer?

3 Why is Wudu' performed before prayer?

EXAM-STYLE QUESTIONS

C Explain **two** reasons Muslims perform Wudu' before prayer. In your answer you must refer to a source of wisdom and authority. (5)

D 'Salah is the centre pillar of Islam.' Evaluate this statement, considering arguments for and against. In your response you should:
- refer to Muslim teachings
- refer to different Muslim points of view
- reach a justified conclusion. (12)

6.4 Sawm

What is sawm?

Sawm literally means 'to abstain'. The term is used in Islam for fasting when Muslims do not eat or drink between sunrise and sunset. Sawm is the Fourth Pillar and the Second Obligatory Act. The Qur'an commands Muslims to fast in Surah 2:183.

> 'You who believe, fasting is prescribed for you, as it was prescribed for those before you, so that you may be mindful of God.'
> *Surah 2:183*

Fasting is a sign of devotion and obedience to Allah. Muslims can fast voluntarily at any time, but it is obligatory during the month of Ramadan because this was when Allah first revealed the message of the Qur'an to Muhammad.

> 'It was in the month of Ramadan that the Qur'an was revealed as guidance for mankind, clear messages giving guidance and distinguishing between right and wrong. **So any one of you who sees in that month should fast, and anyone who is ill or on a journey should make up for the lost days by fasting on other days later.** God wants ease for you, not hardship. He wants you to complete the prescribed period and to glorify Him for having guided you, so that you may be thankful.'
> *Surah 2:185*

The most important purpose of fasting is spiritual development. In addition to that, Muslims believe it is important to fast in Ramadan because they can request the forgiveness of Allah and his mercy. It is a reminder of those who are in need of food and encourages thoughtfulness and charity. It also promotes self-control and strengthens willpower.

By the end of the month of Ramadan a Muslim hopes to be a spiritually stronger person in order to carry out duties to Allah for the rest of the year.

A Muslims will usually end their fasts with dates or water, as Muhammad did.

Why some Muslims don't fast

The Qur'an allows for some Muslims to postpone their fasting. If they are ill, breastfeeding, or travelling, they are allowed to eat and drink but they must fast at another time to make up for the days they have missed before the next month of Ramadan.

> '**Fast for a specific number of days, but if one of you is ill, or on a journey, then on other days later.** For those who can fast only with extreme difficulty, there is a way to compensate – feed a needy person. But if anyone does good of his own accord, it is better for him, and fasting is better for you, if only you knew. '
> *Surah 2:184*

Those who have extreme difficulty in fasting, like the very old or sick, can give 'fidyah' – a donation of food or money to feed the poor as compensation for missing the fast.

The Night of Power

Laylat al-Qadr or The Night of Power is the night that the Prophet Muhammad was first visited by the angel Jibril and the revelation of the Qur'an began. Muslims believe the Qur'an is the final revelation of Allah – the final communication of his guidance for humanity.

Muslims believe the Qur'an was revealed in two different types of revelation. There was a gradual revelation of verses to the Prophet Muhammad by Jibril which took place over a period of 23 years. It was also revealed however in one complete instalment on the Night of Power, when Allah moved the Qur'an from the higher to the lower levels of heaven. This first revelation was an announcement to those in heaven that the final revelation was being made to the last prophet.

B The elderly can make a donation of food or money instead of fasting.

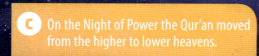

C On the Night of Power the Qur'an moved from the higher to lower heavens.

> ‘We sent it down on the Night of Glory [Power].’
> *Surah 97:1*

Muslims focused on study of the Qur'an during the final days of Ramadan.

History

In 610CE at the cave of Hira on Mount Nur in Makkah, Muslims believe the archangel Jibril appeared to Muhammad and presented him with his first revelation (Surah 96:1–5) and Muhammad's mission as a prophet began. Although unable to read, Muhammad was able to recite the words Allah gave to him so the Qur'an is the Word of Allah.

The experiences of revelation were very often intense and Muhammad would suffer from fatigue. However, he always was able to give advice to the scribes of the Qur'an about the verses and their proper recording.

Importance for Muslims today

Ramadan is the most important celebration for Muslims today. The revelation of the Qur'an forms the basis of Islam. Muslims take guidance, strength, and comfort from its teachings. The exact date of the Night of Power is unclear, but it is believed to be an odd number in the last ten days of Ramadan. During these final nights of Ramadan, Muslims try even harder to observe the fast and hold extra prayers and vigils. Some Muslims spend the final ten days and nights of Ramadan entirely in the mosque, spending their time in prayer and study of the Qur'an.

BUILD YOUR SKILLS

1 a What are the different reasons that Muslims fast?
  b What are the benefits of fasting for Muslims?

2 Write a PEE paragraph summarizing one point in favour of fasting and one point against.

SUMMARY

- Sawm means fasting.
- Sawm is the Third Pillar (Sunni) and the Second Obligatory Act (Shi'a).
- Muslims fast from dawn to sunset during the month of Ramadan which is the month the Qur'an was revealed.
- Fasting brings Muslims closer to Allah and shows devotion, self-control, and charity.
- The Night of Power was when the Qur'an was revealed to the lower levels of heaven, and the first revelation to Muhammad was brought by the angel Jibril.

EXAM-STYLE QUESTIONS

A Outline **three** reasons Muslims fast. (3)
C Explain **two** ways the Night of Power is significant for Muslims. In your answer you must refer to a source of wisdom and authority. (5)

Zakah and khums

What is Zakah?

The meaning of Zakah is 'to purify' and also 'to increase'. The idea behind Zakah is that people purify their wealth by giving a share of it to Allah, through the poor and needy. Zakah purifies possessions and makes them pleasing to Allah. Islam teaches that wealth is given by Allah for the benefit of human beings and should be shared. Zakah is the Third Pillar and the Fourth Obligatory Act.

Shi'a Muslims have always believed Zakah is a personal contribution, rather than one to be controlled by the state. In many Sunni communities it was compulsory for Muslims to pay Zakah to the state. Today, only some countries have compulsory Zakah; most Sunni Muslims now also regard it as a personal contribution.

Zakah began in Madinah after the first battles in the seventh century. The Qur'an gives guidance in Surah 9:58–60 on who should receive Zakah funds, or alms:

> ❝Alms are meant only for the poor, the needy, those who administer them, those whose hearts need winning over, to free slaves and help those in debt, for God's cause, and for travellers in need. This is ordained by God; God is all knowing and wise.❞
> *Surah 9:60*

People pay Zakah if they fulfil required conditions. They must have income and make a profit. The poor are not expected to give Zakah and law schools and lawyers give guidance for Muslims. The amount people pay is not specified within the Qur'an, but traditionally is 2.5 per cent of their wealth and possessions.

What is khums?

The fifth Obligatory Act for Shi'a Muslims is to pay khums, which also translates as 'fifth'. Sunni Muslims also believe in khums, but it is not one of the Five Pillars.

It began as a contribution by the Muslim armies of one fifth of their spoils of war, known as 'ghanima'. Shi'a (and some Sunni) Muslims also believe ghanima covers:

- objects from the sea
- treasure
- mineral deposits
- lawful (halal) property mixed up with unlawful (haram) property
- profit from business
- some land transactions.

Based on Surah 8:36–42, khums is divided into two halves. One half belongs to the **Imam in occultation** which is nowadays used for religious education. The other half is to be given to the poor and the orphaned from among the descendants of the Prophet.

USEFUL TERM

Imam in occultation: the concealed state of living of the 12th infallible Imam of Shi'as. They believe that after this hidden life he will return to restore justice and peace

A Zakah is a way of purifying wealth.

> 'Know that one-fifth of your battle gains belongs to God and the Messenger, to close relatives and orphans, to the needy and travellers, if you believe in God and the revelation.'
> Surah 8:41

Zakah's importance to Muslims

Sunni Muslims believe giving Zakah is a religious duty and is an obligatory tax upon the wealth of Muslims to share Allah's blessing with less fortunate members of the ummah (community). Paying it demonstrates submission to Allah and sincere worship. Zakah should:

- help the poor by redistributing wealth from rich to poor
- help the less fortunate such as widows and orphans
- be used to pay for the maintenance of mosques and Muslim schools.

Zakah is a means of purification and Muslims believe that by purifying their wealth they become closer to Allah.

B Part of the payment of Zakah comes from profits Muslims make in their businesses.

Khums' importance to Shi'a Muslims

Shi'a Muslims today pay 20 per cent of their savings every lunar year, which is split between the Imam and clergy, and the orphaned and poor. This is an important source of income for the clergy and the community. The clergy uses khums money to support religious institutions and students, neither of which receive state funding.

For many Muslims this is a large amount, but because they regard paying khums as a core Obligatory Act, Shi'as believe they are performing obedience to Allah's laws by paying income to support the poor and their leaders. Khums benefits both the organization of Islam and the need of its poorer members. Khums reflects the importance of community to the Islamic faith, and that by supporting the community, Muslims are demonstrating their faith and devotion to Allah.

C Khums supports the poorest in the Islamic community.

BUILD YOUR SKILLS

1 a In pairs, discuss why Muslims may feel they need to purify their wealth.
  b Who benefits from Zakah?

2 a How is khums different to Zakah?
  b Who benefits from khums?

SUMMARY

- Zakah is the Third Pillar (Sunni) and an obligatory tax for the poor for both Sunni and Shi'a Muslims.
- Zakah is a way of purifying one's wealth to please Allah.
- Khums is the Fourth Obligatory Act in Shi'a tradition.
- Khums is a tax of one fifth of surplus income.

EXAM-STYLE QUESTIONS

B Explain **two** ways khums benefits the Muslim community. (4)

C Explain **two** reasons why Muslims believe charitable giving is a central part of Islam. In your answer you must refer to a source of wisdom and authority. (5)

6.6 Hajj

What is Hajj?

The act of pilgrimage is commanded by the Qur'an (Surah 22:25–30). It is the Fifth Pillar of Islam and the Third Obligatory Act. Hajj is a set of rituals that take place in and around Makkah every year over five or six days. The rituals follow the example of the Prophet Muhammad's own pilgrimage of Hajj.

> ❛Proclaim the Pilgrimage to all people.❜
> *Surah 22:27*

Hajj is a duty only to those who have sufficient money to ensure care for their dependants while they are away, and who are physically and mentally fit to undertake the pilgrimage. Muslims are required to undertake Hajj at least once in their lives if possible.

Everything Muslims do on Hajj follows the example and actions of the Prophets Ibrahim and Muhammad, in the very place that they performed them. Makkah was a sacred centre long before Islam and according to Muslims, Adam built a sanctuary at Makkah which was later rebuilt by Ibrahim (Abraham), as described in Surah 2:124–130:

> ❛We made the House a resort and sanctuary for people, saying, "Take the spot where Abraham stood as your place of prayer." We commanded Abraham and Ishmael: "Purify My House for those who walk round it, those who stay there, and those who bow and prostrate themselves in worship."❜
> *Surah 2:125*

The Qur'an talks about walking round the House, and this is an important part of the Hajj ritual. The House, or Ka'bah (cube), has long been a place of pilgrimage for Arab tribes. The Prophet Muhammad re-established the rituals performed at the Ka'bah *c.* 630CE after the liberation of Makkah.

How Hajj is performed

The rituals of Hajj are based on the instructions in Surah 22:27–29 but also follow the actions shown by the Prophet Muhammad himself.

> ❛Then let the pilgrims perform their acts of cleansing, fulfil their vows, and circle around the Ancient House.❜
> *Surah 22:29*

🔍 **SPECIFICATION FOCUS**

Hajj as one of the Five Pillars: the nature, role, origins and significance of Hajj, including Surah 2:124–130, 22:25–30; how Hajj is performed and why Hajj is important for Muslims; benefits and challenges from attending Hajj for Muslims.

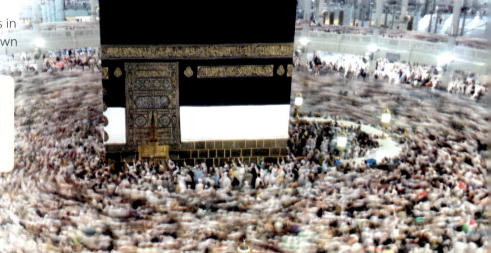

A Muslims circle the Ka'bah seven times in an anti-clockwise direction.

Preparation: Ihram

Ihram means 'to make forbidden'. Muslims undertake a series of cleansing steps to prepare for Hajj. Once they are ready, they need to maintain their purity and certain acts become forbidden.

- The first step is to remove pubic hair and shave underarms.
- Muslims then take a purifying bath.
- Men dress in two pieces of unstitched white cloth and women usually wear clothes which are white. This similarity means that everyone is equal during the Hajj.
- They offer prayers.
- They declare their intention to perform Hajj and recite the Talbiyah, a declaration that their Hajj is only for the glory of Allah.

They are now ready and must avoid the prohibitions of ihram, which include cutting hair or nails, covering the head (men) or face (women), wearing stitched clothing, and using perfume.

Rituals: Tawaf

Muslims visit the Ka'bah which is situated at the centre of the Sacred Mosque. In one of the corners there is a black stone believed to be from heaven and gifted to the prophet Adam. Muslim pilgrims on Hajj walk seven times anti-clockwise around the Ka'bah. As they pass the black stone they try to kiss or touch it if they are near, or stretch out their arm towards it as they pass. Tawaf is completed by prayers at the Place of Ibrahim. Tawaf is undertaken three times during the five or six days of Hajj.

B The golden doors of the Ka'bah are usually covered by hanging curtains.

Rituals: Sa'ya, Arafat, and Ramy al-Jamarat

Muslims perform other rituals in different places around Makkah including:

- the Sa'ya: this is jogging or walking between two hills seven times, done in remembrance of Hagar who was left with Ibrahim's son Isma'il in the desert and ran between two hills seven times searching for water, before it miraculously appeared.
- Wuquf: a day is spent in repentance and prayer at Arafat 'standing before Allah'. Muhammad gave his Farewell Sermon at Arafat in the year he died.
- Ramy al-Jamarat: stones are collected for the ritual of Ramy al-Jamarat, which is repeated three times during Hajj. This is a symbolic stoning of the devil, who tried to tempt Ibrahim three times, where seven stones are thrown at three wide walls.
- Sacrifice: an animal sacrifice is made on behalf of the pilgrims and the meat distributed to the poor. The celebration of Id-ul-Adha takes place around the world at the same time (see 6.8). This remembers the willingness of Ibrahim to sacrifice his son Isma'il at God's command'.
- Halak: after the sacrifice men shave their heads and women dip the ends of their hair.

C The ritual of Ramy al-Jamarat.

Why Hajj is important

Hajj is important to Muslims because the pilgrim has obeyed the command of Allah in the Qur'an and fulfilled the requirements of the Fifth Pillar or Third Obligatory Act. The pilgrim has followed the example and actions of the Prophet in the very place that the Prophet performed these actions. Muslims believe it is a reminder that we are from Allah and will return to Allah in the Akhirah (afterlife).

The places of Hajj are linked with the great prophets of Islam: Muhammad, Adam, Ibrahim, and Isma'il. Muslims on Hajj are inspired by these great prophets to follow their example. Hajj reminds Muslims that Islam is not a new religion but came from Adam.

Benefits and challenges

The benefits of Hajj are:

- the opportunity to repent and have sins forgiven
- bringing Muslims very close to Allah for a whole week
- awareness and unity of Islam as over 2 million Muslims of all races, colours, and cultures perform the same actions in the same place
- meeting new people and learning from them about Islam
- taking part in the holiest event in the Muslim calendar and coming as close to Allah as possible in this life
- achieving the title 'Hajji'. (man) and 'Hajjah' (women). Those who complete Hajj command respect and honour. Their sins are forgiven and they can live life as a perfect Muslim.

Hajj is seen by many Muslims as the crowning achievement of a Muslim's life. If a pilgrim dies on Hajj Muslims believe they go straight to paradise without having to wait for the Day of Judgment.

The challenges of Hajj are that:

- it is a very physically demanding ritual
- there are fatalities every year
- Muslims need time to recuperate after Hajj
- many Muslims delay Hajj until they retire because it is a very expensive and difficult pilgrimage.

SUMMARY

- Hajj is the annual pilgrimage to Makkah and is commanded in the Qur'an.
- It is the Fifth Pillar (Sunni) and the Third Obligatory Act (Shi'a).
- Muslims follow the rituals shown to them by the prophets.
- Hajj is obligatory if a Muslim can afford it.
- Hajj is an opportunity for Muslims to have their sins forgiven and spend time getting closer to Allah.
- Hajj demonstrates the power and unity of Islam as over 2 million gather together.

BUILD YOUR SKILLS

1 a Explain why Hajj is so important to Muslims.
   b Give an example of how the Qur'an encourages pilgrimage.

2 a Summarize the main rituals performed during Hajj.
   b Which ritual do you think brings Muslims closest to Allah? Explain your choice.

EXAM-STYLE QUESTIONS

B Explain **two** reasons for the tradition of Hajj. (4)

D 'Hajj is a personal expression of faith, but more special because it is performed with others.' Evaluate this statement considering arguments for and against. In your response you should:
   - refer to Muslim teachings
   - refer to different Muslim points of view
   - reach a justified conclusion. (12)

6.7 Jihad

What is jihad?

Jihad literally means 'struggle or striving' – to work towards something with determination and effort. Within Islam, it means striving in the name of Allah: 'Those who [...] strove hard in God's way with their possessions and their persons, are in God's eyes much higher in rank; it is they who will triumph' (Surah 9:20). In this verse of the Qur'an Allah advises to strive to be productive both in the way a person lives their life, and in the way they handle their property.

Muslims believe that by constantly trying to be better Muslims, they are showing devotion to Allah. Their acts are not for selfish gain, but done in an unselfish way for his glory. This is an example of greater jihad.

Greater jihad

For Muslims, greater jihad is the struggle of each individual Muslim to be a good and devout Muslim. Muslims often speak about four expressions of jihad. The first three relate to greater jihad:

- Jihad of the Tongue: speaking about their faith
- Jihad of the Hand: expressing their faith in good works
- Jihad of the Heart: making their faith a force for good.

Sunni Muslims perform the Five Pillars as the foundation of their lives; Shi'a Muslims demonstrate the Ten Obligatory Acts. Jihad is to strive against sin and Muslims can engage in greater jihad by becoming the person Allah wants them to be.

As well as observing the Five Pillars of Islam, Muslims must also devote their lives to God by avoiding such temptations and distractions as drugs, alcohol, greed and jealousy. Anything that takes them away from their submission to God must be avoided. Some Muslims go even further and learn the Qur'an by heart, which requires great discipline and patience. Others make great efforts to help others as a way of expressing their faith.

The word jihad has a broad meaning and as such any striving, if done in the name of Allah, can be called jihad; for example the striving of a teenager to attain good examination grades.

The lesser jihad

The fourth expression of jihad relates to lesser jihad:

- Jihad of the Sword: defending their faith when under attack.

Lesser jihad is the struggle to defend Islam, Muslims, and all oppressed people. The key word here is to 'defend': Muslims are encouraged in moderation by the Qur'an.

SPECIFICATION FOCUS

Jihad: the origins, meaning and significance of jihad in Islam; divergent understandings of jihad within Islam, including the difference between lesser and greater jihad; the conditions for declaration of lesser jihad, including reference to Surah 2:190–194 and 22:39; the importance of jihad in the life of Muslims.

A Many Muslims believe that helping others is a way of expressing their faith.

❝Those who have been attacked are permitted to take up arms because they have been wronged—God has the power to help them❞
Surah 22:39

❝Fight in God's cause against those who fight you, but do not overstep the limits: God does not love those who overstep the limits.❞
Surah 2:190

Conditions for declaring lesser jihad

Surah 2:190–194 sanctions a defensive fight. Therefore Muslims can:

- fight those who fight them to remove evil in society and when Islam is in danger
- defend those who are persecuted or oppressed.

It is the view of the majority of Muslims that they may not begin a conflict. Extremist groups use jihad as a justification for their violent activities. They claim they have been provoked into action and that therefore their jihad is legitimate. Many Muslim scholars believe the concept of jihad has been twisted by these groups and does not follow the teaching of the Qur'an, or the hadiths.

The portrayal of jihad as a 'holy war' arose from the way that Islam was engaged in wars during its early establishment. Muslim scholars say the Qur'an does not regard unsanctioned war as a holy act. Islamic law (Shari'ah) lays down strict laws for declaring lesser jihad:

- Muslims must not kill women, children, or weak people.
- Places of religious worship should not be damaged.
- Crops and water supplies should not be destroyed.
- It is forbidden to mutilate bodies.
- Prisoners should be treated with respect.
- Proposals for peace must be accepted.
- Sunni Muslims believe an offensive war can only be sanctioned if there is a chance of success. Shi'a Muslims do not believe in offensive jihad in the absence of the prophet or the infallible Imam. In both cases, it is a governmental decision and cannot be decided by individual persons or organizations.

The importance of jihad for Muslims today

There is an important distinction between the greater and lesser jihad. The root of 'Islam' means 'peace'. The majority of Muslims are upset by the misuse of the concept of jihad by extremists to justify violent attacks which they feel disobey the Qur'an.

In everyday life the most important jihad to Muslims is that of greater jihad: focusing on self-improvement and their improvement of the community. However, Muslims must be prepared to take part in lesser jihad if the need arises. Although jihad is commonly associated with extremist groups, it remains an important obligation for Muslims to defend their faith by force if under attack.

Shari'ah law permits the lesser jihad only if it is fought against an aggressor which threatens Islam and the response is proportionate to the attack.

B Muslims believe they are commanded to defend their fatih, but only to restore peace.

> *Fight them until there is no more persecution, and worship is devoted to God. If they cease hostilities, there can be no [further] hostility, except towards aggressors.*
> *Surah 2:193*

BUILD YOUR SKILLS

1 a Explain the difference between greater and lesser jihad.
   b What might a Muslim consider to be examples of greater jihad?

2 a In pairs discuss how the idea of lesser jihad fits with the idea that Islam is a peaceful religion.
   b Write a PEE paragraph explaining your discussion.

EXAM-STYLE QUESTIONS

A Outline **three** actions that could be considered greater jihad. (3)
B Explain **two** reasons why greater jihad is more relevant to most Muslims today than lesser jihad. (4)

SUMMARY

- Jihad means to strive or struggle in the name of Allah.
- Greater jihad is personal striving against sin.
- Lesser jihad is the defence of Islam on the battlefield.
- Lesser jihad should only be fought to establish the greater jihad. It is the greater jihad that should be the foundation of every Muslim's life.

6.8 Celebrations and commemorations

Id-ul-Adha

Id-ul-Adha is the festival of sacrifice which is celebrated in some countries for up to four days. This festival marks the annual completion of Hajj, and begins on the third day of Hajj (the 10th of the month of Dhul Hijjah) at the same time as the sacrifice in Makkah. The sacrifice at Mina is an event that all Muslims around the world who have been unable to travel to Hajj can now participate in.

- Sacrificing animals is done in commemoration of the prophet Ibrahim's willingness to sacrifice his son Isma'il, as commanded by Allah (Surah 37:77–111).

- The example of the prophet is remembered and celebrated as an example to Muslims of complete obedience and surrender to Allah.

> ❛"Peace be upon Abraham!" This is how We reward those who do good: truly he was one of Our faithful servants.❜
> *Surah 37:109–111*

- Muslims all over the world can enact this part of the Hajj ceremonies on a small scale in their local area.

The main activities of this day include the sacrifice of an animal. The meat of the slaughtered animal is divided into three equal portions: for family, for neighbours and friends, and for the poor. Id-ul-Adha may be the only time when some poor people have meat to eat. In addition:

- Muslims wear new clothes and children are often given presents.
- The mosque will be decorated and special Id prayers are held called **Salat al-Id**.
- The Imam will deliver a sermon which may explain the rules of sacrifice.
- The rest of the day is spent with family and friends, sharing food together.
- Families may choose to visit graveyards to pray for the dead.
- In Muslim countries the day of Id-ul-Adha is usually a public holiday.

SPECIFICATION FOCUS

Celebrations and commemorations: the nature, origins, activities, meaning and significance of the celebration/commemoration of Id-ul-Adha, with reference to Surah 37:77–111, and Id-ul-Fitr in Sunni Islam with reference to their place within Shi'a Islam; and Id-ul-Ghadeer, with reference to Hadith and the interpretation of Surah 5:3, and Ashura in Shi'a Islam with reference to their place within Sunni Islam.

A Muslims remember the dead during their celebrations.

B Indian Muslims offer prayers at the Ferozshah Kotla Mosque during Id ul-Adha in New Dehli.

Id-ul-Fitr

Id-ul-Fitr is celebrated on the first day of Shawwal, the month following the end of Ramadan. Muslims celebrate the end of fasting and give thanks to God for the spiritual blessings and renewal by attending a special prayer called salatul-'Id. Celebrations can last for three days.

Completing Ramadan is a real achievement that brings many blessings and Allah's forgiveness. The festival of Id-ul-Fitr is a celebration of spiritual renewal, although Ramadan has greater religious significance. The main activities of Id-ul-Fitr are joyful:

- Muslims may not fast during the festival so food and drink are enjoyed.
- Muslims wear new clothes and some may exchange gifts and cards.
- Families meet up with each other and may visit graveyards to remember their dead together.
- People give money as a special obligatory charity called Zakah ul-fitr to help the poor and must give at least the value of a full meal to charity.
- Special prayers will be said at the mosque and the Imam may explain the rules of paying Zakah ul-fitr also known as sadaqat ul-fitr.
- Id-ul-Fitr is a public holiday in Muslim countries.

Id ul-Ghadeer

Id ul-Ghadeer is a Shi'a celebration of the Prophet Muhammad's appointment of his nephew Ali ibn Abi Talib as his successor. This happened at a place called Ghadir Khumm, where Muhammad stopped while on his last Hajj pilgrimage with many thousands of Muslims.

Shi'a Muslims believe verses of the Qur'an were revealed to Muhammad alluding to appointment of Ali as the Prophet's successor including Surah 5:3. This verse is believed by Shi'a Muslims to have been revealed after an announcement by Muhammad that Ali was his successor. Most Sunni Muslims do not agree with this idea, and some also suggest the revelation of this verse may have taken place at a different location.

The events of Ghadir Khumm are recorded in hadith. Hadith are given different levels of approval by scholars. Some regard hadith Ghadir Khumm as the highest level of mutawatir, which means many hadith authors have written the events consistently, making it more likely to be accurate and reliable testimony.

Ashura

Ashura means 'tenth' and is a solemn day of remembrance for Shi'a Muslims. On the 10th of the Islamic month of Muharram, Imam Husayn (the grandson of Muhammad) was martyred alongside 72 other companions and family at the battle of Karbala. Husayn refused to swear allegiance to the oppressive new Khalifah Yazid I, who then broke several rules of Islamic military law during the battle that followed. Husayn and his followers were prevented from reaching water, then killed. The Shi'as believe that Husayn accepted a cruel death as an example to Muslims that sacrifice and suffering, as well as the power of an army, are needed to fight evil.

USEFUL TERMS

Ashura: a day of mourning in Shi'a tradition for the martyrdom of Imam Husayn, the grandson of the Prophet Muhammad

Id-ul-Adha: a global celebration which remembers the prophet Ibrahim's willingness to sacrifice his son for Allah

Id-ul-Fitr: a festival to mark the end of Ramadan

Id-ul-Ghadeer: a Shi'a celebration of Muhammad's appointment of his nephew Ali as his successor

Salat al-Id: special Id prayers said at both Id-ul-Adha and Id-ul-Fitr celebrations

'Today I have perfected your religion for you, completed My blessing upon you, and chosen as your religion Islam [total devotion to God]'
Surah 5:3

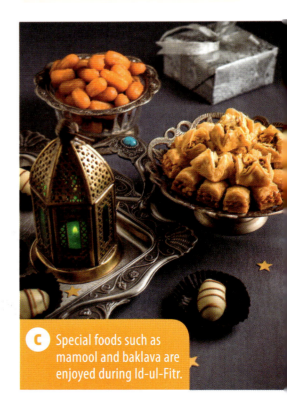

C Special foods such as mamool and baklava are enjoyed during Id-ul-Fitr.

In addition to remembering this tragedy, Sunni Muslims also remember this day to be the day when Musa and the Banu Israil (Moses and the tribes of Israel) were saved from Fir'awn (Pharaoh) in Egypt. They fast two days optionally as recommended by Muhammad.

Activities during Ashura include:

- performing prayers at mosques and religious centres
- mourning ceremonies and eulogies
- wearing dark or black clothes as a sign of respect and grief
- covering mosques in black cloths
- banners and slogans to remind people of the sad occasion they are commemorating
- A pilgrimage to Karbala in Iraq called Arba'een, 40 days after Ashura.

 Ashura is a day of solemn remembrance.

Some people may openly cry and show their emotions while others will refrain from laughing and smiling. There may be chest beating and wailing. Families will gather together and may visit graves. The evening is known as 'Eve of the Distraught'.

To Shi'a Muslims, Id ul-Ghadeer and Ashura keep the memory of two important Muslims alive: Ali as the successor to Muhammad and Imam Husayn, Muhammad's grandson. All Muslims are reminded of the importance of upholding the truth, of justice, and of sacrifice made for the love of Allah.

Significance of festivals

These festivals are significant because they:

- celebrate and commemorate important parts of Islamic history
- demonstrate that Islam encourages both personal practice and community cohesion
- encourage people to offer kindness and give to charity
- show that the priority for a Muslim is to submit to the will of Allah
- promote spiritual development and Islam as a complete way of life.

 BUILD YOUR SKILLS

1 Why is the festival of Id-ul-Adha important?
2 Give three celebratory activities which Muslims take part in during Id-ul-Fitr.
3 Why is the festival of Id-ul-Ghadeer so important to Shi'a Muslims?
4 How is Ashura commemorated by:
   - Shi'a Muslims
   - Sunni Muslims?

EXAM-STYLE QUESTIONS

A Outline **three** ways Id-ul-Adha links to the pilgrimage of Hajj. (3)
D 'Commemorations and celebrations bring the whole Muslim community together.' Evaluate this statement considering arguments for and against. In your response you should:
   - refer to Muslim teachings
   - refer to different Muslim points of view
   - reach a justified conclusion. (12)

 SUMMARY

- Id-ul-Adha is the festival of sacrifice and marks the end of Hajj.
- Id-ul-Fitr marks the end of the month of Ramadan.
- Id ul-Ghadeer is a Shi'a celebration of the day Muhammad appointed his nephew Ali ibn Abi Talib as his successor.
- Ashura is a day of mourning for Muhammad's grandson Imam Husayn who was martyred.
- Ashura reminds Muslims to uphold the truth and strive for a just society to please Allah.

Revision

REVIEW YOUR KNOWLEDGE

1 Name the Ten Obligatory Acts of Shi'a tradition.
2 Explain the Shahadah.
3 Describe the five obligatory times of prayer.
4 Recall the teaching of the Qur'an on Sawm.
5 Describe three ways Muslims prepare for Hajj.
6 Explain why Hajj is important.
7 Describe greater jihad.
8 What is Id-ul-Adha?

USEFUL TERMS

Do you know what these words mean?

Khums   Salah   Sawm   Zakah   Minaret

Mu'adhdhin   Adhan   Jummah

Qiblah   Rak'ah   Imam in Occultation

Ashura   Id-ul-Adha   Id-ul-Fitr

Id-ul-Ghadeer   Salah al-Id   Jihad

EXTEND YOUR KNOWLEDGE: RESEARCH TASKS

For a research task, try to put together a full side of A4 of your own writing on the topics below.

1 Research the work of Muslim charities within the UK and abroad, e.g. Islamic Relief UK or Muslim Aid.
2 Research how Muslims fulfil Salah during everyday life, for example using public prayer rooms or obligations on employers.
3 Research the different views of jihad, including how lesser jihad is interpreted in controversial ways.
4 Research how the celebrations of Id-ul-Fitr, Id-ul-Adha and Id-ul-Ghadeer are celebrated in British Muslim communities.

ONGOING LEARNING REVIEW

It is vital that you keep reviewing past material to make sure you have fully learned and remember it.

1 How do 'Usul ad-Din and the Ten Obligatory Acts connect?
2 Who are the six Beliefs important for?
3 Why is Ibrahim important for Muslims?
4 What happens on the Day of Judgment?
5 Explain six different characteristics of Allah.

See page 288 for answers.

Exam practice

In this exam practice section you will see examples for the exam question types: **a**, **b**, **c** and **d**. You can find out more about these on pages 6–7. Questions (b) and (c) in the **Exam question review** section below show strong student answers. Questions (a) and (d) in the **Improve it!** section need improvement.

Exam question review

(b) Explain **two** reasons why greater jihad is more relevant to most Muslims today than lesser jihad. (4)

Muslims believe greater jihad is important because it is the everyday struggle to become closer to Allah, so it is more relevant because it affects every part of their lives, their decisions and their relationship with Allah.

Muslims can engage in greater jihad by becoming the person Allah wants them to be, so it is more relevant as it helps Muslims to focus on the improvement of themselves. As they become better Muslims this benefits the wider community.

 WHAT WENT WELL

There are two different reasons given here, each explained in detail.

(c) Explain **two** reasons why Muslims believe charitable giving is a central part of Islam. In your answer you must refer to a source of wisdom and authority. (5)

Islam teaches that wealth is given by Allah for the benefit of human beings and so it should be shared. The third pillar of zakah purifies wealth by giving a share of it to the poor and needy.

The fifth Obligatory Act for Shi'a Muslims is to pay khums, based on Surah 8:41 'Know that one-fifth of your battle gains belongs to God and the Messenger.' Based on this khums, the donation of one-fifth of their surplus income is divided between the Imam in occultation and the poor and orphaned, therefore benefitting the clergy and the community.

 WHAT WENT WELL

Question (c) requires the same level of explanation as a question (b), but with the support of a well-chosen source of wisdom or authority. The quotation used is from the Qur'an and shows how it instructs Muslims to share their wealth.

Improve it!

These answers will not get full marks. Can you rewrite and improve them?

(a) Outline **three** Obligatory Acts for Shi'a Muslims. (3)

Praying; struggling; doing good.

(d) 'Commemorations and celebrations bring the whole Muslim community together.' Evaluate this statement considering arguments for and against. In your response you should:
- refer to Muslim teachings
- refer to different Muslim points of view
- reach a justified conclusion. (12)

 HOW TO IMPROVE

Not all of these are accurate, and as one-word answers none of them fulfil the requirement to 'outline', which requires a little more detail, up to about a sentence.

Sad events like Ashura and festivals like Id-ul-Ghadeer, Id-ul-Fitr, and Id-ul-Adha are good because everyone can think about the same things. Lots of things have happened in the history of Islam, which means there are lots of things to think about, even if Sunni and Shia Muslims don't always agree what happened. For example in Id-ul-Ghadeer most Shi'a Muslims believe Muhammad made his nephew the next leader, but not many Sunni Muslims agree, and that is why they are two groups now because they disagreed about this. But what happened at Ghadir Khumm was written down in several hadiths and this is why some Muslims think there is truth because the hadiths agreed, which makes them more likely to be true. In happy festivals there is lot of eating and giving presents to family, so this brings people together.

 HOW TO IMPROVE

Although this answer displays understanding of Id-ul-Ghadeer it gives more detail than is necessary, and offers very little on other festivals or commemoration. Aiming for five or six developed points, covering how celebrations and commemorations might bring Muslims together is a good idea.

Area of Study 2:
Judaism

Study choice
You will study **either** Judaism **or** Islam (Chapters 5 and 6) as your second religion.

Chapter 7: Beliefs and Teachings

Chapter 8: Practices

7.1 The Almighty

The nature of the Almighty

Like Christianity and Islam, Judaism is a monotheistic religion: a religion with one god. The central religious texts are called the **Tenakh**, or Hebrew Bible (see 8.4) and the **Talmud**. The Hebrew name for God is called the tetragrammaton and is made up of four consonants, which translate to YHVH. This is often anglicized to Yahweh meaning 'Lord'. However, Jews believe the name of God is so holy that it should not be spoken aloud or often written – and never erased. Instead Jews use other names, such as Hashem which means 'The Name' or Hakadosh Baruch Hu which means 'The Holy One Blessed be He', when speaking or writing about God.

Jews believe the non-physical nature of God makes it difficult to describe him fully. Jews have other names for God which try to describe some of his different characteristics including:

- El (a powerful and mighty God)
- Elohim (the plural name of El, suggesting that there is more to God than one single part)
- El Shaddai (God Almighty)
- Hashem Tzevaot (Lord of Hosts).

Diversity in Judaism

There are different groups within Judaism, including Orthodox, Liberal, and Reform. There are also secular Jews, who do not affiliate to a religious grouping, but view themselves as Jews because of their cultural or ethnic heritage.

Each group takes a different approach to their faith, although they may share many of the same beliefs, traditions, rituals, and festivals. There is divergence within each group but generally:

- Orthodox Jews believe that tradition and following the commands of the **Torah** in a traditional sense are important. They believe the Torah is the literal Word of God. Ultra-orthodox are the most strict.
- Liberal and Reform (Progressive) Jews believe that the Torah should be understood as a document of its time, and be interpreted in light of modern life and issues. They believe the Torah is the inspired Word of God.

SPECIFICATION FOCUS

The nature of the Almighty: how the characteristics of the Almighty are shown in the Torah, and why they are important in Jewish life today, including One, Creator, Law-Giver and Judge; including reference to Genesis 2.

USEFUL TERMS

Talmud: the 'Oral Torah', or the Oral laws and traditions passed down from Moses, eventually written down as the Mishnah and the Gemara. There are two versions (Jerusalem and Babylonian)

Tenakh: the Hebrew Bible, consisting of the Torah, Nevi'im, and Kethuvim

Torah (1): the Five Books of Moses Bereshit (Genesis), Shemot (Exodus), Vayikra (Leviticus), Bamidbar (Numbers), and Devarim (Deuteronomy)

Torah (2): a wider meaning including the written Tenakh plus the Talmud – the oral law and traditions of Judaism

A Jews believe that God is powerful and mighty.

How the characteristics of the Almighty are shown in the Torah

One

One of the primary expressions of Jewish faith is the Shema (see 8.4), which begins:

Sh'ma Yisra'eil Adonai Eloheinu Adonai echad.

'Hear, O Yisrael: Hashem is our God, Hashem is the one and only.'

- The **Shema** is the most important prayer for Jews and is one of only two prayers commanded in the Torah. It is recited twice daily. It consists of Deuteronomy 6:4–9, 11:13–21, and Numbers 15:37–41.
- God is a single unity who is whole, complete, and invisible. It is impossible to divide God into parts or describe him by physical attributes. To try to do so is simply man's imperfect attempt to understand the infinite. The Tenakh does use physical descriptions when talking about God but this is to help the reader understand what is going on. Phrases such as 'with a strong hand, and with an outstretched arm' (Deuteronomy 4:34) are not meant to be read as a literal description of God.
- God is the only being to whom Jews should offer praise and prayer.

Creator

- As there is just one God, no other took part in Creation. Many Orthodox Jews believe that everything in the universe was created by God.
- Genesis 2:7 illustrates how God created human beings from dust, granting them understanding and speech. Reform and Liberal Jews regard the creation story as a metaphor and believe in evolution, but as beginning with God as the creator.

> ❝And Hashem God formed the man of dust from the ground, and He blew into his nostrils the soul of life; and man became a living being.❞
> *Genesis 2:7*

Lawgiver

The best example of God as a lawgiver is in his gift of the Torah – the Law – to Moses on Mount Sinai. In Exodus the Jewish people were freed from slavery in Egypt but needed guidance. God gave them the Law so that they could live good lives (see 7.4).

- Jews believe that they are children of God; as such he is father-like.
- The phrase Avinu Malkeinu is used in Jewish liturgy which means 'Our father, our king'. Both father and king link to being a lawgiver.
- Only God has the power to rule and judge, to save and destroy.

> ❝For Hashem is our Judge; Hashem is our Lawgiver; Hashem is our King; He will save us.❞
> *Isaiah 33:22*

B Jews study the Torah to learn more of the nature of God.

USEFUL TERM

Shema: the main Jewish declaration of faith

Judge

- Judaism is often seen as a religion of strict Law; however, God's justice is tempered by his mercy and both these qualities are perfectly balanced.

- The name Elohim emphasizes God's might while the tetragrammaton means mercy. Jews use the name Hashem because they do not pronounce YHVH. Together these two names suggest the balance of God's qualities.

- When Moses and the Jewish people accepted the Law, they formed a covenant with God to keep it. Jews believe God judges how well they keep both the ritual and moral laws. Rosh Hashana and Yom Kippur are times of particular judgment during the year for Jews (see 7.7).

The importance for Jewish life today

- The names of the Almighty help bring Jews closer to him, understanding the strength of his nature even if they are unable to fully understand God's greatness.

- Jews worship a single God, although they have plural names for him. This does not mean they believe God is a Trinity, as Christians do, but that God is more complex than a single part.

- Reciting the Shema twice a day reinforces the importance of God as One.

- Understanding God as a Creator, Lawgiver, and Judge helps Jews to act 'in the image of God' with justice and mercy.

C Jews believe that God is just.

BUILD YOUR SKILLS

1. **a** What is the key characteristic of God for Jews?
   b For each of the following, explain how it is shown in the Torah:
   - Oneness
   - Creator
   - Lawgiver
   - Judge.

2. In pairs, discuss different ways Jews might find it helpful in everyday life to reflect on the characteristics of God. What practical uses could it have?

SUMMARY

- God is One, Creator, Lawgiver, and Judge.

- These qualities of God are generally agreed upon by all Jews, although they may interpret them in divergent ways.

- God has many names in the Bible, which helps Jews understand some of the characteristics of God.

- These characteristics and names of God are important in Judaism as they help Jews understand something of the nature of God.

? EXAM-STYLE QUESTIONS

A Outline **three** ways the Oneness of God is important for Jews. (3)

D 'The characteristics of God define the way Jews understand their religion.' Evaluate this statement considering arguments for and against. In your response you should:
- refer to Jewish teachings
- refer to different Jewish points of view
- reach a justified conclusion. (15)

The divine presence

Judaism believes that God created the world, and continues to work in the world. The Shekhinah means 'to settle or dwell' and refers to the divine presence of God within the created world. The divine presence of God is particularly important in relation to:

- the study of the Tenakh and **Talmud**
- the Tabernacle and worship today.

The Shekhinah is not a teaching explicitly contained within the Torah, and although there are some references found in the oral teachings of the Talmud (see 8.2), the divine presence of God is felt in different, subtle ways by Jews: in study, in worship, and in prayer.

Study

Although Jews acknowledge that humans are naturally limited in their ability to understand God, study of the Tenakh and the Talmud is an important part of being Jewish.

- To study is regarded as an act of worship, and as such the Shekhinah is also present.
- Study of the Tenakh is done by both men and women: all Jews are encouraged to connect with God through study. This may take place in a **yeshiva**, but Jews can study at any time.
- The Talmud, the oral law, evolved through and contains discussion between **Rabbis** since the start of Jewish history.

> ❝If two sit together and the words between them are of the Torah, then the Shekhinah is in their midst.❞
> *Rabbi Hananiah ben Teradion (c. 135ce)*

Divergence in understanding

- At some Orthodox yeshiva schools, Torah study is the primary focus. This will take place in the morning, with other subjects such as English, Maths, and Science taking place in the afternoon as a secondary focus.
- Some Hassidic Jews, who are considered the most strict, reject secular (non-religious) study and concentrate on textual learning.

SPECIFICATION FOCUS

The nature and importance of Shekhinah: how the divine presence is shown in the Torah and why it is important including interpretations of 2 Chronicles 7:1–3; the divergent understandings of Shekhinah found in different forms of Orthodox Judaism and the importance of them for Jews today.

USEFUL TERMS

Rabbi: Jewish teacher or religious leader

Talmud: the 'Oral Torah', or the Oral laws and traditions passed down from Moses, eventually written down as the Mishnah and the Gemara. There are two versions (Jerusalem and Babylonian)

Yeshiva: Jewish school of Talmudic study

A In the yeshiva, young Jewish men often work in pairs to study the Torah.

Worship

After God told Moses to lead the Jewish people out of Egypt in search of the Promised Land (Israel), he also instructed him to build the Tabernacle, a portable temple, which God would dwell within as they travelled. It is a key belief of Judaism that God led the Jews out of Egypt.

> ' They shall make a Sanctuary for Me — so that I may dwell among them. '
> *Exodus 25:8*

B Jews believe they can feel the divine presence of God in prayer.

The word mishkan', which means 'tabernacle', comes from Shekhinah. The Tabernacle kept the presence of God with the Jews, and maintained their connection with him.

This connection has continued through to worship today in the synagogue: the modern house of God. As God directed, a light burns in front of the Ark within the synagogue: 'to kindle a lamp continually [...] an eternal decree for their generations, from the Children of Israel' (Exodus 27:20–21).

Prayer

Jews can pray alone or as part of a **minyan**. When Jews pray as a community they believe God is present. Certain prayers such as the **Kaddish** and **Barachu** can only be said with a minyan in the presence of God.

> ' Whenever ten are gathered for prayer, there the Shekhinah rests '
> *Talmud Sanhedrin 39a*

The Tenakh also references the presence of God in response to prayer. In 2 Chronicles 6 Solomon dedicates the newly-built Temple to God, and when he has finished his prayers, he and the Jewish people are overcome with God's power. 2 Chronicles 7:1 says 'the glory of Hashem filled the Temple'. This links to Leviticus 9:24 which relates a similar incident during a sacrifice by Moses and Aaron outside the Tabernacle: 'A fire went forth from before Hashem'.

While early descriptions of the Shekhinah tend to be of a physical nature, contemporary Jewish focus is on a spiritual connection with the divine presence: in worship, prayer, study, or **Tikkun Olam** 'doing good in the world'.

USEFUL TERMS

Barachu: call to prayer

Kaddish: a prayer of praise blessing God's name

Minyan: a group of ten men (Orthodox tradition) or adults (Reform tradition) over the age of 13

Tikkun Olam: acts of kindness performed to repair the world

BUILD YOUR SKILLS

1 Explain the Shekhinah in your own words.

2 Why was the Tabernacle important for Jews?

3 Outline the difference between the Torah and the Talmud.

4 List the different ways in which Jews can experience the Shekhinah.

SUMMARY

- The Shekhinah means the presence of God.
- God is present in every aspect of life.
- Some Jews try to connect with the Shekhinah through study of the Torah, in prayer, and during worship.

EXAM-STYLE QUESTIONS

B Explain **two** reasons the Shekhinah is important. (4)

C Explain **two** ways Jews connect with the Shekhinah. In your answer you must refer to a source of wisdom and authority. (5)

7.3 The Messiah

The nature and purpose of the Messiah

The Mashiach, or **Messiah**, means 'anointed one' and belief in the eventual arrival of the Messiah is a fundamental Jewish belief.

- The Messiah is the one who will be anointed as the king of Israel in the End of Days (Messianic Age).
- The concept is not found in the Torah, but was mentioned frequently by Jewish prophets.

The idea of the Messiah is an ancient one. The Jewish people had been forced into exile from Israel and the prophets reassured them that if they obeyed God then a Messiah, a leader, might come to restore them and improve society.

> ❝ Behold, days are coming [...] a king will reign and prosper and he will administer justice and righteousness in the land. In his days [...] Israel will dwell securely. ❞
> *Jeremiah 23: 5–6*

The nature and role of the Messiah has always caused debate in Judaism. Jews believe he will be:

- a great political leader descended from King David (Jeremiah 23:5)
- well-versed in Jewish law and observe its commandments (Isaiah 11:2–5)
- a charismatic leader, inspiring others to follow his example
- a great military leader, who will win battles for Israel
- a great judge, who makes righteous decisions (Jeremiah 33:15)
- a human being.

How messiahship is shown in the scriptures

In addition to the characteristics of the Messiah described in the **Nevi'im**, there are also indications of what the Messiah will do for the Jewish people:

- He will bring about redemption, both politically and spiritually, by restoring Israel and Jerusalem (Isaiah 11:11–12; Jeremiah 23:8; 30:3; Hosea 3:4–5).
- He will establish a just government in Israel which will be the centre of all government worldwide, for Jews and **gentiles** (Isaiah 2:2–4; 11:10; 42:1).
- He will restore the religious court system of Israel and establish Jewish law as the law of the land (Jeremiah 33:15).
- He will rebuild the Temple and re-establish worship there (Jeremiah 33:18).

SPECIFICATION FOCUS

The nature and purpose of the Messiah: how messiahship is shown in the scriptures including Jeremiah 23:5–8; the nature and significance of the Messianic Age and the Jewish responsibility to bring it about; divergent understandings of the Messiah in different forms of Orthodox and Reform Judaism and the importance of them for Jewish people today.

USEFUL TERMS

Anointed: marked for greatness by a divine power

Gentiles: non-Jews

Messiah: the anointed one, the King sent from God

Nevi'im: 'Prophets' – the second part of the Tenakh

A King David is regarded not only as a great warrior and politician, but as a musician and poet who wrote many of the Psalms.

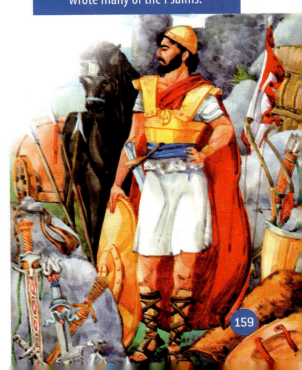

Divergent understandings of Messiah

The idea of a Messiah or a Messianic Age has brought hope and also motivated people to act for change at times of great difficulty. For Orthodox Jews, the Messianic Age means the time when the Messiah has come and is ruling the world. Reform and Liberal Jews believe the Messianic Age will be a better time of peace and harmony.

- The Messianic Age is usually referred to as **Olam Ha-Ba**. It will be a time of peace with no more hatred, intolerance, or war.
- At this time the world will recognize the Jewish God as the only true God and Judaism as the only true religion.
- In the Messianic Age, all Jewish people living in exile will return to their home in Israel (see 7.5).

Jews generally agree upon the *expectations* of the Messiah as written in the Tenakh. However, there are different opinions on *when* the Messiah will come.

- Some Jews believe there is the possibility of the Messiah in every generation.
- Some believe that God has already set a date for the Messianic Age, or that the Messiah will come when when he is most needed, or when he is most deserved.
- Christianity began as an offshoot from Judaism because some thought that Jesus was the Messiah. Jews reject this idea because Jesus did not fulfil their expectations for a Messiah.

Jewish responsibility

Many Jews throughout the ages have felt motivated to improve the world in which they live in order to be active partners in bringing a better world, sometimes understood as hastening the Messianic Age, but also understood in more secular humanist terms. The emphasis for many Reform and Liberal Jews is not on the Messiah, indeed many reject the idea of a personal Messiah, and instead their focus is on the idea of a Messianic Age. They pursue the idea that Jews have an obligation to work to help bring a better world (Tikkun Olam). This is also clear in the participation of members of the Jewish community in activities to promote social, political, and environmental improvements in the world.

B Young Jewish volunteers helping at a shelter for the homeless demonstrate Tikkun Olam.

BUILD YOUR SKILLS

1 Define the term 'Messiah' in Jewish belief.

2 Define what is meant by the 'Messianic Age'.

3 Produce a ten-point fact file on the expected Messiah – only use terms you understand.

4 Mind map the divergent Jewish understandings of the Messiah.

EXAM-STYLE QUESTIONS

A Outline **three** things that Jews believe about the Messiah. (3)

D 'It is the responsibility of Jews today to bring about the Messianic Age.' Evaluate this statement considering arguments for and against. In your response you should:
- refer to Jewish teachings
- refer to different Jewish points of view
- reach a justified conclusion. (15)

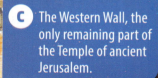
SUMMARY

- The idea of the Messiah is an ancient one in Judaism and is based around a great leader rather than a saviour.
- The Messianic Age means a time when the Messiah is ruling the world.
- The characteristics and tasks of the Messiah are described predominantly in The Nevi'im.
- Jews live in expectation of the Messiah or Messianic Age and live their lives accordingly.

C The Western Wall, the only remaining part of the Temple of ancient Jerusalem.

7.4 The covenant at Sinai

A covenant

A covenant is an agreement between two parties, which benefits both. Both parties need to keep certain conditions or fulfil obligations.

- For Jews, this agreement is between God and the Jewish people.
- It is an agreement formed in love and creates an important relationship. This makes it different from a contract.
- A covenant can only be created and sealed in Judaism with an oath.

Brit olam means 'an everlasting covenant' and makes it clear that Jews believe that God will not break his covenant with the Jewish people. The Jewish people recognize that from time to time they fail to fulfil their obligations and break the law.

> **For you are a holy people to Hashem, your God;** Hashem, your God, has chosen you to be for Him a treasured people above all the peoples that are on the face of the earth.
> *Deuteronomy 7:6*

The covenant at Sinai

God's covenant with Moses and the Jewish people at Mount Sinai followed covenants with the three main patriarchs of Judaism: Abraham, Isaac, and Jacob (Israel). As centuries passed, the descendants of these leaders became slaves in Egypt and suffered greatly under the Pharaohs. Moses was chosen by God to lead the Jewish people out of Egypt.

The nature and history of the covenant

The events leading up to the covenant at Sinai are recorded in the Torah.

- Moses grew up in the household of the Pharaoh, after being rescued from the River Nile. However, he discovered his Jewish heritage and had to leave Egypt after killing an Egyptian taskmaster, then lived in Midian for 40 years.
- God appeared to Moses in the form of a burning bush and told him to return to Egypt to lead the Jewish people to freedom. With the help of his brother Aaron, he spoke to Pharaoh and triggered ten plagues.
- The final plague prompted Pharaoh to allow Moses to leave with the Jewish people. He crossed the **Reed Sea** to freedom and took the people to Mount Sinai.

The Torah states that, at Mount Sinai, God made a covenant with the Jewish people but with an important difference from earlier covenants: Jews who did not follow the agreements would be punished (Deuteronomy 28:15–68).

- The covenant identified the Jewish people as the chosen people of God. By this, it means 'chosen for responsibility'.
- The introductory instructions were the Ten Commandments (the Decalogue), which Moses inscribed on stone.

SPECIFICATION FOCUS

The Covenant at Sinai: the nature and history of the Covenant at Sinai (the Ten Commandments), including Exodus 20; the role and significance of Moses in the Covenant at Sinai; divergent understandings of how and why the Decalogue is important in Jewish life today.

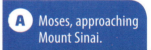
USEFUL TERMS

Olam Ha-Ba: 'The World to Come'; term used for both 1) the Messianic Age and 2) a spiritual afterlife following physical death

Reed Sea: some scholars believe a mistranslation led to this originally being called the 'Red' Sea

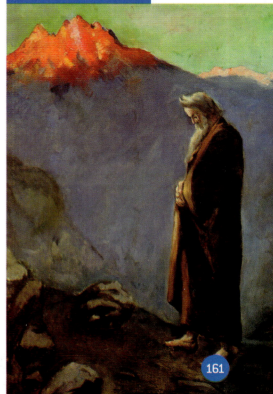

A Moses, approaching Mount Sinai.

B A map showing the land of Israel at the time of the Exodus from Egypt.

- God gave the Jewish people the Torah in its entirety (see 7.1) to help Jews live an obedient life.
- According to Jewish tradition, Moses was also given the Oral Torah, later written down as the Talmud.
- According to Jewish tradition, every Jewish soul that would ever be born was present at that moment, and agreed to be bound to this covenant.

> **The entire people responded together and said, "Everything that Hashem has spoken we shall do!"** Moses brought back the words of the people to Hashem.
>
> *Exodus 19:8*

Why it is important for Jews today

- The Torah is the most important part of the Tenakh as it contains the Law of the covenant. These remain a guide for Jewish living today.
- Jews believe they are bound to follow the teachings in the Torah because of the covenant made by Moses. Obedience will be blessed and disobedience punished.

C The Torah is still read from the traditional scrolls in the synagogue.

- Torah scrolls are stored in the Aron Kodesh or Ark. The most important reading is on the Sabbath when seven members of the congregation are chosen to be called up to the Torah. A designated reader will chant the passage on their behalf.

- Study of the Torah is an important part of Jewish life. This forms a significant part of Jewish education and children can begin from as young as three.

Ultimately, the covenant at Sinai is central to the Jewish understanding of itself as a people, and the gift of the Torah is celebrated every year in the festival of **Shavuot** (see 8.7).

The Ten Commandments

The Ten Commandments (or Decalogue) are the first ten of the 613 commandments given by God to the Jewish people. These commandments are mentioned in order twice in the Torah, in Exodus 20:1–17, and then at Deuteronomy 5:4–21.

> 1. You shall not recognize the gods of others in My presence.
> 2. You shall not make yourself a carved image [an idol].
> 3. You shall not take the name of Hashem, your God, in vain.
> 4. Remember the Sabbath day to sanctify it.
> 5. Honour your father and your mother.
> 6. You shall not kill.
> 7. You shall not commit adultery.
> 8. You shall not steal.
> 9. You shall not bear false witness against your fellow.
> 10. You shall not covet your fellow's house [...] nor anything that belongs to your fellow.
>
> *Exodus 20:3–14*

- During early Jewish times (known as the time of the Second Temple, 516BCE–70CE) they were recited daily. However, this stopped because some Jews started to believe the Ten Commandments were more important than other Mitzvot.

- Today, the Ten Commandments are heard in the synagogue three times a year: in the readings of Exodus and Deuteronomy, and during the festival of Shavuot.

- Many Rabbis will remind Jews that all 613 are important, not just the first ten.

SUMMARY

- In Judaism, a covenant is an everlasting agreement between God and man.
- The Jewish people entered into a covenant with God after Moses had led them out of slavery in Egypt to the Promised Land.
- Moses received the Torah or Law, which continues to play an important role in Judaism today.

USEFUL TERM

Shavuot: commemorates the anniversary of the day God gave the Torah to the entire nation of Israel assembled at Mount Sinai

BUILD YOUR SKILLS

1 Explain in your own words what a covenant is.

2 Rewrite the story of Moses and the covenant at Sinai in five brief bullet points.

3 a Why do you think the Decalogue was so important for early Jews?

  b Do you think these commandments are still relevant for Jews today? Why?

EXAM-STYLE QUESTIONS

B Explain **two** reasons why the covenant at Sinai is important for Jews. (4)

C Explain **two** ways the Torah is a vital part of Jewish life. In your answer you must refer to a source of wisdom and authority. (5)

7.5 The covenant with Abraham

Why is Abraham important?

Abraham founded Judaism. He, his son Isaac, and his grandson Jacob are known as the Patriarchs, and are both the physical and spiritual ancestors of Judaism.

Abraham was born with the name Abram in approximately 1800BCE. Jewish tradition suggests that his father was an idol maker, but from his early childhood Abraham questioned his father's faith and he came to believe that the universe was the work of a single creator. This was unusual as most early religions were polytheistic: they worshipped more than one god.

The nature and history of the Abrahamic covenant

Genesis 12:1–4 records how, in recognition of his faith, God calls to Abraham to leave his home and family. In reward, he said, 'I will make of you a great nation; I will bless you, and make your name great, and you shall be a blessing.'

Abraham does all God asks, and Genesis 17:2–9 recounts God's covenant with Abraham.

Abraham sealed the covenant by **circumcising** himself and all the males in his family. Although the covenant was between God and Abraham, for Jews Abraham represents the Jewish faith and they regard it as the start of a covenant between God and the Jewish people.

Jewish tradition says that Abraham was subjected to ten tests to prove his worthiness for the covenant. The command to leave his home and father was the first test.

In the covenant God promised to 'make of you a great nation', but Abraham and his wife Sarah had no children and both were getting old. Abraham had a son called Ishmael with his wife's maidservant, but God also blessed Abraham and Sarah with a son called Isaac to fulfil his promise that they would create the nation of Israel.

- Isaac's son Jacob would go on to father 12 sons who would establish ten tribes of Israel. Isaac was the son who was the subject of the last test of Abraham's faith.
- God told Abraham to sacrifice Isaac; both Abraham and Isaac were willing to do this, but at the last moment an angel was sent to stop the sacrifice. This was because the test was not about sacrificing a child, but showing obedience to the call of God.

How the covenant affects Jews today

- The idea of the covenant is fundamental to all Jews. There are three parts to the covenant which many Jews believe are still to be fulfilled: the Promised Land (Israel), a great nation, and blessing and redemption.
- Jews believe the covenant with God at Sinai gave them laws to live by, and that obeying them will also fulfil the Abrahamic covenant.
- Jewish men are still circumcised today as a symbol of this covenant.

SPECIFICATION FOCUS

The covenant with Abraham and his descendants: the nature and history of the Abrahamic covenant; the role of Abraham in the covenant, including Genesis 17; why the Promised Land covenanted to Abraham and his descendants is important for Jews today.

USEFUL TERM

Circumcising: removing the foreskin of the penis; 'Brit Milah' is the name of the Jewish ceremony of circumcision

'I will ratify My covenant between Me and you and between your offspring after you, throughout their generations, as **an everlasting covenant, to be a God to you and to your offspring** after you.'
Genesis 17:7

A Abraham is the patriarch of Judaism.

- The birth of Isaac to Abraham and Sarah in their old age shows Jews that God kept his promises and intervened when needed. He was in control of even the processes of nature.

The Promised Land

The Tenakh refers to God's offer of a 'Promised Land' on many occasions. This began with the covenant of Abraham in Genesis. It is described as 'a land flowing with milk and honey' (Exodus 3:8). The Restoration of Israel is part of the belief of the Messianic Age and is an element which can cause disagreement and controversy, with other faiths, and sometimes within Judaism itself.

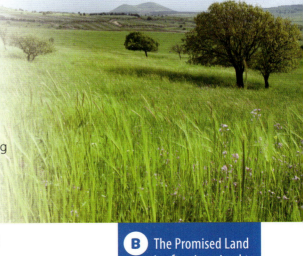

- For much of the time from the period of Judges (about 1200bce) Jews ruled over themselves in the land of Israel. Jews were exiled from the land of Israel by the Romans in 135ce.
- From that time for almost 2,000 years Jews prayed for a return to the land, to 'Zion', and for Jewish sovereignty to be restored. In the nineteenth century the Zionist Movement campaigned for the re-establishment of a Jewish state in their former homeland, desiring self-government and self-defence.
- In 1947 the United Nations voted to divide the land to create two states – one for the Jews and one for the Arabs. In 1948 the State of Israel was created, despite the opposition of Arab countries in the Middle East. Israel's existence today as a democratic state is central to Jewish communities around the world as a guarantor of Jewish survival and expression of religious and cultural life.
- There have been many disputes over this territory since then, including wars, and there is much tension because of the conflict between Israelis and Palestinians.

How this affects Jewish life today

- The land of Israel remains central to Judaism and many laws are tied to the land of Israel and can only be implemented there.
- Prayers for a return to Israel are included in daily Sabbath prayers and festivals.
- Prayers for the State of Israel, alongside prayers for the welfare of the Queen, her government and the leadership of the United Kingdom, are included in Sabbath and festival prayers.
- Living outside of Israel is viewed as a form of exile by some Jews.

 BUILD YOUR SKILLS

1 a Write down five key facts about Abraham.
   b Which two things do you think might be the most important for Jews?
2 What is the Promised Land?
3 a Do you think Jews would consider the covenant at Sinai or Abraham's as more important? Why?
   b How might someone disagree?

 SUMMARY

- God and Abraham entered into a covenant that promised many descendants, a Promised Land, and a blessed nation.
- God showed that he would keep his promises; this remains important to Jews today.
- Israel is the Promised Land which Abraham and Sarah settled.

 EXAM-STYLE QUESTIONS

A Outline **three** reasons Abraham is important to Jews. (3)
C Explain **two** ways the covenant with Abraham affects Jewish life today. In your answer you must refer to a source of wisdom and authority. (5)

7.6 The sanctity of life

The nature and sanctity of human life

Jews believe that human life is the most important (prime) concern because life is given by God and as such is sacred.

The Talmud makes it clear that all people are descended from a single person, and so to take a human life is like destroying the entire world.

> ❛he who destroys one soul of a human being, the Scripture considers him as if he destroys a whole world, and him who saves one soul of Israel, the Scripture considers him as if he should save a whole world. ❜
> *Mishnah (Sanhedrin 4:3)*

Pikuach Nefesh is the name of the principle in Jewish law that states the preservation of human life overrides virtually any other religious law. When a person's life is in danger, almost any mitzvah lo ta'aseh , or 'command to not do an action' of the Torah becomes inapplicable.

> ❛You shall observe My decrees and My laws, which man shall carry out and by which he shall live – I am Hashem. ❜
> *Leviticus 18:5*

The implication here is that Jews should live by Torah law rather than die because of it. For example, if ten Jews break Shabbat rules to save a life they are all praiseworthy, even if only one person may ultimately have been needed.

In the Talmud, Rabbis discussed and approved actions on Shabbat such as rescuing a drowning child, breaking a door to prevent it closing on a child, moving rubble from a collapsed wall to save a child, and extinguishing a fire to save a life (Talmud Yoma 83–84). Almost any Jewish law can be broken to save a human life, which demonstrates how life is valued above all else. The exceptions are murder, idolatry, incest, and adultery. Judaism not only permits, but requires a person to break the commandments to save a human life: 'you shall not stand aside while your fellow's blood is shed' (Leviticus 19:16).

Why human life is holy

The first two chapters of Genesis contain the story of Creation. Judaism teaches that all life comes from God as it clearly states that man is created in God's image.

> ❛And God said, "**Let us make Man in Our image**, after Our likeness. They shall rule over the fish of the sea, the birds of the sky, and over the animal, the whole earth, and every creeping thing that creeps upon the earth." **So God created Man in his Image**. ❜
> *Genesis 1:26–27*

Sanctity of life: the nature and importance of Pikuach Nefesh (primacy of life); why human life is regarded as holy by Jewish people; how life is shown as special and taking precedence over everything, including Talmud Yoma 83–84; divergent understandings of how and why the principle of Pikuach Nefesh is applied by Jews today.

A In Jewish belief, one human life represents every human life.

B Jews believe all human life is holy.

Jews respect life as holy because every life is linked to the first creation of man by God.

Human life in the Torah

The Torah teaches that people who break the rules should be held accountable for their actions. In Leviticus 24:17–18, the consequences of taking human and animal life are set out.

> ❝And a man — if he strikes mortally any human life, he shall be put to death. And a man who strikes mortally an animal life shall make restitution, a life for a life. ❞
> *Leviticus 24:17–18*

Animals are important in Judaism, and should be respected and cared for. However, Genesis 1:26 clearly gives humans 'rule [...] over the animal', which means a man should not be killed for killing an animal.

Regarding human life, Leviticus 24:17–18 is similar to a verse in Exodus 21:23–24: 'But if there shall be a fatality, then you shall award a life for a life, an eye for an eye, a tooth for a tooth.'

- Both verses are written in a way which could be taken literally; however, there is no evidence that this was ever the case in Jewish law.
- Historic Rabbinic understanding of Exodus 21:23–24 is that on one hand it limits a culture of revenge, but on the other it ensures justice through, traditionally, financial compensation.
- The Talmud records a lengthy discussion of Leviticus 24:17–18 (Bava Kama 83b–84a), reinforcing that the Torah is not meant to be read literally and can only be understood in the light of the oral tradition.
- Many Jews believe the Torah is not simply suggesting there should be material payment for injury, but that the perpetrator should reflect on the profound damage caused to his fellow human's quality of life. He or she should beg for forgiveness from the injured part and do **Teshuva** to seek forgiveness from God.

Pikuach Nefesh today

Pikuach Nefesh is important for Jews today and can significantly affect their lives:

- A person who is ill is not permitted to fast on Yom Kippur.
- Doctors are allowed to answer emergency calls on Shabbat.
- Abortions to save the life of a mother are mandatory. The unborn is not yet considered equal to the mother.
- Jews are not permitted to do anything that may hasten death, even to prevent suffering. Euthanasia, suicide, and assisted suicide are strictly forbidden.
- It is sometimes permissible to end artificially prolonged life, for example turning off life support machines when a patient cannot live without it.

Divergent understandings of Pikuach Nefesh

There is divergent understanding among contemporary Jews of how Pikuach Nefesh should affect their actions. It is impossible to say that every Jew in a particular group would feel one way because the issues involved are emotive and individuals may feel very differently, even within a particular tradition. There is a tendency for Orthodox tradition to take a stricter view on what Pikuach Nefesh means, but it should not be assumed that every Orthodox Jew feels this way, or that every Reform Jew would be more liberal.

Judaism does not support assisted dying in any form as human life is holy. However, while suicide is forbidden, it is usually looked upon with understanding and sympathy. Acceptance of abortion is more complicated: while Orthodox Jews only permit it to save a mother's life, for mental health reasons, or in certain very particular conditions; other denominations such as Reform or Liberal would allow wider circumstances such as social, and medical issues to be considered, including the age of the foetus.

Organ donation is also an area of debate among denominations. Liberal and Reform Jews usually permit organ donation. Under certain conditions organ donation is allowed within Orthodox Judaism, but it is very controversial:

- Donation of an organ from a living person where the donor's health is not endangered, and there is a patient waiting is permitted and encouraged.
- Donation from a dead body is also permitted for the purpose of saving life.
- Difficulties arise in defining death because most organs need to be transplanted before the heart stops beating, which suggests their removal causes death. There is an ongoing discussion about what is acceptable.

 C Preserving life may mean acting contrary to some teachings.

BUILD YOUR SKILLS

1   a   Why is human life important to Jews?
    b   List some moral or ethical decisions Jews could face which may be affected by this belief.
    c   Give a reference from the Torah which makes the teaching of Pikuach Nefesh clear.

2   How would Jewish people today understand the phrase from Leviticus 'A life for a life'?

EXAM-STYLE QUESTIONS

C   Explain **two** reasons why the principle of Pikuach Nefesh is so important to Jews. In your answer you must refer to a source of wisdom and authority. (5)

D   'The principle of Pikuach Nefesh means euthanasia is difficult to justify.' Evaluate this statement considering arguments for and against. In your response you should:
    - refer to Jewish teachings
    - refer to different Jewish points of view
    - reach a justified conclusion. (15)

SUMMARY

- The story of Creation in Genesis makes it clear that God is the giver of life, so life is sacred.
- Most Jewish laws can be broken in order to save a person's life in life-threatening circumstances. This is called Pikuach Nefesh.
- Pikuach Nefesh influences how Jews approach moral and ethical decisions such as abortions and euthanasia.

7.7 Moral principles and the Mitzvot

The nature and importance of the Mitzvot

Jewish tradition teaches that there are 613 **Mitzvot** in the Torah. These cover every aspect of life. The **Halakhah** teaches Jews how to perform or fulfil the Mitzvot. Scholars compiled lists of what the 613 Mitzvot are. The primary scholar to do this was Maimonides, an influential medieval Rabbi, in the Mishneh Torah. One of the books of the Mishneh Torah is called Sefer Madda, the 'Book of Knowledge'. This deals with correct belief and explains the idea that the foundation of everything is God, and therefore moral principles should begin from the same point.

Jews believe the Mitzvot were given by God to Moses within the Torah, and that it was part of the covenant at Sinai that the Jewish people would try to observe them. The consequence of disobedience was to be punished.

> 'See, **I present before you today a blessing and a curse.** The blessing: that you hearken to the commandments of Hashem, your God, that I command you today. And the curse: if you do not hearken to the commandments of Hashem, your God, and you stray from the path that I command you today, to follow gods of others, that you did not know.'
> *Deuteronomy 11:26–28*

While Orthodox Jews may think of the Halakhah as having been given on Sinai in the oral and written Torah, Reform Jews view is as something which has evolved through the generations.

The Mitzvot and free will

Many examples in the Torah show God seemingly predetermining the fate of his people; for example, in Genesis 15, God tells Abraham that his descendents will be enslaved, freed, and then return to Canaan. However, Jews do believe they have free will.

Medieval philosophers debated what was human choice and what was hashgahah or 'divine providence' (intervention by God in the human world). God's revelation of the future could be interpreted as a sign of his **omniscience**, rather than his intervention: he knew what would happen rather than that he determined what would happen.

Today, the Jewish tradition is that Jews agreed to live by the Mitzvot God set out: the starting point is that the commandments are correct and set out the best way to live. Everyday decisions are therefore to choose between right and wrong. This is the exercise of free will in Judaism. Those who choose to do good and obey the commandments will be rewarded and those who choose to disobey them will be punished.

SPECIFICATION FOCUS

Moral principles and the Mitzvot: the nature and importance of the Mitzvot, including reference to the Mishneh Torah of Maimonides: Sefer Madda; the importance of the relationship between keeping the Mitzvot and free-will; the Mitzvot between humans and the Almighty, and between humans; divergent understandings of the importance of the Mitzvot between the Almighty and humans, and between humans, for Jewish life today.

USEFUL TERM

Omniscience: complete knowledge of all human actions, past, present, and future

A Rabbi Moshe ben Maimon, 'Maimonides', or 'Rambam'.

B Kosher restaurants help Jews obey the Mitzvot within the context of modern life.

The Mitzvot between humans and the Almighty

Judaism is a system of Mitzvot, daily actions Jews perform or avoid. The Mitzvot reflect Judaism's understanding of what it means to live a Jewish life. The Torah does not always give detailed explanations for all the Mitzvot. Jews will obey them because they believe that God requires it.

- Some commentators suggest that the Law was a kindly gift from God, rather than a set of autocratic rules, sent to help the Jewish people govern themselves after a long period in slavery being ruled by others.
- Observing the Mitzvot is one way that Jews show gratitude for God rescuing them from slavery in Egypt.
- The Mitzvot are acts which show Jews the best way to live their lives. Observing them deepens their relationship with God.

Judaism has sometimes been criticized for having so many rules, suggesting that the Mitzvot removes spirituality from the faith. Most Jews claim this is not the correct way to observe the Mitzvot. They should be used to increase spirituality and an individual's relationship with God; the Mitzvot give religious significance to everyday occurrences such as saying blessings before and after eating, or rules of modesty governing what a Jew may wear.

USEFUL TERMS

Halakhah: the list of 613 Mitzvot which guide Jewish life

Mitzvot: commandments which set rules or guide action (singular: Mitzvah)

There is, however, some divergence in observation of the Mitzvot. Reform Jews have a different view of Rabbanic authority, and also believe that the Torah is divinely inspired rather than the literal word of God. They therefore discuss how the Mitzvot may have been influenced by the cultures in which they were written down, or filtered. This means they are more selective in their observance of some Mitzvot if they feel they do not appear relevant, or more importantly, ethical.

The Mitzvot between humans

The term Mitzvah is also used informally in Judaism to mean 'good deed'. The list of commandments which Jews must follow includes many directions on how they must behave well towards other humans. These are often referred to as gemilut hasadim, or 'acts of loving kindness', and include:

- visiting the sick
- comforting mourners
- feeding the hungry
- clothing the naked (helping the poor).

C A Jew and a Muslim work together for the good of the community.

Acts of loving kindness have no limit on how often they should be performed, and they can be undertaken by anyone, no matter how rich or poor.

The importance for Jews today

Jews believe study of the Torah and Talmud is an act of worship and that the divine presence of God can be felt in this (see 7.2). Rabbis and scholars continue to analyse the Mitzvot.

- This makes Judaism a living religion, which considers the issues of modern life in light of tradition and scripture.
- Many laws are no longer practiced today such as animal sacrifices.
- The Talmud is the starting point for modern day questions such as permissibility of organ donation or abortion.
- Some modern decisions are controversial. There are disputes amongst religious authorities as each Rabbi looks for guidance in ancient texts for modern challenges. The Mitzvot continue to guide Jews in the modern world.

BUILD YOUR SKILLS

1 a What are Mitzvot?
 b How many are found in the Torah?

2 a What is free will?
 b What do Jews believe about free will?

3 'Jews must try to follow all the Mitzvot.' In pairs list why some Jews would agree, and some disagree with this. Find evidence to support your arguments.

SUMMARY

- Mitzvot are commandments; the 613 laws in the Torah form what the basis of the Halakhah, the body of Jewish law and practice.
- Jews follow the Mitzvot as they form part of the covenant between the Jewish people and God.
- Jews believe they have free will and a choice in following the Mitzvot.
- A Mitzvah is also a good deed, and by carrying out good deeds towards other humans, Jews believe they are fulfilling an important part of Jewish life.
- Rabbis and scholars continue to examine the Mitzvot today.

EXAM-STYLE QUESTIONS

A Outline **three** good deeds to humans that some Jews would consider Mitzvah. (3)

C Explain **two** reasons why Jews believe it is important to follow Mitzvot. In your answer you must refer to a source of wisdom and authority. (5)

Life after death

Life after death

Judaism is primarily focused on life here and now, rather than the afterlife. As a result, it does not focus on teachings about life after death. There are different personal opinions among Jews about the possibility of it, but there is general agreement that death is not the end.

- The Jewish afterlife is called **Olam Ha-Ba** (The World to Come).
- Resurrection and reincarnation are traditional Jewish beliefs (see Maimonides' thirteen Principles of Faith, below).
- Temporary (but not eternal) punishment after death in **Gehinnom** is within traditional belief, but there is no concept of eternal punishment.

Jewish teachings about life after death

There is little in the Torah about life after death. Ecclesiastes 12:7 suggests that the soul of an individual returns to God:

> ❝Thus the dust returns to the ground, as it was, and the spirit returns to God Who gave it.❞
> *Ecclesiastes 12:7*

The could be interpreted to mean an afterlife with God, or simply being part of him again: there is no certain teaching. Jewish beliefs are formed mainly through the writings of Rabbis and scholars, such as Maimonides (see 7.7). One of Maimonides' thirteen Principles of Faith based on the Mishneh Torah says:

> ❝I believe with perfect faith that there will be a revival of the dead at the time when it shall please the Creator❞
> *Maimonides, Thirteen Principles of Faith*

Reunited

- The Torah does suggest things such as reunion with people who have died before. Genesis 49:33 describes Jacob as 'gathered to his people' when he dies.
- Exodus 31:14 suggests those who break the Mitzvot will be punished in the afterlife through exclusion: 'that soul shall be cut off', but there is no fixed view on what that punishment would be.

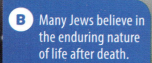
B Many Jews believe in the enduring nature of life after death.

SPECIFICATION FOCUS

Jewish beliefs about life after death: divergent Jewish understandings of the nature and significance of life after death, including reference to different forms of Orthodox and Reform Judaism; Jewish teachings about life after death, including interpretations of Ecclesiastes 12; the nature of resurrection and judgment; why belief in life after death may be important for Jews today.

A Jews will often recite psalms when they visit graves.

USEFUL TERMS

Gan Eden: Garden of Eden – not the same place where Adam and Eve lived, but a pure spiritual heaven

Gehinnom: a place for a set time of purification of the soul, similar to the Christian purgatory (see 1.8)

Olam Ha-Ba: 'The World to Come'; term used for both 1) the Messianic Age and 2) a spiritual afterlife following physical death

Reward and punishment

The idea of **Gan Eden**, a heaven, is not defined within Jewish scripture. The Tenakh speaks more clearly about life after death and the Olam Ha-Ba:

> ❛Many of those who sleep in the dusty earth will awaken: these for everlasting life and these for shame, for everlasting abhorrence. The wise will shine like the radiance of the firmament, and those who teach righteousness to the multitudes [will shine] like the stars, forever and ever.❜
> *Daniel 12:2–3*

The nature of resurrection and judgment

Orthodox Jews believe that the promised Messiah will come to lead a Messianic Age. The righteous will be resurrected and live in a restored Israel. It will be a time of peace when the Temple will be rebuilt. Some Reform Jews share some beliefs in this age to come, but reject the idea of an individual Messiah.

Gan Eden

Ancient Rabbis often talked about Gan Eden as a place where righteous people go after they die. It is unclear from their writings whether they believed that souls would journey to Gan Eden directly after death, or whether they went there at some point in the future for example during the Messianic Age; or even whether it was the resurrected dead who would inhabit Gan Eden at the end of time.

This quotation from Maimonides includes gentiles – the 'pious of all nations' – among those who will be rewarded. Jews believe gentiles (non-Jews) can be judged as righteous if they have followed the Seven Laws of Noah.

> ❛The pious of all nations of the world have a portion in the world to come.❜
> *Moses Maimonides, twelfth-century Rabbi and Jewish philosopher*

Gehinnom

Gehinnom was thought of as a place of punishment for unrighteous souls. The Rabbis believed that those who neglected the Torah and led unrighteous lives would go there, although usually only long enough for their souls to be cleansed before moving on to Gan Eden.

SUMMARY

- Most Jews concentrate on living a righteous life rather than the afterlife.
- Jews do not agree on the nature or form of life after death, but are generally convinced death is not the end.
- Some Jews believe that in the world to come (Olam Ha-Ba), there will be a heaven (Gan Eden) and a place of purification (Gehinnom).
- There is little scripture on life after death and so most teaching comes from ancient Rabbis such as Maimonides.

COMPARE AND CONTRAST

In your exam you may be asked to compare and contrast Jewish beliefs about the afterlife and their significance with Catholic beliefs. Look back at 1.8 for detail on these.

> ❛In the Messianic Age, God will establish peace for [the nations] and they will sit at ease and eat in Gan Eden.❜
> *Exodus Rabbah 15:7*

BUILD YOUR SKILLS

1 Describe in your own words:
   - Gan Eden
   - Gehinnom.

2 a Where does most teaching on life after death for Jews come from?
   b Why do you think many Jews do not focus on life after death but on living a righteous life in the present?

3 Look back at 1.8. In groups discuss the differences and similarities between Jewish and Christian belief in life after death.

? EXAM-STYLE QUESTIONS

B Describe **two** differences in the belief in life after death between Judaism and the main religious tradition of Great Britain. (4)

D 'Jews believe that if they keep the Mitzvot they will reach Gan Eden.' Evaluate this statement considering arguments for and against. In your response you should:
   - refer to Jewish teachings
   - refer to different Jewish points of view
   - reach a justified conclusion. (15)

Revision

REVIEW YOUR KNOWLEDGE

1 What are the four key characteristics of God?
2 What is the term that means 'to settle or dwell'?
3 Name three characteristics of the Messiah.
4 What do Jews understand as a covenant?
5 What two things did God promise to Abraham?
6 Give the term used by Jews to mean the preservation of human life.
7 How many Mitzvot are there in the Torah?
8 What are the two destinations that some Jews believe you go to after death?

See page 288 for answers.

EXTEND YOUR KNOWLEDGE: RESEARCH TASKS

For a research task, try to put together a full side of A4 of your own writing on the topics below.

1 Research the different ways in which Jews today study the Torah including yeshiva, online, or via Apps.
2 Research the work of Jewish charities such as Tzedek or Norwood.
3 Research the full story of the Exodus from the birth of Moses to reaching the Promised Land.
4 Research the different Jewish views on euthanasia and abortion, in connection to Pikuach Nefesh.

USEFUL TERMS

Do you know what these words mean?

Barachu Minyan Tenakh Torah Shema Rabbi Talmud Tikkun Olam Yeshiva
Messiah Shavuot Teshuva Gan Eden Gehinnom Nevi'im Olam Ha-Ba
Circumcision Halakhah Mitzvot Covenant

Exam practice

In this exam practice section you will see examples for the exam question types: **a**, **b**, **c** and **d**. You can find out more about these on pages 6–7. Questions (a) and (b) in the **Exam question review** section below show strong student answers. Questions (c) and (d) in the **Improve it!** section need improvement.

Exam question review

(a) Outline **three** reasons Abraham is important to Jews. (3)

He founded Judaism.

His faith was so strong he was ready to sacrifice his son to God.

His descendants were the 12 tribes of Israel.

WHAT WENT WELL

Question (a) asks you to 'outline' which is slightly more than a one-word answer – up to a sentence for each point. The three answers written here give enough detail to neatly sum up three different reasons.

> (b) Describe **two** differences in the belief in life after death between Judaism and the main religious tradition of Great Britain. (4)

Christians have definite ideas about life after death which include going to either heaven if you have faith in Jesus or hell if you don't. Life after death is not as important to Jews and not all Jews believe in heaven, and none believe in hell.

Some Jews believe that people who need to be cleansed of their sins go to Gehinnom. This is like the Catholic idea of purgatory, the place of purification before going to heaven, but belief in purgatory is not shared by most Christians outside Catholic or Orthodox churches.

✓ WHAT WENT WELL

There are two differences given here, each explaining a point with a good amount of detail, and contrasting the differences in belief.

Improve it!

These answers will not get full marks. Can you rewrite and improve them?

> (c) Explain **two** ways the Torah is a vital part of Jewish life. In your answer you must refer to a source of wisdom and authority. (5)

The Torah is still vital because it contains the 10 Commandments. These tell Jews how to live their lives, even today.

The Torah is still used for prayer and worship.

! HOW TO IMPROVE

The first point is developed as an explanation, but adding an example of one of the Commandments would meet the requirement to refer to a source of wisdom and authority. The second point is not sufficiently developed.

> (d) 'The principle of Pikuach Nefesh means euthanasia is difficult to justify.' Evaluate this statement considering arguments for and against. In your response you should:
> - refer to Jewish teachings
> - refer to different Jewish points of view
> - reach a justified conclusion. (15)

Pikuach Nefesh is the principle of the preservation of human life, which overrides any other religious law.

Justifying euthanasia is therefore very difficult for most Jews. However, ending artificially prolonged life, such as on a life support machine, is acceptable.

Orthodox Jews tend to take a stricter view on Pikuach Nefesh, and maintain all forms of human life are holy.

No actions can be undertaken that hastens death, even if they are dying anyway.

! HOW TO IMPROVE

There are not enough points here, and those included are not sufficiently developed. They may also be inaccurate in places. There is no real chain of reasoning, or a conclusion, which will need to be justified and based on the points made.

8.1 Public acts of worship

SPECIFICATION FOCUS

The nature and purpose of Jewish public acts of worship: the nature, features and purpose of Jewish public worship, including interpretations of Psalm 116:12–19; the nature, features and importance of synagogue services for the Jewish community and the individual.

The nature, features, and purpose of public worship

Avodat Hashem means 'worship of God'. After the destruction of the Temple in Jerusalem, first in 586BCE and again in 70CE, the prayers and worship conducted in the synagogue were considered the most important acts of worship. Still today, the most common form of worship is prayer.

Most services involve reciting the written prayers in the synagogue. This reminds Jews they are part of a community, and individuals are reminded of their place within the context of other Jews. Public worship allows:

- individuals to spend regular time in praise, request, and thanks of God.
- Jews around the world to follow very similar services, which brings a sense of unity.

Public worship in scripture

Some Jews may look to the inspiration contained within Psalm 116 when considering what is important in worship.

> ❛My vows to Hashem I will pay, in the presence, now, of His entire people [...] in the courtyards of the House of Hashem❜
> *Psalm 116:14–19*

Psalm 116:14–19 suggests the value of public worship with others. Historically this would have meant the Temple in Jerusalem; for Jews today this means the synagogue. Prayer as worship was unusual but always existed alongside Temple worship, for occasions of national concern such as drought, famine, or war. After the destruction of the Temple and the exile of the Jews from Israel the idea that the common man could turn to God in prayer became more important.

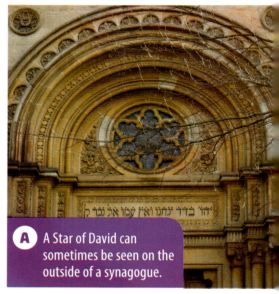

A A Star of David can sometimes be seen on the outside of a synagogue.

Synagogue services

The main public acts of worship that take place within the synagogue are the Daily Prayer services which take place every day, three times a day; the Shabbat (Sabbath) services; and the festival services.

Shabbat

Shabbat begins at dusk on Friday and ends at the appearance of three stars on Saturday. There are Shabbat services in the synagogue on Friday evening and Saturday morning and afternoon. Reform and Liberal denominations tend to focus more on the Shabbat and festival services than the Daily Prayer services.

Prayers such as the Amidah (see 8.4) and Aleinu (see 8.6) are expressed, praising God. The Amidah prayer is adjusted for Shabbat. Instead of

B The congregation usually face towards the Ark.

focusing on personal need, it focuses on the gift of Shabbat and the reasons for Shabbat. A longer reading than usual of the Torah is given, and a sermon by the Rabbi. Lesson 8.6 discusses the Shabbat service in more detail.

The whole family is encouraged to attend, so the service is an opportunity for both families and community to gather together in public worship.

Daily prayers

Jews can pray anywhere, not only in a synagogue, but if there is a minyan present then the additional prayers of the Kaddish, **kedusha**, or those prayers linked with the reading of the Torah can be recited.

Jews are expected to pray three times daily: in the morning (Shacharit), afternoon (Mincha), and evening (Ma'ariv). There are usually services in the synagogue to coincide with these times. In Orthodox synagogues prayers are usually said in Hebrew. In Reform and Liberal synagogues, the balance of prayers in Hebrew and English varies.

- Jews often stand to say prayers as a reminder of God's presence.
- Prayers are usually said silently when praying alone.
- The **Siddur** contains the daily prayers which vary throughout the calendar.

The importance of synagogue services

The synagogue services unite the local community in prayer and study, while reminding them of their place within the worldwide Jewish community. Jews throughout the world use broadly similar prayer books, although there is diversity between denominations. Jews pray towards Israel. In Israel they pray towards Jerusalem and in Jerusalem towards the site of the Holy Temple.

Private prayer usually consists of three elements: thanksgiving, prayers of praise, and prayers that ask for things. Jews believe that God will take action and respond to their prayers, perhaps not always in the way they expect, but prayer is never in vain.

A sermon by the Rabbi will usually relate to a part of the service or to a topical issue which may affect the ways Jews should live their lives.

C Jews pray silently when alone.

SUMMARY

- Prayer is the most important part of Jewish worship; synagogues play an important role in this.
- Shabbat, festival, and the Daily Prayers are the most important services that take place publicly in the synagogue.
- These unite the community while providing time for the individual to offer their own prayer of praise and thanksgiving.

8.2 The Tenakh and Talmud

SPECIFICATION FOCUS

The Tenakh and the Talmud: the nature, features, purpose and significance of the Tenakh (the written law) and Talmud (the oral law) for Jews in daily life today, with reference to Perkei Avot 2; the nature and purpose of Jewish laws: food laws, kashrut, including kosher, and treifah and the separation of dairy and meat, including reference to Deuteronomy 14:3–10; the divergent implications of the Jewish food laws for Jews today.

The nature and purpose of the Tenakh

The Tenakh is the Jewish Bible. The name is formed from the first letters of each of the Tenakh's three divisions:

- the **T**orah: the Pentateuch or Five Books of Moses (see 7.1)
- the **N**evii'im: the Prophets (in two groups: Former and Latter)
- the **K**etuvim: the Writings (Books of Wisdom, 'The Five Scrolls', Book of Prophecy, and Books of History).

The Torah is the most sacred object in Judaism and takes the form of a handwritten parchment scroll that is kept in the Ark (a special cupboard) in the synagogue. A printed copy is called a *Chumash*.

Orthodox Jews regard the Torah as the literal word of God which was revealed to the Jewish people at Mount Sinai in around 1280BCE. As such, the Torah is considered divine and timeless; it cannot be altered. The rest of the Tenakh shows how the Jewish people lived during the times of the Prophets and how they tried to keep them on the right path.

Many Reform Jews believe that the Torah is a human creation – written by their ancestors and inspired by their understanding of themselves and the place of God in their lives.

The nature and purpose of the Talmud

The Talmud is the record of the Oral Tradition and literally means 'instruction or learning'. Orthodox Jewish tradition says that this instruction was also given to Moses at Mount Sinai as a detailed teaching in how the Torah should be interpreted. Over 1,000 years later it was written down so it wouldn't become distorted by time or by being passed on by word of mouth. Reform Jews see the Talmud as a human creation, reflecting the distilled wisdom of many generations of the Jewish people.

- The two parts of the Talmud are called the Mishnah (the core text) and Gemara (the Rabbinical analysis).
- It is divided into sections called tractates and in standard print is over 6,200 pages long.
- It the source of all Jewish legal teaching and decision.
- The Mishnah is written in Hebrew, the Gemara is written in Aramaic, a language spoken by the Jews in ancient Israel.
- The Mishnah was compiled in around 200CE and the Gemara in around 500CE.

The Talmud contains the teaching and opinion of thousands of early Rabbis on many topics including law, ethics, philosophy, customs, and history.

A A page from the Talmud. The text of the Mishnah and Gemara is in the centre, and Rabbinic discussion is placed around them.

The importance of their use in daily life and worship

The differing views on the authority of the Torah have led to separation between Orthodox and Reform Jews in both worship and practice. However, the centrality of Torah reading and study is common to all synagogues.

- One scroll is taken from the Ark and sections are read four times a week in Orthodox synagogues (on Mondays, Tuesdays, Saturday mornings and Saturday afternoons) and once a week in Reform and Liberal synagogues (on Saturday/Shabbat).
- Over the course of the year, the whole Torah is read in sequence.

The Talmud is regarded as central to Orthodox Jewish life and all Jews are encouraged to study it. Perkei Avot or 'Ethics of the Fathers' is a set of ethical teachings within the Mishnah. Chapter 2 commends the value of study:

> 'If a man has acquired a good name he has gained something which enriches himself; but if he has acquired words of the Torah he has attained afterlife.'
> *Perkei Avot, Ch2:8*

Regular study and lectures are held in synagogues. There are international study programmes such as Daf Yomi ('a page a day'), in which Jews across the world study in unison.

Many Reform and Liberal Jews view the Talmud as a rich source of study and learning about Jewish values and the evolution of Jewish thought. They may study it without giving it the same authority as many Orthodox Jews. Other Jews do not see the Talmud as important and choose not to study it. Some feel Aramaic is an inaccessible language, or that many of the debates within the Talmud took place in the sixth century and so are irrelevant to Jews today. Modern English versions have become popular with some Jews and make the Talmud more accessible for them.

The nature and purpose of Jewish food laws

For many people, the Jewish food laws are an opportunity to bring kedusha, or holiness, to one of the most essential areas of existence. The Torah and Talmud provide Jews with laws and detailed guidance on how to keep them. Kashrut is the term for the laws relating to food.

Food that is acceptable to Jews is called kosher; it literally means 'fit' or 'correct'. Food that is not kosher is called treifah which means 'torn' and was used originally for animals that had been attacked by a predator. These laws are found in the Torah, so Jews believe they come from God. Deuteronomy 14:3–10 lists some animals which can and cannot be eaten – pigs cannot. Some food combinations such as dairy at the same time as meat are avoided.

- Some have suggested that kosher food laws benefit health. For example, not eating animals that are unconscious before they are killed reduces the risk of eating an unhealthy animal.

> 'Moses revealed the Torah at Mount Sinai and handed it to Joshua, Joshua to the elders, the elders to the prophets, and the prophets to the men of the Great Assembly.'
> *Ethics of the Fathers Authorised Daily Prayer Book*

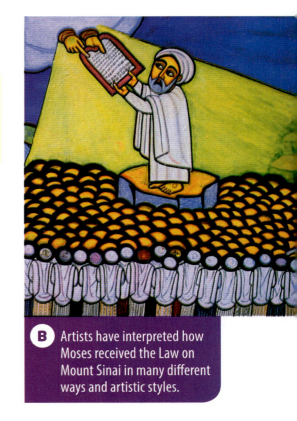

B Artists have interpreted how Moses received the Law on Mount Sinai in many different ways and artistic styles.

- Pigs in Israel also used to carry a lot of disease, and again it would have been unwise to eat them.
- Many Jews keep the laws simply because they believe they came from God.

> 'These are the animals that you may eat: the ox, sheep, and goat [...] and every animal that has a split hoof, which is completely separated in two hooves, that brings up its cud [...] But this shall you not eat [...] the camel, the hare, and the hyrax, for they bring up their cud, but their hoof is not split – they are unclean to you.'
> *Deuteronomy 14:4–7*

Their application in Jewish life today

Orthodox Jews continue to believe that these rules are important to keep, but some Reform and Liberal Jews believe they are outdated. Many Jews continue to refrain from pork even if they do not observe all dietary laws. As certain combinations of food are prohibited, such as meat and dairy, a three-hour gap must be observed after meat before eating dairy. Additionally, Orthodox Jewish families would have separate utensils for each. This creates challenges for Jews when eating out; not only does the food need to be kosher, but so do the cooking methods.

During the week of Passover, Jews do not eat anything containing yeast. Often a deep clean of the house takes place to remove all foodstuffs that won't be eaten during this time. Separate crockery and cutlery are used to avoid contamination.

While some Reform Jews may believe that some rules of kashrut are outdated others aim to take the principles of kashrut and find ways of making them meaningful. For some Reform Jews certain principles of kashrut are important as a way of expressing kedusha and a sense of connection with God.

There are Jews, including both Reform and Orthodox, who observe what is called 'eco-kashrut' – aiming to bring contemporary ethical and ecological issues into a consideration of what it is fit to eat. For example, a cow may be kosher according to the letter of the law, but has it also been raised in an ethical manner?

 C Kosher food is identified by different symbols on packaging.

 BUILD YOUR SKILLS

1 Complete a table comparing and contrasting the Tenakh and Talmud. Include key facts about each and how each is used.

2 **a** What is the purpose of kashrut?
  b In groups, create a mind map with the words 'kosher' and 'treifah' in the middle. Add as much information as possible about Jewish food laws, including relevant quotations.

? **EXAM-STYLE QUESTIONS**

C Explain **two** ways the Talmud is used by Jews. In your answer you must refer to a source of wisdom and authority. (5)

D 'The laws of kashrut provide many challenges for Jews today' Evaluate this statement considering arguments for and against. In your response you should:
- refer to Jewish teachings
- refer to different Jewish points of view
- reach a justified conclusion. (12)

 SUMMARY

- The Torah is the most important and holy book for Jewish people. It contains the Law of Moses. It forms part of the Tenakh.
- The Talmud is the Oral Law and contains information on how the Torah's laws should be interpreted. It is widely studied by Jews.
- Food that is acceptable to Jews is called kosher; unacceptable food is called treifah.
- Some Jews continue to observe the food laws, believing they come from God. Others do not observe them as strictly.

8.3 Private prayer

The nature of prayer in the home and of private prayer

As many Jews cannot attend the synagogue daily, often individual prayers in the home will replace them. These may be carried out individually or as a family. Private, or individual, prayer is also encouraged and considered an important part of Jewish worship:

> ❛ Tremble and sin not; reflect in your hearts while on your beds and be utterly silent, Selah. ❜
> *Psalms 4:5*

Jews are encouraged to clear their minds before they begin to pray so they can focus only on God. Psalm 4:5 says 'reflect in your hearts', which means an individual should forget the world around them and look inwards, into their heart, to connect with God. It is this connection which is most important during prayer.

Shabbat prayer

Prayers are important as part of the Shabbat rituals. On a Friday night, the Shabbat meal is prepared before candles are lit to welcome Shabbat. Prayers are recited before the meal begins. The **Kiddush** is a prayer of sanctification which:

- celebrates God's creation of the universe
- remembers the release of their ancestors from slavery in Egypt.

After the Kiddush is recited over the wine and other blessings are made, the food is eaten. The meal can take several hours, with stories being told and songs being sung. The connection of family, and sometimes friends, through prayer and thanksgiving is considered to be of great value.

Prayer three times a day

Jews believe they are instructed to pray three times a day:

> ❛ Evening, morning, and noon, I supplicate and moan; and He has heard my voice. ❜
> *Psalm 55:18*

The formal morning, afternoon, and evening prayers are important parts of the day for Jews. They keep God in the forefront of a Jew's thoughts. Many Jews recite the Shema upon retiring at night. Upon waking, Jews say **Modeh ani** which is a short prayer thanking God for the gift of life.

SPECIFICATION FOCUS

The nature and purpose of prayer in the home and of private prayer: the nature, features and purpose of prayer three times a day; the importance of having different forms of prayers, including interpretations of Psalm 55:16–23.

USEFUL TERMS

Kiddush: prayer of sanctification

Modeh ani: 'I give thanks', a prayer recited upon waking

A The Shabbat meal is an important time for the family to gather together.

B Morning prayers are important for Jews to start the day with God.

181

When prayer might be used and why

Jews pray for a wide variety of reasons including to praise, request, and thank. Praying in a group brings Jews together as a community. The Torah commands Jews to join together to thank God. In doing so, they may also strengthen their personal relationship with him.

Jews also believe in constant prayer beyond the three set times for daily prayer, by acknowledging God in every dimension of their day. This might be when something good or bad happens, or simply just to connect with God for a moment. Jews also say blessings before and after they have eaten, as instructed in the Torah:

> 6 You will eat and you will be satisfied, and bless Hashem, your God, for the good Land that He gave you. 9
> *Deuteronomy 8:10*

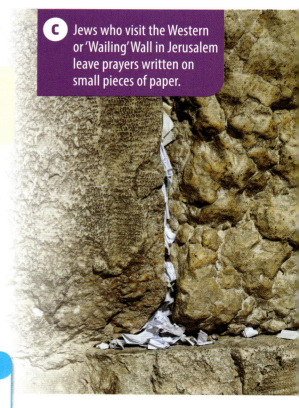

C Jews who visit the Western or 'Wailing' Wall in Jerusalem leave prayers written on small pieces of paper.

The importance of having different forms of prayers

The different types of prayer – daily, individual, constant, Shabbat and festivals – allow Jews to connect with God in different ways.

- Daily prayer allows regular prayer, sometimes connecting in faith as a family.
- Individual prayer allows personal reflection and solitary time with God.
- Constant prayer keeps God in an individual's heart and mind and allows spontaneous opportunity for thanksgiving.
- Shabbat prayer brings family and friends together in regular celebration.

BUILD YOUR SKILLS

1 a List the ways Jews may pray in private.
   b For each way, explain the different benefit or purpose.

2 a How many times a day do many Jews pray?
   b Why do they do this?

3 What might Jews reflect upon during times of private prayer?

SUMMARY

- Jews are encouraged to pray at least the daily prayers in the home if they cannot attend synagogue.
- Formal, personal, and constant prayer are important to the everyday lives of Jews.
- The Hebrew word for prayer can also mean 'reflection' showing how Jews use prayer to consider their lives and how they can be better people.

? EXAM-STYLE QUESTIONS

A Outline **three** different forms of private prayer. (3)

C Explain **two** reasons why prayer in the home or private prayer are important to Jews. In your answer you must refer to a source of wisdom and authority. (5)

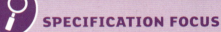

Examples of the different types of prayer

The Shema

> 'Hear, O Israel: Hashem is our God, Hashem is the One and Only.'
> *Deuteronomy 6:4*

This is the opening of the Shema which is the most important prayer in Judaism. It is usually recited twice a day in the morning and evening services in the synagogue. It declares the most fundamental principle of the Jewish faith: the belief in one God. Judaism was an unusual faith when it began in that it recognized only one God; prior to this, religions often worshipped many different gods.

The first paragraph of the Shema contains many important teachings about God:

> 'Hear, O Israel: Hashem is our God, Hashem is the One and Only. You shall love Hashem, your God, with **all your heart**, with **all your soul**, and with **all your resources**. And these matters that I command you today shall be on your heart. **You shall teach them thoroughly to your children** and you shall speak of them while you sit in your home, while you walk on the way, when you retire and when you arise. Bind them as a sign upon your arm and let them be ornaments between your eyes. And write them on the doorposts of your house and upon your gates.'
> *Deuteronomy 6:4–9*

The remainder of the Shema is found in Deuteronomy 11:13–21 and Numbers 15:37–41.

The **tallit** is worn by men and some boys over barmitzvah at every morning service. A tallit is a fringed shawl and the fringe on the corner reminds the wearer of the commandments in the Torah They are also used to cover the head during prayer to help focus..

Tefillin are two small black boxes with straps which contain four specific sets of verses from the Torah. They are worn on the forehead and arm, but not during Shabbat or festivals. The wearing of these comes from the part of the Shema where Jews are told to bind the prayers on their arms and foreheads (Deuteronomy 6:8), which symbolically connects the heart and mind, emotion and intellect to God. Tefillin are only worn on weekday mornings. Women may wear tallit and tefillin in Reform and Liberal communities.

The Shema is also kept in a **mezuzah**, which is a container found on the right-hand doorpost outside Jewish homes, and on every doorpost within that leads to a habitable room. These remind Jews of God's presence.

USEFUL TERMS

Mezuzah: a small box set on a doorpost containing a copy of the Shema

Tallit: a fringed prayer shawl

Tefillin: small boxes worn on head and arm containing verses from the Torah, including the Shema

A A mezuzah contains the Shema, following the commandment in Deuteronomy 6:9.

B Tefillin contain handwritten prayers.

The Amidah

The Amidah is the core part of every Jewish worship service, and is therefore also referred to as the HaTefillah, or 'the prayer'. It literally means 'standing' and refers to a series of blessings which are recited while standing up.

Importance of having different forms of prayer

Jewish prayer was originally unstructured. Individual Rabbis would generate the specific words of the Amidah blessings and select relevant readings from the Torah. However, eventually the format and themes were formalized and standard versions of prayers were settled upon.

Morning prayer

Thanks for the use of the body are given. Psalms and selections from the Tenakh are chosen which help focus the mind on God. The Shema and the Amidah with 19 blessings from God are also recited.

Afternoon prayer

Psalm 145 ('Praise', by David) is always read during these prayers, followed by the Amidah, and ending with the Aleinu (see 8.6).

Evening prayer

The Shema, Amidah, and Aleinu are recited.

Other prayers include:

- **The Kaddish:** A prayer of praise which is usually used after a Rabbi's teaching. A longer version is used at funerals called the Mourner's Kaddish.
- **Barkhu:** The call to prayer at the start of a synagogue service by the prayer leader.

These different prayers are used in different circumstances and ways, and allow Jews to connect with God in different ways: sometimes praising, sometimes thanking, sometimes simply communicating.

C Liberal Rabbi, Alina Treiger, wearing the tallit.

 COMPARE AND CONTRAST

In your exam you may be asked to compare and contrast Jewish practices and worship with Catholic practices and worship. Look back at 2.2 for detail on these.

 BUILD YOUR SKILLS

1 Make a list of the key Jewish beliefs stated in the Shema.

2 What three items would Jews use to help them pray? Explain each in your own words.

3 How and when are the Shema and Amidah prayers said?

4 a Describe the daily prayer schedule that some Jews may follow.
  b Why do you think some Jews may not follow this?

 SUMMARY

- Daily prayer is an important part of Jewish life; it may take place in the synagogue or privately.
- The Shema is the most important Jewish prayer and describes the core beliefs about God.
- The Amidah consists of three sections: praise, request, and thanks. It is a core part of Jewish prayer services and contains a number of blessings from God.
- Prayers are used within tefillin and mezuzot.

? EXAM-STYLE QUESTIONS

B Describe **two** differences in the types of prayer said during public worship between Judaism and the main religious tradition of Great Britain. (4)

C Explain **two** ways the Shema is said within Jewish worship. In your answer you must refer to a source of wisdom and authority. (5)

8.5 Ritual and ceremony

The importance of ritual for Jews today

Rituals are grounded in Jewish law which includes the mitzvot as well as Rabbinic laws and traditions. It doesn't govern just religious life, but also daily life. Observance shows gratitude to God, provides a sense of Jewish identity, and brings God into everyday life.

Important moments in the life of a Jew are marked by customs, many of which go back to biblical times and have been developed in accordance with Halakhah (religious law) and local traditions.

Birth

For Jews, despite the soul existing in the womb, the life of the child begins when it is halfway emerged from the mother's body. The child is then born pure and entirely free from sin.

Leviticus 12 outlines rituals during Temple times for purification of a mother after giving birth. If she had a boy she 'may not touch anything sacred and she may not enter the Sanctuary' (Leviticus 12:3) for 7 days plus 33 days. If she had a girl the time was extended to 14 days plus 66 days. This is because the mother was thought to take longer to recover after having a girl because she had created another creator, which reflects the holiness surrounding the gift of creation.

In ancient times, a mother would have made offerings at the Temple after these days and 'become purified' (Leviticus 12:8). Today, she will attend the **mikvah** once she has stopped bleeding. This cannot be sooner than 7 days (after a boy) or 14 days (after a girl).

Children are always given a Hebrew name although they will often have English names which they use in the secular world. A girl's name is officially given in the synagogue when the father takes an aliyah (a reading from the Torah) after her birth. In Reform communities there may also be a Simchat Bat, 'Rejoicing for a daughter' celebration. A boy's name is given during the Brit Milah (ritual circumcision).

Brit Milah

The Brit Milah, or 'covenant of circumcision', is one of the most universally observed mitzvot. Even secular Jews almost always observe these laws. It is an outward physical sign of God's everlasting covenant.

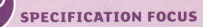

SPECIFICATION FOCUS

The importance of ritual for Jews today: the nature, features and purpose of the birth, marriage, Bar and Bat Mitzvah ceremonies, including interpretations of Genesis 21:1–8 and Leviticus 12; the nature, purpose and importance of mourning ceremonies; the distinct importance of the funeral, shiva, avelut and yahrzeit for Jews today; divergent understandings of the importance of each ritual for different forms of Orthodox and Reform Judaism today.

USEFUL TERM

Mikvah: ritual bath for purification

A Carrying the baby to his Brit Milah is an honour.

Abraham was commanded to circumcise himself and his descendents in Genesis 17:10-12. He kept this promise when his son, Isaac was born:

> ❝Abraham circumcised his son Isaac at the age of eight days as God had commanded him.❞
> *Genesis 21:4*

The removal of the foreskin of the penis is itself a religious ritual that must be performed by someone religiously qualified, called a mohel.

The ritual of Pidyon ha-ben or 'Redemption of the Son' applies if the firstborn is male, and born by natural birth. Historically, the firstborn son of a family would provide service to the Temple. The child is redeemed from that service by paying a small sum (five silver shekels in biblical times) to a kohein, a priest and descendant of Aaron. This ritual is not usually observed in Reform communities.

Bar and Bat Mitzvah ceremonies

The Bar and Bat Mitzvah (Son and Daughter of Commandment) ceremonies take place for boys aged 13 and girls aged 12 in Orthodox communities and 13 in Reform and Liberal. These are seen as a 'coming of age'. The young people, in the eyes of the Jewish faith, are then able to take responsibility for their own actions and faith.

After the Bar Mitzvah, the boy can lead the synagogue service or take an active part in the service, and can be included in a minyan or read as part of a service. These rights are granted to any Jewish boy on their 13th birthday. Reform and Liberal Jews would also grant these rights to a girl on her Bat Mitzvah. Liberal synagogues have a further ceremony of Kabbalat Torah at the age of 15 when boys and girls confirm their acceptance of a Jewish way of life.

Only in the last 100 years or so, have Bat Mitzvah celebrations for girls taken place.

For both, young Jews are expected to study and prepare carefully. They will read various texts, especially boys, who will often be called to read from the Torah scroll in the synagogue on their Bar Mitzvah. Girls will also undertake a variety of learning, volunteering, and charitable tasks, which may include learning how to bake **challah** bread for Shabbat observance, emphasizing their important role in the Jewish home. In Reform and Liberal communities, both boys and girls will read from the Torah, and boys will also often undertake the same tasks as girls.

Marriage

The Torah provides very little teaching on marriage. However the Talmud explains how to find a partner, the form the wedding ceremony should take, and the nature of the marital relationship. The Kiddushin, or betrothal, is a binding engagement and the first part of marriage. Nisuin is the name for full marriage.

The ceremony is often around half an hour including a message to the bride and groom from a Rabbi. The couple stand under a huppah, a canopy that represents the beginnings of a new home. In Reform ceremonies both exchange rings. In Orthodox

B Bar and Bat Mitzvah celebrations are proud moments in Jewish life.

ceremonies, the plain metal ring is traditionally placed on the bride's right forefinger as in Jewish law, a marriage becomes official when the chatan (groom) gives an object of value to the kallah (bride).

Sheva Brechot or 'seven blessings' are recited in the presence of guests or the Rabbi. In Orthodox marriages, two religiously observant male witnesses are needed for the signing of the Ketubah: the marriage contract. In Reform and Liberal two Jewish adults, either male or female can witness. The Ketubah's nature is different for Orthodox, Reform, and Liberal traditions.

The groom stamps on a small glass (to symbolize the destruction of the Temple) before they retire briefly to another room to spend some time alone together and to complete the nisuin. This is then usually followed by a meal and party, which has religious significance as well. In Reform and Liberal synagogues same-sex marriage is now possible.

C The items from a wedding ceremony.

Mourning ceremonies

Mourning ceremonies aim to help the bereaved return to normal life after the loss of a loved one.

The Jewish word for mourning is avelut. Many Orthodox Jews will make a tear in their clothes upon hearing of the death of a loved one, following the example of Jacob.

> 6 Then Jacob tore his clothes, put on sackcloth and mourned for his son many days. 9
> *Genesis 37:34*

USEFUL TERMS

Eulogy: speech of praise and remembrance for someone who has died

Challah: plaited bread prepared before Shabbat begins

Reform Jews might wear a torn black ribbon or cut a tie. Both Reform and Orthodox Jews will then make a blessing to God referring to him as true judge and show their acceptance of God taking the person's life.

There are five periods of avelut:

- *Aninut*: from death to burial.
- *Shiva*: the first seven days of mourning; the day of burial is day one.
- *Sheloshim*: the first thirty days from the day of burial, including the shivah; the complete mourning period for all (except when mourning for a parent).
- *Yud-bet chodesh*: the 'year of mourning' for a parent, the twelve Hebrew months following the day of death.
- *Yahrzeit*: the anniversary date of the death, according to the Jewish calendar.

After the funeral, the mourners return to the home where ritual mourning will take place to eat a 'meal of consolation', traditionally a hard boiled egg and a beigel, a circular roll, seen to symbolize the cycle of life.

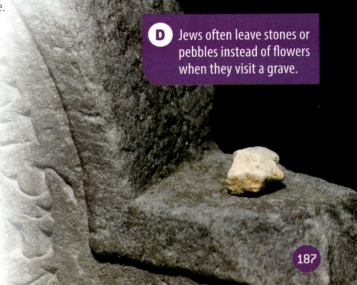

D Jews often leave stones or pebbles instead of flowers when they visit a grave.

The next seven days are called sitting shiva which means a period of intense mourning. Mourners:

- stay at home, sitting on low stalls or the floor
- do not wear leather shoes, shave or cut hair, wear cosmetics, or work
- don't do things that bring comfort or pleasure
- usually wear the clothes they wore to the funeral
- pray three times daily with friends, family, and neighbours making up the minyan.

After this is the period of Sheloshim or 'lesser mourning' which ends 30 days after the person's death. Normal life resumes, but mourners do not attend parties, listen to music, or shave or cut their hair. Male mourners try to recite the Mourner's Kaddish daily in the synagogue.

In the case of a parent, the period of mourning lasts 11 months in Yud-bet chodesh. After this period, formal mourning stops but on the anniversary a Yahrzeit candle is lit and the men (and in Reform and Liberal communities, women) recite the Mourner's Kaddish.

Yahrzeit candles are widely used by Jews today in memory of the dead, both those known personally to the individual and on occasions such as Yom Kippur and Yom HaShoah, when those who died in the Holocaust are remembered.

The funeral

Jews are traditionally buried rather than cremated, ideally within 24 hours of death. Some Reform and Liberal communities also permit creation. Candles are lit and the body is never left alone while awaiting burial as a sign of respect.

- The body is washed and wrapped in a linen shroud.
- Men are also wrapped in their tallit. The tassels which signify the commandments to remember are often cut off, no longer being necessary.
- Plain coffins are used, which show an equality in death between rich and poor.

Jews believe the synagogue is a place for the living, so the funeral takes place entirely at the cemetery. Here, a short service takes place with psalms, prayers, and a short **eulogy** by the Rabbi about the deceased. After the coffin is lowered, mourners shovel earth onto the coffin.

Everyone who attends washes their hands in a ritual outside the cemetery. The hands are washed by pouring water from a cup over each hand alternatively three times. This symbolizes leaving death behind.

E A Yahrzeit candle is lit in remembrance of a loved one.

BUILD YOUR SKILLS

1 a Create a basic timeline for the life of a Jew indicating the key rituals and ceremonies that may take place.
  b For each, add three key bullet points about what happens.
  c Pick two rituals or ceremonies and explain why they would be particularly important to Jews.

2 Which rituals or ceremonies are not kept by all Jews? Why do you think this is?

EXAM-STYLE QUESTIONS

C Explain **two** important features of the Jewish ritual of Brit Milah. In your answer you must refer to a source of wisdom and authority. (5)

D 'All Jews celebrate the same rites and rituals.' Evaluate this statement considering arguments for and against. In your response you should:
  - refer to Jewish teachings
  - refer to different Jewish points of view
  - reach a justified conclusion. (12)

SUMMARY

- Rituals are an important part of Jewish life representing the significant moments of both religious and daily life.
- Birth, 'Coming of Age', marriage, and death all have rituals associated with them for Jews.
- Brit Milah is an outward sign of a Jew's covenant with God.
- Most rituals are followed by all Jews but there may be slight differences within what they say and do.

8.6 Shabbat

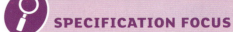

SPECIFICATION FOCUS

The nature, features, history and purpose of celebrating Shabbat: the nature, features and purpose of the celebration of Shabbat in the home and in the synagogue, including interpretations of Exodus 31:12–18; why the celebration of Shabbat is important for the Jewish community and the individual today.

The nature, features, history, and purpose of celebrating Shabbat

Shabbat is a special day, characterized by time to relax; spending time with family and community, and worshipping at the synagogue.

Jews believe that God instructed them to observe the Sabbath and keep it holy. This is repeated several times within the Torah. It includes worship in both the synagogue and the home.

> ' God blessed the seventh day and sanctified it because on it He abstained from all His work which God created to make. '
> *Genesis 2:3*

It begins on Friday evening at dusk, and then ends when three stars appear in the sky on the Saturday. This is the end of the week for Jews. This can be a challenge in the winter in countries where the light fades before the working day has finished. Some Reform Jewish communities allow their members to observe the Shabbat as 6:00pm Friday to 6:00pm Saturday to help ease the conflict between modern society and faithful religious observance. They believe that being flexible is a good way to bring more Jews into observance.

How it is celebrated

> ' Between Me and the Children of Israel it is a sign forever that in a six-day period Hashem made heaven and earth, and on the seventh day He rested and was refreshed. '
> *Exodus 31:17*

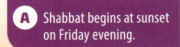

A Shabbat begins at sunset on Friday evening.

The home

Historically people only ate two daily meals on working days. As Shabbat is a special day of rest, there are traditionally three meals that take place in the home during Shabbat: on the Friday evening, Saturday morning, and late Saturday afternoon. The Friday evening meal begins with a Kiddush blessing and further blessing upon the challah bread. The end of Shabbat is marked on the Saturday with the **havdalah** blessing over wine, when a special candle is lit.

The home will usually be cleaned and tidied ready for Shabbat, and sometimes is decorated with flowers. Candles will be lit before Shabbat begins, as kindling lights is one of the activities forbidden on Shabbat. A meal is then served and the singing of special Shabbat hymns is common.

As Jews abstain from work during Shabbat, careful preparation of food is needed: cooking is forbidden for most Jews as they need to ignite the cooker, which counts as work and is forbidden within Exodus:

> ❝You shall not kindle fire in any of your dwellings on the Sabbath day.❞
> *Exodus 35:3*

There are 39 categories of action classified as work and therefore forbidden. Anything not listed needs to be decided upon, and there is not always agreement amongst Jews; for example, whether texting a friend on a mobile phone would create an electrical connection – an 'ignition' and therefore be work.

The synagogue

The main Shabbat services can last around two hours. Some parts are similar to other weekday services, but there are also some differences. A Shabbat service would consist of the following:

- The Amidah, or standing prayer, is recited as the congregation face Jerusalem.
- The Torah is removed from the Ark as the first part of the Shema is recited.
- From the **bimah**, a section of the Torah is chanted in Hebrew. In Reform synagogues this is also translated into English. A **yad** is used to follow the words.
- After the reading, the Torah is returned to the Ark.
- The Rabbi will then deliver a sermon, which is always in the language of the congregation (even in Orthodox synagogues).
- The Shabbat service will then end with prayers including the Aleinu prayer, which expresses a Jew's duty to praise God: 'Let us now praise the Sovereign of the universe, and proclaim the greatness of the Creator…'
- The Kaddish follows, a prayer that acknowledges that God knows best: 'Exalted and hallowed be God's great name, in the world which God created, according to plan…'
- The final act is to sing the hymn of Adon Olam – 'Master of the World'.

USEFUL TERMS

Havdalah: closing ceremony of Shabbat; it means 'separation'

Bimah: raised platform from which readings are made and sermons given

Yad: a pointer for following text

B Two loaves of challah are prepared (sometimes home-baked) ready for Shabbat.

Shabbat's importance today

Observing Shabbat is a core part of the Jewish faith. Jews believe it is one of the Ten Commandments given to Moses by God, and to honour this is fundamental. Modern Jews frequently live in countries where Judaism is not the predominant faith, which provides challenges in observing Shabbat as strictly as they may wish. Additionally, the nature of society and work in particular has changed greatly since the time of Moses.

Rabbinical study of the Torah and Talmud continues to help modern Jews address these new issues, and decide what can and cannot be done during Shabbat.

There is much difference in opinion: Orthodox Jews may turn off their phone as they consider answering it to be work. Others will not drive a car as the ignition of the engine could be interpreted as work: this means many would try to live within easy walking distance of the synagogue. Some Conservative and Reform Jews would argue it is more important to attend the synagogue on Shabbat than to not drive a car. Modern life involves compromise for some Jews.

Regardless of some difficulties, Shabbat remains a day of enjoyment for Jews today and a time to connect with family. Many Jews attend synagogue services and will join Torah study groups. Youth groups will often meet on Shabbat afternoons for discussions and social interaction. Ultimately, by observing Shabbat, Jews are following God's commandment of resting and keeping the day holy.

C Lighting the Shabbat candles marks the beginning of the Sabbath for Jews.

BUILD YOUR SKILLS

1 a When does Shabbat begin and end?
  b How does tradition suggest that Shabbat should be a special day?

2 Give a detailed account, from the perspective of a Jew about:
  - what happens in the home during Shabbat
  - what happens in the synagogue
  - why these things are important.

SUMMARY

- Shabbat is observed from Friday evening to Saturday evening.
- It is celebrated in the home on the Friday with a special meal and in the synagogue on either Friday evening or Saturday morning.
- Modern life can make strict observance of Shabbat challenging for Jews.
- The day is important for both family time and Torah study; it is keeping God's commandment.

EXAM-STYLE QUESTIONS

A Outline **three** things that would happen in a Jewish home to celebrate Shabbat. (3)

D 'Driving a car breaks Shabbat.' Evaluate this statement considering arguments for and against. In your response you should:
  - refer to Jewish teachings
  - refer to different Jewish points of view
  - reach a justified conclusion. (12)

8.7 Festivals

Festivals: the nature, origins, and purpose of festivals

For Jews, there is a time for happiness (celebrations) and sadness (commemoration), as this passage from the Ketuvim illustrates:

> 'Everything has its season, and there is a time for everything under the heaven [...] a time to weep and a time to laugh'
> *Ecclesiastes 3:1–4*

- Festivals occur at set times within the Jewish calendar, but vary slightly as the dates are based on a lunar calendar.
- Most festivals are based on the history of the Jewish people, remembering a happy event from Jewish history.
- Joyful events celebrate God's involvement and intervention on their behalf.
- Some festivals focus on God as creator (Shabbat) and others on relationships with God (Yom Kippur).
- Festivals are usually celebrated both at home and in the synagogue, involving the whole community.

Why festivals are important for Jews today

By their nature, the festivals remain important lessons in the history of Judaism for Jews today. Connecting with other Jewish people is important to sustain and help one another's faith as they have done throughout history. Jews believe it is important to commemorate the Passover of over 3,000 years ago, as well as more modern events such as the Holocaust.

Festivals provide an opportunity for families and synagogue communities to come together and share their common past. Tradition is an important part of Jewish life, and for Orthodox Jews simply continuing the way of life from their forefathers is vital. Reform Jews observe festivals, with some innovation and adaptation to modern living, believing this gives them greater relevance and meaning for their communities.

A Festivals allow Jews to connect to the traditions of their ancestors, for example building a sukkah for Sukkot.

Rosh Hashanah

Rosh Hashanah literally means the 'head of the year'. It is the first day of the Jewish year and is used to remember the story of creation at the start of the Torah. It is also the first of the '**Days of Awe**'. Orthodox Jews celebrate over two days; for Liberal Jews and some Reform Jews it is just one day.

Rosh Hashanah is considered the anniversary of creation and the Mishnah says on this day God writes down the deeds of a person, judges them, and makes decisions about the year to come. Rosh Hashanah is therefore a time for Jews to evaluate their behaviour, reflect on the past year, to make peace, and to ask forgiveness of others before the judgment of God is finalized on Yom Kippur. The celebration is instituted in Leviticus:

> 'Speak to the children of Israel, saying: in the seventh month, on the first of the month, there shall be a rest day for you, a remembrance with shofar blasts, a holy convocation. You shall not do any laborious work, and you shall offer a fire-offering to Hashem. '
> *Leviticus 23:24–25*

After visiting the synagogue, Jews wish each other L'shanah tovah, 'a good year'. A festive meal is celebrated in the home, with the addition of fruit which symbolizes renewal. After the Kiddush, slices of apple dipped in honey are eaten in the hope of a 'sweet' new year. A pomegranate may be eaten to symbolize the wish that good deeds will be plentiful like the seeds in a pomegranate.

Jews also attend the synagogue the following morning, and Jews who do not regularly attend make the effort to do so on this morning. The **shofar** is blown 100 times.

In the afternoon, the Tashlikh ceremony takes place when families visit a tream or river, recite prayers and symbolically empty their pockets to represent the casting off of sins.

Yom Kippur

The second of the 'Days of Awe', the 'Day of Atonement' is the holiest day in the year. It is a day to reflect on sins and to seek forgiveness from God, in order to become 'at one' with God. In the ten days before Yom Kippur, beginning with Rosh Hashanah Jews seek forgiveness from others for any wrong they may have done them, as forgiveness from other people must precede seeking forgiveness from God.

Many Jews undertake 25 hours of fasting following the instruction in Leviticus 16 to 'deny themselves'. Some Jews believe this builds self-control, some believe it helps focus their mind on the important prayers of the day, and others simply fast because it is a mitzvah.

Jews also regard Yom Kippur as a joyful experience, repairing their relationship with God. Leviticus 16:20–22 details how a goat was led into the desert carrying the sins of the Jewish people. On Yom Kippur Jews try to replicate this by

B A shofar heralds important events.

C Wearing white at Yom Kippur symbolizes purity.

confessing and atoning for their sins before God seals the book of judgment containing the decisions made on Rosh Hashanah about an individual's future.

The services begin in the evening with Kol Nidre or 'All Vows' when Jews cancel any vows they have made to God they cannot keep. Jews often wear white as a symbol of purity and avoid leather shoes which suggest luxury. Jews will spend a large part of the day in the synagogue in prayer and reflection. The doors of the Ark are opened for most of the final service of the day and are then closed; a single blast of the shofar is sounded, almost as a finale, and the congregation says aloud: 'Next Year in Jerusalem rebuilt'.

The first pilgrim festival: Pesach

There are three Pilgrim Festivals – Pesach, Shavuot and Sukkot – when Jews would have visited the Temple in Jerusalem to bring gifts, as commanded in the Torah. All of these festivals have both an agricultural and historical significance.

Pesach is usually referred to as the Passover, as it is based on the night that God 'passed over' Egypt killing every firstborn male, but not those of the Jewish people. Jews try to gather together as a family, and include members of the community who cannot be with their own relatives.

The festival coincides with the barley harvest in ancient times but primarily celebrates the liberation of the Jewish people from hundreds of years of slavery in ancient Egypt. It was the start of their journey to nationhood. Pesach is a reminder of God's love for the oppressed and weak members of society in every generation. Jews will remember all those deaths connected to their freedom, both Jewish and Egyptian.

- Today, all **chametz** (**leaven**) is removed from the home as it is not eaten for seven days.
- The home must be thoroughly cleaned before Pesach to remove all traces of chametz.
- The festival lasts eight days in total for Orthodox Jews, and seven days for Reform or Liberal traditions, with the Seder meal being the most important event.

> 🔑 **USEFUL TERMS**
>
> **Chametz:** foods containing wheat, barley, and oats, left to soak for over 18 minutes
>
> **Leaven:** meaning risen – food that has been fermented with a raising agent such as yeast, prohibited during Pesach
>
> **Haggadah:** a Jewish book which sets out the rituals of Pesach

Zeroa and **Baytzah**
A shank bone (Zeroa) and roasted egg (Baytzah) are reminders of the sacrifices Jews used to make at the Temple.

Chazaret
Chazaret is another type of Maror, usually made of grated fresh horseradish.

D A seder plate: every item is symbolic

Karpas
A green, leafy vegetable (usually celery or parsley/ lettuce), dipped in salt water, to represent tears.

Maror and Charoset
Maror (bitter herbs for the bitterness of slavery) are dipped in charoset (sweet apple, cinnamon, nut and wine mix) to symbolize the mortar used in buildings by slaves. The sweetness represents freedom.

Seder literally means 'order' because everything that happens during the seder meal follows the order set out in the **Haggadah**. Everything on the seder plate is symbolic of a part of the seder service, for example a small bowl of salt water symbolizes the tears of the Jewish people as they struggled in slavey in ancient Egypt.

The seder service is a reflection on the banquets of free men in the ancient world. Freed from slavery, Jews celebrate in the way free men would.

Four cups of wine (or grape juice) are drunk as four symbols of freedom. When the wine is being poured, guests pour for each other, just as free people had servants do in ancient times. Although four cups of wine should be drunk, a fifth cup, for Elias, is poured and left undrunk. Jews live in the hope he will return to announce the arrival of the Messiah during Passover. At the end, Jews together wish that they will celebrate the meal together in Jerusalem the following year.

The second pilgrim festival: Shavuot

This festival celebrates the giving of the Law on Mount Sinai, as well as marking the wheat harvest in ancient Israel.

- Historically the second pilgrim festival, where Jews would travel to offer wheat from the harvest at the Temple.
- It marks the seven-week or 49-day counting period between Passover and Shavuot.
- To celebrate the gift of the Torah, Jews may take time to explore texts in community learning programmes.
- Several customs have evolved including the eating of dairy and decorating the synagogue in greenery.

The third pilgrim festival: Sukkot

Sukkot begins four days after Yom Kippur but it is very different in mood and content. It marks the end of the summer and ushers in the autumn fruit harvest.

Sometimes known as the Feast of the Tabernacles or Feast of the Booths, it is a reminder of the dwellings the Jewish people lived in during the wilderness years – little booths or huts. It is celebrated for eight days and this is seen as a holiday period for Jews observing it, and a time of particular hospitality to others.

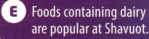

E Foods containing dairy are popular at Shavuot.

 BUILD YOUR SKILLS

1 a Give three reasons why Jews celebrate festivals.
  b Which of these do you think is the single most important?

2 Write down two key facts to learn for each of:
  - Rosh Hashanah
  - Yom Kippur
  - Pesach
  - Shavuot
  - Sukkot.

EXAM-STYLE QUESTIONS

B Explain **two** ways festivals connect Jews with their past. (4)

D 'Festivals are important because the Tenakh instructs Jews that they must celebrate certain events.' Evaluate this statement considering arguments for and against. In your response you should:
  - refer to Jewish teachings
  - refer to different Jewish points of view
  - reach a justified conclusion. (12)

SUMMARY

- Festivals are an important part of Jewish life and are used to remember happy times in Jewish history.
- They are a time for families and wider Jewish communities to unite and celebrate their faith.
- Rosh Hashanah and Yom Kippur are generally regarded as the most important festivals; Jews' observance of other festivals varies depending on whether they are Reform, Liberal, or Orthodox and where they live in the world.

8.8 Features of the synagogue

SPECIFICATION FOCUS

Features of the synagogue: the nature, history and purpose of the different design of the synagogues in Liberal, Reform and Orthodox Judaism, including facing Jerusalem, layout of seating, the Ark and the bimah and with reference to Proverbs 14:28; how and why the synagogue is used by the different communities, including reference to Exodus 27:20–21; how and why objects of devotion are used within the synagogues, including a yad, Torah Scroll, ner tamid and menorah.

The nature and history of the synagogue

The Jewish place of worship is called the synagogue, which literally means 'bringing together'. Proverbs 14:28 refers to the strength of Judaism being in the gathering of Jews together: 'A multitude of people is a king's glory.' Whilst praying in a minyan is the minimum size for public prayer, the greater the number involved, the more honour to God. Synagogue design is focused on facilitating worship together, as a whole people, focusing on the bimah in the centre where the Torah is read.

- The synagogue is sometimes called shul, meaning 'school', which reflects the role of education in the lives of Jews.
- Synagogues can be identified by a Star of David or menorah on the outside.

Synagogue design

Many features of synagogues are the same in the Orthodox and Reform traditions because they play an important part in worship. There will always be an Ark and bimah. The design of the seating and position of the bimah may vary slightly: Orthodox synagogues often have seating on three sides facing a central bimah, while the Ark takes up the fourth side. There may also be a separate balcony area for women. This layout can be replicated in Liberal or Reform synagogues, or they may place the bimah at the front of the hall before the Ark. Seating would be angled towards the front of the hall. Some modern Jewish synagogues are different shapes, but the positioning of seating towards the bimah and Ark remain important.

The synagogue should face towards Jerusalem, so those in the UK face east. This does not need to be exact, and sometimes they may face other directions for structural reasons; however, the community will usually try to face Jerusalem when standing for prayer.

Objects of devotion

The Ark

The Aron Kodesh, or 'Ark' is the most important element of the prayer hall and is set in the wall which faces Jerusalem. It is where the Torah scrolls are kept, in honour of the Holy of Holies in the Temple which contained the Ark of the Covenant and the Ten Commandments. The doors or curtain are only opened when the Torah Scrolls are taken out during worship or on occasions such as Yom Kippur.

Ner tamid

The ner tamid or 'eternal light' is kept burning at all times in front of or above the Ark. This is set out as a requirement in Exodus 27:20–21, 'to kindle

A In an Orthodox synagogue, women sit apart from the men in the balconies.

a lamp continually' before God, for all eternity. This light reflects God's eternal nature, and the menorah, a seven-branched candlestick, was always kept burning in the Temple because of this commandment. Exodus 25:31–40 gives specific instructions on the design of the menorah, including its seven branches.

The bimah

Much of synagogue design reflects the design of the ancient Temple, and in this respect the bimah represents the Temple altar.

- The Rabbi leads the service from the bimah.
- The Torah scrolls are removed from the Ark, placed on the bimah, and read from there.
- The words of the Torah are followed using a yad, a long pointer shaped at the end with a pointed finger. This is used so the Torah is not touched directly by the reader, respecting the special status of the sacred Scripture.

The synagogue within the community

As well as being a place of worship and education, the synagogue also serves as a community centre. There are often Hebrew classes, adult education classes, youth clubs, and charity events, alongside regular worship and celebrations of festivals and rites of passage such as Bar and Bat Mitzvahs.

Traditions within synagogues

Just as the design of synagogues may vary between traditions, what happens during services will also vary:

- Men and women sit together in Reform synagogues but separately in Orthodox.
- Married women will cover their heads in Orthodox synagogues for modesty. In Liberal and Reform, women are encouraged to wear tallit and sometimes a kippah as a sign of equal obligation.
- Musical instruments may be used in Reform and Liberal services but not in Orthodox.
- Women take an active part in Liberal and Reform services but not in Orthodox.

B Ner tamid burning above the ark.

C The bimah can be of simple or ornate design.

BUILD YOUR SKILLS

1 a Plan a virtual guided tour of the synagogue. Create bullet point notes for each feature and object of devotion.
  b Which features/objects would you particularly emphasize? Why?

SUMMARY

- The synagogue is the Jewish place of worship.
- The synagogue has features that remind Jews of the Temple in Jerusalem.
- Orthodox, Reform, and Liberal synagogues share many similarities such as the Ark and bimah but can vary in layout.
- The Ark and bimah are the most important features.

EXAM-STYLE QUESTIONS

A Outline **three** key features of the synagogue. (3)
B Describe **two** differences between Orthodox and Reform synagogues. (4)

Revision

REVIEW YOUR KNOWLEDGE

1. Name the three main occasions that Jews will go to the synagogue.
2. What three parts make up the Tenakh?
3. What do Jews understand Psalm 55:18 to mean?
4. What are the two most important Jewish prayers?
5. How are the ceremonies for people becoming Son or Daughter of Commandment usually referred?
6. When does Shabbat take place?
7. Name three Jewish festivals you have studied.
8. What is the Ark?

* See page 288 for answers.

USEFUL TERMS

Do you know what these words mean?

Kaddish Kedusha Kiddush Siddur
Mezuzah Tallit Tefillin Mikvah
Havdalah Bimah Yad Days of Awe
Shofar Chametz Haggadah Leaven
Challah Seder Aron Kodesh

EXTEND YOUR KNOWLEDGE: RESEARCH TASKS

For a research task, try to put together a full side of A4 of your own writing on the topics below.

1. Research the operation of Jewish restaurants / food shops – how do they follow kashrut?
2. Research in detail the different aids to prayer: tallit, tefillin, mezuzah, the Siddur
3. Research one ritual or ceremony from 8.5 and identify differences in celebration between Jews.
4. Research an example of a synagogue, its history and key features, for example Bevis Marks in London or the Hurva Synagogue in Jerusalem.

ONGOING LEARNING REVIEW

It is vital that you keep reviewing past material to make sure you have fully learned and remember it.

1. How are the characteristics of God important to Jews today?
2. In what ways can Jews connect with the Shekhinah?
3. How does the Covenant at Sinai affect Jewish practices?
4. Give two examples of how Pikuach Nefesh could override Shabbat laws.
5. How do Orthodox and Reform Jews interpret the Mitzvot differently?

Exam practice

In this exam practice section you will see examples for the exam question types: **a**, **b**, **c** and **d**. You can find out more about these on pages 6–7. Questions (a) and (d) in the **Exam question review** section below show strong student answers. Questions (b) and (c) in the **Improve it!** section need improvement.

Exam question review

(a) Outline **three** things that would happen in a Jewish home to celebrate Shabbat. (3)

The house would be cleaned and tidied, and may be decorated with flowers.
A special meal is served on the Friday evening.
There will be no work carried out.

> (d) 'Festivals are important because the Tenakh instructs Jews that they must celebrate certain events.' Evaluate this statement considering arguments for and against. In your response you should:
> - refer to Jewish teachings
> - refer to different Jewish points of view
> - reach a justified conclusion. (12)

For Jews there are times for happiness and times for commemoration, and many of these are based on teachings in the Tenakh. However, not all are because some link to historical or community events such as the harvest festivals.

Festivals are usually celebrated at home and in the synagogue. They are important because they help Jews remember their history: Pesach is a reminder of the escape to freedom written in Exodus, as well as the barley harvest festival. Rosh Hashanah is the Jewish New Year and celebrating it is specified in Leviticus 23:24–25 when it says the first day of the seventh month must be a holy day.

Yom Kippur is based on Leviticus 16:20–22 when a goat was sent into the desert carrying the sins of the Israelites. It is also called the Day of Atonement and Jews reflect on their sins and seek forgiveness.

While most Jews will celebrate festivals such as Yom Kippur, some like Sukkot may not be celebrated, or celebrated for less time than the specified 8 days. Orthodox Jews may feel festivals are important to continue as they are traditional. Reform and Liberal Jews may feel they help Jews today understand their faith better.

In conclusion, I think festivals are not only important because they are in the Tenakh, but because they also help Jews understand their history and connect Jews in worldwide celebration.

Improve it!

These answers will not get full marks. Can you rewrite and improve them?

> (b) Explain **two** reasons synagogue services are important to Jews. (4)

The word synagogue literally means 'bringing together' and is where the local community come together to pray. They are reminded they are part of a wider global community. It is also a reminder of the Temple.

> (c) Explain **two** reasons why prayer in the home or private prayer are important to Jews. In your answer you must refer to a source of wisdom and authority. (5)

Many Jews cannot attend the synagogue daily, so they need to pray in the home. Psalm 4:5 says 'reflect in your hearts while on your beds and be utterly silent.'

Deuteronomy 8:10 makes it clear that it is important to pray before eating food.

WHAT WENT WELL

The three answers written here give just enough detail to neatly sum up three different and relevant activities.

WHAT WENT WELL

This answer contains a series of detailed points which evaluate the statement thoroughly. Relevant sources of wisdom and authority are quoted. Different Jewish points of view are discussed and considered before arriving at a justified conclusion.

HOW TO IMPROVE

An answer needs two developed points; it is also good to put them as two separate paragraphs to make this clear. The second point is not developed to explain how the synagogue is linked to the Temple.

HOW TO IMPROVE

Two sources of wisdom have been included but the second point is not developed. How do Jews put this scripture into practice? You will not be penalised for including two sources, but you will not get full marks if you do not include two well-explained points.

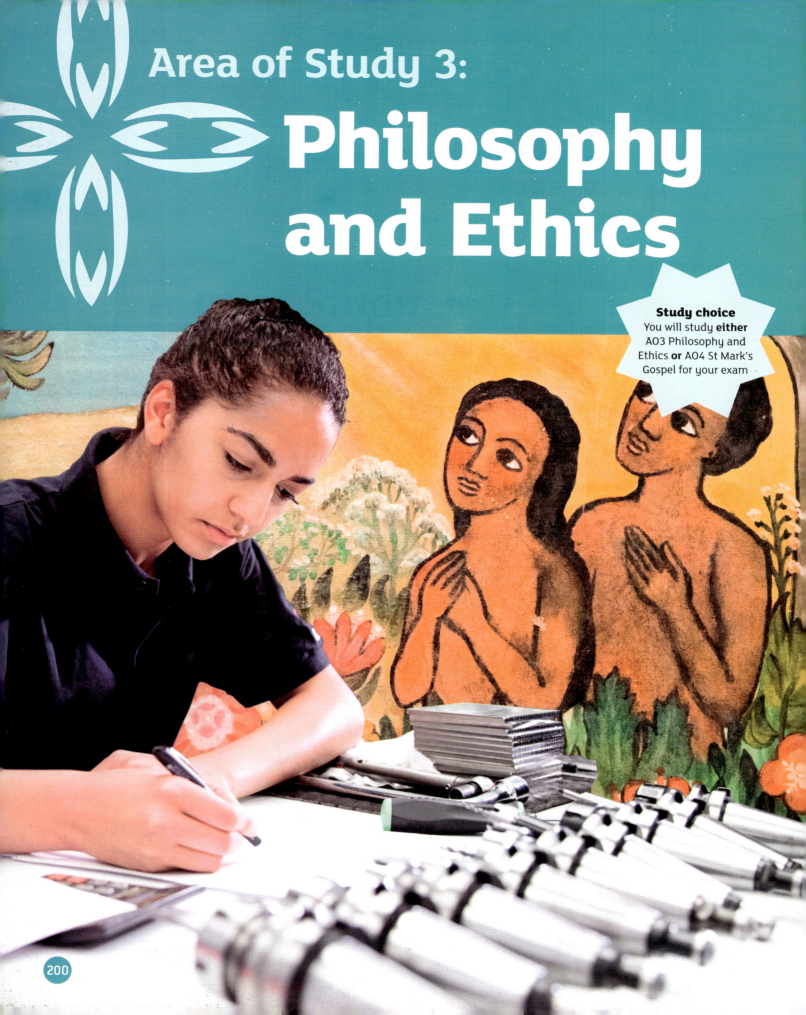

Area of Study 3:
Philosophy and Ethics

Study choice
You will study **either** AO3 Philosophy and Ethics **or** AO4 St Mark's Gospel for your exam

Chapter 9: Arguments for the Existence of God

Chapter 10: Religious Teachings on Relationships and Families in the 21st Century

9.1 Revelation

The nature of revelation

To reveal something is to uncover something that was previously hidden. In ordinary life, people sometimes say this when they learn something surprising about another person: 'Well, that was a revelation!'

When Catholics speak about revelation they mean the way in which God has made himself known to humans. Revelation is when God speaks to humans and tells them the things about himself that they could not otherwise know.

Revelation as proof of God

It is important to understand Christians do not believe God is trying to prove he exists: revelation is about God communicating and teaching. In doing so however, Christians believe revelation inevitably provides proof of his existence.

- Christians believe revelation is important because without it, humans cannot know who God is, which they believe is the meaning and purpose of being a human.
- Revelation is also a proof for Christians of God's love for humans. People only share stories and their inner life with people they love. Christians believe God also does this through revelation.

Jesus Christ as the culmination of God's revelation

Christians believe that God first revealed himself to the people of Israel. In the story of Moses, God speaks from a burning bush and first tells humans his name.

> 6 Moses said to God, "If I come to the people of Israel and say to them, 'The God of your fathers has sent me to you,' and they ask me, 'What is his name?' what shall I say to them?" God said to Moses, "I am who I am." And he said, "Say this to the people of Israel, 'I am has sent me to you.' 9
> *Exodus 3:13–14*

Catholics believe that Jesus is the final revelation of God – that God no longer spoke at a distance to his people but came down to earth through him and walked and ate with them as friends.

SPECIFICATION FOCUS

Revelation as proof of the existence of God: the significance of Jesus Christ as the culmination of God's revelation; what the revelation of Jesus Christ shows about the nature of God for Catholics, including reference to Hebrews 1:1–4.

A A revelation often uncovers a hidden truth.

B Moses was spoken to by God through the Burning Bush.

> ❝In many and various ways God spoke of old to our fathers by the prophets; but in these last days he has spoken to us by a Son, whom he appointed the heir of all things, through whom also he created the world.❞
> *Hebrews 1:1–2*

Jesus' physical presence as the Son is concrete proof for Christians of the existence of God. He was a man who could be seen and heard by all; this is why Jesus is sometimes called a gift – because he was the presence of God on earth: 'He reflects the glory of God and bears the very stamp of his nature' (Hebrews 1:3).

C Catholics believe that through scripture, the revelation of God can be better understood.

- Catholics believe this revelation of God through Jesus was first given to the apostles. These apostles then trusted the story of this revelation to the community now called the Church.
- The record of this encounter with God through Jesus is found in an authoritative way in the Bible – in the Old and New Testaments. The Bible is a book guaranteed by the Church to be a faithful record of God's revelation to humans.
- Catholics believe that still today, through the Church and the Bible, people can encounter Jesus and thus the revelation of God.

What the revelation of Jesus shows about God

The revelation of Jesus shows that God acts with love. In the Gospel of John, the Bible explains that:

- sending Jesus was a sacrifice for God
- God sent Jesus out of love for humans
- God sent Jesus to save humans and lead them back to faith.

> ❝'For **God so loved the world that he gave his only Son**, that whoever believes in him should not perish but have eternal life. For God sent the Son into the world, not to condemn the world, but that the world might be saved through him.❞
> *John 3:16–17*

SUMMARY

- Revelation is God revealing or showing something of himself.
- Revelation allows Christians to know what is true.
- Jesus is the complete and final revelation of God.
- The Bible is the most important source of revelation and is important today to lead Catholics to God.
- Revelation strengthens belief.

BUILD YOUR SKILLS

1. Explain, in your own words, what revelation means for Catholics.

2. **a** Choose a reason why revelation may lead people to believe in the existence of God and write one paragraph of an essay using PEE.
   b Write another paragraph for a reason why revelation may not lead people to believe in the existence of God.

EXAM-STYLE QUESTIONS

B Explain **two** examples of revelation in the Bible. (4)

D 'Revelation is the only way Catholics can know that God truly exists.' Evaluate this statement, considering arguments for and against. In your response you should:
- refer to Catholic teachings
- reach a justified conclusion. (15)

9.2 Visions

The nature and importance of visions

A vision may be seen as a form of private revelation; however, they do not always clearly explain something about the nature of God. For Catholics the content of these private revelations can only be accepted if they do not contradict anything taught by the Church.

- The Church has recognized some visions (for example, those of St Bernadette and Joan of Arc), which gives Catholics permission to believe in their truth.
- Visions may be of Jesus, Mary, one or more saints, or of angels. They may also take other forms and be only understood by the believer within their own personal context.

There are two main forms of visions that occur:

- **Corporeal visions** where people physically see something.
- **Imaginative visions** where people see something in their imagination or dreams.

Visions are important because they can:

- prompt action or greater faith from the person who experiences the vision and those around them
- suggest a direct calling from God or a possible vocation
- show the loving part of God's nature as a Father, offering guidance through visions
- demonstrate the mystery of God, setting a challenge or a test of faith, or prompting action which will mean a great change in a person's life.

Biblical and non-biblical examples of visions

Old Testament

One of the earliest visions in the Old Testament is that of Abraham, who is visited by God. He promises to protect and reward Abraham for his devout obedience to God.

> ❛After these things the word of the Lord came to Abram in a vision, "Fear not, Abram, I am your shield; your reward shall be very great."❜
> *Genesis 15:1*

New Testament

The transfiguration of Jesus in Matthew 17:1–13 is a key New Testament vision. Moses and Elijah appear to Jesus, Peter, James and John, and the voice of God is heard to speak:

This vision provides evidence for Christians that Jesus was the Son of God, and the presence of the Old Testament figures of Moses and Elijah confirms Jesus as the fulfilment of the Old Testament prophesies.

SPECIFICATION FOCUS

Visions as proof of the existence of God: the nature and importance of visions for Catholics; biblical and non-biblical examples of visions, including Joan of Arc and Genesis 15 and Matthew 17:1–13; reasons why they might lead to belief in God and Catholic responses to non-religious arguments (including atheist and Humanist) which maintain that visions are hallucinations and provide no proof that God exists.

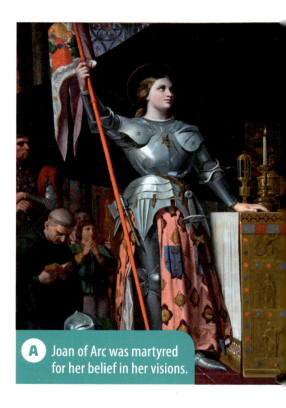

A Joan of Arc was martyred for her belief in her visions.

> ❛a voice from the cloud said "This is my beloved Son, with whom I am well pleased; listen to him".❜
> *Matthew 17:5*

Non-biblical

In 1424 a French peasant girl named Joan had visions of St Michael, St Catherine, and St Margaret who told her she must force the English from her French homeland. Joan had heard the voices of these saints from an early age, but this was the first time she received instruction. It took some time to convince the military leaders of her use but she eventually helped the army capture many French towns during the Hundred Years War. Eventually she was captured and sold to the English, who burnt her at the stake as a heretic in 1431 at the age of 19. She was made a saint in 1920.

Reasons why visions might lead people to believe in God

- Visions can be a powerful, personal experience, giving great strength and faith.
- There are many examples in the Bible and throughout history which allow people to interpret visions in a religious way.
- Private revelations are rare but, if they are authentic, may prove the existence of God. Richard Swinburne (1934–) claims that if God exists, we would expect him to make contact on occasion.

Arguments against visions as proof that God exists

Arguments against visions as proof that God exists are sometimes made by non-religious groups who suggest that:

- there is often no lasting or physical proof that visions have taken place
- they could be explained as hallucinations, misunderstanding, or simply made up
- even if the vision is believed to be genuine, there is no reason to see this as proof for God's existence
- dreams could simply be our subconscious wanting to have a religious experience.

Catholics argue that visions are only accepted if they do not contradict Church teaching, therefore visions are never considered in isolation and are supported by evidence for God's existence found in sources of authority such as the Bible.

B Our Lady of Walsingham: this is now the National Shrine for Catholics in England and Wales following eleventh century visions of Mary to a local noblewoman.

BUILD YOUR SKILLS

1 a Explain why visions are an important part of God's relationships with people in the Bible.
  b Outline an example from the Bible.

2 Write two paragraphs to explain why non-biblical religious experiences may or may not lead people to believe in the existence of God.

EXAM-STYLE QUESTIONS

A Outline **three** examples of religious visions. (3)

D 'Religious visions have no relevance for Catholics today.' Evaluate this statement, considering arguments for and against. In your response you should:
- refer to Catholic teachings
- refer to non-religious points of view
- reach a justified conclusion. (15)

SUMMARY

- Visions can be life-changing, affect belief, and lead to a calling or vocation.
- Visions have been reported since Old Testament times and many believe they continue today.
- Many Catholics believe they demonstrate a way of God communicating with Christians, showing his loving and mysterious nature.
- Critics suggest that a lack of proof, or alternative explanations mean visions do not prove God exists.

9.3 Miracles

The nature and importance of miracles

A miracle is something that seems to break the laws of science and makes people think that only God could have done it. Miracles are recorded throughout history from the earliest times, and claims of miracles are still made today. They always involve a religious experience of some kind.

- If a person witnesses an event that they believe that God has caused or created, their faith is likely to be strengthened.
- For Catholics, the miracles that Jesus performed were clear signs of his divine nature and of the nature of God's kingdom. Jesus' miracles are often categorized into different types:
  – healing: such as curing people from illness
  – natural: such as calming the sea, generating more food or wine
  – **exorcisms**: the casting out of demons or evil spirits.

Biblical and non-biblical examples of miracles

Biblical

Miracles are evidenced throughout the Old Testament, including the miracle performed by God through Moses, as he leads the Israelites out of Egypt and parts the Red Sea.

> ❛Then Moses stretched out his hand over the sea; and the Lord drove the sea back by a strong east wind all night, and made the sea dry land, and **the waters were divided. And the people of Israel went into the midst of the sea on dry ground**, the waters being a wall to them on their right hand and on their left.❜
>
> *Exodus 14:21–22*

According to John's Gospel, the first miracle that Jesus performed was at a wedding in Cana. As the wine began to run out, Mary asked Jesus to help.

> ❛Now six stone jars were standing there […] Jesus said to them, "Fill the jars with water." And they filled them up to the brim. He said to them, "Now draw some out, and take it to the steward of the feast." So they took it [and] **the steward of the feast tasted the water now become wine.**❜
>
> *John 2:6–9*

SPECIFICATION FOCUS

Miracles as proof of the existence of God: the nature and importance of miracles for Catholics; biblical and non-biblical examples of miracles, including those at Lourdes and John 4: 43–54; reasons why they might lead to belief in God and Catholic responses to non-religious arguments (including atheist and Humanist) which maintain that miracles can be scientifically explained and provide no proof that God exists

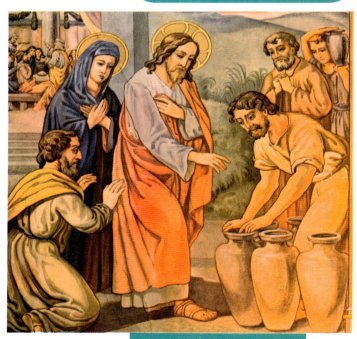

 Jesus turned water to wine at a wedding in Cana.

CATECHISM OF THE CATHOLIC CHURCH

'The signs worked by Jesus attest that the Father has sent him. They invite belief in him.'
CCC 548

Many of Jesus' most memorable miracles are those of healing (see 11.4); Mark 8:22–26 recounts the story of the blind man healed at Bethsaida. The man was physically healed and would have been welcomed back into the community (those with afflictions were often outcast as sinners). To be healed would suggest the forgiveness of his sins.

> ❝ And they came to Beth-sa'ida. And some people brought to him a blind man, and begged him to touch him. [...] Then again he laid his hands upon his eyes; and he looked intently and was restored, and saw everything clearly. ❞
> *Mark 8:22–25*

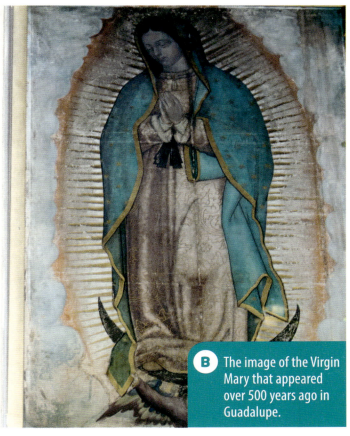

B The image of the Virgin Mary that appeared over 500 years ago in Guadalupe.

Non-biblical

Our Lady of Guadalupe: In 1531, in Mexico City, Juan Diego said the Virgin Mary appeared to him. She asked him to build a church where he stood and to collect a bundle of flowers. When he opened his robes, the flowers fell away to reveal an image of Mary. This can still be seen today in the Basilica of Our Lady of Guadalupe in Mexico City.

The painting remains as colourful today as it did 500 years ago, despite the Mexican heat, damage which strangely disappeared, and a bomb which damaged the altar but left the image unharmed.

Lourdes: In Lourdes in 1858 Mary appeared to a young girl called Bernadette Soubirous (1844–1879) 18 times. Mary pointed to a spring of water which Bernadette dug out and drank from. Lourdes has become a major place of Roman Catholic pilgrimage with over 5 million pilgrims visiting every year. It is connected to healing and a number of miracles have been attributed to the water.

Serge Francois had lost almost all the mobility in his left leg after complications from two operations. He made a pilgrimage to Lourdes in 2002 to pray for healing, drank the water, and washed his face in water from the spring. His healing was unrelated to any form of treatment and Francois made a 975-mile walking pilgrimage in thanksgiving for his recovery. This was declared a miracle in 2011.

Reasons why miracles might lead people to believe in the existence of God

- Since miracles have no natural scientific explanation, people see this as proof of God's existence.
- Those who were part of, or witnessed the miracle, may feel they have had direct contact with God.
- If there is no other possible explanation, even an atheist or **agnostic** may look to God as an answer.

🔑 **USEFUL TERMS**

Agnostic: a person who does not believe it is possible to know whether God exists or not

Exorcism: removal of evil spirits who have possessed a person

Arguments against miracles as proof that God exists

Arguments against miracles as proof that God exists are sometimes made by non-religious groups who suggest:

- Miracles could simply be coincidences, or unusual/uncommon events. Even if the probability is very low, very unusual things can still occur.
- Scientific and medical knowledge is limited, but always developing. Just because something is unexplainable now, does not mean it will always be unexplainable.
- Just because something is unexplainable, the explanation is not necessarily God, or proof that God exists.

Catholic responses

Catholics believe miracles are one way God communicates or interacts with humans and that they reveal the omnipotent nature of God. Both biblical and non-biblical miracles reflect events of unexplainable power, and healing miracles exemplify God's love for humans.

Because there are so many miracles within the Bible, Catholics believe it is not unreasonable to expect them to be possible today. John 4:48 suggests that Jesus said miracles were necessary to help Christians to believe: 'Unless you see signs and wonders you will not believe'. Examples in the Bible where miracles were difficult, or when the person in need was not present, such as the official's son in John 4:43–54 demonstrate the need for faith. This is not a quality which can be explained or justified by science.

> ❛Jesus said to him, "Go; your son will live." The man believed the word that Jesus spoke to him and went his way.❜
> *John 4:50*

Some Christians and non-Christians struggle with the idea that not every request for healing is granted, or that miracles fail to happen in times of crisis. Many Catholics explain God cannot say yes to every request, and that a denial may be part of a bigger plan for that individual which only an omniscient God can understand (see 9.7, 9.8, and 2.4 for further discussion).

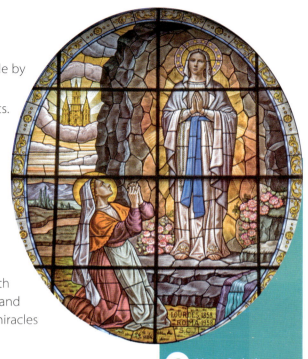

 C Many Catholics believe that healing miracles such as those at Lourdes reveal God's love.

✐ BUILD YOUR SKILLS

1 Explain in your own words:
- what a Catholic understands a miracle to be
- why they are important.

2 Explain why some people are sceptical of miracles.

 EXAM-STYLE QUESTIONS

B Explain **two** reasons why a miracle may lead someone to believe in God. (4)

C Explain **two** reasons why some Catholics see non-biblical miracles as good evidence for God's existence. In your answer you must refer to a source of wisdom and authority. (5)

SUMMARY

- A miracle is an event that appears to break the laws of science.
- Catholics and other Christians may claim God is the only explanation.
- Catholics believe that miracles provide evidence of God interacting with humans. They offer an explanation for the unexplainable.
- Critics argue that they are still not proof that God exists. There may be other answers and explanations, even if people don't know them yet.

9.4 Religious experiences

The nature of religious experiences

It is hard to know the true number of religious experiences; however, a survey in the USA in 2006 by Ipsos found that 47 per cent of the people they asked had had a religious or mystical experience. There are similar surveys in the UK, and the number of experiences reported has been steadily increasing since the 1960s.

Catholics would be cautious about the term 'mystical experience' however, which would not be the same thing as a religious experience if it did not feature the presence of God.

- A religious experience, sometimes described as **numinous**, is a feeling of the presence of God which fills a person with awe and sometimes fear.
- This may occur in a religious building, a beautiful place, or when witnessing the natural world.
- People may feel an awareness of something greater than them and this, they feel, is God. This may go beyond their usual use of the five senses.
- It is often described as an experience of *transcendence* which means going beyond human experience and existing outside of the material world.
- For Catholics, it can be an important reminder of the omnipresence of God. It may also confirm God's role as creator and designer of the world.
- The experiences often build faith, or give people a sense of encouragement.

Religious experience and revelation

Catholics believe that Jesus was the final and complete revelation. Therefore religious experiences cannot be regarded as revelations. However, the Catholic Church suggests in CCC 66–67 that the revelation of Jesus could be further *explained*, and some private revelations have been recognized by the Church.

SPECIFICATION FOCUS

Catholic attitudes towards religious experiences and its use as a philosophical argument for the existence of God: the nature of religious experience and why not all religious experiences are approved by the Church, including reference to Catechism of the Catholic Church 66–67; Catholic responses to non-religious (including atheist and Humanist) arguments that religious experiences do not provide proof that God exists.

USEFUL TERM

Numinous: having a mysterious, spirit, or holy quality

A The beauty and power of nature can inspire a feeling of the numinous.

In this way, the Catholic Church accepts God may wish to continue to communicate with Christians, but maintains that anything he reveals should be interpreted as:

- secondary to the revelation of Jesus
- only able to provide insight to understand what has already been revealed.

Private revelations will contain no new revelation.

The Catholic Church cannot investigate every religious experience reported to them, but they do rigorously examine some, before recognizing any as authentic.

Philosophical arguments

Whether a religious experience is recognized or not, individuals may feel they provide a philosophical argument for the existence of God. Christian philosopher Richard Swinburne said that it is reasonable to believe that the world is probably as we experience it to be; this is his Principle of Credulity. Therefore, unless we have a specific reason to question a religious experience, we ought to accept that it is at least possible that it is evidence for the existence of God. He suggested that religious experiences increase the probability of God's existence, even if they are not strong evidence on their own.

Why religious experiences may not be proof that God exists

Laws of nature

However, many people do not believe that religious experiences are strong evidence, and argue that they provide no useful evidence when arguing for the existence of God. David Hume (1711–1776) criticized miraculous religious experiences because they defy the laws of nature by which every human exists. He argued the following:

- Miracles contradict the laws of nature.
- Laws of nature are unbreakable – every human can observe they are true without exception.
- Therefore this means there is more evidence in favour of the laws of nature (every human experience) than in miracles (the experience of a small number of humans).
- A wise man should 'proportion his belief to the evidence', so it is unreasonable to believe a miracle has occurred.

Lack of evidence

For many religious experiences, there is no testable evidence to prove the truth of what happened. Often the event is brief, and only experienced by one or a small number of people. It is simply not possible to test religious experiences in the way a sceptic would want to.

Use of stimulants

There are various drugs which relax the user and may make them more open to religious experiences. Drugs which cause hallucinations or strengthen the senses may provide experiences similar to religious experiences. Other drugs

CATECHISM OF THE CATHOLIC CHURCH

'no new public revelation is to be expected before the glorious manifestation of our Lord Jesus Christ. Yet even if Revelation is already complete, it has not been made completely explicit; **it remains for Christian faith gradually to grasp its full significance** over the course of the centuries.'
CCC 66

CATECHISM OF THE CATHOLIC CHURCH

'Throughout the ages, there have been so-called "private" revelations, some of which have been recognized by the authority of the Church. They do not belong, however, to the deposit of faith.'
CCC 67

B Miracles defy the laws of nature.

could produce a vision or a feeling of the numinous. Peyote is a drug used by indigenous Americans intentionally to provide meditative spiritual experiences.

Hallucinations

Hallucinations are usually vivid, substantial, and realistic. They can take many forms and involve a variety of the senses. They may appear to be of a religious nature and similar to a religious experience, sometimes including visions.

- They can be caused by a wide variety of conditions including anxiety, stress, grief, migraine, narcolepsy, Parkinson's disease, and epilepsy.
- Hallucinations could be mistaken for visions.

Wish fulfilment

Psychologist Sigmund Freud (1858–1939) saw religious experiences as 'wish fulfilment', claiming religious humans revert to childlike feelings and have great delusions. Others claim that humans yearn for a being that will satisfy all their dreams and desires. As such, humans can be encouraged to believe religious experiences because they have an inner desire to do so. Dreams can also be part of the subconscious and such a dream with religious content may well be simply part of the 'wish fulfilment'.

Catholic responses to the question of proof

- As an omnipotent being God is not bound by the laws of nature, so it is to be expected that miracles or religious experiences can and do break them.
- Just because an experience leaves no evidence, doesn't mean it didn't happen. Many Catholics believe that faith does not require proof.
- Catholics do not disagree that drugs, hallucinations, and wish fulfilment can have similar effects to religious experiences. For these, and other reasons, the Church does not lightly recognize religious experiences as true private revelations.

C A modern crime scene can be tested in many different ways, unlike most religious experiences.

D Hallucinations could have religious content; are these religious experiences?

BUILD YOUR SKILLS

1 a Explain what a Catholic may understand as a religious experience.
  b Why are they sometimes hard to describe?

2 Create a mind map of reasons for and against religious experiences being used to convince a non-believer of God's existence.

SUMMARY

- A religious experience is a feeling of the divine presence of God.
- Catholics believe it is confirmation of God's role in the world.
- Religious experiences have occurred from Biblical times. Many claim they still happen today.
- Some critics argue miraculous religious experience defies the laws of nature.
- There is often a lack of credible evidence for religious experiences.
- It is hard to prove anything about God from them: they may be explainable as just wish fulfilment, or hallucinations caused by stimulants or illness.

EXAM-STYLE QUESTIONS

A Outline **three** reasons some people do not think religious experience is proof for God's existence. (3)

D 'Religious experience is genuine proof of God's existence.' Evaluate this statement, considering arguments for and against. In your response you should:
- refer to Catholic teachings
- refer to non-religious points of view
- reach a justified conclusion. (15)

The design argument

The classical design argument

The design argument suggests that because so much of the natural world appears to be deliberately designed with order and purpose, there must be a designer, and that this designer is God.

- It is sometimes called the **teleological** argument, and is found in many different philosophy and belief systems.

- The earliest recorded versions feature in both ancient Greece and Rome. Roman philosopher Cicero (106–43BCE) said: 'What could be more clear or obvious when we look up to the sky and contemplate the heavens, than that there is some divinity or superior intelligence?'

- Catholic theologian St Thomas Aquinas wrote at length about the design argument as one of 'Five Ways' to prove the existence of God (see 9.6). He argued that even things that 'lack knowledge' such as plants are 'directed to their end' by God: they have direction and purpose. He gives the metaphor of the arrow – on its own it can't know where to aim, but an archer gives it purpose.

- William Paley (1743–1805), an Anglican vicar, made an important argument using an analogy of a watch. If you came across a watch in a field and examined it, you would not assume the parts had come together by chance; it is clearly something which has been designed with purpose. Therefore you should not assume the order of the universe is accidental; he believed it was designed with purpose, as explained within the Bible.

The strengths of the argument

It is based on our own experience of design

- There appear to be many designed, ordered, or purposeful objects.
- These are things which everyone can observe.

It complements a Christian view of the nature of God

- It suggests purpose for human lives, which strengthens faith.
- Philosophers say a designer must be omnipotent and omniscient which supports the Catholic view of God.
- It provides a complete explanation of the design in the universe.

It encourages scientific examination of the universe

- The argument brings science and religion to agreement.
- It encourages and deepens the study of science and nature.
- Attempts by science to discover the underlying rules of the universe make sense if they were created by an intelligent designer.

SPECIFICATION FOCUS

Design argument: the classical design argument for the existence of God and its use by Catholics as a philosophical argument for the existence of God; understandings of what the design argument shows about the nature of God for Catholics including Romans 1:18–24; Catholic responses to non-religious (including atheist and Humanist) arguments against the design argument as evidence for the existence of God.

USEFUL TERM

Teleology: the study of a thing's purpose or design

❝Ever since the creation of the world his invisible nature, namely, his eternal power and deity, has been clearly perceived in the things that have been made.❞
Romans 1:20

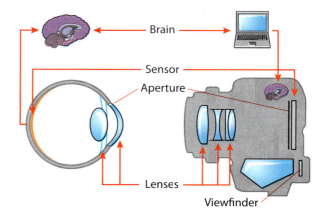

A The SLR camera and the human eye share striking resemblance in design. Is one designed and the other the product of evolution?

Evidence against the design argument

The uniqueness of the universe

- David Hume was a key critic of the design argument. He said the universe is unique and not like anything else, so we cannot use an analogy to explain it.

- Catholics would argue that just because something is unique doesn't mean evidence and experience can't be applied to it to explain it.

The existence of evil and suffering

- Evil and suffering are either signs that God is a poor designer, or that there is no designer.
- If a benevolent, omnipotent God is the designer of the universe, why is it not perfect?

- Catholics would argue that humans can learn goodness from their experience of suffering or evil.

B Aquinas argued that only the archer gives an arrow purpose.

There is no order – just the appearance of order

- Richard Dawkins (1941–) suggests that people see the world with 'purpose coloured spectacles': they only see order because they look for it.

- Catholics would argue that science and evidence support the concept of order.

Evolution as an explanation of order and purpose

- Evolutionary theory suggests that complex organisms have developed through genetic mutation and natural selection and not through design.
- There have been many evolutionary 'dead ends' resulting in extinctions in the natural world. If the universe is designed, why have there been so many design failures?

- Catholics would argue that science suggests the world could not exist as it currently does without the specific evolution that has taken place, therefore it must have been directed.

 BUILD YOUR SKILLS

1 **a** Note down examples of things in the natural world which appear to be designed.
   b Which two of these do you think are the best examples of design? Why?

2 Choose one of the weaknesses of the design argument and write one PEE paragraph of an essay explaining it.

? EXAM-STYLE QUESTIONS

B Explain **two** ways a non-religious person would argue the appearance of design in the world is not evidence of God's existence. (4)

C Explain **two** ways Catholics would argue the design argument is a strong argument for God's existence. In your answer you must refer to a source of wisdom and authority. (5)

SUMMARY

Strengths:
- The design argument is based on human experience.
- It gives Catholics a sense of meaning and purpose, and encourages scientific exploration of the universe.

Weaknesses:
- Humans cannot compare the universe to other things because it is unique.
- Evolution / natural selection can explain order and purpose in the universe.
- The world seems poorly designed to contain suffering.

9.6 The cosmological argument

The **cosmological** argument is the idea that there was something which began or started the universe. The ancient Greeks Plato (428–348BCE) and Aristotle (384–322BCE) called this something a **prime mover**.

St Thomas Aquinas wrote five arguments to explain the existence of God called the 'Quinque viæ'. Three of these connect to the cosmological argument and the idea of a first cause as an explanation for everything that exists.

The cosmological argument proposes that cause and effect are key features of our world, therefore:

- the very existence of the universe requires an explanation or 'first cause' (Aquinas' Argument of the Unmoved Mover)

- God is this first cause of the universe (Aquinas' Argument of the First Cause)

- without a first cause, the chain of cause and effect would stretch infinitely backwards into the past (called 'infinite regress'). This seems impossible: logic suggests there must have been a first cause (Aquinas' Argument from Contingency).

> ❝Now in efficient causes it is not possible to go on [back] to infinity … therefore **it is necessary to admit a first cause, to which everyone gives the name God**. ❞
> *St Thomas Aquinas*

The strengths of the cosmological argument

It is based on our own experience

- Everyone can see the evidence that all things in the universe we can investigate have a cause.

- It is difficult to deny that cause and effect exist in the world.

- Catholics believe that this disproves arguments that the universe does not need a cause.

It is more logical than the alternative

- It makes sense and fits with our experience of events within the universe.

- Believing in an infinite chain of causes and effects seems impossible.

- Catholics believe that this logic means there can be a total explanation of everything that exists, disproving arguments that a total explanation is impossible.

🔍 **SPECIFICATION FOCUS**

Cosmological argument: the cosmological argument for the existence of God and its use by Catholics as a philosophical argument for the existence of God, including reference to Thomas Aquinas' First Three Ways of showing God's existence; understandings of the nature and importance of what the cosmological argument shows about the nature of God for Catholics; Catholic responses to non-religious (including atheist and Humanist) arguments against the cosmological argument as evidence for the existence of God.

🔑 **USEFUL TERMS**

Cosmological: relating to the history, structure and dynamics of the universe

Prime mover: the first mover or first cause of all other moving things

A As a domino falls, it causes the next one to fall. Who caused the first one to fall?

It is compatible with scientific evidence

Most scientists argue that the universe does have a beginning (and that the Big Bang is the strongest theory), which is in-keeping with the cosmological argument that the universe needs a first cause. This makes it compatible with scientific thinking.

What the cosmological argument reveals about God's nature

Catholics believe the cosmological argument shows the omnipotent nature of God. Omnipotence is the belief that God is all-powerful. The cosmological argument shows that God has the power to do all things – to create a universe from nothing. Therefore his power is limitless.

Evidence against the cosmological argument

The impossibility of a total explanation

- Bertrand Russell (1872–1970ᴄᴇ) argued that a total explanation of everything that exists was impossible as all explanations rely on other earlier explanations.
- Humans should just accept the universe is here.

The universe as a whole does not need a cause

- Russell also said that just because everything in the universe needs a cause, it does not mean the universe as a whole needs a cause. We have no experience of universes being caused and created, so we cannot assume it needs a cause.
- David Hume said there is nothing wrong in claiming things can come into existence without a cause.

The first cause doesn't have to be God

- Some scientists are happy to use the Big Bang Theory as a suitable explanation for the start of the universe without the need for God.
- Catholics would explain everything starts somewhere, and only an omnipotent God could be the absolute beginning.

CATECHISM OF THE CATHOLIC CHURCH

'Of all the divine attributes, only God's omnipotence is named in the Creed. […] We believe that his might is universal, for **God who created everything also rules everything and can do everything**.'
CCC 268

B A visual interpretation of the Big Bang.

BUILD YOUR SKILLS

1 a In pairs, write down three examples of the universal law of cause and effect: "X happened because of Y".
  b Which of these would support the cosmological argument? Why?

2 Explain the key weaknesses of the cosmological argument.

EXAM-STYLE QUESTIONS

B Explain **two** strengths of the cosmological arguments for Catholics. (4)

D 'The universe needs a first cause. This is God.' Evaluate this statement considering arguments for and against. In your response you should:
  - refer to Catholic teachings
  - refer to non-religious points of view
  - reach a justified conclusion. (15)

SUMMARY

- The cosmological argument follows the universal law of cause and effect.
- St Thomas Aquinas proposed God was the first cause of the universe.
- Catholics believe the argument reveals God's omnipotent nature.
- Atheists argue that the world does not necessarily need a first cause, and there is also no certain proof that the first cause is God.

9.7 The existence of suffering

The issue of suffering for Catholics

Catholics believe that there is only one God who reveals himself as a Trinity of persons: Father, Son, and Holy Spirit. All **theists**, Catholics included, believe God possesses:

- **omnipotence:** unlimited power
- **omniscience:** complete knowledge of all human actions, past, present, and future
- **omnibenevolence:** unlimited goodness and love.

These create problems for Catholics, because if God is omnipotent, he has the power to stop suffering; if he is omniscient, he is aware of its existence in the world; and if he is omnibenevolent, he would surely want it to stop. This is often referred to as the classic 'problem of evil'.

The problem predates Christianity; the Greek philosopher Epicurus (341–270BCE) suggested that since there is evil in the world, there cannot logically be an omnipotent, omniscient, and omnibenevolent god.

The Christian theologian Lactantius debated the issue of suffering in around 300CE.

> ❝if He is both willing and able, which alone is suitable to God, from what source then are evils? or why does He not remove them? [...] He does not take them away, because He at the same time gives wisdom [...] **unless we first know evil, we shall be unable to know good.** ❞
> *Lactantius, Ch13, Treatise on the Anger of God*

The prophecy of Isaiah 45 suggests that God will grant favour to the good and punish rebels. Therefore some Catholics would believe that if the good suffer, they should keep faith because there is a purpose for this which only God understands.

Examining or rejecting belief in God

Suffering was introduced as one of the weaknesses of the design argument (see 9.5). David Hume suggested that the problem of evil is the 'rock of atheism', that is: its strongest argument against the existence of God. The philosopher J. L. Mackie presented the concept of the inconsistent triad considering how evil can exist if God is omnipotent and omnibenevolent.

The combination of any two of these positions leads to the third being logically impossible. For many, it is clear that evil and suffering do exist, therefore they come to the conclusion that either God does not exist or he is not worthy of worship.

SPECIFICATION FOCUS

Issues raised by the existence of suffering and God as all-loving: the issues it raises for Catholics about the nature of God, including Isaiah 45; how the problem and its basis as a philosophical argument may lead some to examine and others to reject their belief in God.

USEFUL TERM

Theist: a person who believes in the existence of God(s)

A The devastation of natural events can cause people to feel bewildered about the power of God.

Evil exists

Inconsistent triad

God is omnipotent • God is omnibenevolent

B The inconsistent triad.

God is frequently referred to as 'Father' within the Christian faith. Just as a good parent will discipline their child, so many Christians believe God does not stop bad things happening so humans can learn from their mistakes.

Natural evil

Natural evil leads to suffering which comes from natural events in the world which humans cannot control. These include:

- natural disasters like tsunamis and earthquakes
- illness and disease.

Natural evil often seems incomprehensible. Even if you accept that a person might suffer because of the actions they take, suffering because of natural evil does not seem a just punishment for victims if there has been no crime. Individual Catholics might feel that these are ways to test faith, and to challenge those who must face such difficulties, in order to make them stronger, and to make them appreciate the good in the world. Lactantius explained that without evil, humans cannot know good: that is why suffering remains in the world.

Moral evil

Moral evil causes suffering from actions carried out by humans, such as murder, theft, assault, and terrorism. Humans question whether, with omnipotent and omniscient powers, God could prevent the terrible actions which people carry out.

Catholics argue that humans have free will, and therefore must be allowed to act as they choose. Despite the sometimes evil consequences, it is a price you pay for true free will. Free will is an important idea for humans; indeed the suggestion that an individual does not control their own future is unthinkable for many. There are conflicting ideas about free will in the Bible but Catholics are guided by CCC 1730.

CCC 1713 explains that God has given man a conscience; in this way it could be argued that God constantly encourages humans to act in the right way, but they have the choice whether or not to listen.

C An individual may wonder why God did not stop a crime if he is omnipotent.

CATECHISM OF THE CATHOLIC CHURCH

'God created man a rational being, conferring on him the dignity of a person who can initiate and control his own actions.'
CCC 1730

CATECHISM OF THE CATHOLIC CHURCH

'Man is obliged to follow the moral law, which urges him "to do what is good and avoid what is evil". This law makes itself heard in his conscience.'
CCC 1713

BUILD YOUR SKILLS

1 **a** Outline the characteristics of God.
   b Explain how these create a potential challenge for Catholics.

2 Describe the types of evil. Do these need different solutions? Why or why not?

SUMMARY

- Evil in the world suggests there cannot be an omnipotent, omniscient, and omnibenevolent God.
- Lactantius argued that you must know evil to know good.
- Catholics believe in free will, and that suffering can be a consequence.
- Moral evil and natural evil present different problems for Catholics.
- Some Catholics question or reject God over the issue of evil and suffering.

EXAM-STYLE QUESTIONS

A Outline **three** reasons Catholics might give for the existence of suffering in the world. (3)
B Explain **two** reasons linked to suffering that a non-religious person may use to reject God. (4)

9.8 Solutions to the problem of suffering

Catholic responses to suffering

'For everything created by God is good.'
1 Timothy 4:4

Catholics believe that God is creator of all, and that all of his creation was good. It is therefore important to consider how Catholics, and other Christians, reconcile obvious suffering or evil with a belief in God. Catholics do not believe that evil is a thing in itself, but an absence of good, or a wrong choice – just as darkness is not a thing in itself, more an absence of light.

Biblical responses

Job: The Book of Job is an epic poem about a righteous man named Job who is allowed by God to be tested and tormented by Satan. The story of Job can give individuals who are suffering strength, but it also emphasizes that suffering and the reasons for suffering are not something that can always be understood by humans. God suggests it is arrogant to assume that they can: 'Shall a faultfinder contend with the Almighty?' (Job 40:2).

Psalms: The Psalms make it clear that it is correct to believe in a God who is:

- omnipotent: 'Whatever the Lord pleases he does, in heaven and on earth' (Psalm 135:6).
- omniscient: 'Great is our Lord, and abundant in power; his understanding is beyond measure' (Psalm 147:5).
- omnibenevolent: 'For the Lord is good; his steadfast love endures for ever' (Psalm 100:5).

Psalm 119 also teaches Christians that they can learn from their previous suffering: 'It is good for me that I was afflicted, that I might learn thy statutes' (Psalm 119:71).

New Testament: Christians believe the New Testament reveals a God who suffered in Jesus. For Catholics, the answer to any problem of evil has Christ at the heart of the answer: that there must be a higher purpose to suffering, which may not be comprehensible to humans.

Theoretical responses

St Irenaeus (130–202CE) was a bishop who argued that God was responsible for allowing evil, but that it was justified in its existence. He argued humans had two stages: first, made in the image of God, but incomplete; second, growing towards perfection, to be like God through their exercise of free will.

SPECIFICATION FOCUS

The solutions offered to the problem of suffering and a loving and righteous God within Catholicism: biblical, theoretical and practical responses – Psalms, including reference to Psalm 119, Job, free will (St Augustine), as a way for humans to develop (St Irenaeus), prayer, and charity; divergent understandings within Christianity of their success in solving the problem.

USEFUL TERM

Theodicy: a theory/defence of why God permits evil

 A Job lost everything during his trials.

St Irenaeus said evil and suffering exist because these are the best way for humans to develop: without them, people cannot learn to make the correct moral choices.

St Augustine of Hippo (354–430ᴄᴇ), another bishop, concluded that evil exists in the world because humans have abused their free will and corrupted goodness. He said that humans must use their free will to choose the right actions and reject evil to improve their soul, no matter how hard: the reward is heaven.

Philosophers and theologians continue today to try to explain how the existence of God can be reconciled with the suffering that exists in the world. John Hick (1922–2012) updated Irenaeus' **theodicy** and Alvin Plantinga (1932–) has developed a 'free will defence' using parts of Augustine's theodicy.

Practical responses

Prayer

Catholics are given the opportunity to share their suffering with God in prayer, and this may give a sense of relief. During the Mass, prayers of intercession are offered for those locally, nationally, and internationally who are suffering. The community shares in the suffering and asks God to help those in need. For some Catholics, prayer may be the only meaningful response.

Charity

Catholics believe Jesus calls them to help those in need because helping others is the same as helping Christ. Matthew 25:31–46, the Parable of the Sheep and Goats, makes it clear that those who help others will be rewarded with a place in heaven (see 2.7 and 2.8).

Success of solutions

For many Christians, the Bible is a reminder not only of the suffering of Jesus on the cross, but of many of the early Christians and the people of God in the Old Testament. Some may look at the theoretical solutions found in the study of philosophy; others dedicate their lives to practical solutions. For many, suffering remains a mystery.

- There were approximately 2.2 billion Christians in the world as of 2011 (Pew Research Center), which suggests the problem of suffering is one that many are able to overcome, even if they struggle with it.
- However, it remains a key factor in some Christians ceasing to practise their faith.

B For some, prayer can ease suffering.

'When we see children suffer it wounds our hearts: it is the mystery of evil [...] we must not deny our failure but rather open ourselves trustingly to hope in God, as Jesus did.
Pope Francis – The Infinite Tenderness of God

EXAM-STYLE QUESTIONS

C Explain **two** ways Catholics might respond to the problem of suffering. In your answer you must refer to a source of wisdom and authority. (5)

D 'The Bible offers the best solutions to the problems of suffering.' Evaluate this statement considering arguments for and against. In your response you should:
- refer to Catholic teachings
- refer to different Christian points of view
- reach a justified conclusion. (15)

BUILD YOUR SKILLS

1. a Identify three biblical responses to suffering.
   b Outline one theoretical solution.
   c Describe two practical solutions Catholics might offer.
2. Pick the most successful solution and explain why you have chosen it.

SUMMARY

- The Bible shows God is omnipotent, omniscient, and omnibenevolent, and tells of individuals who suffered greatly but remained faithful.
- St Irenaeus and St Augustine tried to solve the problem of evil and suffering in their theodicies.
- Charity and prayer can be practical solutions for many Catholics.

Revision

REVIEW YOUR KNOWLEDGE

1. What is the most important source of revelation for Catholics?
2. Identify two reasons why visions may not lead someone to religious belief.
3. Define a miracle.
4. Recall the term used to describe a feeling of the divine presence of God.
5. Name a scholar who argued for the Design Argument as proof that God exists.
6. Name a scholar who argued against the Design Argument as proof that God exists.
7. Give two examples of the different types of evil.
8. What is a theodicy.

* See page 288 for answers.

EXTEND YOUR KNOWLEDGE: RESEARCH TASKS

For a research task, try to put together a full side of A4 of your own writing on the topics below.

1. Research Padre Pio of Pietrelcina and the sources of his faith: visions and miracles.
2. Research Father Georges Lemaître and his contribution to the Big Bang theory.
3. Research the response of a Catholic agency to a natural disaster, e.g. CAFOD, Trócaire, or SCIAF.
4. Research the work of Sister Helen Prejean and her work with those who have carried out acts of moral evil.

USEFUL TERMS

Do you know what these words mean?

Agnostic   Exorcism   Numinous   Teleology   Cosmological   Prime Mover   Theist   Theodicy

Atheist   Omnipotence   Omniscience   Benevolence   Revelation   Nature miracles

Exam practice

In this exam practice section you will see examples for the exam question types: **a**, **b**, **c** and **d**. You can find out more about these on pages 6–7. Questions (b) and (c) in the **Exam question review** section below show strong student answers. Questions (a) and (d) in the **Improve it!** section need improvement.

Exam question review

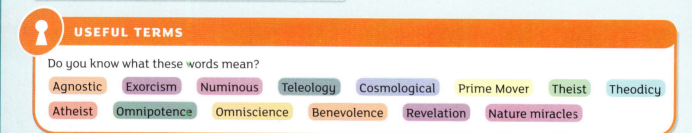

(b) Explain **two** reasons why a miracle may lead someone to believe in God. (4)

Since miracles have no natural or scientific explanation, they can be seen as proof of God's existence. An example could be a miraculous healing in Lourdes that doctors cannot explain.

People who directly experienced the miracle would feel like God has made direct contact with them and this would strengthen their belief, some may even become a priest or nun.

(c) Explain **two** ways Catholics would argue the design argument is a strong argument for God's existence. In your answer you must refer to a source of wisdom and authority. (5)

The design argument is a strong argument as it relies on evidence in the world around us. We can observe the complex parts of nature, such as the human eye, which indicate to Catholics there must be a designer.

The idea of purpose and design are made very clear in the book of Genesis when it describes the design of the world and its being made in 6 days by God. It even makes clear that humans were designed in the image of God to have dominion over creation.

Improve it!

These answers will not get full marks. Can you rewrite and improve them?

(a) Outline **three** examples of religious visions. (3)

St Bernadette in Lourdes and Joan of Arc.

(d) 'The Bible offers the best solutions to the problems of suffering.' Evaluate this statement considering arguments for and against. In your response you should:
- refer to Catholic teachings
- refer to different Christian points of view
- reach a justified conclusion. (15)

Catholics need to respond to the problem of suffering.

St Irenaeus said that suffering allowed people to grow towards perfection. Evil in the world helps people to learn to make the right decisions, one example would be their reaction to a natural disaster and giving to charity.

St Augustine said that it was the result of free will. Adam and Eve chose to disobey God and all of mankind must now suffer.

These theoretical solutions are useful and still used by philosophers today, as they help people understand why suffering exists.

10.1 Marriage

The importance and purpose

Catholics believe that God instituted (established) marriage as part of creating the world. On the sixth day, in the first creation story, God creates man and woman and tells them: 'Be fruitful and multiply, and fill the earth and subdue it' (Genesis 1:28).

- The Bible teaches that marriage is not just a human institution or legal arrangement, but something God established from the beginning of the world. This is why it is one of the seven sacraments in the Catholic Church.
- St Paul says that marriage bears witness to the everlasting love of Christ for his Church. Therefore, husbands should love their wives, 'as Christ loved the church and gave himself up for her, that he might sanctify her' (Ephesians 5:25–26). Wives, too, are called to love their husbands as the Church loves Christ (Ephesians 5:22–23).

For Catholics, the purposes of sacramental marriage are included in what the Church calls the marks, or external signs, of marriage.

- **Loving:** having a relationship of love and faithfulness
- **Lifelong:** having the lifelong support and comfort of each other
- **Exclusive:** being committed to only one marriage partner
- **Fruitful:** having the opportunity to procreate, have their own children, and the opportunity to bring up a Christian family. Infertile couples are not excluded from this. CCC 1654 explains 'their marriage can radiate a fruitfulness of charity, of hospitality, and of sacrifice'.

Catholics make promises to one another in the marriage ceremony to commit to these marks of marriage. Although they are known as marriage vows, they are actually promises, as vows are made to God.

Catholic teachings about marriage

Catholics believe that marriage comes as a gift from God. As a result, the vision of marriage is based on the Bible and is shown in the teachings and practices of the Church. It has these main elements:

- Marriage unites a couple in faithful and mutual love.
- Marriage opens a couple to the giving of new life.
- Marriage is a way to respond to God's call to holiness.
- Marriage calls the couple to be a sign of Christ's love in the world.

In all marriages that take place, the spouses make a legal contract with one another by signing the register. In a Catholic, sacramental marriage, the couple also enters into a covenant in which their love is sealed and strengthened by God's love. The legal contract can be dissolved. The covenant cannot – a true marriage cannot be brought to an end by human power.

A A Catholic marriage always takes place in a Catholic Church.

The Catholic Church teaches that marriage is union between a man and a woman because Genesis makes clear that man and woman were created for one another: 'a man leaves his father and his mother and cleaves [attaches] to his wife, and they become one flesh' (Genesis 2:24). CCC 1601 sets out the Church's view of marriage as a sacrament.

In 2014 Pope Francis led an interfaith conference *Humanum: An International Interreligious Colloquium* to discuss the views on marriage of different faiths. They included Catholic, Evangelical, Anglican, Pentecostal, Eastern Orthodox, Anabaptist, Mormon, Jewish, Muslim, Jain, Buddhist, and Hindu representatives, and the result was a book called *Not Just Good, But Beautiful* which celebrates the benefits of marriage. It strongly represents the Catholic view of marriage as a cornerstone of healthy families, communities, and societies.

Marriage in society

- Religious marriage ceremonies of all kinds reflect the individual set of beliefs of each faith.

- Christians believe in the sanctity, or holiness, of religious marriage. Non-religious people may argue a civil marriage is just as important and special for the couple involved. Secular Humanists have campaigned for Humanist marriages to be legally recognized to allow 'non-religious people the same choice that religious people have of a meaningful ceremony composed by a person who shares their values and approach to life' (British Humanist Association).

- Marriage also remains a legal ceremony. Catholics who undertake a sacramental marriage in a church do also get married legally: this is when they sign the registers. A legal marriage establishes rights and obligations between the couple, and with their children. It establishes protection if one of the couple dies, or decides to end the marriage. This is why the legal marriage is important in society.

- For many people (particularly the non-religious, secular Humanists, or same-sex couples) civil marriage is important as a time to make a public declaration of the love and commitment between persons.

Different views of marriage

Before 2014 same-sex couples could not marry, they could only undertake a civil partnership. Mixed sex couples had (and still only have) a choice of either a civil marriage or a religious marriage. Same-sex marriage became legal in England, Wales, and Scotland in 2014. The marriage ceremonies for these couples, and other civil marriage ceremonies between men and women, are non-religious and must be conducted by a civil registrar.

Some same-sex couples are religious and wish to have a religious marriage ceremony. In England and Wales, no one has a legal right to demand a Church performs a same-sex marriage. The Anglican and Catholic Churches do not permit them, but other religions may grant permission for a marriage ceremony in their religious building if they choose.

✝ **CATECHISM OF THE CATHOLIC CHURCH**

'The matrimonial covenant, by which a man and a woman establish between themselves **a partnership of the whole of life**, is by its nature ordered toward the good of the spouses and the procreation and education of offspring; this covenant between baptized persons has been raised by Christ the Lord to the dignity of a sacrament.'
CCC 1601

B A civil marriage allows a couple to share their commitment without religion.

Secular Humanists believe they should be allowed to be married by a Humanist celebrant, rather than a civil registrar. Humanist and non-religious wedding ceremonies are not legally binding unless performed by a registrar.

Not all couples wish to marry. Same-sex couples can undertake a civil partnership, which is a legal union with the same rights and responsibilities as marriage. Any couple can choose to simply cohabit (live together), but their legal rights are not automatically protected as they would be after a civil partnership or marriage (for example the right to inherit property).

Cohabiting families are, proportionately the fastest growing family type in the UK, with 3.2 million families in 2015 increased from 3 million in 2013, against 12.5 million families increased from 12.3 million of married/civil partnership type (ONS 2013, 2015 Changing nature of family type). This could suggest the importance of marriage within society is diminishing.

The Catholic Church forbids cohabitation as it tempts couples into premarital sex. It teaches that a sacramental marriage between one man and one woman is the only authentic way to form a partnership and raise a family.

C Humanist wedding ceremonies can be held in many different locations.

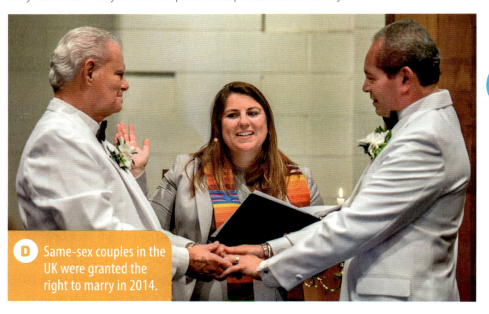

D Same-sex couples in the UK were granted the right to marry in 2014.

BUILD YOUR SKILLS

1 **a** What do Catholics believe the Bible teaches about marriage?

   b Why might a Catholic decide to get married within the Church?

   c How does this make the marriage different to other marriages?

2 **a** What other types of marriage take place?

   b Fully explain why the Catholic Church does not recognize same-sex marriage.

SUMMARY

- For Catholics, marriage is established through the creation story in Genesis.
- The Church sees marriage as uniting a couple and opens the couple to procreation.
- Catholics believe marriage is one of the building blocks of society and the best environment in which to bring up children.
- Marriage is important in society as it provides legal rights and responsibilities for the couple and their children.

EXAM-STYLE QUESTIONS

A Outline **three** features of a Catholic marriage. (3)

B Explain **two** ways non-religious views about marriage are different to Catholic views. (4)

Marital, unitive, and procreative

The Catholic Church teaches that sexual relations:

Unitive

Marital

'bring together a man and woman who are married for the purpose of having children.'

Procreative

The Church recognizes there are other positive things that arise from a sexual relationship within a sacramental marriage, including: increased spiritual connection, selflessness, happiness and pleasure.

Relationships outside marriage

The Catholic Church is clear on its teaching that sex should only take place between a man and woman married to one another. Therefore sex outside of marriage is wrong:

- **Premarital:** this is sex before marriage. The Church believes that sex is a gift from God to be enjoyed by a married couple to unify them as one and create children, so couples should abstain until married.

- **Cohabitation:** this is when a couple lives together before marriage. Usually they are also in a sexual relationship.

- **Same-sex:** this is sex between two men or two women. The Catholic Church teaches that to be homosexual is not a sin; however, homosexual sexual relationships are. The Church teaches that homosexuals should remain **celibate**.

- **Extramarital sex:** this is adultery – sex outside of marriage with a person who is not your husband or wife. This breaks the promises of matrimony, and would be grounds for a civil divorce. A sacramental marriage cannot be dissolved, and a divorced Catholic couple would still be married in the eyes of the Church.

SPECIFICATION FOCUS

Catholic teaching about the importance of sexual relationships: Catholic teaching about sexual relationships as marital, unitive and procreative, including Catechism of the Catholic Church 2360–2365; Catholic teaching on sexual relationships outside of marriage and homosexuality; divergent Christian, non-religious (including atheist and Humanist) attitudes to sexual relationships, including the acceptance of sexual relationships outside marriage and homosexuality and Catholic responses to them.

CATECHISM OF THE CATHOLIC CHURCH

'In marriage the physical intimacy of the spouses becomes a sign and pledge of spiritual communion.'
CCC 2360

CATECHISM OF THE CATHOLIC CHURCH

'the truly human performance of these acts fosters the self-giving they signify and enriches the spouses in joy and gratitude. Sexuality is a source of joy and pleasure.'
CCC 2362

A The Church teaches that having children is a key part of sexual relations.

B The Church believes cohabitation can encourage pre-marital sex.

225

Different attitudes towards relationships

- Since the 1960s family life in the UK has changed. Previously it was expected that people would not have sex until marriage, be married in church by the age of 25, live as a **nuclear** family, and not divorce. This is not the case now.
- Many people in the UK do not wait until marriage to have sex. Approximately 50 per cent of 17 year olds have had sex (Unicef, 2001).
- In the UK today, nearly half of babies are born to people who are not married: 47.5 per cent in 2012 (ONS, 2013), which indicates how many couples choose to cohabit.
- Same-sex marriage is legal in England, Wales, and Scotland due to changes in the law in 2014. This reflects a growing attitude of acceptance and tolerance.

Views of non-religious groups

Non-religious groups such as secular Humanists believe that individuals should behave morally, but that they should be allowed freedom within the limits of morality. This means that a sexual relationship between two consenting adults is perfectly acceptable to many, whether they are married or not. However, most humanists believe morality would suggest this should be a carefully thought-through decision, that contraception should be used, and couples should be faithful.

- Catholics would not agree sex before marriage was acceptable.
- The Catholic Church teaches that all forms of contraception are wrong (see 10.5).
- Catholics agree that couples should be faithful.

Catholics and many secular Humanists also agree with the principle of treating others as you would like to be treated (Luke 6:31). As a humane principle, it underpins how the majority of Humanists believe they should behave.

BUILD YOUR SKILLS

1. a What is the key teaching on sexual relations in the Church?
   b What three things can be identified from this?

2. a Describe four types of relationships that exist outside of Catholic marriage.
   b How might other Christians and non-religious people respond to people in these relationships? Why?

SUMMARY

- The Church teaches that sexual relationships bring together a man and a woman who are married for the purpose of having children.
- The Church teaches that sex connects couples in a spiritual and loving way.
- Today there are many types of sexual relationships that are acceptable.
- Non-religious groups such as secular Humanists often believe consensual and careful sex before marriage is acceptable.

USEFUL TERMS

Celibate: unmarried; and therefore not engaging in sexual activity

Nuclear: a married couple and their own children; a 'unit' of society

The 20-year-switch

How sexual activity has changed

Average number of partners of opposite sex over the lifetime (people aged 16–44)

1990–1991 survey

9 partners

4 partners

2010–2012 survey

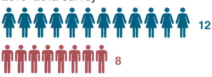

12

8

C Attitudes to relationships constantly change within society.

EXAM-STYLE QUESTIONS

C Explain **two** reasons why sexual relationships are important for Catholic married couples. In your answer you must refer to a source of wisdom and authority. (5)

D 'Non-religious and wider Christian attitudes towards sexual relationships conflict with Catholic teachings.' Evaluate this statement considering arguments for and against. In your response you should:
- refer to Catholic teachings
- refer to different Christian points of view
- refer to non-religious points of view
- reach a justified conclusion. (12)

10.3 The family

Procreation, security, and education

Catholics believe that the family was created by God as the basic unit of society, and as such is the place where children should be brought up.

- The family is the principal place for the education of children in morals – learning right from wrong.
- The family is where children first experience the Catholic faith and learn to pray.
- Pope Benedict XVI called the family 'a communion of love' (*Angelus*, 27 December 2009), which offers a secure and caring environment in which children can grow.
- The family is often called 'the domestic church' (CCC 1666), and is where children learn the love of God.

Catholic teaching is influenced by:

- the Holy Family of Jesus, Mary, and Joseph, who provide a model of family living: being faithful and obedient to God, protective, and dedicated to family life, serving the needs of the family before themselves
- sharing in the mission of the Church: family life is seen as a vocation for lay Catholics
- the purposes of the family, which are similar to marriage:
  - lifelong relationships of love and faithfulness
  - support and comfort of each other
  - to procreate and have children
  - to bring up a Christian family who receive the sacraments
  - to be a sign of Christ's love in the world.

'**The family is the best school at which to learn to live out those values which give dignity to the person** and greatness to peoples. In the family sorrows and joys are shared, since all feel surrounded in the love that exists at home, a love that stems from the mere fact of belonging to the same family.'
Pope Benedict XVI, Angelus, 27 December 2009

SPECIFICATION FOCUS

Catholic teaching about the purpose and importance of the family: Catholic teaching about the purpose and importance of families including: procreation; security and education of children; Catholic responses to the different types of family within 21st century society (nuclear, single parent, same-sex parents, extended and blended families), including *Familiaris Consortio*, 36–85.

CATECHISM OF THE CATHOLIC CHURCH

'The Christian home is the place where children receive the first proclamation of the faith. For this reason **the family home is rightly called "the domestic church,"** a community of grace and prayer, a school of human virtues and of Christian charity.'
CCC 1666

A Catholics believe the family has a responsibility to nurture and educate its children in faith.

The purpose of family

There are a wide variety of family types in society, but the purpose of family is often agreed upon – at least in part – by religious and non-religious groups.

The British Humanist Association for example states that: 'a family is any unit committed to sharing resources and to mutual support [and] the welfare of children' (*A Humanist Discussion of Family Matters*). The atheism commentator Austin Cline suggests that: atheists are concerned about] 'things like love, kindness, mutual respect, sacrifice, and building a better future together as a community [...] Families are defined by the love they have for each other and the work they do together.'

The goals some atheists and Humanists reflect many of those set out by the Catholic Church, but there are two key differences: Catholics take their beliefs from the teachings of God; the Church teaches that families should be formed as a consequence of a marriage between a man and a woman.

Catholics are called to faithfulness, so when a person faces difficulty they can receive the help and support of family. Catholics are called to seek marriage counselling in order to reconcile their own relationships for the benefit of their children. Forgiveness is a key part of Jesus' teaching.

Different types of family

The Church recognizes that different family types exist in society, but it believes the nuclear family is still the best type in which to raise a faithful Catholic family.

In 1981 Pope John Paul II produced an apostolic exhortation on the family called Familiaris Consortio. This communication aimed to reaffirm the Catholic Church's position on the meaning and role of marriage and the family.

Part 3 (36–64) is concerned with the role of the Christian family, including the rights and duties of parents to 'serve life' and educate their children as Catholics. Part 4 (65–84) concerns the pastoral care of the family, and includes what the Church should do to support couples before and after marriage.

- Despite some Catholics being outspoken about issues concerned with cohabitation, same-sex marriages, divorce, and remarriage, the Church has not changed any of its teaching on this topic.

- While reaffirming the Catholic Church's position that homosexual acts were sinful, but homosexual orientation was not, Pope Francis famously said in 2013, 'If a person is gay and seeks God and has goodwill, who am I to judge?'

- In early 2015, Pope Francis sent a questionnaire to all bishops in the world to seek input from Catholics of all levels, including lay men and women from all walks of life, about how the Church should respond to the sometimes difficult and controversial situations faced by modern families. These include same-sex marriage, divorce, and contraception. This was in preparation for a Synod on the Family in late 2015. The Synod made no significant changes to the teaching of the Church, but emphasized the pastoral responsibility the Church has for those who have struggled to live up to Church teaching.

B It is important to remember that these are not the only types of family. Many families are unique in their construction.

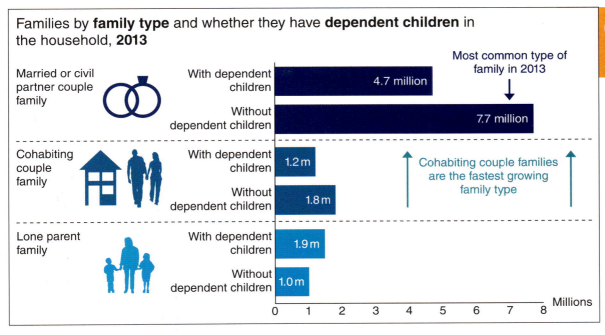

Families by **family type** and whether they have **dependent children** in the household, 2013

Married or civil partner couple family
- With dependent children: 4.7 million
- Without dependent children: 7.7 million — Most common type of family in 2013

Cohabiting couple family
- With dependent children: 1.2 m
- Without dependent children: 1.8 m

Cohabiting couple families are the fastest growing family type

Lone parent family
- With dependent children: 1.9 m
- Without dependent children: 1.0 m

Millions 0 1 2 3 4 5 6 7 8

C The changing nature of family type, ONS 2013.

Modern society includes a variety of family types in addition to the 'nuclear family' including: single parent, same-sex parents, extended, and blended. It can often be hard to categorize families and diversity has always existed in domestic arrangements.

In other countries or cultures, extended families with many generations living together are common. There have always been single-parent families created through the death of a parent or separation, and blended families created when such single-parent families unite in a new marriage.

The social differences and acceptance are the biggest change, particularly with single-parent families created through choice or separation, and same-sex parent families. However, some of these families still face discrimination, financial or emotional difficulties; but these are not problems that only affect the 'newer' types of family. Every family can face difficulties, and the Catholic Church recognizes that every family needs support whatever its type (*Familiaris Consortio* 77–85).

SUMMARY

- Catholics believe that the family was created by God and should be a faithful place for the upbringing of children.
- The family is the 'domestic church' that should be a community of faith, hope, and charity.
- Religious and non-religious groups share some ideas about the purpose of family.
- There are a great variety of family structures in the UK.
- Every family can face difficulties, and the Church says it should support every family, whatever its type.

BUILD YOUR SKILLS

1 a Explain the following three terms in the context of Catholic families:
   • procreation
   • security
   • education.
  b Which of these could be considered the most important? Why?

2 a Why do you think changes in family in the 21st century have occurred?
  b How did Popes John Paul II and Francis suggest Catholics treat families in difficult situations?

EXAM-STYLE QUESTIONS

A Outline **three** ways the family is 'the domestic church'. (3)
C Explain **two** reasons why the family is important for Catholics. In your answer you must refer to a source of wisdom and authority. (5)

10.4 Support for the family

Supporting families

Families are naturally important to parish life. Parents are often the current full members of the Church, and in time many of their children will be confirmed and become active members, living out the sacraments themselves.

A parish will often have many diverse activities and services for both parents and children, to encourage them to participate in the wider family life of the Church.

- The Catholic Church teaches that family life is important, and therefore each local Catholic church or parish is called to provide practical and spiritual support to families where possible.
- The Church realizes that there are many pressures and potential difficulties for Catholic families in modern society. Catholics are not immune from difficulties that are experienced in wider society and can struggle with relationship issues and parenting problems. This may include debt, domestic violence, separation, or infidelity.
- The parish is the local and immediate source of support and help.

Family worship

- Attending the Mass is an opportunity for a family to be together. In a society where many families don't even eat together, going to the Mass may be the only time in the week where the whole family sits down together.
- A liturgy more suitable for children also encourages attendance at the Mass for younger families.

Classes for parents

- These are often part of Catechesis programmes such as those for baptism or first Holy Communion. Parents are welcomed into the parish to learn about the sacraments, which can help them better understand Catholic teaching.
- Some parishes offer specific training on how to bring up children in the Catholic faith and how to be a good Catholic parent.

Family Group Movement

Family Groups are parish friendship groups and any member of the parish is welcome to join them. They encourage monthly meetings where members take part in a low-cost activity, and enjoy time together in support of each other and love of Jesus. Their inclusive nature encourages families, couples, and individuals to come together.

SPECIFICATION FOCUS

Support for the family in the local Catholic parish: how and why the local parish tries to support families, including through family worship, the sacraments, classes for parents, groups for children and counselling, with reference to the Family Group Movement and Catechism of the Catholic Church 2226; the importance of the support of the local parish for Catholic families today.

A Family worship encourages children to be present in church and allows families a chance to be together.

B Special sessions for parents will often be part of catechesis programmes.

> 'Family Groups offer our Catholic communities the chance to become more family-sensitive, friendly and welcoming, in line with the objectives of the Bishops' collaborative pastoral initiative: Everybody's Welcome.'
> *Bishop Peter Doyle, Patron*

 Children's liturgy can encourage young Catholics to think about their faith for themselves.

Groups for children

- There is often a range of groups that exist within the parish, from mother and toddler groups for the youngest members of the parish, to youth clubs, Girl Guide and Scout affiliated groups, and even young adult discussion groups. These allow children to socialize with other young Catholics even if they do not attend Catholic schools.
- 'Children's liturgy' during the Mass, when children leave the main service for their own liturgy, allows parents time to worship and helps children grow their own faith.

Counselling

- The parish priest is the first point of contact (and is usually trained in counselling) and may be supported by a pastoral team of volunteers within the parish or on a diocese level.
- Organizations such as Marriage Care provide free counselling for couples experiencing issues with their relationship. This is organized either by the parish, or independently by the couple.
- Natural family planning is promoted at diocesan level and often forms part of marriage preparation courses.

Other help

- Catholic charities such as St Vincent de Paul might help provide furniture for a struggling family who have been rehomed or are facing financial hardship.

CATECHISM OF THE CATHOLIC CHURCH

'Family catechesis precedes, accompanies and enriches other forms of instruction in the faith. **Parents have the mission of teaching their children to pray and to discover their vocation as children of God.** The parish is the Eucharistic community and the heart of the liturgical life of Christian families.'
CCC 2226

BUILD YOUR SKILLS

1. a Why does the Catholic Church see it as important to support the family?
   b Why do you think this is increasingly important in the 21st century?
   c Create a simple table that divides the different types of help:

Parents	Parents AND Children	Children

   d Which do you think would be the most important? Why?

SUMMARY

- Families are a core part of the larger Church family.
- Supporting family life is an important role of the parish. Families experience many difficulties and the parish is often the first source of help.
- Parishes may offer classes, groups for children, and counselling for the community. These will often help families overcome their problems.

EXAM-STYLE QUESTIONS

A Outline **three** ways the Catholic Church provides support for the family. (3)
B Explain **two** ways that children are supported by the Catholic Church. (4)

10.5 Family planning

Catholic teaching

The Catholic Church teaches that all forms of contraception are wrong. The Church encourages responsible spacing of births using the natural method of avoiding sex during the stage of a woman's menstrual cycle in which she is fertile and may conceive.

This teaching is important because the Church feels that contraception undermines sexual relations as unitive *and* procreative; the two things cannot be separated.

Papal teaching

In 1968 Pope Paul VI wrote an encyclical called *Humanae Vitae* (On Human Life). This encyclical confirmed the Church's position on family planning and the regulation of births. The Pope explained that preventing pregnancy 'contradicts the will of the Author of life'. Therefore Catholics who use contraception are defying God's will.

Since the papal encyclical, subsequent popes have reaffirmed its teaching. Catholic teaching suggests that contraception encourages sex outside marriage. Pope Benedict XVI explained this worries the church because 'if only the body is satisfied, love becomes a commodity' (*Deus Caritas Est*, 2005).

The Catholic position is not that Catholics should be forced to have children they cannot responsibly raise and support, but that Catholics should be responsible in their behaviour and remain faithful to the teachings of the Church and Jesus.

Sanctity of life

Abortion was expressly forbidden by *Humanae Vitae*. Pro-life groups campaign for the rights of unborn babies; sometimes these are religious groups, and sometimes they are secular. In the UK abortion is legal under certain conditions, but in some Catholic countries such as Ireland, abortion is only allowed when it is necessary to save a woman's life.

SPECIFICATION FOCUS

Catholic teaching on family planning and the regulation of births: Catholic teaching about artificial contraception and natural family planning, including reference to *Humanae Vitae*; divergent Christian, non-religious (including atheist and Humanist) attitudes to family planning, including acceptance of artificial methods of contraception by some Protestant Churches and the application of ethical theories, such as situation ethics, and Catholic responses to them.

✝ CATECHISM OF THE CATHOLIC CHURCH

'The regulation of births represents one of the aspects of responsible fatherhood and motherhood. Legitimate intentions on the part of the spouses do not justify recourse to morally unacceptable means (for example, direct sterilization or contraception).' *CCC 2399*

🔑 USEFUL TERM

Situation ethics: where right and wrong depend on the circumstances of a situation

A Pope Paul VI explained the position of the church regarding family planning.

Divergent attitudes to family planning

Like Catholics, some secular Humanists believe in family planning and the regulation of births. They believe in the importance of responsibility, and have always strongly advised the use of family planning. They believe having a baby is an important decision, but unlike Catholics, they believe that people, particularly teenagers, should be informed and assisted in obtaining contraception. The British Humanist Association states: 'If contraception results in every child being a wanted child, and in better, healthier lives for women, it must be a good thing.'

Atheists are often keen for individuals to make their own decisions based on rational thought. As they do not believe in God, some suggest that 'morality is a biological phenomenon and not imposed on us by a "supernatural" authority' (Atheism UK). This means humans should decide whether something is moral or right – or not. This includes the debates on contraception, family planning, and abortion.

Other Christian attitudes

Opinion between, and within, Christian denominations regarding family planning is varied. Some Protestant churches allow non-abortive contraception methods – preventing pregnancy rather than terminating it. The Church of England says 'Contraception is not regarded as a sin or going against God's purpose' and it also directs Christians to their conscience when deciding on having children: 'a responsibility […] laid by God upon the consciences of parents' (Church of England website). Individual Christians may feel that **situation ethics**, where right and wrong depend on the circumstances of a situation, or primacy of conscience (see 3.8) should play a part in their decision. Listening to their personal conscience, informed by Christian teachings, this may lead some to use artificial contraception to control pregnancy.

The Catholic Church does not agree with certain Christian or non-religious positions. They believe that:

- humans do not have the power to contradict the will of God regarding life
- sex outside marriage is wrong.

B Anti-abortion protestors include both religious and non-religious individuals.

BUILD YOUR SKILLS

1 List examples of contraception not allowed by Catholic teaching.
2 What is the natural method?
3 Outline the issues for Christian couples regarding:
- sexual activity
- pregnancy with a child with a disability
- pregnancy with a risk to the mother's life.
4 How might situation ethics apply in the above situations?

SUMMARY

- The Catholic Church believes any form of contraception is wrong.
- The Catholic Church believes only the natural method of family planning is acceptable.
- Some Protestant Churches such as the Church of England do not regard contraception as a sin.
- Many Humanists advocate contraception as responsible and better for everyone.
- Many atheists believe individuals should make their own rational choices, including when it comes to family planning.

EXAM-STYLE QUESTIONS

C Explain **two** reasons why the Catholic Church believes contraception is wrong. In your answer you must refer to a source of wisdom and authority. (5)
D 'For Christians, natural family planning is the most faithful way of avoiding pregnancy.' Evaluate this statement considering arguments for and against. In your response you should:
- refer to Catholic teachings
- refer to different Christian points of view
- refer to non-religious points of view
- refer to relevant ethical arguments
- reach a justified conclusion. (12)

10.6 Divorce, annulment, and remarriage

The meaning of divorce, annulment, remarriage

In the UK, a divorce is the legal ending of a marriage by a court. Some Christian denominations permit remarriage, but a Catholic sacramental marriage is a lifelong commitment. Although a Catholic couple could obtain a civil divorce in a court, in the eyes of the Catholic Church their sacramental marriage would stil exist.

An annulment is a declaration that a marriage was never valid and therefore never existed. You can apply for a civil or religious annulment but there are strict limitations on what events might make a marriage invalid. Annulment is relatively rare; 1 in every 20,000 Catholics gets an annulment each year, while the divorce rate is about 1 in 90 in any given year. To get an annulment you also need to have a legal divorce.

Remarriage is where one or both people getting married have been married before. The Catholic Church does not allow remarriage to anyone married in the Church. Matrimony is a sacrament and as a result of the vows, the only way that the marriage ends is when one of the partners dies, or it is declared never to have existed, and is annulled.

Church teaching

The Old Testament's teaching on divorce is clear: 'I hate divorce, says the Lord the God of Israel' (Malachi 2:16).

In the New Testament, it is apparent that any divorce that has taken place is wrong and a result of people's stubborn refusal to obey God. In the Gospel of Matthew, Jesus makes the teaching on divorce clear.

- The Catholic Church does not believe that a valid Catholic marriage can be dissolved because God has joined the man and woman together (CCC 2382).
- The Church does allow for legal separation and civil divorce if this is in the interests of the safety or health of the couple and children, e.g. if a parent is abusive or alcoholic (CCC 2383).
- However, the couple remain married in the eyes of God and the Church and so cannot marry anyone else (CCC 2384).
- This teaching is because
  - Jesus taught that divorce was wrong, and Catholics should follow this.
  - Matthew 19:8 says God does not want divorce to take place and any reference to it being allowed was when people stubbornly refused to obey God's law.
  - A covenant is made during the sacrament of marriage that cannot be broken by any earthly power.

SPECIFICATION FOCUS

Catholic teaching about divorce, annulment and remarriage: Catholic teaching on divorce, annulment and remarriage, including Catechism of the Catholic Church 2382–2386; divergent Christian, non-religious (including atheist and Humanist) attitudes to divorce, annulment and remarriage, including the application of ethical theories, such as situation ethics, and Catholic responses to them.

> "But I say to you that every one who divorces his wife, except on the ground of unchastity, makes her an adulteress; and whoever marries a divorced woman commits adultery."
> *Matthew 5:32*

> He said to them, "For your hardness of heart Moses allowed you to divorce your wives, but from the beginning it was not so."
> *Matthew 19:8*

A A civil divorce does not end a sacramental marriage.

Different attitudes to divorce

Other Christian attitudes

Most other Christian churches do allow divorce if the marriage has broken down. Many also allow remarriage within church, often after meeting with a priest or minister for counselling and repentance. This teaching is because:

- Some suggest Jesus allowed divorce when someone has been adulterous (Matthew 5:32).
- Christianity is based on forgiveness so people should be allowed a second chance if they confess and are truly repentant; this also applies to marriage.
- Christians sometimes need to pick *the lesser of two evils* and the effects of remaining in a broken-down marriage are, some would say, worse than getting divorced.

This final point is an example of situation ethics. Moral values influence the decision, but situation ethics suggests the greater goods of love and justice are the most important guiding principles. As love is at the heart of Christian belief, it is an ethical theory with a similar motivation.

Non-religious attitudes

The British Humanist Association believes that, 'Though marriage is a useful social institution, Humanists do not believe that it is "sacred", recognize that some relationships fail, and so support liberal divorce laws.' Most secular Humanists do not object to remarriage.

Catholic response

- Matrimony is a sacrament and should be preserved. The church offers help and support for couples, including counselling, to try to help them work through problems together.
- Catholics believe the needs of the family and children come above the needs of the individual.
- The effects on the couple and their children can be significant and long-lasting in an unhappy family home. It is sometimes important to end the civil marriage and relationship in the civil court.

B Unhappiness in marriage is a difficult issue.

✝ CATECHISM OF THE CATHOLIC CHURCH

'If civil divorce remains the only possible way of ensuring certain legal rights, the care of the children, or the protection of inheritance, it can be tolerated and does not constitute a moral offense.'
CCC 2383

✏ BUILD YOUR SKILLS

1. In your own words, define
   a) divorce, b) annulment,
   c) remarriage.

2. Which of these does the Catholic Church allow?

3. a What was Jesus' teaching on divorce?
   b Why do some Christians still not agree with divorce?

SUMMARY

- The Church does not believe divorce from sacramental marriage is possible.
- Annulment can only take place under strict circumstances.
- The Church recognizes civil divorce may sometimes be necessary.
- Other Christians do not encourage divorce, but allow it and remarriage as Christianity teaches forgiveness.
- Non-religious groups usually allow divorce and remarriage but encourage action in a family's best interests.

? EXAM-STYLE QUESTIONS

A Outline **three** reasons the Catholic Church does not allow divorce? (3)

D 'Divorce is not permitted by the Bible.' Evaluate this statement considering arguments for and against. In your response you should:
- refer to Catholic teachings
- refer to different Christian points of view
- refer to non-religious point of view
- refer to relevant ethical arguments
- reach a justified conclusion. (12)

10.7 Equality of men and women in the family

Equality in Catholicism

The Catholic Church teaches that men and women should have equal roles in life and equal rights in society. Both men and women can teach catechesis; distribute the Eucharist in the Mass and other locations such as the home of the sick; and perform many other jobs and lay roles with the Church. However, women cannot be ordained.

Attitudes in the Bible

The Old Testament is a story of election: people chosen by God. In Genesis Adam and Eve are chosen equally by God yet sin equally by both disobeying God. The narratives in Genesis can be interpreted in different ways to emphasize either the similarity or difference between men and women:

- It is clear in Genesis that both men and women are in the image of God, and as such equal:

  ❝So God created man in his own image, in the image of God he created him; male and female he created them.❞
  Genesis 1:27

- Eve was created from the rib of Adam (Genesis 2:22) for them to complement and fulfil one another's needs. By God's design and purpose neither is superior, although they are different.
- In the account of the Fall (Genesis 3), both Adam and Eve are cursed for their disobedience.

  ❝"I will greatly multiply your pain in childbearing; in pain you shall bring forth children [...] cursed is the ground because of you; in toil you shall eat of it all the days of your life.❞
  Genesis 3:16–17

The role of men and women in the family

The Catechism emphasizes the equality of men and women within the family in CCC 2207. Both the husband and wife are called to 'give themselves' in commitment both towards making their marriage work, and to create children. Neither one is given more or less importance, but the emphasis is on partnership. The Catechism refers to 'fraternity within society' meaning 'friendship', which further indicates the necessity of equality.

SPECIFICATION FOCUS

Catholic teaching about the equality of men and women in the family: Catholic teaching about the role of men and women in the family with reference to Catechism of the Catholic Church 2207, including the dignity of work within the home; divergent Christian teachings and attitudes about the equality and roles of men and women in the family and Catholic responses to them.

CATECHISM OF THE CATHOLIC CHURCH

'The family is the original cell of social life. It is the natural society in which husband and wife are called to give themselves in love and in the gift of life. Authority, stability, and a life of relationships within the family constitute the foundations for freedom, security, and fraternity within society.'
CCC 2207

A Adam and Eve were both punished in the Garden of Eden.

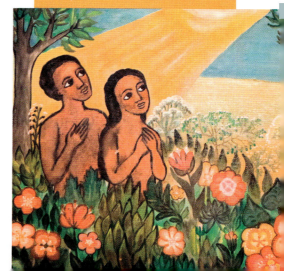

Dignity of work in the home

The phrase 'dignity of work within the home' does not mean the Church believes women should be confined to domestic work. Domestic work is of enormous value and can be done by either a man or a woman. Whoever does it, it is not less valuable than the work that is done in the world to generate income.

> ❝A just valuing of the work of women within the family is required. In this way, women who freely desire will be able to devote the totality of their time to the work of the household without being stigmatized by society or penalized financially, while those who wish also to engage in other work may be able to do so with an appropriate work-schedule, and **not have to choose between relinquishing their family life or enduring continual stress**, with negative consequences for one's own equilibrium and the harmony of the family.❞
>
> *Letter to the Bishops of the Catholic Church on the Collaboration of Men and Women in the Church and in the World*

Divergent Christian views

Other Christian denominations do have female clergy or ministers, such as the Church of England and Methodists. They would agree with the importance and equality of both men and women within the family, using the Bible as a reference for their belief.

Many Christians would agree that women should be supported as they attempt to juggle home and working life, as the Catholic 'Letter to the Bishops' above suggests. Others would also strongly argue that men should be equally supported in their work/home balance.

The importance of the family is agreed upon by all Christian denominations, and men and women are important as equal partners to the success of a family. This is increasingly accepted and promoted by mainstream Christian groups, reflecting the attitudes of society.

 'Dignity of work' means all work should be valued equally wherever it is performed.

 BUILD YOUR SKILLS

1 **a** What does the Catechism teach about the family?
  b What does it teach about the roles of men and women within the family?

2 Why is it important to the Catholic Church to promote equality within the family?

3 How might other Christian attitudes differ to those of the Catholic Church?

 **SUMMARY**

- The Catholic Church teaches that men and women should have equal roles in life and equal rights in society, except ordination.
- Genesis shows the equality but difference of man and woman: created in God's image.
- The Catholic Church believes that men and woman have an equal role in the family, and that they should be supported in a life outside the family too.
- Many other Christian denominations also believe in equality between men and women within the family.

 EXAM-STYLE QUESTIONS

A Outline **three** ways women are shown as equal in the Bible. (3)

C Explain **two** reasons why the Catholic Church promotes equality within the family. In your answer you must refer to a source of wisdom and authority. (5)

Gender prejudice and discrimination

What are gender prejudice and discrimination?

- **Gender prejudice:** believing people of one gender are inferior or superior purely on the basis of their sex.
- **Discrimination:** treating people less favourably because of their gender, ethnicity, colour, sexuality, age, class, etc.

Prejudice is the *thought*, and discrimination is the *action* that results from the thought. It is impossible to make thoughts against the law but discrimination can lead to prosecution.

Catholic opposition to prejudice and discrimination

> ❝There is neither Jew nor Greek, there is neither slave nor free, there is neither male nor female; for **you are all one in Christ Jesus.**❞
> *Galatians 3:28*

Galatians 3 makes it clear that neither the man nor the woman has a special advantage in being a Christian. God does not choose men in preference to women, or relate to men more directly.

Some people may cite references to women found in the New Testament which may seem to support gender inequality:

> ❝Wives, be subject to your husbands, as to the Lord. For the husband is the head of the wife as Christ is the head of the church, his body, and is himself its Savior.❞
> *Ephesians 5:22–23*

However, this comes straight after a passage that suggests *everyone* should be submissive to God and husbands should likewise submit to their wives: 'Be subject to one another out of reverence for Christ' (Ephesians 5:21).

In 1 Corinthians 14 St Paul speaks positively about the praying and prophesying of women yet within this same letter he says 'the women should keep silent in the churches. For they are not permitted to speak, but should be subordinate' (14:34). Many scholars suggest that it was St Paul's attempt to reduce the chaos in some early Church services. That is why Catholics oppose gender prejudice and discrimination.

SPECIFICATION FOCUS

Catholic teachings about gender prejudice and discrimination: Catholic opposition to gender prejudice and discrimination, including theology of the body; examples of Catholic opposition to gender prejudice and discrimination, including Catechism of the Catholic Church 1938; divergent Christian attitudes to gender differences, including the role of women in the Church, prejudice and discrimination and Catholic responses to them.

✝ **CATECHISM OF THE CATHOLIC CHURCH**

'Excessive economic and social disparity between individuals and people of the one human race is a source of scandal and militates against social justice, equity, human dignity, as well as social and international peace.'
CCC 1938

A Jesus did not make a distinction between men and women.

There are many examples of Jesus combatting the prejudice and discrimination of his time. However, many scholars argue the most striking feature is that these interactions with women are recorded in the first place. Jesus does not make any declarations about the role of women, he just treats them with respect and as individuals (see 12.7). A few examples include:

- the Samaritan woman at the well (John 4:4–26)
- the woman taken in adultery (John 7:53–8:11)
- the Greek woman (Matthew 15:21–28 and Mark 7:24–30).

The Catechism teaches that sexual discrimination is 'sinful' and 'open contradiction' of the teaching of the Gospels (CCC 1938). It suggests everyone should work towards fairer conditions for all because it affects the whole of humanity.

Between 1979 and 1984, Pope John Paul II gave a series of lectures on the meaning of the human body and sexuality known as the 'Theology of the Body'. One of the most important themes he considered was the original creation of man and woman as equal, complimentary partners for one another.

Divergent Christian attitudes

Some Christian denominations are keeping pace with secular attempts to wipe out prejudice and discrimination within religion and society. Some Baptist and Pentecostal denominations have been ordaining women for nearly a century. The Church of England ordained its first women priests in 1994, and its first women Bishop in 2014, although this was not without controversy within the Church of England. Some priests left the church to join the Catholic Church as a result.

The Catholic and Orthodox Churches do not believe in the ordination of women, nor do some Evangelical denominations. They suggest that Bible teachings from St Paul such as Ephesians 5:23, and the fact that Jesus did not have female disciples means women should not lead the Church. In 1994 Pope John Paul II issued an Apostolic Letter confirming the Church's belief that because of this 'the Church has no authority whatsoever to confer priestly ordination on women' (*Ordinatio Sacerdotalis*).

Women still play an active role in other parts of church life within Christian churches. In Catholic churches this includes teaching catechesis and distributing the sacrament of Holy Communion during the Mass (see 10.7).

 The Right Reverend Ruth Worsley, the Church of England's Bishop of Taunton.

 BUILD YOUR SKILLS

1 a In your own words, define a) prejudice, b) discrimination.
   b Give two examples of each.

2 Describe Jesus' attitude to women in the Bible using at least two examples.

3 Explain how a piece of scripture could be understood in different ways:
   - to support equality
   - to highlight difference.

? EXAM-STYLE QUESTIONS

B Explain **two** reasons why Catholics oppose prejudice and discrimination. (4)

D 'The Bible contains more teaching against gender prejudice than in favour of it.' Evaluate this statement considering arguments for and against. In your response you should:
   - refer to Catholic teachings
   - refer to different Christian points of view
   - reach a justified conclusion. (12)

 SUMMARY

- Sexism is discriminating against people because of their gender.
- Some passages in the Bible can be interpreted to suggest gender inequality, but others suggest men and women should support each other.
- Jesus did not discriminate against women, and set an example for Catholics today to follow.
- Christian denominations vary in the roles they allow women within their churches.

Revision

REVIEW YOUR KNOWLEDGE

1. What is the book Pope Francis wrote about marriage?
2. List the three things the Catholic Church teaches about sexual relationships.
3. What has been called 'the domestic church'?
4. Describe at least three of the ways the Church supports families.
5. What is the natural method of avoiding pregnancy?
6. Explain an annulment.
7. Name some of the activities both men and women can do in the Church.
8. Provide two examples of Jesus treating women with respect in the Gospel.

* See page 288 for answers.

USEFUL TERMS

Do you know what these words mean?

Celibate Nuclear Catechesis Atheist Sin

Denominations   Secular   Situation ethics

EXTEND YOUR KNOWLEDGE: RESEARCH TASKS

For a research task, try to put together a full side of A4 of your own writing on the topics below.

1. Research organisations such as Catholic Marriage Care or Explore Marriage. Explain how they help people before and during marriage.
2. Research Pope John Paul II's lectures on the 'Theology of the Body' 1979–84.
3. Research the roles of women in the Catholic Church before and after Vatican II.
4. Research the Church of England's change of rules to allow female ordination.

ONGOING LEARNING REVIEW

It is vital that you keep reviewing past material to make sure you have fully learned and remember it.

1. How is Jesus important as God's revelation?
2. What is Aquinas' contribution to the Cosmological argument?
3. What can Catholics learn from the story of Job?
4. Explain the inconsistent triad.
5. What are the arguments against religious experiences as proof that God exists.

Exam practice

In this exam practice section you will see examples for the exam question types: **a**, **b**, **c** and **d**. You can find out more about these on pages 6–7. Questions (c) and (d) in the **Exam question review** section below show strong student answers. Questions (a) and (b) in the **Improve it!** section need improvement.

Exam question review

(c) Explain **two** reasons why the family is important for Catholics. In your answer you must refer to a source of wisdom and authority. (5)

Catholics believe the family was created by God, as seen in Genesis 1 when Adam and Eve were created as partners. This means it is important and holy.

The family is also important because it is the place where children are taught the Catholic faith. The Catechism makes it clear that the family is the 'domestic church' where parents have the responsibility to bring up the children faithfully.

> (d) 'The Bible contains more teaching against gender prejudice than in favour of it.' Evaluate this statement considering arguments for and against. In your response you should:
> * refer to Catholic teachings
> * refer to different Christian points of view
> * reach a justified conclusion. (12)

The Catholic Church teaches that men and women should be treated equally, this means there should not be gender prejudice or discrimination. However the teaching in the Bible is not always clear and can be interpreted in different ways.

Catholics may refer to Galations 3:28 where it says 'There is neither male nor female, you are all one in Christ Jesus' to make it clear that there is no distinction between the sexes.

Jesus also treated women in a different way to others living at the time. For example, he saved the woman who was caught in the act of adultery and about to be stoned to death.

Some Christians feel it is right to keep women as second to men and use St Paul in 1 Corinthians 14 when he said, 'women should keep silent'.

Other Christians, such as those in the Church of England, may feel Catholics do not treat women equally as they do not have women priests, and therefore there is still gender prejudice justified by the Bible.

The magisterium of the Catholic Church guides Catholics on this issue by saying that sexual discrimination is 'sinful' (CCC 1938). Therefore Catholics should not interpret the Bible as supporting gender prejudice.

In conclusion, the messages in the Bible can seem confusing, but it is important to remember the historical context. Most Christian churches are clear that women should be treated equally, without prejudice, following the example that Jesus set.

Improve it!

These answers will not get full marks. Can you rewrite and improve them?

> (a) Outline **three** features of Catholic marriage. (3)

Loving and unitive.

> (b) Explain **two** ways that children are supported by the Catholic Church. (4)

Children going out during Mass.

 WHAT WENT WELL

Question (c) requires the same level of explanation as a question (b), but with the support of a well-chosen source of wisdom or authority. This answer has used two references; while this won't get you any extra marks, it demonstrates how references can be helpful to help you explain a point you wish to make.

 WHAT WENT WELL

It's a good idea to aim to write five or six well-developed points, covering the different points of view listed in the question bullet points. This answer achieves that, uses appropriate quotations, and considers the points of view against the question, arriving at a justified conclusion.

 HOW TO IMPROVE

Are these two different features, or the same one expressed differently? Two more features are needed, with a little more detail for all three – up to one sentence each.

 HOW TO IMPROVE

Always try to use proper terms, e.g. 'Children's liturgy'. This answer then needs an explanation of what that is, and how it shows support for children. The answer also needs a second developed point.

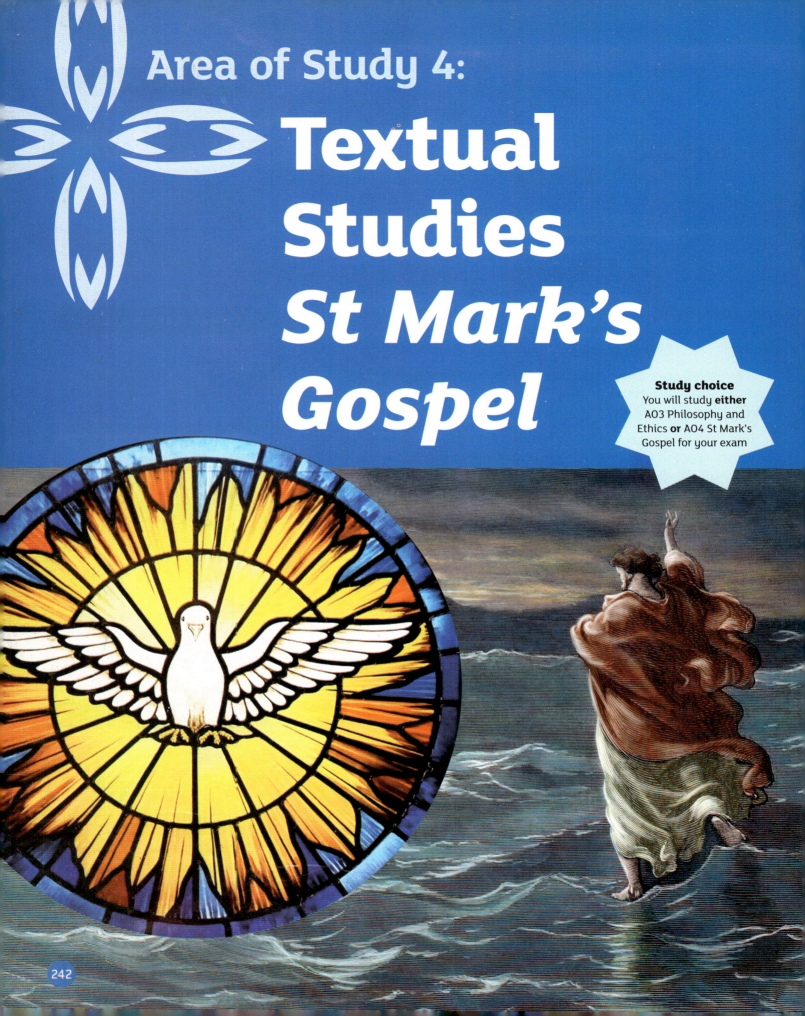

Area of Study 4:

Textual Studies
St Mark's Gospel

Study choice
You will study **either** AO3 Philosophy and Ethics **or** AO4 St Mark's Gospel for your exam

Chapter 11: Who is Jesus?

Chapter 12: The Nature of Discipleship

11.1 The Messiah and the Son of Man

SPECIFICATION FOCUS

The Messiah and the Son of Man: the expectations of the Messiah at the time of Jesus based on the Old Testament (Isaiah 53); what the use of these titles shows about Jesus; the title 'Son of Man'; the meaning of the title including reference to Daniel 7:13, its use in Mark's Gospel and what it shows about Jesus; the significance of Jesus as Messiah and Son of Man for different Christians today.

What does the Messiah mean?

The idea of a messiah had developed before the time of Jesus. Messiah is Hebrew for 'anointed one'; Christ is the Greek translation of Messiah and so means the same. Kings and queens are anointed – that is, marked with holy oil – at coronations. This action is performed to invoke a divine influence and to indicate being set aside for a specific task or mission. These were ideas that followed King David's reign, a thousand years before. Jewish people thought of David as the great role model for the Messiah.

What were the expectations of a Messiah?

By the time of Jesus, the idea was that the Messiah would be a religious leader sent from God who would free the Jewish country of Israel from the Romans. Jesus used the title but meant by t a humble leader sent from God. The arrival of the Messiah was a longed-for event: Jews believed the Old Testament prophesied the coming of a leader and saviour. However, many Jews did not see Jesus as the fulfilment of these ancient prophesies.

What does the use of the title Messiah show about Jesus?

One of the interpretations of the Messianic secret (see 11.5) was that Jesus knew the term would be regarded with suspicion. Jews had been waiting a long time for the Messiah and it would be difficult to believe he had finally arrived.

Jesus accepted the title of Messiah when he was questioned by the High Priest (Mark 14:62) because he believed he was the Messiah. No one can know how much knowledge of God's ultimate plan Jesus had, but the key is that he demonstrated the faith in God that he asked from his followers.

As a Jew himself, Jesus' idea of the Messiah would have been influenced by the Jewish scriptures (the Old Testament). The prophet Isaiah spoke of a 'suffering servant' Isaiah 52:13) and of a gentle leader. This may have influenced his actions as reported in Mark's Gospel.

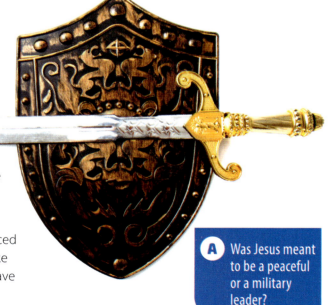

A Was Jesus meant to be a peaceful or a military leader?

> ❛He will not cry or lift up his voice, or make it heard in the street; a bruised reed he will not break, and a dimly burning wick he will not quench; he will faithfully bring forth justice. ❜
> *Isaiah 42:2–3*

Isaiah 53 describes the nature and suffering of a rejected Messiah, which reflects the suffering and rejection which Jesus endured during the Passion and crucifixion. The passage talks at length about the Messiah carrying the 'transgressions' of humankind – the things that they had done wrong, and by doing so, saving humankind:

> ❝But he was wounded for our transgressions, he was bruised for our iniquities; upon him was the chastisement that made us whole, and with his stripes we are healed. ❞
> *Isaiah 53:5*

Who is the Son of Man?

The **Son of Man** was a title that Jesus used. It is not frequently used in the New Testament apart from in the Gospels. It is a curious title to understand and Christian commentators have suggested two main interpretations:

- It suggests the ordinary humanity of Jesus.
- It suggests the cosmic divinity of Jesus.

When Psalm 8 and the prophet Ezekiel used the phrase, it referred to the ordinariness of humans before God. However, the title in the Book of Daniel refers to a supernatural figure with cosmic authority.

> ❝[...] and behold, with the clouds of heaven there came one like a son of man [...] his dominion is an everlasting dominion, which shall not pass away, and his kingdom one that shall not be destroyed. ❞
> *Daniel 7:13–14*

B Mark 10:38 suggests that Jesus knew that he would suffer as the Messiah.

🔑 **USEFUL TERM**

Son of Man: a title connected with the Messiah used in Daniel 7 in the Old Testament

C The way Jesus behaved suggests he believed a Messiah should be a humble servant.

In Mark's Gospel, Jesus is reported as calling himself the Son of Man, as well as being referred to as the Son of Man by Mark. Many Catholics believe Jesus used the title because it was mysterious and multi-layered, with a unique set of associations.

Jesus may therefore have used this phrase as a way to both conceal and reveal his identity. As noted, he was apparently not open about the belief he had that he was the Messiah. Scholars suggest that this secret needed to be kept until an appropriate moment. By using the phrase 'Son of Man' with its elusive meaning, he knew that people would have different responses to the words.

Hence in Mark's Gospel, by using the curious title 'Son of Man' Jesus is being revealed as someone who is human, but also someone who is divine and has been given authority by God to establish an everlasting kingdom (Daniel 7:13–14).

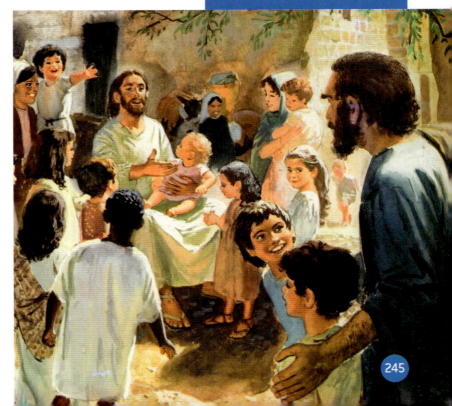

The significance of the Messiah and the Son of Man for Christians today

Some commentators say that Jesus especially used the title Son of Man to stress the idea of God's rule. There is a link here with the idea of the Kingdom of God and the Messiah. For Christians today, this title shows the idea of Jesus as a mighty ruler sent from God.

As Jesus put it in Mark 8:31, 'The Son of man must suffer many things.' The cross is a symbol for Christians of the sacrifice Jesus made so that the salvation of the world could be accomplished. He was prepared to make that sacrifice, enduring suffering and costing his life.

Christians today should understand what this teaches them about Jesus; that he was a divine leader sent with the mission of salvation.

BUILD YOUR SKILLS

1 a What does the term 'Messiah' mean for Christians?
   b What does the term 'Son of Man' mean?

2 a What evidence is there that Jesus is human in Mark's Gospel?
   b What evidence is there that Jesus is divine in Mark's Gospel?

3 What challenges do Christians face if they believe Jesus is both divine and a human?

SUMMARY

- Christians believe the Messiah is a prophet, priest, and servant king sent from God to save them.
- Isaiah 53 suggests the Messiah will willingly take on the sins of humankind.
- Mark's Gospel tells us that the Son of Man is one of the titles Jesus uses about himself.
- This title was used by the prophet Daniel and can be a way of talking about a special being sent from and connected to God.

EXAM-STYLE QUESTIONS

B Explain **two** meanings of the title 'Son of Man'. (4)

D 'Jesus was not the type of messiah that the Jewish people were expecting.' Evaluate this statement considering arguments for and against. In your response you should:
- refer to St Mark's Gospel
- reach a justified conclusion. (15)

The baptism of Jesus

Who was John the Baptist?

John was a preacher who began his public ministry before Jesus began his. He called people to repentance, offering baptism for the forgiveness of their sins. People from Judaea and from Jerusalem came to hear him preach.

For Mark, John recalled a promise of the prophet Isaiah, who had predicted a forerunner before the Messiah:

> "Behold, I send my messenger before thy face, who shall prepare thy way; the voice of one crying in the wilderness: Prepare the way of the Lord, make his paths straight."
> *Mark 1:2–3*

John lived a very simple lifestyle, wearing clothes made of camel's hair and a belt around his waist. Mark says he ate wild honey and locusts. He lived out the message he had to share which included the revelation that the one to come was greater than him:

> After me comes he who is mightier than I, the thong of whose sandals I am not worthy to stoop down and untie. I have baptized you with water; but he will baptize you with the Holy Spirit.
> *Mark 1:7–8*

Jesus' baptism

Jesus was baptized by John in the River Jordan. The Jordan was an important place to the Jews as it had been here that Joshua had parted the river when they were returning from Egypt.

After John had baptized Jesus, Mark tells us two important details:

> And when he [Jesus] came up out of the water, immediately he saw the heavens opened and **the Spirit descending upon him** like a dove; and **a voice came from heaven**, "Thou art my beloved Son; with thee I am well pleased."
> *Mark 1:10–11*

- The dove is a sign of the Holy Spirit, which comes down to Jesus.
- The voice from heaven is explained as God the Father. The words used are a quotation from Psalm 2:7, which David had written to celebrate his coronation as king. Many scholars see the baptism of Jesus as like a coronation, an announcement of his being the Messiah. From this moment Christians believe the ministry of Jesus began.

SPECIFICATION FOCUS

The baptism of Jesus (Mark 1:2–11): the events of the baptism; divergent understandings of its significance, including marking the beginning of the ministry of Jesus, what it shows about him, and its significance for Christians today.

A The Holy Spirit came down to Jesus during his baptism.

The significance of the baptism for Christians today

For Christians today, the baptism of Jesus is significant for four particular reasons.

- **It shows Jesus' divine origin and his divine command.**
  When God speaks at the baptism of Jesus, this reveals the divine origin of Jesus as God's 'beloved Son' (Mark 1:11).

- **It is one of only a few passages in the New Testament where there is reference to the presence of the Father, the Spirit, and the Son.**
  This is significant because it influenced the development of the doctrine of the Trinity as the early Church began to understand the relationship of God, the Son and the Holy Spirit.

- **It is an indication of Jesus' willingness to take on the sins of humanity, since he himself is sinless and therefore not in need of baptism.**
  Jesus was born free from original sin because of the immaculate conception of his mother, Mary. John offered baptism for the forgiveness of sins, therefore Jesus' baptism meant something else: solidarity with those he had come to save.

- **It gives an example for Christians to follow.**
  For all Christians today, baptism is important as the beginning of their life like Jesus as beloved children of God.

B Baptism is the beginning of the Christian journey.

 BUILD YOUR SKILLS

1 a In pairs, discuss:
- why Jesus wanted to be baptized
- what the baptism revealed about the purpose of Jesus
- what it revealed about the Trinity.
b On your own, write a paragraph summarizing each point.

2 Explain why baptism is an important sacrament for Catholics today.

3 Can a person who is baptized automatically be said to be a Christian? Give reasons for your answer.

 EXAM-STYLE QUESTIONS

A Outline **three** things the baptism of Jesus revealed to Christians. (3)

C Explain **two** reasons commentators have suggested that his baptism was a major turning point in the story of Jesus. In your answer you must refer to a source of wisdom and authority. (5)

 SUMMARY

- The Bible says that the baptism of Jesus also involved the Holy Spirit and God the Father.
- Mark's Gospel suggests the voice from heaven showed that Jesus was sent from God.

Nature miracles in Mark's Gospel

What are nature miracles?

Miracles can be divided into several categories. A **nature miracle** is one where the usual order of life is either suspended or surpassed by the activity of God. They include feeding an extraordinary number of people, calming the weather, and walking on water.

Examples of nature miracles in Mark's Gospel

Jesus calms the storm

Mark 4:35–41 describes how Jesus calmed a storm as he and his disciples were travelling across the lake of Galilee one night. According to Mark's story, Jesus was asleep with his head on a pillow as the storm raged. Many commentators see this as an important reminder that Jesus was human.

When awakened by the disciples, Jesus 'rebuked the wind, and said to the sea, "Peace! Be still!"' (Mark 4:39). The storm obeyed. The disciples reacted with wonder: 'they were filled with awe, and said to one another, "Who then is this, that even wind and sea obey him?"' (Mark 4:41).

- This was a sign that Jesus was God as he was able to control the storm, to bring peace into the chaos.
- It links to the story of Creation when God made all things and displayed his power over all.
- Many commentators also suggest that this story is a message of comfort to the original audience of Mark's Gospel: the community of Christians living in Rome undergoing persecution. It is suggested that whenever they felt as if Jesus was distant or uncaring in the face of their own persecutions, they could remember this miracle and take strength from it.

The feeding of the five thousand

Mark 6:32–44 describes how Jesus fed 5,000 followers with only five loaves and two fish.

- The 12 baskets were an important image, as 12 was a number that stood for the tribes of Israel.
- Jesus' action of breaking and blessing bread to feed the 5,000 is repeated when he shares his body as the bread of life for all of the Jewish people at the Last Supper: 'he took bread, and blessed, and broke it, and gave it to them, and said, "Take; this is my body"' (Mark 14:22).

SPECIFICATION FOCUS

Nature miracles in Mark's Gospel: what they show about Jesus, including the calming of the storm (Mark 4:35–41); the feeding of the five thousand (Mark 6:32–44) and the walking on the water (Mark 6:45–52) and divergent understandings of their significance for different Christians today; Christian responses to non-religious arguments (including atheist and Humanist) which maintain that miracles can be scientifically explained and provide no proof of Jesus as divine.

> ' he looked up to heaven, and blessed, and broke the loaves [...] they all ate and were satisfied. And they took up twelve baskets full of broken pieces and of the fish. '
> *Mark 6:41–43*

A How could 5,000 people be fed from five loaves and two fish?

- The fact there were baskets full of leftovers suggests that God can be relied upon to provide the things that people need, as he did when he provided manna for Moses and the Israelites when they were in the desert.
- The baskets of food can also be seen as a metaphor for the word of God – even after it is shared among all Jesus' followers, there is still plenty left for others.

Jesus walks on the water

Mark 6:45–52 describes the event when Jesus walks across the Sea of Galilee to his disciples who are caught in a storm in their boat, unable to row to shore. The disciples believe he is a ghost but Jesus reassures them: '"Take heart, it is I; have no fear." And he got into the boat with them and the wind ceased' (Mark 6:50–51).

- This miracle is important as it shows the divine nature of Jesus.
- It might also link with the Genesis Creation story: 'the Spirit of God was moving over the face of the waters' (Genesis 1:2).
- Jesus again shows a command of nature by calming the wind.

The reaction of the disciples is also important: 'they were utterly astounded […] but their hearts were hardened' (Mark 6:51–52). Despite witnessing amazing events, the disciples still struggle to understand what they are witnessing in Jesus.

The meaning of these miracles for Christians today

All three of these miracles show why Christians can proclaim Jesus as God, as creator, and as Lord of nature. He can do things that show his divine status – such as walk on water – as well as show his human nature, such as falling asleep.

- These stories show Christians that Jesus is both human and divine.
- They encourage Christians to keep faith in difficult times and to trust God.
- They show that the kingdom of God is among them in Jesus, and a sign and promise of the kingdom to come.

Non-religious arguments sometimes suggest that miracles can be scientifically explained (see 9.3), or if they cannot, that the answer is not automatically that Jesus is divine and therefore capable of performing miracles. Coincidence and chance could also play a part in any miraculous event. Christians believe that there must be an answer, and Jesus' divinity is reasonable given the number and variety of miracles he performed.

 B Does Jesus walking on the water prove he is divine?

 USEFUL TERM

Nature miracles: acts of God which seem to suspend or change the way nature normally works

 BUILD YOUR SKILLS

1 Explain a potential challenge in believing that Jesus performed miracles of nature.
- How would a non-religious person respond?
- How would a Christian respond?

2 How have Christians used nature miracles to strengthen faith?

? EXAM-STYLE QUESTIONS

B Explain **two** nature miracles performed by Jesus and their meaning. (4)

D 'Nature miracles prove that Jesus is divine.' Evaluate this statement considering arguments for and against. In your response you should:
- refer to St Mark's Gospel
- refer to non-religious points of view
- reach a justified conclusion. (15)

 SUMMARY

- Nature miracles are where the natural order of life is surpassed by the activity of God.
- Christians believe that the miracles Jesus performs are evidence that he was sent from God.
- Nature miracles encourage Christians to keep faith and trust in God no matter how unusual the events.

Healing miracles in Mark's Gospel

What are healing miracles?

Healing miracles are acts of God which return people to full physical, mental, or spiritual health. Many Christians believe healing miracles still take place today, such as those witnessed after pilgrimages to Lourdes for example (see 2.6). Mark's Gospel is full of healing miracles and a key aspect of Jesus in Christianity is his role as a healer, which is a sign of his divine power; and in Mark's Gospel, a sign and promise of the kingdom of God.

Examples of healing miracles in Mark's Gospel

The healing of Legion

Mark 5:1–20 describes Jesus' encounter with a man violently **possessed** by the demons of Legion. He lived in darkness 'Night and day among the tombs' and was 'always crying out, and bruising himself with stones' (Mark 5:5). As Jesus approached him, he ordered Legion out.

> ❝ And when he saw Jesus from afar […] he said, "What have you to do with me, Jesus, Son of the Most High God?" ❞
> *Mark 5:6–7*

It is significant that the demon greeted Jesus in this way recognizing Jesus for who he truly was, when the disciples still struggled to understand.

Jesus drove the demons out into a herd of pigs, who then drowned themselves in the sea. The pig is an unclean animal and the flight of the pigs into the sea is also a symbol of Jesus being the herald of the kingdom. Before him all is cleansed – the demoniac and the land itself. The healed man now sat in the light with Jesus. When he asked to accompany Jesus he was given another task instead: "'Go home to your friends, and tell them how much the Lord has done for you, and how he has had mercy on you'" (Mark 5:19).

This event took place in Gerasa, which was a **gentile** area on the edge of Israel. It is probable therefore the possessed man was not a Jew, yet this did not prevent Jesus from healing him by exorcising the demon. One of the reasons Jesus was condemned by the Pharisees was his association with 'unclean' gentiles.

- This story shows Christians that Jesus is from God, as the power to remove evil can only come from God.
- The most 'unworthy' are often the ones who recognize Jesus as the Messiah, such as the demons in this story, and in the exorcism in Mark 1:24. They represent the gradual revealing of Jesus' Messianism.
- The healing Jesus performs brings people out of darkness into the light of faith.

SPECIFICATION FOCUS

The healing miracles in Mark's Gospel: what they show about Jesus, including the healing of Legion (Mark 5:1–20); the raising of Jairus' daughter (Mark 5:21–43) and divergent understandings of their significance for Christians today.

USEFUL TERMS

Gentiles: non-Jews

Healing miracles: acts of God which return people to full physical, mental, or spiritual health

Possessed: taken over by evil spirits

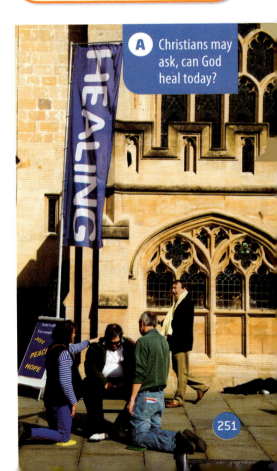

A Christians may ask, can God heal today?

The raising of Jairus' daughter

Mark 5:21–43 recounts the raising of a girl from the dead, and a woman who was healed of a haemorrhage. A leader of the synagogue called Jairus asked Jesus to cure his ill daughter: On the way, Jesus encountered a woman who had bled for 12 years. Many commentators point out that the haemorrhage was most likely a disordered menstrual bleeding. This interpretation is helpful as it explains many elements of the story:

- how a person can bleed for twelve years and yet not die
- a menstruating woman was seen as unclean; touching Jesus would have made him unclean too; therefore she was afraid that Jesus would be angry with her for touching his cloak.

The opposite is true; he says: 'Daughter, your faith has made you well' (Mark 5:34).

The miracle has several layers of significance: an overturning of the purity laws; a sign of Jesus' divine power; and a so a sign that in the kingdom of God it is the outcast and those on the margins who show faith who are of most significance.

As he continued on his way, people from Jairus' house came and said that the girl had died. Jesus reassured Jairus by saying, 'Do not fear, only believe' (Mark 5:36) and the child rises from death.

- This account shows Christians that Jesus has power over death.
- This story can be seen as a claim to a resurrection, a story which prepares the reader for Jesus' ultimate example.

The meaning of these miracles today

These miracles show:
- Jesus has the power to defeat evil and death.
- Jesus' power is bound to the faith of the individual.
- The kingdom of God is present in Jesus.

The demons of Legion obeyed Jesus' command to leave because they recognized him as 'Son of the Most High God'. The woman who touched the hem of his clothes was cured not just by his power, but because she showed faith. When Jesus encountered people of little faith, he was unable to perform miracles (Mark 6:5–6).

The healing miracles above are therefore important for Christians today as they show that no matter how desperate things might seem, through faith in Jesus there is the possibility of healing and renewal.

SUMMARY

- Christians believe that healing miracles show Jesus' authority.
- According to Mark's Gospel, miracles can only occur when faith is also present.
- For Christians, healing is about bringing wholeness and peace to the whole person.

B Did Jesus heal the woman, or was it her own faith?

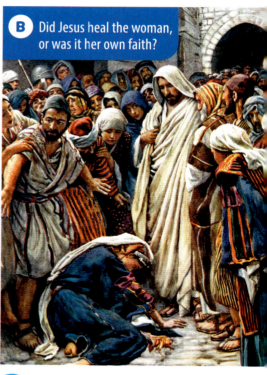

BUILD YOUR SKILLS

1. How does Mark's Gospel present the exorcism of Legion as a healing miracle? Consider:
   - the suffering of the possessed man
   - the result of Jesus' actions.

2. What does the way Legion responds to Jesus suggest about Jesus?

3. What similarities are there between the accounts of the exorcism and the healing of the woman/raising of Jarius' daughter?

? EXAM-STYLE QUESTIONS

A. Outline **three** things the healing miracles of Jesus show Christians about him. (3)

C. Explain **two** ways the healing miracles of Jesus are relevant for Catholics today. In your answer you must refer to a source of wisdom and authority. (5)

11.5 Peter's confession

SPECIFICATION FOCUS

Peter's confession at Caesarea Philippi (Mark 8:27–33): what this shows about Jesus and his purpose; ideas about the Messianic secret in Mark's Gospel.

'Who do men say that I am?'

Jesus took his disciples near to the city of Caesarea Philippi, outside of Galilee. Jesus asked his disciples whom the people following them thought he was. They answered by giving a list of alternatives:

> ❝"Who do men say that I am?" And they told him, "John the Baptist; and others say, Eli'jah [Elias]; and others one of the prophets." And he asked them, "But who do you say that I am?" **Peter answered him, "You are the Christ."** And he charged them to tell no one about him. ❞
> *Mark 8:27–30*

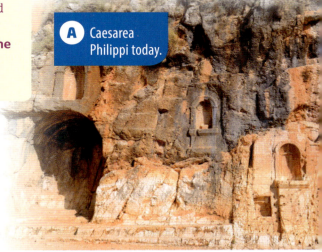

A Caesarea Philippi today.

The answers given by the disciples reflected the mystery surrounding Jesus – some believed he was a reincarnation of Elias, who according to Jewish tradition would return from heaven to reveal the identity of the Messiah. Some believed he was a prophet, at odds with the religious leaders of the day because he had been sent by God to make people return to the truth. Only Peter gave the correct answer: 'You are the Christ' (the Messiah).

This was the first time one of the disciples had used such a title: this is Peter's confession.

Jesus and his purpose

Peter's confession was the prompt for Jesus to begin to teach his disciples that the Son of Man had to suffer and die, and that on the third day after his death, he would rise again. Given his profession of Jesus as the Christ, Peter was filled with the Messianic hopes of the time – that Jesus would be a warrior king like David who would restore political autonomy and rule of Israel. Jesus' talk of suffering and death at this point would have been the absolute opposite of what Peter expected. This is one of the key points at which popular expectations of the Messiah and Jesus' understanding of his own messianism come into sharp contrast.

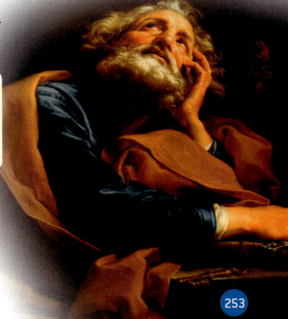

B Peter, like the other disciples, failed to understand what kind of Messiah Jesus would be.

> ❝And he said this plainly. And Peter took him [aside], and began to rebuke him. But turning and seeing his disciples, he rebuked Peter, and said, **"Get behind me, Satan!** For you are not on the side of God, but of men." ❞
> *Mark 8:32–33*

Jesus was beginning to reveal his ultimate purpose: as a sacrifice for the salvation of humanity. This was hard for the disciples to take in because this was not what they understood the Messiah to be. Jewish tradition spoke of a messiah as a saviour who would restore the kingdom of Israel and liberate Jews from oppression, not as someone who would suffer and die.

The Messianic secret

A scholar named Wilhelm Wrede proposed that St Mark's Gospel contains an explanation for why Jesus was not recognized as the Messiah during his lifetime. Wrede argued that Jesus never claimed to be the Messiah and that the early Christian claims that he *was* the Messiah had to account for the fact that Jesus never made such a claim. Wrede also assumes his eventual acceptance of the title is a non-historical edit by the author Mark.

Most commentators reject Wrede's explanation but recognize the secret as a genuine feature of Mark's Gospel. There are many instructions from Jesus to his followers or those he helps to keep his status as the Messiah a secret.

- After Jesus brings Jairus' daughter back from the dead he instructs her parents not to tell anyone (Mark 5:43).
- After Peter confesses he believes Jesus to be the Messiah, Jesus warns his disciples 'to tell no one about him' (Mark 8:30).
- When exorcising demons, 'he would not permit the demons to speak, because they knew him' (Mark 1:34).

Commentators explain it by stating that Jesus is reluctant to accept the title early in his ministry since he is aware of the misunderstandings of messianism which were common at the time. They argue that his vision of himself a a suffering servant had to be gradually revealed or else it would be misunderstood.

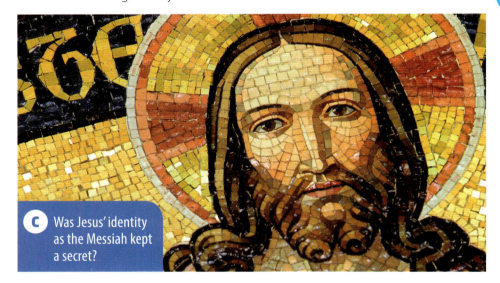

C Was Jesus' identity as the Messiah kept a secret?

BUILD YOUR SKILLS

1 a List and explain the other titles the disciples use for Jesus in Mark 8:27–33.
  b Why is the title of Christ the most important?

2 Why is Peter's confession so important to Catholics?

3 a Explain the Messianic secret.
  b In pairs, discuss why you think this secret is part of Mark's Gospel.
  c What effect does the secret have on the way Mark's Gospel might be viewed by those reading it?

SUMMARY

- Peter's confession is that Jesus is the Christ (Messiah).
- Peter's confession prompts Jesus to reveal the end of his life to his disciples.
- For Catholics, Peter's confession of faith suggests that he is the most important leader of the early Church.
- The Messianic secret is the idea of keeping Jesus' identity as the Messiah a secret.

EXAM-STYLE QUESTIONS

B Explain **two** results of Peter's confession of Jesus as Messiah. (4)
C Explain **two** things Peter's confession reveals about Jesus. In your answer you must refer to a source of wisdom and authority. (5)

11.6 The transfiguration

The transfiguration

Six days after the confession at Caesarea Philippi, Jesus took the inner group of disciples – Peter, James, and John – to a high mountain where they were alone. Traditionally, these lonely places were where people went to pray, as a mountain was nearer to heaven. The cloud or mist around mountains was often used as a symbol of the presence of God.

At this point, something extraordinary happened – the transfiguration:

> ❛he was transfigured before them, and his garments became glistening, intensely white❜
> *Mark 9:2–3*

The whiteness demonstrated the divine purity of Jesus. This was his glorified state and was the revelation of the 'kingdom of God come with power' (Mark 9:1). This was a glimpse of the kingdom Jesus would bring as the Messiah, Jesus' true identity, and his future resurrected and exalted status.

The Law and the prophets show their support for Jesus

Peter, James, and John must have been surprised by this but then something else occurred. Two people from Israel's past appeared – Moses and Elias. These two great religious leaders talked to Jesus. They had great symbolic importance: Moses represented **the Law** given by God and the rescue from Egypt's slavery; Elias was seen as the greatest of **the prophets**.

Elias challenged kings who were not true to the religion of Israel. He had been taken up to heaven in a chariot sent from God, which was a sign that he would return to earth to signal the coming of the Messiah. The message is clear: both the key figures of the Old Testament were there to say that Jesus was the fulfilment of God's purpose.

Peter was confused and frightened by what was happening and spoke rather oddly.

> ❛"Master, it is well that we are here; let us make three booths, one for you and one for Moses and one for Eli'jah [Elias]." For he did not know what to say, for they were exceedingly afraid.❜
> *Mark 9:5-6*

This may be a reference to the Feast of Tabernacles, when little booths (shelters) were built and lived in for seven days (Leviticus 23:34).

🔍 **SPECIFICATION FOCUS**

The transfiguration (Mark 9:1–10): what this event shows about Jesus; the reasons and importance of the appearance of Moses and Elias in relation to Moses' role as lawgiver and the Old Testament prophecy of Elias; divergent understandings of its significance for Christians today; Christian responses to non-religious arguments (including atheist and Humanist) which maintain that visions, such as the transfiguration, provide no proof that Jesus is the Messiah.

🔑 **USEFUL TERMS**

The Law: the commandants given to Moses by God and taught through the Torah

The prophets: the spokespeople of God such as Isaiah and Daniel

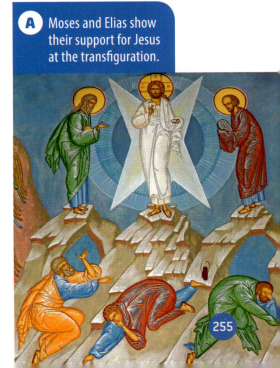

A Moses and Elias show their support for Jesus at the transfiguration.

A cloud appeared and from this, a voice said, 'This is my beloved Son; listen to him!' (Mark 9:7). The cloud was a symbol of the presence of God. The voice was God, telling the disciples to follow Jesus. Moses and Elias left them, returning to God.

Once again Jesus 'charged them to tell no one what they had seen, until the Son of man should have risen from the dead' (Mark 9:9). This evidently confused the disciples, as Mark says, 'they kept the matter to themselves, questioning what the rising from the dead meant' (Mark 9:10). Death and resurrection did not fit with their view of the Messiah.

The significance of the transfiguration

The transfiguration of Jesus is certainly one of the strangest events in Mark's Gospel, but it makes two important connections:

- Moses and Elias are there to show that the Old Testament's teachings of the Messiah are fulfilled in Jesus
- the voice from heaven and the presence of the cloud are there to show that Jesus has authority to speak for God the Father because he is God the Son.

For Christians today, this shows that Jesus is not a break with the Old Testament: he fulfils its prophecy. This could only be done if he is uniquely from God.

Non-religious arguments suggest that visions, including the transfiguration, provide no proof that Jesus is the Messiah or of a divine nature (see also 9.2). In the case of the transfiguration, Christians might argue that it was witnessed by more than one disciple, which increases its authenticity. It also challenged the beliefs of the disciples which suggests it is unlikely to be an instance of wish-fulfilment.

B Many Christians visit this mountain in Israel, believed to be where the events of the transfiguration happened.

BUILD YOUR SKILLS

1 a Research the lives of Moses and Elias and explain why they are important biblical figures.
  b How might their appearance at the transfiguration affect the way Christians view the vision?

2 a What do non-religious people think about visions?
  b How might they explain the transfiguration?

EXAM-STYLE QUESTIONS

A Outline **three** events from the transfiguration. (3)

D 'The transfiguration is as important an event in the life of Jesus as his death on the cross and the resurrection.' Evaluate this statement considering arguments for and against. In your response you should:
  - refer to St Mark's Gospel
  - refer to non-religious points of view
  - reach a justified conclusion. (15)

SUMMARY

- The transfiguration was a glimpse of the kingdom Jesus would bring as the Messiah.
- Christians believe that the voice from heaven present at Jesus' transfiguration is God the Father, who calls Jesus his son.
- Christians believe the presence of Moses and Elias shows that Jesus is the fulfilment of the Old Testament hopes for a messiah.

The conflicts of Jesus in Mark's Gospel

Healing the paralysed man

In Mark 2:1–12 is given the story of the paralysed man. In Capernaum a large crowd gathered around where Jesus was preaching.

Four men arrived, carrying a paralysed man. They wanted Jesus to heal their friend but it was impossible to get close. They walked up the stairs to the roof, made a hole in it, and lowered him on a stretcher.

> ❝And when Jesus saw their faith, he said to the paralytic, "My son, your sins are forgiven."❞
> *Mark 2:5*

This angered some of the teachers of the law who felt that Jesus had committed blasphemy, as they said only God could forgive sins. Mark says that they were 'questioning in their hearts', and that Jesus perceived 'in his spirit that they thus questioned' him (Mark 2:8).

Jesus challenged them about what difference it made which words he used, when the effect was still the same – the man would be healed:

> ❝Which is easier, to say to the paralytic, "Your sins are forgiven," or to say, "Rise, take up your pallet and walk"?❞
> *Mark 2:9*

Jesus told them that the Son of Man did have authority to forgive sins, and that he would prove it.

This story shows the authority of Jesus and is the first of a series of direct encounters or conflicts with the religious authorities.

Observing the Sabbath

Mark 2:23–3:6 recounts Jesus' disagreement with the **Pharisees** about the Sabbath. The Sabbath was the special holy day that God had decreed that the people of Israel should keep in the fourth of the Ten Commandments that had been given to Moses, which included a prohibition on doing any work.

When his disciples picked grain to eat on the Sabbath, the Pharisees said they were acting unlawfully. Jesus made the point that when King David was in need he ate the sacred bread in the Temple. He concluded, 'The sabbath was made for man, not man for the sabbath; so the Son of man is lord even of the sabbath' (Mark 2:27–28). Jesus was claiming to be one with the God who had brought the Sabbath

A Picking grain on the Sabbath brought Jesus into conflict with the Pharisees.

🔍 **SPECIFICATION FOCUS**

The conflicts of Jesus in Mark's Gospel: the healing of the paralysed man (Mark 2:1–12); disagreements about the Sabbath (Mark 2:23–3:6) and their link with Old Testament understandings of the Sabbath; and the cleansing of the Temple (Mark 11:15–18), what these show about Jesus and why they might be important in the narrative of Mark's Gospel.

B Should the Sabbath be honoured today?

into existence at Creation, not just a man defying a rule. As he explained when he healed the paralysed man, as the Son of Man he has the authority to forgive sins and rewrite the Sabbath laws.

Jesus the controversialist

The Temple was the holy building of Israel, a sacred place of God's presence. It was here that people came to give sacrifices to God to atone for their sins.

Mark 11:15–18 recounts how, when Jesus arrived in Jerusalem the week he was executed, he went to the Temple and drove out those who were changing money. Jews had to change money to buy temple sacrifices, and the money changers took the opportunity to make an unjustified profit – some of which went to priests. As he overturned the tables, Jesus said, 'Is it not written, "My house shall be called a house of prayer for all the nations"? But you have made it a den of robbers' (Mark 11:17). Mark 11:18 reveals the reaction of the priests: 'the chief priests and the scribes heard it and sought a way to destroy him; for they feared him'.

Fear has been suggested as an enemy of faith (see Mark 11.3 and 11.4). In this situation, the priests' reaction makes their fear appear selfish – for their loss of power. But was this reaction accurate?

Jesus certainly challenged the power of the priests, the **Sadducees** and Pharisees, who were then important religious groups in Jewish society. However, Mark's Gospel was written for a particular audience: persecuted Roman Christians. Some commentators have suggested the context in which Mark's Gospel was written affected how some people were portrayed.

The scribes and Pharisees are often presented as villains, who 'sought a way to destroy him' or as Pontius Pilate is said to believe, acted 'out of envy' when they delivered Jesus to him for punishment (Mark 15:10). The Romans were the group who crucified Jesus, yet they are not portrayed in the same manner as the Jewish authorities.

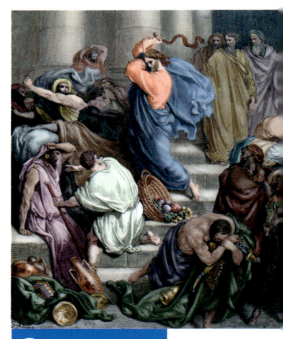

C Jesus was angry about the corruption in the Temple courts.

It is hard to know the truth of exactly how everyone behaved. Modern interpretation of the Gospels rejects anti-Semitic ideas that could suggest that all the Jewish people are for evermore responsible for the death of Jesus, and use the whole of the New Testament as a source when drawing conclusions. Some commentators believe the Jewish authorities reacted as would be expected – Jesus did break some of the laws which people were accustomed to keeping, and he made claims that would have amounted to blasphemy had Jesus not been the Messiah.

The significance of these conflicts

Jesus was unafraid to take on the false religiosity of his day, to challenge those in power who were failing to live to the highest standards. He did not avoid conflict which often seemed inevitable. The narrow keeping of laws which meant that there was no concern for helping people in need was not acceptable to him. Jesus tried to teach the key idea of Christianity through his actions – serving God and others in love.

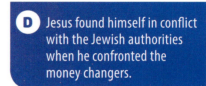

D Jesus found himself in conflict with the Jewish authorities when he confronted the money changers.

The narrative of Mark's Gospel

The Gospel of Mark is an account of Jesus' adult life. The first half recounts the ministry of Jesus as he performs miracles, preaches, and moves around. The second half begins with Peter's confession of Jesus as Messiah, and the Gospel then moves into a new phase where Jesus is moving towards the end of his life and the inevitable suffering he must endure. Jesus' actions in the Temple were a direct rebuke to the Jewish authorities, and brought him closer to his arrest and crucifixion.

BUILD YOUR SKILLS

1 a List the reasons that Jesus and the religious leaders of his day were often in conflict.
  b In pairs, discuss why Mark's Gospel suggests the religious leaders were reluctant to believe Jesus was the Messiah.

2 Explain how Jesus answered an objection to healing on the Sabbath.

SUMMARY

- Christians believe that Jesus challenged the religion of his day.
- Mark's Gospel shows that this brought him into conflict with powerful Jewish groups over issues like the Sabbath and the Temple.

EXAM-STYLE QUESTIONS

B Explain **two** ways in which Jesus came into conflict with the religious leaders of his day. (4)

C Explain **two** ways the conflicts of Jesus' life contradict the Christian idea that he is the 'Prince of Peace'. In your answer you must refer to a source of wisdom and authority. (5)

SPECIFICATION FOCUS

The last days of Jesus' life: reasons for his arrest; the Last Supper (Mark 14:12–31); the prayers in Gethsemane (Mark 14:32–42); the betrayal and arrest (Mark 14:43–52); the trial before the High Priest (Mark 14:53–65); the trial before Pilate (Mark 15:1–15); the Passion (Mark 15:21–39; 16:1–8), what these events show about the purpose of Jesus' life, and how they may differ from other Gospel accounts, what these events show about Jesus; divergent understandings of the significance of these events for different Christians today.

The Last Supper

Mark describes how Jesus met with the disciples to celebrate Passover. This ceremony began the sacrament of Eucharist.

> ❛And as they were eating, he took bread, and blessed, and broke it, and gave it to them, and said, "Take; **this is my body**." And he took a cup, and when he had given thanks he gave it to them, and they all drank of it. And he said to them, "**This is my blood** of the covenant, which is poured out for many.❜
> *Mark 14:22–24*

He described his blood as being 'poured out for many' (Mark 14:24). This was Jesus' way of explaining that his sacrifice was to restore the covenant between God and his people as a way to establish the kingdom of God. Jesus also revealed one disciple (Judas) would betray him and that Peter would deny knowing him in the coming hours.

The prayers in Gethsemane

After eating, they went to the Garden of Gethsemane. Jesus took the inner group of Peter, James, and John to pray. He was troubled and prayed for God the Father to change his plan: 'Abba, Father, all things are possible to thee; remove this cup from me' (Mark 14:36). The cup of suffering was an image from the Old Testament, a sign of judgment to come.

Jesus asked the disciples to stay awake with him: 'Watch and pray that you may not enter into temptation' (Mark 14:38), but none of them were able and they left Jesus alone in his troubles.

After he was betrayed by Judas' kiss and seized, Jesus said, "'But let the scriptures be fulfilled." And they all forsook him, and fled' (Mark 14:49–50). He was abandoned by his disciples in his time of need. The events in Gethsemane emphasize the solitary path Jesus endured as the Messiah.

A In the Eucharist today, Catholics believe the body and blood of Christ is present in the bread and wine.

Why was Jesus arrested?

Mark describes in 14:1 how the chief priests and scribes 'were seeking how to arrest him by stealth, and kill him'. The use of 'stealth' suggests they knew their actions would not be supported by everyone, but it also implies that their actions were unjustified or wrong.

There were different groups who all wished for Jesus' death, probably for slightly different reasons:

- The Sadducees were the priestly class who saw Jesus' attacks on the Temple as a threat to both their religious authority and their inherited wealth.

- The Herodians were supporters of Roman rule who saw his popularity as potentially politically destabilising.
- The Pharisees were politically radical but religiously conservative. For them Jesus' breaking of the law would have been viewed as an offence to God.

The trials of Jesus

Jesus was tried at the High Priest's house. The High Priest asked Jesus if he was the Messiah and Jesus said 'I am', then added, 'you will see the Son of man sitting at the right hand of Power' (Mark 14:62). This infuriated the council who 'all condemned him as deserving death' (Mark 14:64) and sent him to the Romans.

To say 'I am' was to recall the revelation to Moses of God at the Burning Bush, when God said 'I am who I am' (Exodus 3:14). Jesus was claiming equality with God by using this phrase.

Blasphemy was not a Roman criminal offence, but treason was. Pilate was told that Jesus said he was a king, and so was a threat to Caesar. He was therefore put on trial again in Pilate's court. One of the meanings of 'messiah' is a type of king, so here they emphasized the idea of Jesus as being an earthly king, not the political leader expected by the Jewish faith. Mark suggests Pilate did not believe this and tried to get Jesus released under an old tradition, but the crowd chose a murderer, Barabbas, to be released instead.

Mark's Gospel is the only one of the four in which Jesus is reported to admit he is the Messiah to the High Priest. In Matthew, Luke and John he gives a more ambiguous answer: '"tell us if you are the Christ, the Son of God." Jesus said to him, "You have said so"' (Matthew 26:63–64).

The Passion

In Christianity 'passion' means suffering. Mark 15:21–39 and 16:1–8 describe the final suffering of Jesus as he was taken to Golgotha, crucified, and died, then rose from the dead.

Crucifixion

Jesus was crucified at Golgotha between two criminals: 'And the inscription of the charge against him read, "The King of the Jews."' (Mark:15:26). Crucifixion was a painful and shameful method of execution.

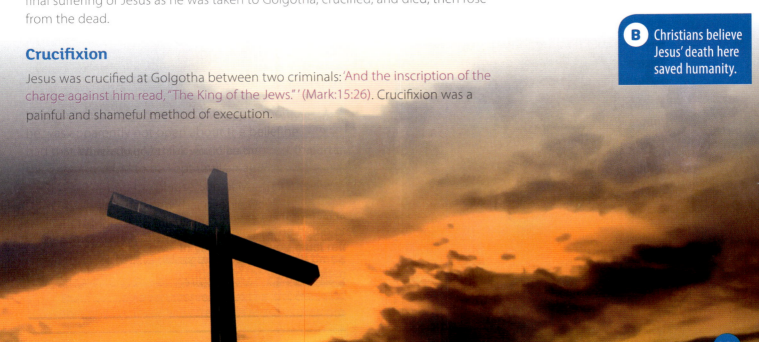

B Christians believe Jesus' death here saved humanity.

At the moment he dies 'the curtain of the temple was torn in two, from top to bottom' (Mark 15:38). This event is significant because of the importance of the curtain as a divide in the Temple. The curtain sealed the *Sanctum Sanctorum* or **Holy of Holies** from all but the High Priest. The tearing of the curtain is a sign of the free invitation to all to enter God's presence – something previously reserved to the High Priest.

Mark tells us that the centurion in charge of Jesus said "Truly this man was the Son of God!" (Mark 15:39) and was the first to recognize who Jesus was.

Jesus' women followers watched his crucifixion and with Joseph of Arimathea, they arranged that Jesus' body be taken down from the cross and buried.

The Gospels of Matthew and Luke also report that the Temple curtain ripped in two, but John's Gospel does not include this detail.

C When the women arrived at Jesus' tomb, the stone had been moved.

Resurrection

On Sunday morning, Mary Magdalene, Mary (James' mother), and Salome went to anoint Jesus' body with spices. The large stone that had been rolled in front of the tomb had been moved. A young man was standing there who said that Jesus was raised from the dead and that he was going to Galilee, so Peter and the disciples should go back to meet him. Matthew's Gospel agrees that there was one angel, but the Gospels of John and Luke report two.

The story ends with this verse: 'And they went out and fled from the tomb; for trembling and astonishment had come upon them; and they said nothing to any one, for they were afraid' (Mark 16:8). Many commentators believe this is the original ending, but most copies of the Bible then have either one or two other endings probably added by later Christians. In the Gospels of Matthew, Luke and John, the women do go and tell the disciples. Only in Luke and John does a disciple respond and go to the tomb: Peter in Luke and Peter and another in John.

The purpose of Jesus' mortal life

Why did the Son of God become human as Jesus? Christians believe Jesus was God made man so he could truly redeem humanity. Most Christians, including Catholics, believe that Jesus' death and resurrection saved them from sin and brought the kingdom of God. One view is called 'penal substitution' which suggests that humanity needed to make a payment for their redemption, and so Jesus needed to be human in order to make that payment on their behalf.

Another view proposes that salvation could only be achieved if God entered into the full experience of what it is to be human. In order to defeat death, God, in Jesus, had to die. Jesus' sacrifice on the cross was willing sacrifice. In the Garden of Gethsemane, Jesus experienced human fear and struggled to answer God's call, but by the end of the night he resolved his strength, accepted God's plan, and declared, 'the hour has come'.

It is clear in the Gospels that the purpose of Jesus' life from his own perspective, was to establish the kingdom of God. Having experienced it first-hand, Jesus understood what it means to be a human. It would only be after the resurrection that his disciples would come to fully understand how Jesus was God.

USEFUL TERM

Holy of Holies: the sacred inner sanctuary of the Temple where God was believed to dwell

The significance of these events for Christians today

The events during the last days of Jesus are vital to Christianity. Although the birth of Jesus often seems like the main event of Christianity, it is the celebration of Christ's sacrifice and resurrection at Easter which is the most important part of the Christian calendar. Jesus' death and resurrection was the revelation of truth:

- Jesus was the Messiah
- what he said was true
- the way Jesus behaved was the right path to follow.

Christians believe that they will be saved from sin by the grace of God, if they accept his offer of salvation. But they should seek to follow the example of Jesus so that they might show their commitment to God, not simply to obtain salvation.

D Artists have tried to imagine what the Last Supper would have been like.

Symbols

- The bread and wine of the Last Supper are the core part of communion and Mass services in Christian churches. In this way the sacrifice of Jesus is regularly remembered (and for Catholics re-presented) and brings Christians together to recall the love that God showed the world in the life, death, and resurrection of Jesus.

- The cross has become a core symbol for Christians of all denominations because it is believed to be the place where salvation was achieved.

- The reality of Jesus' death shows Christians that God has entered into a human body and has come to experience suffering as Jesus, God made flesh, bringing him closer to them.

- The empty tomb shows Christians that death is not the end. The resurrection of Jesus foreshadows the resurrection of the dead at the end of time.

- The core message of Jesus was love – Christians today believe acts of sacrifice, following his example, are demonstrations of Christian love. In this way Jesus guides and motivates Christians by the things he said and, more importantly, the things he did.

BUILD YOUR SKILLS

1 Consider each stage of the last days of Jesus' life:
   - summarize why each one is important for Christians in one or two bullet points
   - find a key quotation from Mark's Gospel for each stage.

2 List the reasons why Jesus' death on the cross is important to Christians.

3 How are the events of the last days remembered in Christian worship today?

4 Explain a potential challenge for Christians today in believing in the resurrection.

SUMMARY

- Christians believe that the death and resurrection of Jesus atoned for the sins of the world.
- Christians believe Jesus' death on the cross brought salvation to the world and established the kingdom of God.
- Christians believe the resurrection is proof that Jesus was God and defeated death.
- At the Last Supper, Jesus began the sacrament of Eucharist with his blood and body.

EXAM-STYLE QUESTIONS

A Outline **three** significant events during the evening of Jesus' arrest in Mark's Gospel. (3)

D 'No resurrection, no Christianity.' Evaluate this statement considering arguments for and against. In your response you should:
   - refer to St Mark's Gospel
   - reach a justified conclusion. (15)

Revision

REVIEW YOUR KNOWLEDGE

1 Name the prophet who predicted John the Baptist would be the forerunner of Jesus.

2 Describe how all three persons of the Trinity were at the baptism of Jesus.

3 Define what a nature miracle is.

4 Name the synagogue official whose daughter Jesus brought back from the dead.

5 How was the woman with a haemorrhage healed?

6 What did Peter reply to Jesus' question 'But who do you say I am?'?

7 Define what is meant by the Sabbath.

8 What did Jesus say about the bread and the wine at the Last Supper?

* See page 288 for answers.

EXTEND YOUR KNOWLEDGE: RESEARCH TASKS

For a research task, try to put together a full side of A4 of your own writing on the topics below.

1 Research the suggestions of who might be the author of St Mark's Gospel.

2 Research the idea of the Messianic secret.

3 Research Catholic Church teaching on St Peter and his role in the leadership of the Church.

4 Research the significance of Moses and Elijah for Jews at the time of Jesus.

USEFUL TERMS

Do you know what these words mean?

Son of Man   Nature miracle   Healing miracle   Gentile   Possessed   The Law   The prophets

Sadducees and Pharisees   Holy of Holies   Baptism   Crucifixion   Discipleship   Messiah

Resurrection   Sabbath   Transfiguration

Exam practice

In this exam practice section you will see examples for the exam question types: **a**, **b**, **c** and **d**. You can find out more about these on pages 6–7. Questions (a) and (b) in the **Exam question review** section below show strong student answers. Questions (c) and (d) in the **Improve it!** section need improvement.

Exam question review

(a) Outline **three** reasons miracles are important to Catholic belief. (3)

Miracles show Jesus as both human and divine.
Miracles encourage Christians to have faith in God.
Miracles show the kingdom of God is present in Jesus.

WHAT WENT WELL

Question (a) asks you to 'outline' which is slightly more than a one-word answer – up to a sentence for each point. The three answers written here give enough detail to neatly sum up three different reasons.

(b) Explain **two** reasons why the baptism of Jesus was an important event. (4)

The baptism of Jesus was important as it revealed Jesus as divine. When the voice of God speaks from heaven he calls Jesus 'my beloved son', therefore revealing his divine status.

The Holy Spirit descends from heaven like a dove and God's voice is heard as Jesus is baptized. This is the clearest Biblical example of the Trinity being present together which identifies the event as being of great importance.

WHAT WENT WELL

There are two different reasons given here, each explaining a different point with a good amount of detail.

Improve it!

These answers will not get full marks. Can you rewrite and improve them?

(c) Explain **two** ways the healing miracles of Jesus are relevant for Catholics today. In your answer you must refer to a source of wisdom and authority. (5)

The healing miracles show that if you have faith in Jesus his powers to help you are endless.

They also show that Jesus has the power to defeat evil and death.

HOW TO IMPROVE

These are relevant points to make, but they lack the development explaining exactly how and why they are relevant for Catholics today. Try to add examples to show full understanding of the question. The answer also lacks the required source of wisdom or authority.

(d) 'The Transfiguration is as important an event in the life of Jesus as his death on the cross and the resurrection.' Evaluate this statement considering arguments for and against. In your response you should:
- refer to St Mark's Gospel
- refer to non-religious points of view
- reach a justified conclusion. (15)

The Transfiguration occurred on a mountain where Jesus and the disciples were praying. A voice from heaven speaks to the disciples and tells them that they should listen to Jesus as he is God's son. It can be argued to be an event that shows Jesus' true identity.

However other Christians will argue that there are more significant events such as the resurrection, and only a small number of disciples were present so it could not have been that important.

When Jesus dies a Roman centurion says he was the Son of God, but an atheist who is non-religious wouldn't agree with that because they believe Jesus was just a man.

HOW TO IMPROVE

The number of marks available for a question can guide you to how much you need to write. This answer is not enough aiming for five to six well-developed points, which cover both religious and non-religious points of view would be a good idea. There are glimpses of potential, but the answer fails to make and link arguments in a meaningful and analytical way – it recounts the events of the transfiguration and offers opinion with no sources of wisdom or authority. A conclusion is missing.

The call of the first disciples

The call

Mark 1:14–20 relates how Jesus began to gather his disciples after John the Baptist had been put in prison for challenging the behaviour of the Roman-appointed King Herod. Jesus went to Galilee to start his ministry. The area of Galilee was where Jesus was brought up and it was a place of ordinary working people such as fishermen and farmers, not the rich or powerful.

He called on the people to realize that they should repent of their sins and that the kingdom of God was at hand. First, he called to two fishermen, Simon and his brother Andrew:

> ❛Follow me and I will make you become fishers of men.❜
> *Mark 1:17*

Two more brothers, James and John, who were working on their nets, answered Jesus' call without hesitation. All four men left their livelihoods and families.

Mark's Gospel does not give an explanation as to why they followed immediately, but it illustrates the nature of discipleship as an unhesitating response to the call of Jesus.

A key theme of Mark's Gospel is that the disciples did not always fully grasp what Jesus was trying to teach them, or misinterpreted what he meant.

In Mark 2:13–17, Jesus calls a tax collector called Levi to follow him. Levi is significant because of his job. Tax collectors were not popular, as they were seen as collaborators with the Romans, frequently mixing with gentiles, which made them unclean according to Jewish law. When the local religious leaders see Jesus eating 'with sinners and tax collectors', they are appalled and question the disciples. Jesus replies:

> ❛Those who are well have no need of a physician, but those who are sick; I came not to call the righteous, but sinners.❜
> *Mark 2:17*

> ### SPECIFICATION FOCUS
>
> **The call of the first disciples (Mark 1:14–20, 2:13–17):** how this shows the nature of discipleship in showing the willingness to immediately follow Jesus regardless of consequence and how this might affect a Christian today; the sending out of the Twelve (Mark 6:7–13), how this shows the nature of discipleship including the command to take nothing for the journey and the responsibility to preach and serve; divergent ways in which it affects ideas about Christian living today.

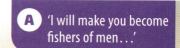

A 'I will make you become fishers of men…'

The addition of Levi as a disciple shows that Jesus was preaching an inclusive message. Including a despised tax collector showed everyone that:

- the kingdom of God was open to everyone who believed in Jesus
- Jesus was preaching a different message to the one they currently received from their leaders.

Relevance today

- Christians today believe they can learn from the unhesitating response which the disciples gave to Jesus.
- To follow Jesus is to live in a way where the disciple might be called at any time to give up their normal home or career for the kingdom of God.
- Jesus showed that those who were rejected could find a place with him and be transformed.
- Whether you are a fisherman or a tax collector, Jesus calls everyone to serve the kingdom: no one will be discriminated against.

Sending out of the Twelve

A disciple is a person who follows the discipline of a teacher. In Mark 6:7–13, Jesus sent out the **twelve disciples** he had gathered, in pairs, with disciplined instructions that they must follow. The Twelve are symbolic of the twelve tribes of Israel – so first, they had to go to the Jews.

> This would have encouraged people to put donations in it.

> They needed to show their trust and faith in God, not wealth.

> ❝ He charged them to take nothing for their journey except a staff; no bread, **no bag, no money in their belts**; but to **wear sandals and not put on two tunics**. And he said to them, "**Where you enter a house, stay there until you leave the place**. And if any place will not receive you and they refuse to hear you, when you leave, **shake off the dust that is on your feet for a testimony against them**." ❞
>
> *Mark 6:8–11*

> They should have a simple lifestyle, committed to enduring physical hardship for the Gospel.

> Washing the dirt off their feet of any place that didn't welcome disciples or their message was a way of saying that rejecting Jesus and his message would bring judgment.

> Disciples should accept hospitality.

> **USEFUL TERM**
>
> **Twelve disciples:** the inner group of Jesus' followers who represent the 12 tribes of Israel

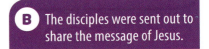

B The disciples were sent out to share the message of Jesus.

The sending out of the Twelve was a coordinated effort to begin to announce that the kingdom of God had arrived. The disciples were entrusted with the responsibility to call people to repent, heal the sick, and were given the power to cast out demons: 'authority over the unclean spirits' (Mark 6:7).

However, this power was set against the list of instructions which Jesus then gave them, insisting the disciples committed to an austere life with little physical comfort and relying on the hospitality of others. The dedication of the disciples shows their continued faith in Jesus, and that they were willing to make sacrifices for their faith. This reflects the sacrifices Jesus made – he didn't ask them to do more than he was prepared to do.

C The twelve tribes of Israel are descended from the sons and grandsons of Jacob, who was given the name of 'Israel' by God.

The meaning of this for Christians today

The sending out of the Twelve was an important moment. Jesus was sharing the responsibility and authority of announcing the arrival of the kingdom of God. The disciples shared in Jesus' authority to heal and remove evil. Christians today can share too in that authority to heal and to confront evil. The work of the Church today is to continue to communicate that message in its teachings and actions within the world.

- The Catholic Church believes that it should evangelize and tell others of the good news of the Gospel and how it can transform lives.
- Evangelical Christian groups also believe that public witness to faith is important in sharing the message of Christ.
- Other Christians may exercise discipleship in their everyday lives through the command to serve others (see 12.5).

 BUILD YOUR SKILLS

1 What does Jesus' choice of disciples suggest about his kingdom?

2 What was the purpose of the hardships the disciples endured?

3 What do Christians today believe the example of discipleship teaches them?

 EXAM-STYLE QUESTIONS

B Explain **two** instructions which Jesus gave to the disciples when he sent out the Twelve. (4)

C Explain **two** reasons for Jesus' teaching that whoever wants to be first must serve others. In your answer you must refer to a source of wisdom and authority. (5)

SUMMARY

- The nature of discipleship is to answer Jesus' call without hesitation.
- Jesus chose a wide variety of people to be disciples, not always people who would seem to be naturally good or religiously pure.
- Being a disciple involves sacrifice and hardship.

12.2 Parables

What are parables?

Parables are powerful stories which Jesus used to explain the ideas of the kingdom of God: the rule of God in human beings' hearts.

The parable of the tenants

Mark 12:1–12 recounts the Parable of the **Tenants** which Jesus told to the religious leaders in Jerusalem. A man rents his vineyard to tenants, but when he sends servants to collect a share of the harvest they are all attacked or murdered by the tenants. Finally the man's son is sent and killed. Jesus explains how the story will end: 'What will the owner of the vineyard do? He will come and destroy the tenants, and give the vineyard to others' (Mark 12:9). The image of the vineyard had been drawn from Isaiah 5 in the Old Testament. Jesus often drew upon the Old Testament for his images and teachings.

The parable was a warning to the religious leaders that they should submit to the will of God.

- The servants represented the prophets.
- The owner represented God.
- The Son was Jesus.
- The tenants were the religious leaders of Israel.

Jesus is saying that the kingdom that is offered to, and rejected by Israel would be taken from them and given to gentiles. Mark's Gospel says that the religious leaders understood Jesus' meaning: 'they perceived that he had told the parable against them' (Mark 12:12).

SPECIFICATION FOCUS

Parables: The Parable of the Tenants (Mark 12:1–12): how this story shows the potential cost of discipleship and its relationship to Christians today; the Parable of the Sower (Mark 4:1–20), how each group shows different types of Christians; the nature of discipleship as shown in each group and in the role of the sower; its significance for Christians today; the importance of these parables with reference to the Kingdom of God and divergent ways in which that is variously understood as realised and in the future.

USEFUL TERM

Tenants: residents or renters of a property

A The Parable of the Tenants contained a warning for those listening.

Cost of discipleship

Jesus was in many ways a dangerous man to associate with. He spoke out against the religious leaders of the day, and challenged their authority. Mark 12:12 says the leaders 'tried to arrest him'. As associates of Jesus, the disciples also risked arrest, and punishment.

For Christians today, this story shows that God sent Jesus to save humanity. It reveals that there is persecution for those who would share the message of God, even today. Jesus calls his disciples not to make the same mistake: to accept his message and stand up for their belief, rather than reject him and endure judgment.

The Parable of the Sower

Mark 4:1–20 recounts the Parable of the Sower, which was told to a gathering of ordinary people. A man sows seed in a field. As he scatters it, it falls in different places and grows with differing amounts of success. The seed represents God's message. Each area represents a different response to the message:

1 'some seed fell along the path, and the birds came and devoured it' (Mark 4:4) – these are people who hear the message but do not listen; it does not penetrate their hearts at all.

2 'Other seed fell on rocky ground […] since it had no root it withered away' (Mark 4:5–6) – these are people who listen and respond at first, but for whom the response has no depth, so as soon as the hot sun of persecution rises, their faith withers and dies.

3 'Other seed fell among thorns and the thorns grew up and choked it' (Mark 4:7) – these are people who listen and respond at first, but other worldly distractions choke their faith.

4 'other seeds fell into good soil and brought forth grain' (Mark 4:8) – these are people who hear and respond to the Gospel.

The kingdom of God

Parables are stories with a hidden meaning. The people listening to Jesus lived in an agricultural world, therefore they would have recognized references to vineyards and seed, and how different types of soil were better or worse for growing crops.

Yet, the Parable of the Sower was clearly not easy to understand: people stayed behind to ask Jesus what he meant. Jesus' explains the parable to those who asked and refers to them being given 'the secret of the kingdom of God' (Mark 4:11).

This begins to divide people into those who have understood his message and those who have not. The 'insiders' are the last group of people in the parable: the good soil, for whom the benefits of hearing the message will be 'increasing and yielding thirtyfold and sixtyfold and a hundredfold' (Mark 4:20). The outsiders who remain confused are the first three groups of the path, rocky ground, and thorns. Jesus said:

> ❛for those outside everything is in parables; so that they may indeed see but not perceive, and may indeed hear but not understand.❜
> *Mark 4:12*

Some Christians find the idea of division an uncomfortable one. Is the kingdom of God inclusive as Jesus suggests by his choice of disciples and companions? Or is it exclusive as the Parable of the Sower suggests?

The key to this parable is that Jesus is the sower, the messenger of God, offering the message or seed to everyone. The seed is good: it is the soil that determines how well it grows. This places a responsibility on those who hear the message to perceive and understand before they can enter the kingdom of God.

 B The struggle humans sometimes face to follow Jesus is just as applicable today as it was 2,000 years ago.

The meaning of the parables and the kingdom of God for Christians today

There is divergent understanding within Christianity about whether the arrival of Jesus brought about the kingdom of God on earth now, or whether it is still to come. Many Christians believe *both* are true: that Jesus began the fulfilment of the promise of a kingdom, but that it will not be completed until he returns. Mark 1:15 says 'the kingdom of God is at hand', not that it is here but that it draws near.

Some commentators argue that the kingdom is a vocation, not a location. It misses the point to think of the kingdom as a place when it is grace – life lived in God's love. It begins now but will only be completely experienced in the age to come.

The parables show that there are struggles to face by following Jesus: persecution, suffering, temptation, the desire for security and the comforts of life. Christians believe that if the word of God is taken seriously and lived out, it will transform their lives immeasurably, enabling them to begin living as part of the kingdom of God.

SUMMARY

- The Parable of the Tenants shows that Jesus believed his message would be rejected by the Jewish authorities.
- The Parable of the Tenants also shows that this rejection meant the invitation would be extended to gentiles.
- The Parable of the Sower shows the different reactions to the Gospel message of Jesus.
- Mark's Gospel says that parables are designed to confuse as well as explain, in order to reveal the truly faithful (Mark 4:10–13).
- Parables are designed to explain what it means to be part of the kingdom of God, the rule of God in people's lives.

12.3 The story of the rich man

The story of the rich man

Mark 10:17–31 tells the story of the rich man, who knelt before Jesus and asked, 'Good Teacher, what must I do to inherit eternal life?' (Mark 10:17). He wanted to know how to secure his place in heaven.

Jesus listed some of the commandments he must follow, according to which the man agreed he had lived. Jesus then revealed the only remaining action for the man: 'You lack one thing; go, sell what you have, and give to the poor, and you will have treasure in heaven; and come, follow me' (Mark 10:21). The man left, feeling very sad as he was very rich.

The key teaching of the story is in the exchange that follows between Jesus and his disciples in 10:23–26. He says 'How hard it will be for those who have riches to enter the kingdom of God!' Then he has to repeat himself because the disciples were 'amazed' by what he said. At the time of Jesus, a huge proportion of the population were poor, heavily taxed, and living in hard conditions. Wealth was the only way ordinary people could improve their situation: the rich man was someone to aspire to be. Many also believed (as reflected in the Book of Job) that wealth was a sign of God's favour. It confused listeners because it reversed their understanding of who was worthy and who was not.

Jesus told them that 'trust in riches' will prevent their entering the kingdom of God, which is why they asked in shock and confusion, 'Then who can be saved?' (Mark 10:26) meaning, 'Well, if there's no hope for the great and rich, then there's no hope for ordinary people like us.'

Jesus explains that humans cannot create their own salvation, only God can offer that: 'With men it is impossible, but not with God; for all things are possible with God' (Mark 10:27).

This is very important. It is one of the earliest indications of the tension between the Jewish Law and the Gospel. By the standards of the Torah the rich young man was clearly righteous and justified, but Mark's Gospel explains that the keeping of the Law is not enough for membership of the kingdom. In fact a complacent presumption of righteousness was the one thing Jesus criticizes most often.

Peter was confused and spoke for all the disciples: 'Lo, we have left everything and followed you' (Mark 10:28). Jesus tries to reassure the disciples that their sacrifice will be recognised:

> 'there is no one who has left house or brothers or sisters or mother or father or children or lands, for my sake and for the gospel, who will not receive a hundredfold now in this time, houses and brothers and sisters and mothers and children and lands.'
> *Mark 10:29–30*

SPECIFICATION FOCUS

The story of the rich man (Mark 10:17–31): how this shows the nature of discipleship in the command to sell all things and how it will affect Christian discipleship today in different ways; its significance for Christians today with reference to the Kingdom of God and divergent ways in which that is variously understood as realised and in the future.

> It is easier for a camel to go through the eye of a needle than for a rich man to enter the kingdom of God.
> *Mark 10:25*

A Jesus used vivid imagery such as the camel and needle to help explain his message to his followers.

B The world is still divided into rich and poor.

Jesus ended the parable with a phrase that still perplexes people: 'But many that are first will be last, and the last first' (Mark 10:31). This was Jesus' teaching against complacency and is often interpreted to give further reassurance to Peter and the disciples: that although they were poor and lowly (the last) in this world, they were dearer to him than the religious leaders or those high in society (the first). In the kingdom of God, these positions would be reversed.

The meaning of this story for Christians today

The story of the rich young man contains many challenges for Christians today:

- Should Christians should sell everything they have?
- Are possessions a barrier to the kingdom of God?

Some commentators try to resolve this by saying that Jesus is talking to a specific person – possessions and money are *this* man's barrier; for another person it might be their anger. The disciples had made tremendous sacrifices to follow Jesus, but that would be true of anyone who truly followed Jesus. To follow the kingdom of God is to be willing to give up all for the rule of God. In this way, many Christians believe they become part of the kingdom of God now through their actions, but that they will be ultimately rewarded when the kingdom finally comes in its entirety.

There is also the wider interpretation of the man's presumption of righteousness when he replies he has kept the commandments: 'all these I have observed from my youth' (Mark 10:20).

Christians therefore should make no assumptions about their own righteousness, but concentrate on doing good through their actions instead. Some people like Mother Teresa of Calcutta decide they need to live with the poor in order to help them and are prepared to give up their comforts to do so. Others have suggested that we need to live with fewer possessions and less money so that others can be helped; that it is not wealth on its own that is a problem, but how it is used for good.

SUMMARY

- Jesus challenged the rich man to think about the power of money.
- Disciples must realize material riches mean nothing in the kingdom of God.
- Jesus promised his followers that he would bless them if they were prepared to sacrifice for him.
- Everyone is welcome in the kingdom of God, rich or poor, but everyone must make sacrifices.

BUILD YOUR SKILLS

1   a   What was the reaction of the disciples to Jesus' announcement about the rich?
    b   In pairs, discuss why they felt this way.
    c   What did Jesus do to reassure them?

2   Jesus does not list all Ten Commandments in Mark 10:19. Find the tenth commandment in Exodus 20. Why might this one have a special relevance to the story of the rich man?

EXAM-STYLE QUESTIONS

A   Outline **three** things Jesus' teaching to the rich man teaches Christians. (3)

D   'Rich people can never be good disciples.' Evaluate this statement considering arguments for and against. In your response you should:
- refer to St Mark's Gospel
- reach a justified conclusion. (12)

12.4 The spirit cast out of the boy

SPECIFICATION FOCUS

The spirit cast out of the boy (Mark 9:14–29): the problems of discipleship as shown in the efforts to cure the boy, and its significance for Christians today.

The spirit cast out of the boy

Mark 9:14–29 tells the story of a miracle which Jesus performs after leaving the Mount of Transfiguration (see 11.5). The scene below is in stark contrast to the wondrous sight they have just witnessed:

> ❛And when they came to the disciples, they saw a great crowd about them, and scribes arguing with them. And immediately all the crowd, when they saw him, were greatly amazed, and ran up to him and greeted him.❜
> *Mark 9:14–15*

Jesus was mobbed, and a man explains, 'Teacher, I brought my son to you, for he has a dumb spirit […] I asked your disciples to cast it out, and they were not able' (Mark 9:17–18).

Jesus' reply is an interesting one:

> ❛O faithless generation, how long am I to be with you? How long am I to bear with you? Bring him to me❜
> *Mark 9:19*

Commentators have variously suggested Jesus could have been talking to the father of the possessed boy, the crowd, the disciples, the scribes or the wider Jewish community. Given the theme of criticism of the disciples within Mark's Gospel, it would seem most likely to be them.

There is also debate on *how* Jesus might have spoken. Some commentators suggest that this was an expression of frustration or weariness; Jesus is human after all. He's just come down from a wonderful moment where God announced, 'This is my beloved Son; listen to him' (Mark 9:7), only to find the disciples he left behind have been unable to exorcise an unclean spirit and are arguing with the local scribes.

Certain words in his reply (Mark 9:19) can suggest the purpose of what he said:

- 'faithless': it was the lack of faith of those present which meant the exorcism failed.
- 'how long am I to be with you?': Jesus asked how long it would take for the message to sink in.
- 'How long am I to bear with you?': Jesus was repeating to those around that he had said before that faith was the key. He was asking how long he should be patient.

A The spirit cast out of the boy emphasizes the importance of faith to the success of miracles.

When the father asked Jesus for help, he revealed his lack of faith: '*if you can do anything, have pity on us and help us.*" And Jesus said to him, "If you can! All things are possible to him who believes." Immediately the father cried out, "I believe; help my unbelief!"' (Mark 9:22–24).

Problem of discipleship

Jesus cast the unclean spirit from the boy and saved him. The disciples asked why they could not do it. Jesus replied: 'This kind cannot be driven out by anything but prayer and fasting' (9:29). The implication is that the disciples were not faithful enough.

When Jesus sent out the Twelve, he gave them the authority to cast out spirits; they should have been able to help the boy, but their faith was not strong enough. Mark's Gospel often shows the disciples as weak in faith, or at least unable to grasp the whole truth of Jesus' teaching.

The meaning of this story for Christians today

The lack of faith and prayer that the disciples and others showed was rebuked by Jesus. If people want to see miracles, he taught, faith, fasting, and prayer are essential. Ultimately, spiritual healing is only possible when God shows his authority.

- There is no force so powerful or so evil that faith in Jesus cannot defeat it, something which should give Christians hope in the face of difficulties.
- Some Christians use the sentence of the father, 'Lord, I believe, help my unbelief,' as the basis of a prayer to grow in faith.

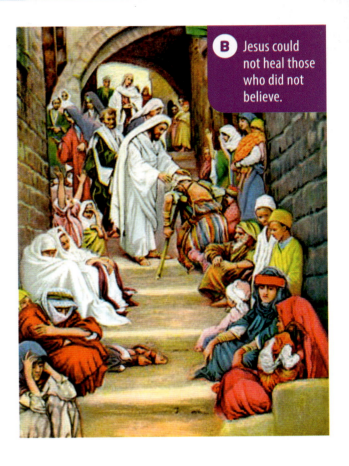

B Jesus could not heal those who did not believe.

BUILD YOUR SKILLS

1 a In pairs, identify all the incidents of faith or faithlessness within this story.
   b What do they suggest about the success of miracles?
2 Compare this story with another about demon possession such as the story of Legion in Mark 5:1–20. How are they similar and how are they different?

SUMMARY

- This story demonstrates that Jesus has the authority to exorcise evil spirits.
- He granted this authority to the disciples but they could not use it without faith.
- Jesus shows that faith is the necessary quality to make miracles happen.

EXAM-STYLE QUESTIONS

B Explain **two** things the story of the spirit cast out of the boy reveals about Jesus' disciples. (4)
C Explain **two** teachings which Christians can take from the story of the spirit cast out of the boy. In your answer you must refer to a source of wisdom and authority. (5)

12.5 Jesus' teachings on service

🔍 **SPECIFICATION FOCUS**

Jesus' teachings on service (Mark 10:41–45): the purpose of discipleship as shown in the command to serve; its implications and significance for Christians today.

The command to serve

The call to serve Christ came with costs.

- The fishermen like Peter and Andrew as well as the tax collectors like Levi gave up their businesses to follow Jesus.
- The disciples became travellers, leaving the friendships and family relationships that were important to them.
- Following Jesus meant giving up money and possessions, as he acknowledged to them when they encountered the rich man: 'It is easier for a camel to go through the eye of a needle than for a rich man to enter the kingdom of God' (Mark 10:25) (see 12.3).
- Jesus promised rewards for the sacrifices but acknowledged that his followers would face persecution and suffering.

The price of service

James and John, two of his disciples, asked Jesus for a reward when the kingdom of God came: 'Grant us to sit, one at your right hand and one at your left, in your glory' (Mark 10:37). They wanted to be princes when he was king.

Why do James and John make this request?

- They thought the kingdom of God would be earthly, not spiritual: that Jesus would be a king on Earth and by his side they could wield genuine power.
- They were ambitious; despite Jesus' teaching about abandoning wealth, they remained seduced by the idea of power.
- They hadn't grasped the idea that Jesus had come as a servant, not a leader.

Their request suggests a genuine ignorance among the disciples of the kingdom of God, and the nature of the sacrifice Jesus would make for humanity. They were influenced by Jewish ideas of messiahship, which were different to the ones that Jesus was offering.

Jesus challenged them, but first he acknowledged their ignorance: 'You do not know what you are asking' (Mark 10:38). He was warning them to be careful what they wished for by asking whether they could deal with the suffering that he was to experience: 'drink the cup that I drink' (Mark 10:38). They confidently said, 'We are able,' and Jesus acknowledged their willingness to sacrifice by saying, 'The cup that I drink you will drink' (Mark 10:39).

This foretold that James and John would both indeed suffer on their road to the kingdom of God: James was the first of the apostles to be martyred (murdered by King Herod, Acts 12:2) and John was exiled and the last of the disciples to die.

Jesus pointed out, however, that God alone has the authority to choose who rules in the kingdom: 'but to sit at my right hand or at my left is not mine to grant' (Mark 10:40).

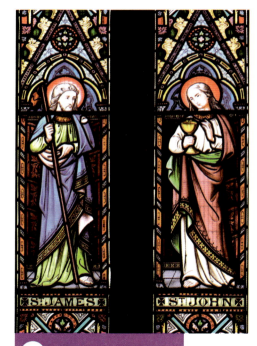

A James and John asked to sit beside Jesus in glory.

Serving, not being served

The other disciples were angry with James and John when they heard about this request. Jesus realized this and, calling them together, explained what discipleship truly meant.

> ❛"whoever would be great among you must be your servant, and **whoever would be first among you must be slave of all. For the Son of man also came not to be served but to serve**, and to give his life as a ransom for many."❜
> *Mark 10:43–45*

He explained that the Son of Man was characterized by selflessness and service; so then should his disciples be, particularly if they wanted to be the greatest of all.

The meaning of this discipleship for Christians today

Christians today believe the command to serve is something everybody can participate in.

The civil rights activist and Baptist minister Martin Luther King suggested that we often are like the drum major in a parade, banging our own drum, drawing attention to ourselves in order that we get the praise we feel we deserve.

This is not what being a disciple is about. If the Son of Man has come to serve, then his followers can do nothing less. For Catholics today, this call to discipleship is influenced by Catholic Social Teaching (see 2.7). It might involve giving their lives in service of the poor or oppressed, or giving money or possessions to help others. Above all, it will be about serving others first as a way to show love to God, not seeking prestige, status, or acclaim.

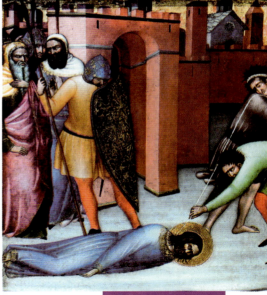

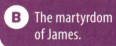
B The martyrdom of James.

BUILD YOUR SKILLS

1. Write a job description for a disciple, using the teachings of Jesus.
2. Explain two challenges disciples today might face when living out Jesus' teaching.

SUMMARY

- The Bible says that discipleship is about following Jesus and his teaching.
- Jesus teaches his followers discipleship involves sacrifice.
- James and John wanted the glory and power of Jesus, but he taught them that they must be willing to endure the same hardships as him.
- Mark 10:41–45 shows that part of sacrifice is service to others.

EXAM-STYLE QUESTIONS

B Explain **two** of Jesus' teachings on discipleship. (4)
D 'When Christ calls a man, he bids him come and die.' Evaluate this statement considering arguments for and against. In your response you should:
- refer to St Mark's Gospel
- reach a justified conclusion (12)

12.6

Peter's denial

SPECIFICATION FOCUS

Peter's denial (Mark 14:66–72): the challenges that the denial brings and what it teaches about the problems of discipleship, and its significance for Christians today as an example and warning; Christian responses to non-religious arguments (including atheist and Humanist) which suggest that religious observance, such as discipleship, can be seen to be unnecessary.

Peter's denial

Jesus foretold that Peter would deny knowing him: 'this very night, before the cock crows twice, you will deny me three times' (Mark 14:30). When Jesus was arrested, Mark tells us that Peter tried to follow. He arrived outside where Jesus was on trial, standing outside the High Priest's house in the courtyard. One of the High Priest's serving girls approached Peter:

> 'She looked at him, and said, "You also were with the Nazarene, Jesus." But he denied it, saying, "I neither know nor understand what you mean."'
> *Mark 14:67–68*

Peter tried to move away, but she saw him again and told others he was a follower of Jesus, 'But again he denied it' (Mark 14:70). However, the bystanders continued to question him. Under pressure from those around him, Peter panicked:

> 'But he began to invoke a curse on himself and to swear, "I do not know this man of whom you speak." And immediately the cock crowed a second time. And Peter remembered how Jesus had said to him, "Before the cock crows twice, you will deny me three times." And he broke down and wept.'
> *Mark 14:71–72*

The challenges of Peter's denial

Peter's denial highlights the faults of human beings:

- pride when he assures Jesus he will not betray him 'Even though they all fall away, I will not' (Mark 14:29)
- inattention when he cannot stay awake with Jesus at Gethsemene 'Watch and pray that you may not enter into temptation; the spirit indeed is willing, but the flesh is weak' (Mark 14:38)
- fear when he betrays Jesus by denying him.

Mark illustrates that all the disciples let Jesus down through their human flaws because it was not easy to be a disciple. The challenge of Peter's denial is how he can be redeemed after such a monumental failure.

Peter's forgiveness

Mark tells us that at the time of the resurrection, the women at the tomb are told to go to Peter: 'But go, tell his disciples and Peter that he is going before you to Galilee' (Mark 16:10). Peter's denial does not leave him excluded from news of the resurrection.

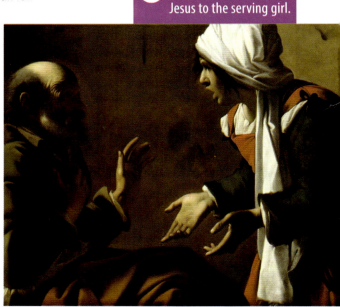

A Peter denied he knew Jesus to the serving girl.

Many commentators suggest that Peter was one of the sources for Mark's Gospel. People are often more critical of themselves than others are of them; it is possible that Peter's telling of the story picks out his own faults and emphasizes them. Mark's Gospel does not record any details of how Peter may have been forgiven by Jesus, but clearly he *was* redeemed because he went on to lead the Church.

The meaning of Peter's denial for Christians today

Peter failed Jesus badly in the story of his denial as he was motivated by fear for his own life, rather than to demonstrate faith in Jesus. This makes him very important to Christians today. If a man who failed so spectacularly can become one of the leaders of the Church, then Christians feel that God can use them.

After the cock crows Peter breaks down and cries (Mark 14:72). This is a picture of the guilt that Christians believe can be overcome if sin is repented. The importance of confession to Catholics, where guilt and sin are formally admitted and repented, is in seeking absolution and restoration with God and realizing the truth.

This experience was key to making Peter the leader that he was to become. He could have become crippled by his own guilt but instead, he was released to serve. Many commentators think that Peter told the writer of Mark's Gospel the full story of what had happened to him that night, so that it would serve as an example. At the time Mark's Gospel was written, the persecuted Christian community held Peter as a hero of faith, and may even have witnessed his martyrdom. The reported failure of Peter might have offered them comfort – showing that even a friend who disappointed Jesus could still be a disciple.

Non-religious attitudes to discipleship

Non-religious groups such as secular Humanists believe that humans are responsible for their own 'salvation', although they would not regard salvation in a religious sense. Therefore discipleship which follows the authority of a God would not be seen to be helpful in achieving this. Non-religious individuals may feel humans should look to their own conscience for guidance in how to act and become the best person they can be (see 3.8). Christians do not believe discipleship is passive submission to another individual, but an active, positive path to being a better Christian, and therefore a better person. They believe Jesus is the supreme example to follow because as the Son of God and the Son of Man, he shows Christians how to be truly human.

 B After Jesus' ascension, Peter became a dynamic leader.

BUILD YOUR SKILLS

1 Rewrite the story of Peter's denial from his point of view, remembering to explore the different emotions he would have been going through at the time.

2 Mark's Gospel reveals Peter to have many weaknesses, but what strengths does it also show?

3 How might a non-religious person interpret Peter's actions as a disciple?

 SUMMARY

- Mark's Gospel shows Peter failed Jesus by denying him.
- The guilt which Peter feels at his failure can be understood by Christians today who should repent and seek forgiveness for their own sins.
- Peter is possibly presented as a failure to comfort the original audience of Mark's Gospel: persecuted Christians.
- Non-religious groups such as secular Humanists do not believe discipleship is the best path towards being a better person.

? EXAM-STYLE QUESTIONS

A Outline **three** results of Peter's denial. (3)

C Explain **two** reasons why Peter's denial of Jesus makes him an example for Christians today. In your answer you must refer to a source of wisdom and authority. (5)

12.7 Women in the ministry of Jesus

Jesus and women

In Jesus' time, women were often treated badly. Jesus, however, showed respect and care for them.

The Greek woman

Mark 7:25–30 recounts the story of a Greek woman, a gentile, who approached Jesus to help her possessed daughter. Jesus replies:

> 'Let the children first be fed, for it is not right to take the children's bread and throw it to the dogs.'
> *Mark 7:27*

By children, Jesus means the Jews; the dogs represent the gentiles; and the bread is his message and salvation. Commentators have argued whether Jesus was dismissing the woman by suggesting he needed to help the Jews before he would help a gentile child, or whether he was testing her faith by suggesting she should be helped after the Jews.

Her response demonstrates her faith: 'Yes, Lord; yet even the dogs under the table eat the children's crumbs' (Mark 7 28). She doesn't argue with his assessment of her needs as secondary, nor contradict his description of her as a dog; she continues the analogy to suggest she should be allowed to share in the faith, as dogs would eat the crumbs under the table.

Whatever his initial intention, Jesus heals her daughter: 'For this saying you may go your way; the demon has left your daughter' (Mark 7:29).

In this story Jesus was saying to the Greek woman that his duty was to the Jews first, but she persuaded him to act to help her daughter. Her faith impressed him.

The anointing at Bethany

Mark 14:3–9 recounts that when Jesus was at the house of his friend Simon, a woman came to Jesus and poured 'an alabaster jar of ointment of pure nard, very costly' (Mark 14:3) over his head. Some people grew angry that the woman had spent so much money on this, when the money could have gone to the poor.

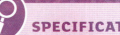

SPECIFICATION FOCUS

Women in the ministry of Jesus as shown in Mark's Gospel: the discipleship and importance of women including the Greek woman (Mark 7:25–30); the anointing at Bethany (Mark 14:3–9); the crucifixion, burial and resurrection (Mark 15:40–47, 16:1–11); divergent understandings of its significance for Christians today.

A The Greek woman appealing to Jesus.

Jesus' reaction was different.

> ❝Let her alone; why do you trouble her? She has done a beautiful thing to me. For you always have the poor with you, and whenever you will, you can do good to them; but you will not always have me. **She has done what she could; she has anointed my body beforehand for burying.**❞
> *Mark 14:6–8*

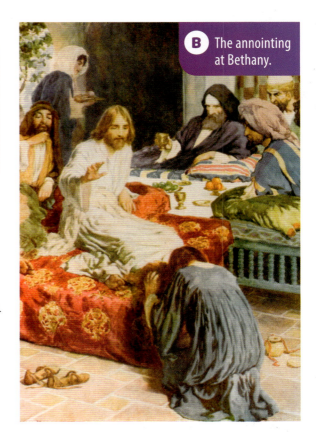

B The annointing at Bethany.

Unlike the male disciples, the woman has thought to carry out an action purely for the benefit of Jesus as she anoints the Anointed One, the Messiah. She is therefore important because she showed him love, and carried out an act of prophetic compassion; an act which foreshadows the burial of Jesus to come. Bodies were anointed with oil and spices before burial, but because Jesus dies on a Friday there is no time to anoint his body. The Jewish Sabbath which prohibits work begins on a Friday evening. Jesus says the woman will be remembered forever for her kindness to him: 'what she has done will be told in memory of her' (Mark 14:9).

Witnesses to key events – women at the cross and the resurrection

The women who followed Jesus were at the crucifixion:

> ❝There were also women looking on from afar, among whom were Mary Mag'dalene, and Mary the mother of James the younger and of Joses, and Salo'me [...] and also many other women who came up with him to Jerusalem.❞
> *Mark 15:40–41*

C Women at the resurrection of Christ.

It is the women who witness his death, not his male disciples. 'Witness' can mean someone who can give a first-hand account of an event, but it can also mean someone who publicly affirms their faith.

Both Marys accompany Jesus' body to his tomb (Mark 15:47) but the only man to take part in the burial of Jesus is 'Joseph of Arimathe'a, a respected member of the council, who was also himself looking for the Kingdom of God' (Mark 15:43).

The women return to the tomb to anoint Jesus on the Sunday, where they meet 'a young man [...] in a white robe' (Mark 16:5) and receive instruction from him. The resurrection is a crucial moment in the Paschal Mystery, and yet so many of those closest to Jesus were not there for the first moment when it was announced. It is important that it was the women who stayed with Jesus during his death that were then the first to hear this news.

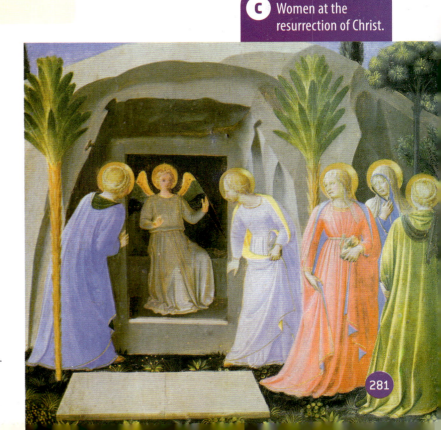

D What roles do women today have in the Church?

> ❝Do not be amazed; you seek Jesus of Nazareth, who was crucified. He has risen, he is not here; see the place where they laid him. But go, tell his disciples and Peter.❞
> *Mark 16:6–7*

It is also important that they are not asked to summon the disciples, but the young man tells them to *tell* his disciples and Peter: they are authorized to share the good news, as apostles and evangelizers to bear the testament themselves. It is interesting that when Mary Magdalene does do this, 'they would not believe it' (Mark 16:11). Some Christians interpret these events to suggest a greater significance for women within Christianity; others feel it shows that the faithful, whoever they might be, will be rewarded.

The significance for Christians today

What do these stories about the importance of women in the ministry of Jesus teach Christians today? Faith. Love. Strength.

- In the story of the Greek woman is a person whose faith, however low down in the social order she might be, makes her an example of the need to trust God.
- The anointing of Jesus at Bethany shows an act of love and compassion, which should be replicated by Christians today who wish to behave in a truly Christian way.
- The women present at the crucifixion and the resurrection showed strength and devotion in moments of great challenge. They stayed constant witnesses, when the male disciples did not. They are examples of courage for Christians today.

SUMMARY

- Mark's Gospel shows women were important followers of Jesus.
- Jesus treated women with respect and prophetic compassion.
- Women demonstrate faith, love, and strength through their connection with Jesus.
- Women were the first witnesses to news of the resurrection of Jesus and communicated that news to the disciples.

BUILD YOUR SKILLS

1 What does Jesus mean when he says the actions of the woman at Bethany 'will be told in memory of her'?

2 **a** What is Jesus' attitude to:
- the Greek woman
- the woman at Bethany
- the women at his crucifixion and resurrection?

b What can Christians learn about Jesus' overall attitude to women from the stories in Mark's Gospel?

EXAM-STYLE QUESTIONS

A Outline **three** ways Jesus shows compassion towards women in Mark's Gospel. (3)

D 'Women are vital to the story of Jesus.' Evaluate this statement considering arguments for and against. In your response you should:
- refer to St Mark's Gospel
- reach a justified conclusion. (12)

Discipleship in the 21st century

Being a disciple today

Being a disciple in the 21st century is a costly experience. To try to follow the teachings of Jesus is a challenge in a world where people follow other religions or have no religious faith at all. Many people are hostile to the idea of religion, observing the extremism cultivated by some groups. This section considers the lives of two people from the twentieth century who inspire Christians today to be disciples of Jesus.

Dietrich Bonhoeffer

Dietrich Bonhoeffer was a Lutheran Christian writer and leader born in Germany in 1906. When Adolf Hitler came to power in 1933, Bonhoeffer spoke out against the Nazi regime. When the Nazis took over the Lutheran church to which Bonhoeffer belonged, he defied the laws that said Hitler's book *Mein Kampf* should be placed alongside the Bible. He refused to take an oath to support Hitler.

In his book *The Cost of Discipleship*, he spoke against what he called 'cheap grace', by which he meant a faith that took for granted the love of God, rather than actively seeking to be transformed by it. He believed people did not truly understand the cost of being a disciple. As he put it, 'When Christ calls a man, he bids him come and die.'

Bonhoeffer was part of the German Resistance and imprisoned for helping Jews escape from persecution as well as trying to recruit allies. He was linked to a plot to assassinate Hitler and executed in April 1945. He had felt compelled to make a stand in the name of Jesus against the evil he had seen. In this way Bonhoeffer showed that discipleship means standing firm in the face of opposition and speaking out against tyranny. It sometimes means being willing to die for what you believe.

Mother Teresa

Mother Teresa was a Catholic nun born in Albania. When she became a member of a religious order, to begin with she was a teacher but she felt that God was calling her to work with the poor and the oppressed in India. She founded a charity called The Missionaries of Charity in 1946.

> ❝I was to give up all and follow Jesus into the slums – to serve him in the poorest of the poor.❞
> *Mother Teresa*, A Simple Path

She and the nuns would go out onto the street, feeding and trying to care for the poor where they lived. They set up shelters to care for the dying. She said each person who was dying should be treated as if they were Jesus himself.

SPECIFICATION FOCUS

Discipleship in the 21st century: divergent understandings of how discipleship is shown in the lives of individual Christians today; specific examples should show how a person's life reflects on the demands of discipleship outlined in Mark's Gospel, including Mark 8:34 and the examples of either Dietrich Bonhoeffer, Oscar Romero or Mother Teresa.

A Dietrich Bonhoeffer paid a price for being a disciple.

B Mother Teresa felt called to help the very poorest in the world.

> ❛The poverty in the West is a different kind of poverty – it is not only a poverty of loneliness but also of spirituality. There is a hunger for love, as there is a hunger for God.❜
> *Mother Teresa*, A Simple Path

She died in 1997 and at her funeral, the Indian government arranged that her body should be taken to its resting place on the same carriage that had taken Mahatma Gandhi to his resting place. Ghandi had led India to independence from British rule and this was an incredible honour. Mother Teresa's work amongst the poor continues today through the Missionaries of Charity family of Sisters, Brothers, Fathers, and Co-Workers which she helped establish.

After her death it was revealed that Mother Teresa suffered greatly in her religious beliefs. However, although she did not always feel a closeness to God, she did not doubt his existence, and she believed God worked through her.

Mother Teresa showed that discipleship can mean the devotion of an entire life in the name of Jesus. She lived a life of positive action to directly help those in need on the streets of India. However, her life also shows that being a disciple is not an easy task. Faith in God is not always effortless, no matter how deeply an individual believes. In 2016 Pope Francis announced Mother Teresa would be declared a Saint.

Being a disciple today

St Mark's Gospel calls for self-sacrifice in the name of discipleship:

> ❛And he called to him the multitude with his disciples, and said to them, "If any man would come after me, let him deny himself and take up his cross and follow me".❜
> *Mark 8:34*

C Mother Teresa dedicated her life to serving the poor of India.

There are many challenges for the disciples of Jesus today. There is the problem of trying to live a simple lifestyle, one not obsessed with money and possessions. The modern disciple may find that the Christian message of love and forgiveness is rejected by a world where hatred and revenge are glorified in entertainment.

Staying true to a religious message may also be seen by some as dangerous: Christians continue to be persecuted around the world including in North Korea, Iraq, and Afghanistan. Some of the problems might be different, but many remain much the same. Bonhoeffer is an example of courage for Christians who live within these persecuted areas, but he should also be an inspiration for those who live outside them and could indeed stand up and speak against those who would oppress others, whether Christians or not.

Mother Teresa did not always feel close to God but she did not doubt he was there. The disciples did not always understand or hear Jesus' message. He berated them for their faithlessness on several occasions, yet they continued to follow him.

This is the belief of all modern Christians: that any obstacle, even doubts in faith or understanding, can be overcome by learning from the teachings of Jesus.

D Christians in Pakistan protest after suicide bombers killed 80 people attending Mass.

BUILD YOUR SKILLS

1 In groups discuss:
  a What marks of a good disciple do you think a 21st century follower of Jesus should have?
  b How does Dietrich Bonhoeffer illustrate these qualities?
  c How does Mother Teresa illustrate these qualities?

2 Can a person today live out all of Jesus' teaching on discipleship? Give reasons for your answers using the examples you discussed above.

SUMMARY

- Dietrich Bonhoeffer demonstrated that there was a cost to being a disciple.
- Mother Teresa reflected the call to 'deny himself' to live out a life for others.
- Mother Teresa showed that faith was not always easy.
- The Bible teaches that disciples of Jesus should have a special concern for the poor.

EXAM-STYLE QUESTIONS

A Outline **three** things accomplished in the life of one person you think has shown discipleship. (3)

C Explain **two** ways Christian discipleship challenges people to become less selfish. In your answer you must refer to a source of wisdom and authority. (5)

Revision

REVIEW YOUR KNOWLEDGE

1 Name the first two disciples to be called by Jesus, according to St Mark's Gospel.
2 Describe what happened at the Mount of Transfiguration.
3 Define a parable.
4 Name the two disciples who asked Jesus if they could rule with him in the kingdom of God.
5 What was the job the first two disciples did?
6 Name the three women who went to the tomb of Jesus on Easter Sunday.
7 Name a parable which shows the importance of faith to healing.
8 What did Jesus say to Peter when Peter said Jesus should not suffer as the Messiah?

* See page 288 for answers.

USEFUL TERMS

Do you know what these words mean?

Twelve disciples   Tenants   Kingdom of God

Parables   Anointed   Discipleship   Evangelizing

Sacrifice   Messiah   Salvation

EXTEND YOUR KNOWLEDGE: RESEARCH TASKS

For a research task, try to put together a full side of A4 of your own writing on the topics below.

1 Research what different views of the kingdom of God there are among Christians.
2 Research non-religious ideas about discipleship and positive role models.
3 Research the role of women in the time of Jesus and in the early church.
4 Research the life of another remarkable Christian such as Dorothy Day or Oscar Romero.

ONGOING LEARNING REVIEW

It is vital that you keep reviewing past material to make sure you have fully learned and remember it.

1 What does the title Son of Man reveal about Jesus?
2 How do the disciples react to Jesus' miracles?
3 How does the healing of Legion link to the idea of the Messianic secret?
4 Why does Jesus clash with the Jewish authorities at the Temple?
5 How does the importance of discipleship differ between Christians and the non-religious?

Exam practice

In this exam practice section you will see examples for the exam question types: **a**, **b**, **c** and **d**. You can find out more about these on pages 6–7. Questions (c) and (d) in the **Exam question review** section below show strong student answers. Questions (a) and (b) in the **Improve it!** section need improvement.

Exam question review

(c) Explain **two** reasons why Peter's denial of Jesus makes him an example for Christians today. In your answer you must refer to a source of wisdom and authority. (5)

Peter denied knowing Jesus out of fear for his own life. He is a good example for Christians today because his failure didn't destroy his faith. It gives hope for ordinary people today who may struggle to be faithful Christians.

Peter showed instant remorse – repentance – as soon as he betrayed Jesus: 'he broke down and wept' (Mark 14:72). Today Catholics are taught to repent for their sins through the sacrament of reconciliation. As a result their sins are forgiven and their relationship with God is repaired.

 WHAT WENT WELL

This is a detailed answer with thorough good explanation of each reason, and a well-chosen quotation to illustrate Peter's repentance.

> (d) 'Women are vital to the story of Jesus.' Evaluate this statement considering arguments for and against. In your response you should:
> - refer to St Mark's Gospel
> - reach a justified conclusion. (12)

I agree that women are vital to the ministry of Jesus as his exchanges with them show his compassionate nature. In Jesus' time women were treated badly, however Jesus always treats women with respect and they offer him the same.

In the anointing at Bethany, a woman pours 'an alabaster jar of ointment (Mark 14:3) over his head. This angered some but Jesus commended the woman's actions saying, 'She has done a beautiful thing to me' (Mark 14:6). She represents love. The act of anointment also foreshadows his death and burial, so in this way a woman was able to see what Jesus own disciples could not.

However, in Mark 7, a Greek woman asks for his help in healing her possessed daughter. Jesus appears dismissive of the woman saying to her, 'Let the children first be fed.' By this it is understood that Jesus is saying he should help the Jews before the Gentiles. The woman agrees with him asking for a 'crumb' or share in the faith too. Her faith impresses Jesus and he heals her child.

Women are witnesses to Jesus' birth, death and resurrection. This suggests their importance when – as the first to witness his resurrection – they are instructed to go and tell the others as ministers of the good news.

To conclude, Jesus' treatment of women shows how vital they are in his story. The women show Christians today how to act as examples of faith, devotion, and love. They also symbolise the courage of all Christians to spread good news today.

 WHAT WENT WELL

It's a good idea to aim to write five or six well-developed points, covering the different points of view listed in the question bullet points. This answer achieves that, and considers the points of view against the question, arriving at a justified conclusion.

Improve it!

These answers will not get full marks. Can you rewrite and improve them?

> (a) Outline **three** things accomplished in the life of one person you think has shown discipleship. (3)

Dietrich Bonhoeffer showed courage against the Nazis as a German resistance fighter during WWII. He said Jesus bids his disciples to 'come and die' which means disciples should die bravely.

> (b) Explain **two** reasons why Jesus had disciples. (4)

Jesus chose disciples so that he would help in sharing the kingdom of God. He believed that the people of Israel needed to be reached with the message and so that was their first responsibility.

 HOW TO IMPROVE

The student has misunderstood the type of question they are being asked. This answer really only explains one accomplishment, so two more succinct things are needed.

 HOW TO IMPROVE

These are relevant points to make, but they lack the development explaining exactly how and why Jesus had disciples. Try to add examples to show full understanding of the question, and split points into two paragraphs.

Answers

Chapter 1: Review your knowledge page 34
1 God the Father; God the Son; God the Holy Spirit. **2** As a literal, factual account of creation; as metaphorical stories. **3** God takes on a physical human form in order to be accessible to, and save humanity. **4** Blasphemy is insulting God. The High Priest found Jesus guilty of this and sentenced him to death. **5** The Passion, death and resurrection of Jesus. **6** Jesus' death and resurrection restores the relationship between God and humans. **7** Eternal life a) comes through belief in Jesus, b) is only possible because of his sacrifice. **8** Omnipotent; benevolent; omniscient.

Chapter 2: Review your knowledge page 60
1 Baptism; Confirmation; Eucharist. **2** Liturgical worship is how humans take part in the work of God. **3** Vigil of the Deceased; funeral liturgy (either just the Liturgy of the Word, or with the Liturgy of the Eucharist); Rites of Commendation and Committal. **4** A powerful prayer to help and encourage a deceased person. **5** Formal: using the words and structure of Church traditions; extempore: using unplanned words. **6** Celebration or worship of God that is not part of official Church liturgy. **7** A journey made to religiously significant places with a spiritual purpose. **8** To love God completely; to treat other people in the way you would want to be treated.

Chapter 3: Review your knowledge page 84
1 Law; History; Prophets; Writings; Gospels; Letters; Revelation. **2** Inspired Word of God; literal Word of God; liberal view; source of guidance. **3** The authority to teach, possessed by the Pope and bishops. **4** The Second Vatican Council or Vatican II. **5** The Body of Christ. **6** One; Catholic; Holy; Apostolic. **7** The conception of Mary, the mother of Jesus, free of sin in her mother's womb. **8** Fulfil it.

Chapter 4: Review your knowledge page 104
1 Mass (public worship) and private prayer. **2** Lectern; altar; crucifix; tabernacle; baptismal font; confessional; stations of the cross; statues; water stoop; Lady altar. **3** Items used during the liturgy, including sacred vessels. **4** 'The Creation of Adam' by Michelangelo (fresco); 'The Return of the Prodigal Son' by Rembrandt (painting). **5** Kneeling before them; touching or kissing them; lighting candles before them; praying before them. **6** Matthew = Human/Angel; Mark = Lion; Luke = Ox; John = Eagle. **7** Mystery Plays and Passion Plays. **8** 'He who sings prays twice.'

Chapter 5: Review your knowledge page 128
1 Surrender; obedience; submission; peace. **2** Unity of Allah (Tawhid); belief in Angels; books of Allah; faith in the prophets; belief in the Day of Judgment and life after death. **3** Unity or Oneness of Allah (Tawhid); Divine Justice ('Adl); Prophethood (Nubuwwah); Successors to Muhammad (Imamah); Day of Judgment and Resurrection (Mi'ad). **4** Muslims look to the behaviour and actions of prophets in order to improve the way they live their lives in obedience to Allah. **5** The Qur'an is the most holy book of Islam; it had supreme authority for Muslims and guides their lives. **6** Angels teach Muslims the importance of worship, obedience and submission to Allah's will. **7** The belief of predestination – that the universe follows the divine master plan of Allah. **8** The Qur'an teaches that death is not the end, but the beginning of the life to come. Muslims will be judged and rewarded (in paradise) or punished (in hell) according to their decisions during life.

Chapter 6: Review your knowledge page 150
1 Salah; Sawm; Zakah; Hajj; Khums; Jihad; Amr bil-Ma'raf; Nahy anil-Munkar; Tawalla; Tabarra. **2** The Muslim declaration of faith that there is no God except Allah, and that Muhammad is the messenger of Allah. **3** Fajr (dawn); Zuhr (midday); Asr (late afternoon); Maghrib (sunset); Isha (between sunset and midnight). **4** 'You who believe, fasting is prescribed for you, as it was prescribed for those before you, so that you may be mindful of God' (Surah 2:183). **5** Shave pubic hair; take a purifying bath; men wear two pieces of unstitched white cloth; women wear white; prayers are offered; intention to perform Hajj is declared; Talbiyah recited. **6** Hajj is an opportunity for Muslims to have their sins forgiven; spend time getting closer to Allah; unify with other Muslims; follow the actions of Muhammad. **7** For Muslims, greater jihad is the struggle of each individual to be a good and devout Muslim. **8** Id-ul-Adha, the festival of sacrifice, marks the annual completion of Hajj and begins on the third day of Hajj at the same time as the sacrifice in Makkah.

Chapter 7: Review your knowledge page 174<
1 One; Creator; Lawgiver; Judge. **2** Shekhinah. **3** Political leader; military leader; judge; charismatic; inspirational; human; knowledgeable about Jewish law. **4** A covenant is an agreement between the Jewish people and God, which benefits both. Both the Jews and God need to keep certain conditions or fulfil obligations. **5** Land and a son (or many descendants). **6** Pikuach Nefesh. **7** 613. **8** Gan Eden (heaven) and Gehinnom (similar to Purgatory).

Chapter 8: Review your knowledge page 198
1 Shabbat; Daily Prayers; Festivals. **2** Torah; Nevi'im; Ketuvim. **3** Praying three times a day. **4** Shema and Amidah. **5** Bar and Bat Mitzvah. **6** Every week – from dusk on Friday to the appearance of 3 stars in the sky on the Saturday – or 6pm to 6pm in some communities. **7** Rosh Hashanah; Yom Kippur; Pesach; Shavuot; Sukkot. **8** Where the Torah scrolls are kept in the synagogue.

Chapter 9: Review your knowledge page 220
1 The Bible. **2** Lack of proof; misunderstandings; made-up; dreams; hallucinations. **3** An event that appears to break the laws of science. **4** Religious experience. **5** St Thomas Aquinas; William Paley. **6** Richard Dawkins; David Hume. **7** Examples of moral evil could include murder, theft, assault or terrorism; examples of natural evil could include tsunamis, hurricanes or floods. **8** An attempt to justify God's existence in spite of the evil and suffering that exists.

Chapter 10: Review your knowledge page 240
1 Not Just Good, But Beautiful. **2** Unitive (bring together); procreative (creating children); marital (within marriage). **3** The family. **4** Family worship; sacraments; classes for parents; groups for children; Family Group Movement; counselling. **5** Avoiding sex during stages in the women's menstrual cycle when she is most fertile and may conceive. **6** A declaration that a marriage was never valid in the first place and therefore never existed. **7** Catechesis; distribute the Eucharist (in Mass and to the sick); give the readings in Mass (as lector). **8** Samaritan woman at the well; the woman taken in adultery; the Greek woman.

Chapter 11: Review your knowledge page 264
1 Isaiah. **2** Jesus as the Son was baptized, the Father spoke and the Holy Spirit appeared like a dove. **3** A miracle where natural forces are shown to be under the control of Jesus, such as the walking on the water or the calming of the storm. **4** Jairus. **5** Her own faith – she believed touching the hem of Jesus' cloak was enough to heal her. **6** 'You are the Christ.' **7** The day of rest when no work is done; the seventh day of creation. **8** 'This is my body. This is my blood.'

Chapter 12: Review your knowledge page 286
1 Simon Peter and his brother Andrew. **2** Moses and Elias appeared, showing that Jesus was the fulfilment of Biblical prophecy. There was a voice from heaven confirming that Jesus was the Son of God and that people should listen. **3** A story with a meaning which explains the ideas of the kingdom of God. **4** James and John. **5** Fishermen. **6** Mary Magdalene, Mary the mother of James and Joses, and Salome. **7** Woman cured of a haemorrhage; spirit cast out of the boy. **8** 'Get behind me, Satan.'

Glossary

A

Acrostic: where the first letter of each word in a sentence together make a separate word with particular meaning

Adhan: in Islam, the words of the call to prayer

'Adl: belief in Allah's justice and fairness

Agnostic: a person who does not believe it is possible to know whether God exists or not

Akhirah: in Islam, everlasting life after death, spent in either paradise or hell

Allah: the Islamic name for God

Al-Qadr: predestination, a future already decided by Allah

Annunciation: the announcement by the angel Gabriel that Mary would conceive Christ

Anointed: marked for greatness by a divine power

Apostolic Succession: the belief that the tradition from the apostles has been handed down in the Church through the Pope and bishops and gives them authority

Apostolic Tradition: the wisdom inspired by the Holy Spirit which influences the words and practices of the Church

Ascension: the moment the resurrected Jesus is taken up to heaven

Ashura: a day of mourning in Shi'a tradition for the martyrdom of Imam Husayn, the grandson of the Prophet Muhammad

Assumption: the taking of Mary, body and soul, to heaven at the end of her life

Atheist: a person who does not believe in the existence of God(s)

Atonement: to make up for; in Christianity the restoration of the relationship between God and humans which as mended by Christ's sacrifice

B

Baptism: ceremony using water as a sign of the washing away of sin and new life in Christ

Baptisteries: special separate buildings containing the font or baptismal pool, popular in Italy

Barachu: Jewish call to prayer

Barzakh: meaning 'barrier'; it is the state between death and the Day of Judgment

Basilica: the name given to certain long, oblong churches granted special privileges by the Pope

Benevolence: the belief that God is loving and good

Bible: the Christian scriptures, consisting of the Old and New Testaments

Bimah: raised platform from which readings are made and sermons given

Blasphemer: someone who claims the attributes of God or shows contempt or a lack of reverence for God

Blasphemy: saying something about a sacred being which is not permitted by a religion

Blessed Sacrament: the real presence of Jesus in the consecrated bread and wine, either to be consumed or adored

C

Canonical: authoritative parts of the Bible approved by the Catholic Church

Catechesis: teaching, usually in classes such as for confirmation or Holy Communion. Its focus is an increase in understanding of the faith for those who have already been baptized or accepted the faith

Catechism: a single authoritative book containing the doctrines of the Roman Catholic Church concerning faith and morals

Celibate: unmarried; and therefore not engaging in sexual activity

Chalice: cup for consecrated wine

Challah: plaited bread prepared before Shabbat begins

Chametz: foods containing wheat, barley, and oats, left to soak for over 18 minutes

Charismatic movement: an active style of Christian worship may include dancing and lively music (also sometimes called full body worship)

Christ: means 'anointed one' in Greek, the same as the word 'Messiah' in Hebrew

Circumcising: removing the foreskin of the penis; 'Brit Milah' is the name of the Jewish ceremony of circumcision

Cosmological: relating to the history, structure and dynamics of the universe

Crucifixion: the death of Jesus on the cross

Crusades: religious military campaigns to the Holy Land

D

Days of Awe: days of repentance; Rosh Hashanah and Yom Kippur

Denominations: different groups or churches within Christianity

Deuterocanonical: belonging to the second canon, a later addition to the Bible

Devotions: practices which create a sense of devotion, love, and affection for God

Discipleship: following the teaching and the example of Jesus

Doctrine: a belief held by the Church

Dogma: doctrines which have been infallibly defined by an ecumenical council or pope, which all Catholics must accept

Doxology: expression of praise of God

E

Ecumenical council: a worldwide gathering of all the bishops of the world with the Pope, or his approval

Ecumenism: the idea that there should be one unified Christian Church

Efficacious prayer: *efficax* is Latin for powerful and effective; in the funeral rite it is prayer to help and encourage the deceased person

Eucharist: the sacrament in which Catholics receive the bread and wine which has become the body and blood of Jesus. It is also the name given to the consecrated bread and wine which are received during this sacrament

Eulogy: speech of praise and remembrance for someone who has died

Evangelizing: proclaiming and living out the Gospel or good news of Jesus

Ex cathedra: means 'from the chair' and refers to the authority the pope has in inheriting the 'chair' of St Peter, as an heir would inherit a throne

Excommunicate: exclude someone from sacramental participation in the Church

Exorcism: removal of evil spirits who have possessed a person

F

Frescoes: murals painted on fresh plaster

G

Gan Eden: Garden of Eden – not the same place where Adam and Eve lived, but a pure spiritual heaven

Gehinnom: a place for a set time of purification of the soul, similar to the Christian purgatory

Gentiles: non-Jews

Genuflect: to bend the knee or touch the ground (usually with one knee) as a gesture of respect

Grace: the blessing and mercy of God

H

Hadith: sayings of the Prophet Muhammad. An important source of Islamic law

Haggadah: a Jewish book which sets out the rituals of Pesach

Hail Mary: a prayer addressed to Jesus' mother, Mary. Catholics believe closeness to Mary is closeness to Christ

Hajj: the annual pilgrimage to Makkah, which all Muslims must undertake at least once if possible

Halakhah: the list of 613 Mitzvot which guide Jewish life

havdalah: closing ceremony of Shabbat; it means 'separation'

Healing miracles: acts of God which return people to full physical, mental, or spiritual health

Holy of Holies: the sacred inner sanctuary of the Temple where God was believed to dwell

Holy Land: the original Land of Israel, which is now divided between modern Israel, Palestine, Lebanon, Jordan, and Syria

Homily: a commentary that follows a reading of scripture explaining and teaching the meaning of God's Word

I

'Ibadah: loving obedience, submission, and devotion to Allah

Iconoclasm: the destruction of religious icons and other images for religious or political motives

Id-ul-Adha: a global celebration which remembers the prophet Ibrahim's willingness to sacrifice his son for Allah

Id-ul-Fitr: a festival to mark the end of Ramadan

Id-ul-Ghadeer: a Shi'a celebration of Muhammad's appointment of his nephew Ali as his successor

Imam: 1) Sunni leader of communal prayer; 2) Shi'a religious and political leader, the successor of the Prophet

Imam in occultation: the concealed state of living of the 12th infallible Imam of Shi'as. They believe that after this hidden life he will return to restore justice and peace

Iman: faith arrived at by knowledge and understanding

Incarnate: made flesh

Incarnation: God the Son taking human form as Jesus Christ

Inerrant: containing no errors

Intercessions: prayers which request help or relief

J

Jihad: to struggle or strive. This could be a spiritual or physical struggle

Jummah: Friday prayer

K

Ka'bah: a building in the centre of Islam's most sacred mosque in Makkah, regarded as the house of Allah

Kaddish: a prayer of praise blessing God's name

Kedusha: the third section of all Amidah recitations

Khalifah: (sometimes Caliph) an elected religious and political leader

Khums: the payment by Shi'as of one fifth of their surplus income for good causes

Kiddush: prayer of sanctification

Kingdom of God: the rule of God over all creatures and things.

Kitab al-iman: Book of Faith

L

Leaven: meaning risen – food that has been fermented with a raising agent such as yeast, prohibited during Pesach

Lectionary: a book which contains the passages of scripture which are to be read at Mass, listed in the order of the liturgical year for each Sunday or weekday

M

Makkah: the most holy city of Islam, the city where Prophet Muhammad was born

Messiah: the anointed one, the King sent from God

Mezuzah: a small box set on a doorpost containing a copy of the Shema

Mikvah: ritual bath for purification

Minaret: the spire of the mosque from where the call to prayer is broadcast

Minyan: a group of ten men (Orthodox tradition) or adults (Reform tradition) over the age of 13

Mitre: pointed bishop's hat

Mitzvot: commandments which set rules or guide action for Jews

Modeh ani: 'I give thanks', a prayer recited upon waking

Monotheism: the belief in one God

Monstrance: a decorative frame used to hold and display the consecrated host

Mu'adhdhin: the person who leads and recites a mosque's call to prayer

Mystery of the Rosary: the Joyful Mysteries, Sorrowful Mysteries, and Glorious Mysteries concentrate on joyful, sorrowful, and glorious moments in the life of Christ or Mary. In 2002 the Pope introduced five new mysteries, the Luminous Mysteries

N

Nature miracles: acts of God which seem to suspend or change the way nature normally works

Nevi'im: 'Prophets' – the second part of the Tenakh

Nicene Creed: the Christian profession of faith

Non-theist: someone who is uncommitted towards a belief in God

Novena: nine days of public or private prayer for special occasions or intentions

Nuclear: a married couple and their own children; a 'unit' of society

Numinous: having a mysterious, spirit, or holy quality

O

Olam Ha-Ba: 'The World to Come'; term used for both 1) the Messianic Age and 2) a spiritual afterlife following physical death

Omnipotence: the belief that God is all-powerful

Omniscience: complete knowledge of all human actions, past, present, and future

Ordained: take holy orders as a priest, bishop or deacon

Orthodox: traditional beliefs of religion

P

Parables: 'earthly stories with a heavenly meaning', told by Jesus to illustrate his teaching

Passion: Jesus' arrest, trial, and suffering

Paten: plate for the consecrated host

Penance: a punishment or act of reparation which shows repentance

Penitent: the person acknowledging sorrow or sin

Pilgrimage: a journey made for religious reasons

Pontifical: relating to the Pope (the Pontiff)

Possessed: taken over by evil spirits
Prime mover: the first mover or first cause of all other moving things
Purgatory: a place or state of purposeful suffering where the souls of sinners are purified before going to heaven

Q

Qiblah: the direction of the sacred shrine of the Ka'bah in Makkah
Qur'an: the Holy Book of Islam, as revealed to the Prophet Muhammad by God through the angel Jibril

R

Rabbi: Jewish teacher or religious leader
Rak'ah: a sequence of ritual prayer movements
Ramadan: the ninth month of the Islamic calendar in which the Qur'an was revealed to Muhammad
Redemption: the forgiveness of sins through Jesus' sacrifice; redemption is part of salvation
Reed Sea: some scholars believe a mistranslation led to this originally being called the 'Red' Sea
Relics: an object connected with a saint such as physical remains, belongings, or something they used/touched
Repentance: saying sorry to God for sins
Requiem: a Mass to remember someone who has died. Usually celebrated as part of the funeral but not always
Responsorial: a chant recited in parts which includes a response by the congregation between each part
Resurrection: 1) in Christianity; Jesus' rising from the dead in a transformed body; 2) in Islam, raising from the dead
Revelation: truth or knowledge revealed by a deity; the way God makes himself known to believers
Roman Curia: a body of administrative groups and officials which carry out the official work of the Church

S

Sabbath: the holy day of Judaism, which begins at sunset on Friday and finishes when the stars appear on Saturday; also the name given to the holy day of rest for Christians which is now a Sunday
Sacrament: a religious ceremony; a visible sign of God's grace
Sacrifice: to make an offering of yourself or a gift at some cost
Sadducees and Pharisees: influential groups within the ancient Jewish community
Salah: worship of Allah through regular prayer. The Second Pillar of Sunni and First Obligatory Act of Shi'a tradition
Salat al-Id: special Id prayers said at both Id-ul-Adha and Id-ul-Fitr celebrations
Salvation: the process of being saved from sin and returning to God through his grace
Sanctifying grace: a state in which God shares his life and love
Sawm: obligatory fasting during Ramadan
Scripture: sacred writings, believed in Christianity to be the Word of God, set down in human writing under the inspiration of the Holy Spirit
Secular: concerned with the physical world alone, rather than the spiritual
Shahadah: the Islamic creed or profession of faith. The first pillar of Islam
Shari'ah: the moral and religious law which Muslims must obey, based directly on the Qur'an and sunnah
Shavuot: commemorates the anniversary of the day God gave the Torah to the entire nation of Israel assembled at Mount Sinai
Shema: the main Jewish declaration of faith
Shirk: believing in things other than Allah or as equals to Allah
Shofar: an ancient instrument made of ram's horn which is blown to herald important events and to call Jews to repentance

Siddur: book of daily prayers; literally means 'order' or 'sequence'
Sins: acts against the will of God
Situation ethics: where right and wrong depend on the circumstances of a situation
Son of Man: a title connected with the Messiah used in Daniel 7 in the Old Testament
Stole: a priest's silk garment worn over the shoulders and hanging down to the knee or below. Its colour reflects the occasion for which it is worn
Sunnah: the teachings and deeds of Muhammad
Tableaux: freeze-frame scenes, sometimes accompanied by music

T

Tallit: a fringed prayer shawl
Talmud: the 'Oral Torah', or the Oral laws and traditions passed down from Moses, eventually written down as the Mishnah and the Gemara. There are two versions (Jerusalem and Babylonian)
Tawhid: the oneness and unity of Allah
Tefillin: small boxes worn on head and arm containing verses from the Torah, including the Shema
Teleology: the study of a thing's purpose or design
Temple: the holiest building of Judaism, built on Temple Mount in Jerusalem and destroyed in 586BCE by the Babylonians, then again after rebuilding in 70CE by the Romans
Tenakh: the Hebrew Bible, consisting of the Torah, Nevi'im, and Kethuvim
Tenants: residents or renters of a property
Teshuva: returning to God; repentance
Theist: a person who believes in the existence of God(s)
Theodicy: a theory/defence of why God permits evil
The Law: the commandants given to Moses by God and taught through the Torah
The prophets: the spokespeople of God such as Isaiah and Daniel
Tikkun Olam: acts of kindness performed to repair the world
Torah: 1) the Five Books of Moses Bereshit (Genesis), Shemot (Exodus), Vayikra (Leviticus), Bamidbar (Numbers), and Devarim (Deuteronomy); 2) a wider meaning including the written Tenakh plus the Talmud – the oral law and traditions of Judaism
Transfiguration: a change in appearance or form; the unveiling of Jesus as Messiah alongside the support of Moses and Elias
Twelve disciples: the inner group of Jesus' followers who represent the 12 tribes of Israel

U

Unrepented sin: sins which have not been acknowledged/faced up to, and for which the individual may not feel sorry

V

Vatican II: the Second Vatican Council – an ecumenical council held between 1962 and 1965
Vestments: long robe worn by priest over his clothes
Vigil: time spent awake to keep watch or to pray
Virtue ethics: considering the moral character of a person to help analyse their ethical decisions
Votive: a vow, wish, or desire

W

Wudu': ritual cleansing or ablution with water

Y

Yad: a pointer for following text
Yeshiva: Jewish school of Talmudic study

Z

Zakah: purification of wealth by giving to the poor

Index

Acknowledgements

The publisher would like to thank the following for permission to use their photographs:

COVER: Baloncici/iStockphoto; p4: Lolostock / Shutterstock; p6: Tang Yan Song / Shutterstock; p7: Sutichak / Shutterstock; p8: age fotostock / Alamy Stock Photo; p8: duchy / Shutterstock; p11: Terry Healy / iStockphoto; p12: Image Source / Alamy Stock Photo; p13: The Bridgeman Art Library; p13: The Bridgeman Art Library; p14: Universal History Archive/UIG via Getty Images; p15: MasPix / Alamy Stock Photo; p16: The Bridgeman Art Library; p17: © Nicholas Rous / Alamy Stock Photo; p18: Christopher Futcher / Shutterstock; p19: ivan-96 / iStockphoto; p19: Lena Sergeeva / iStockphoto; p20: SolStock / iStockphoto; p21: ROMEO GACAD/AFP/Getty Images; p22: Niday Picture Library / Alamy Stock Photo; p23: Chronicle / Alamy Stock Photo; p23: freya-photographer / Shutterstock; p24: AF archive / Alamy Stock Photo; p25: Heritage Image Partnership Ltd / Alamy Stock Photo; p26: Colin Underhill / Alamy Stock Photo; p27: robertharding / Alamy Stock Photo; p29: robertharding / Alamy Stock Photo; p28: Friedrich Stark / Alamy Stock Photo; p30: Chronicle / Alamy Stock Photo; p31: Granger Historical Picture Archve / Alamy Stock Photo; p32: Robert Adrian Hillman / Shutterstock; p33: Bob Daemmrich / Alamy Stock Photo; p36: ShutterDivision / Shutterstock; p37: David H. Wells / Getty Images; p38: MarioPonta / Alamy Stock Photo; p39: Godong/UIG via Getty Images; p40: Sergio Azenha / Alamy Stock Photo; p41: age fotostock / Alamy Stock Photo; p42: Sally and Richard Greenhill / Alamy Stock Photo; p43: Godong / Alamy Stock Photo; p44: AXINITE / Alamy Stock Photo; p45: Aubord Dulac / Shutterstock; p45: Volt Collection / Shutterstock; p46: Marmaduke St. John / Alamy Stock Photo; p46: Zvonimir Atletic / Shutterstock; p48: Martin Holek / Shutterstock; p50: FILIPPO MONTEFORTE/AFP/Getty Images); p49: Zvonimir Atletic / Shutterstock; p51: www.BibleLandPictures.com / Alamy Stock Photo; p52: Sample / Alamy Stock Photo; p52: WDG Photo / Shutterstock; p53: 67photo / Alamy Stock Photo; p54: Joe Raedle/Getty Images; p56: CAFOD; p55: DOE Photo / Alamy Stock Photo; p57: Friedrich Stark / Alamy Stock Photo; p58: WordonFire; p58: neneo / shutterstock; p59: ZUMA Press, Inc. / Alamy Stock Photo; p63: OPIS / iStockphoto; p65: classicpaintings / Alamy Stock Photo; p65: Godong / Alamy Stock Photo; p64: North Wind Picture Archives / Alamy Stock Photo; p67: Phil Wills / Alamy Stock Photo; p68: Ishara S.KODIKARA/AFP/Getty Images; p69: epa european pressphoto agency b.v. / Alamy Stock Photo; p70: duchy / Shutterstock; p71: Corbis; p72: Spencer Platt/Getty Images for Caritas; p73: Pierre-Yves Babelon / Shutterstock; p74: imageBROKER / Alamy Stock Photo; p76: robertharding / Alamy Stock Photo; p75: ASP Religion / Alamy Stock Photo; p77: Renata Sedmakova / Shutterstock; p78: The Bridgeman Art Library; p79: Shawn Hempel / Shutterstock; p79: federicofoto / iStockphoto; p80: NOEL CELIS/AFP/Getty Images; p81: AoS / www.apostleshipofthesea.org.uk; p82: INTERFOTO / Alamy Stock Photo; p83: Nemeziya / Shutterstock; p86: Ian G Dagnall / Alamy Stock Photo; p86: Scott Olson/Getty Images; p87: zodebala / Getty Images; p88: Justyna Pszczolka / Alamy Stock Photo; p88: Alejandro Mendoza R / Shutterstock; p89: MarioPonta / Alamy Stock Photo; p89: age fotostock / Alamy Stock Photo; p90: small_frog / iStockphoto; p90: Felipe Caparrós Cruz / iStockphoto; p91: Grzegorz Galazka\Archivio Grzegorz Galazka\Mondadori Portfolio via Getty Images; p92: Olga_Anourina / Shutterstock; p93: © 2008 Sr Mary Stephen CRSS and McCrimmon Publishing Co. Ltd.; p93: federico rostagno / 123RF; p93: Cosmin-Constantin Sava / 123RF; p94: Corbis; p95: Mark Schwettmann / Shutterstock; p96: federicofoto / 123RF; p96: Zvonimir Atletic / Shutterstock; p97: Brigida Soriano / Shutterstock; p97: Dariush M / Shutterstock; p98: Linda Kennedy / Alamy Stock Photo; p98: oriontrail / Shutterstock; p99: PjrTravel / Alamy Stock Photo; p99: Jeffrey Blackler / Alamy Stock Photo; p100: PURPLE MARBLES YORK 1 / Alamy Stock Photo; p100: Kippa Matthews/REX/Shutterstock; p101: Kippa Matthews/REX/Shutterstock; p102: Agencja Fotograficzna Caro / Alamy Stock Photo; p102: Phoenix Tenebra / Shutterstock; p103: Spencer Grant / Alamy Stock Photo; p106: hikrcn / Shutterstock; p106: NOAH SEELAM/AFP/Getty Images; p108: James R. Martin / Shutterstock; p109: Q2A Media; p110: Bianda Ahmad Hisham / Shutterstock; p111: jeep2499 / Shutterstock; p112: Paul Quezada-Neiman / Demotix / Demotix/Press Association Images; p113: Tom Gowanlock / Shutterstock; p113: Shutterstock; p114: wayfarerlife / Shutterstock; p115: Fresnel / Shutterstock; p115: oversnap / Getty Images; p116: Aviator70 / iStockphoto; p117: Calavision / Shutterstock; p118: ollirg / Shutterstock; p119: Leila Ablyazova / Shutterstock; p120: BERKO85 / iStockphoto; p121: Roman Sakhno / Shutterstock; p121: Astrid Gast / iStockphoto; p122: ZUMA Press, Inc. / Alamy Stock Photo; p123: Juanmonino / iStockphoto; p124: Corbis; p126: bikeriderlondon / Shutterstock; p127: Yavuz Arslan/ullstein bild via Getty Images; p130: Pawel Bienkowski / Alamy Stock Photo; p131: Mansoreh / Shutterstock; p131: nakorn / Shutterstock; p132: Matyas Rehak / Shutterstock; p132: The Bridgeman Art Library; p133: VIDALUZ/ullstein bild via Getty Images; p134: Peter Horree / Alamy Stock Photo; p135: AfricaImages / iStockphoto; p136: hikrcn / Shutterstock; p137: Grapheast / Alamy Stock Photo; p138: Jacques van Dinteren / iStockphoto; p138: Romolo Tavani / Shutterstock; p139: Joel Carillet / iStockphoto; p140: Julio Etchart / Alamy Stock Photo; p141: gaborbasch / iStockphoto; p141: ton koene / Alamy Stock Photo; p142: Ozkan Bilgin/Anadolu Agency/Getty Images; p143: Abid Katib/Getty Images; p143: rasoul ali / Getty Images; p143: epa european pressphoto agency b.v. / Alamy Stock Photo; p144: ASIF HASSAN/AFP/Getty Images; p145: Maskot / Getty Images; p146: MARCO LONGARI/AFP/Getty Images; p147: epa european pressphoto agency b.v. / Alamy Stock Photo; p147: mirzavisoko / Shutterstock; p148: JOAT / Shutterstock; p149: Peter Macdiarmid/Getty Images; p152: VlLevi / iStockphoto; p154: trubavin / iStockphoto; p155: Samuel Perry / p156: graphixmania; p157: Eitan Simanor / Alamy Stock Photo; p158: Joel Carillet / iStockphoto; p159: ArtMari / Shutterstock; p160: Jim West / Alamy Stock Photo; p160: photo.ua / Shutterstock; p161: The Bridgeman Art Library; p162: Duncan Walker / iStockphoto; p162: Burgeon / iStockphoto; p164: Art Directors & TRIP / Alamy Stock Photo; p165: asafta / iStockphoto; p166: LiAndStudio / Shutterstock; p167: VlLevi / iStockphoto; p168: Design Pics/Ron Nickel/Getty Images; p169: Fulcanelli / Shutterstock; p170: TravelCollection / Alamy Stock Photo; p171: Jim West / Alamy Stock Photo; p172: Ira Berger / Alamy Stock Photo; p172: robert_s / Shutterstock; p176: Elizabeth Leyden / Alamy Stock Photo; p176: Gregory Rec/Portland Press Herald via Getty Images; p177: Image Source / Alamy Stock Photo; p178: Israel Images / Alamy Stock Photo; p179: david sanger photography / Alamy Stock Photo; p180: Kosher, London Bet Din; p181: Richard T. Nowitz / Getty Images; p181: Lara65 / iStockphoto; p182: SchalkKlee / iStockphoto; p183: Terry Wilson / iStockphoto; p183: Ira Berger / Alamy Stock Photo; p184: dpa picture alliance archive / Alamy Stock Photo; p185: Eitan Simanor / Alamy Stock Photo; p187: Mishella / Shutterstock; p186: Nancy Louie / iStockphoto; p186: Design Pics Inc / Alamy Stock Photo; p187: JosefPirkl / Shutterstock; p188: R. Roth / Shutterstock; p189: r.classen / Shutterstock; p190: S1001 / Shutterstock; p191: Ethan Myerson / iStockphoto; p192: Chameleons Eye/REX/Shutterstock; p193: Alamy Stock Photo; p193: Yevgenia Gorbulsky / Alamy Stock Photo; p194: Liudmila Chernova / iStockphoto; p195: Craevschii Family / Shutterstock; p196: Fat Jackey / Shutterstock; p196: Eddie Gerald / Alamy Stock Photo; p197: Godong / Alamy Stock Photo; p197: V. Dorosz / Alamy Stock Photo; p200: Eval Bartov / Alamy Stock Photo; p200: Monkey Business Images / Shutterstock; p202: BlueSkyImage / S̶̶̶̶̶; p202: FineArt / Alamy Stock Photo; p203: Richard Lowthian / Shutterstock; p2̶̶̶̶ ̶̶̶̶̶ ̶̶̶̶̶ny Stock Photo; p205: CountrySideCollection - Homer Sykes / Alamy Stock Phot̶ ̶̶̶̶̶ ̶̶̶̶/ Shutterstock; p207: Noradoa / Shutterstock; p208: jozef sedmak / Alamy Sto̶ ̶̶̶̶̶̶̶soeva / Shutterstock; p210: Paladin12 / Shutterstock; p211: Eddies Images / Shu̶̶ ̶̶̶̶̶ean Drobot / Shutterstock; p213: David Carillet / Shutterstock; p214: 3Dalia / Shutterstock; p215: DE̶̶̶̶ ̶̶N RAVENSWAAY/SCIENCE PHOTO LIBRARY; p216: Dustie / Shutterstock; p217: Lisa S. / Shutterstock; p218: winnond / Shutterstock; p219: Design Pics Inc / Alamy Stock Photo; p222: Chris Clark / Alamy Stock Photo; p223: Patrick Ward / Alamy Stock Photo; p224: Sipa Press/REX/Shutterstock; p224: Marmaduke St. John / Alamy Stock Photo; p225: Flashon Studio / Shutterstock; p225: bikeriderlondon / Shutterstock; p227: Phase4Studios / Shutterstock; p227: Christopher Futcher / Getty Images; p228: Vikulin /

Shutterstock; p228: Donna Day / Getty Images; p228: India Picture / Shutterstock; p228: Monkey Business Images / Shutterstock; p230: OJO Images Ltd / Alamy Stock Photo; p230: Photographee.eu / Shutterstock; p231: Godong / Alamy Stock Photo; p232: Kais Tolmats / iStockphoto; p232: Rolls Press/Popperfoto/Getty Images; p233: Stephen Barnes/Society / Alamy Stock Photo; p234: OUP RF; p235: Photographee.eu / Shutterstock; p236: Eyal Bartov / Alamy Stock Photo; p237: Alena Ozerova / Shutterstock; p237: Monkey Business Images / Shutterstock; p239: jon ryan / Alamy Stock Photo; p238: The Bridgeman Art Library; p242: Godong / Alamy Stock Photo; p242: PRISMA ARCHIVO / Alamy Stock Photo; p244: aquariagirl1970 / Shutterstock; p245: Mike Flippo / Shutterstock; p245: The Bridgeman Art Library; p247: Godong / Alamy Stock Photo; p248: Ed Buziak / Alamy Stock Photo; p249: Anneka / Shutterstock; p250: PRISMA ARCHIVO / Alamy Stock Photo; p251: Richard Wayman / Alamy Stock Photo; p252: Art Directors & TRIP / Alamy Stock Photo; p253: Yuriy Chertok / Shutterstock; p253: The National Trust Photolibrary / Alamy Stock Photo; p254: Joe Vogan / Alamy Stock Photo; p255: jozef sedmak / Alamy Stock Photo; p256: irisphoto1 / Shutterstock; p257: Cultura Creative (RF) / Alamy Stock Photo; p258: Ros Drinkwater / Alamy Stock Photo; p258: PRISMA ARCHIVO / Alamy Stock Photo; p259: Ozornina / Shutterstock; p260: photo.ua / Shutterstock; p261: Andrey_Kuzmin / Shutterstock; p262: doulos / iStockphoto; p263: The Bridgeman Art Library; p266: Ekkachai / Shutterstock; p267: Corbis; p268: PhotoStock-Israel / Alamy Stock Photo; p269: Isaac gil / Shutterstock; p270: Maslov Dmitry / Shutterstock; p270: pzAxe / Shutterstock; p270: S. M. Beagle / Shutterstock; p270: VAV / Shutterstock; p271: SAFIN HAMED/AFP/Getty Images; p272: KenTannenbaum / iStockphoto; p273: Peter Treanor / Alamy Stock Photo; p274: CHOATphotographer / Shutterstock; p275: Lebrecht Music and Arts Photo Library / Alamy Stock Photo; p276: Colin Underhill / Alamy Stock Photo; p277: Peter Horree / Alamy Stock Photo; p278: The Bridgeman Art Library; p279: The Bridgeman Art Library; p280: The Bridgeman Art Library; p281: Chronicle / Alamy Stock Photo; p281: DEA PICTURE LIBRARY / Getty Images; p282: Studio-Annika / iStockphoto; p282: Lisa S. / Shutterstock; p283: Granger Historical Picture Archive / Alamy Stock Photo; p284: Tim Graham / Alamy Stock Photo; p284: Alenq / Shutterstock; p285: epa european pressphoto agency b.v. / Alamy Stock Photo;

We are grateful to the authors and publishers for use of extracts from their titles and in particular for the following:

Scripture quotations taken from The Revised Standard Version of the Bible: Catholic Edition, copyright © 1965, 1966 the Division of Christian Education of the National Council of the Churches of Christ in the United States of America. Used by permission. All rights reserved; Excerpts from Catechism of the Catholic Church, http://www.vatican.va/archive/ccc_css/archive/catechism/ccc_toc.htm (Strathfield, NSW: St Pauls, 2000). © Libreria Editrice Vaticana. Reproduced with permission from The Vatican; Excerpts from The Qur'an OWC translated by M. A. S. Abdel Haleem (Oxford University Press, 2008). © M. A. S. Abdel Haleem 2004, 2005. Reproduced with permission from Oxford University Press; Excerpts from The Stone Edition of the Tanach (Mesorah Publications, 2010). Reproduced with permission from ArtScroll/Mesorah Publications, Ltd; A. Cline: Religion, Atheism, Family Values: Are Religion & God Needed for Family Values? (About Inc., 2016). Reproduced with permission from About.com; St Teresa of Avila: The Collected Works of St Teresa of Avila, Volume One, translated by Kieran Kavanaugh and Otilio Rodriguez (Institute of Carmelite Studies, 1976). © 1976 Washington Province of Discalced Carmelites.www.icspublications.org Reproduced with permission from the Institute of Carmelite Studies; Bishop P. Doyle: A Word from Family Groups' Patron, http://www.catholicfamily.org.uk/related-work/parish-family-groups (Catholic Bishops' Conference of England and Wales, 2014). Reproduced with permission from Marriage & Family Life Project Officer, Catholic Bishops' Conference of England and Wales; British Humanist Association: A Humanist Discussion of… Environmental Issues, http://humanismforschools.org.uk/pdfs/Family%20Matters.pdf (British Humanist Association, 2016). Reproduced with permission from the British Humanist Association; British Humanist Association: A Humanist Discussion of… Family Matters, http://humanismforschools.org.uk/pdfs/environmental%20 issues.pdf (British Humanist Association, 2016). Reproduced with permission from the British Humanist Association; British Humanist Association: Marriage Laws, https://humanism.org.uk/campaigns/human-rights-and-equality/marriage-laws/ (British Humanist Association, 2016). Reproduced with permission from the British Humanist Association; CAFOD: CAFOD website, www.CAFOD.org.uk (CAFOD, 2016). Reproduced with permission from CAFOD; Church of England: Medical Ethics & Health and Social Care Policy: Contraception (Church of England, 2016). © Archbishops' Council 2016. Reproduced with permission from The Archbishops' Council; Congregation for the Doctrine of the Faith: The Nicene-Constantinople Creed Formula to adopt from now on in cases in which the Profession of Faith is prescribed by law in substitution of the Tridentine formula and the oath against modernism, 17th July 1967 (The Vatican, 1967). © Libreria Editrice Vaticana. Reproduced with permission from The Vatican; Council of Trent: Session XXV "On the Invocation of Saints", 1563, (The Vatican, 2016). © Libreria Editrice Vaticana. Reproduced with permission from The Vatican; Libreria Editrice Vaticana, Secretary of State: Pontifical Yearbook 2013, (The Vatican, 2013). © Libreria Editrice Vaticana. Reproduced with permission from The Vatican; Dr C. Mercer: Average Number of Partners (graphic), (NATSAL, 2016). Reproduced with permission from Dr Catherine Mercer for the NATSAL team; Pew Research Center: Number of Christians Rises, But Their Share of World Population Stays Stable, 22nd March 2013, (Pew Research Center, 2013). Reproduced with permission from Pew Research Center; Pontifical Biblical Commission: The Interpretation of the Bible in the Church, presented to Pope John Paul II on 23rd April 1993, (The Vatican, 1993). © Libreria Editrice Vaticana. Reproduced with permission from The Vatican; Pope Benedict XVI: Angelus, Feast of the Holy Family, 27 December 2009, (The Vatican, 2009). © Libreria Editrice Vaticana. Reproduced with permission from The Vatican; Pope Benedict XVI: Deus Caritas Est, December 25th 2005 (The Vatican, 2005). © Libreria Editrice Vaticana. Reproduced with permission from The Vatican; Pope Francis: The Infinite Tenderness of God: Meditations on the Gospels, (Word Among Us Press, 2016). © Libreria Editrice Vaticana. Reproduced with permission from The Vatican; Pope Francis: Evangelii Gaudium, On the Proclamation of the Gospel in Today's World, November 24th 2013, (The Vatican, 2013). © Libreria Editrice Vaticana. Reproduced with permission from The Vatican; Pope Francis: Press Conference of Pope Francis During the Return Flight, Papal Flight 28th July 2013 (The Vatican, 2013). © Libreria Editrice Vaticana. Reproduced with permission from The Vatican; Pope John Paul II: Letter to the Bishops of the Catholic Church on the Collaboration of Men and Women in the Church and in the World, 31st July 2004 (The Vatican, 2004). © Libreria Editrice Vaticana. Reproduced with permission from The Vatican; Pope John Paul II: Apostolic Letter, 22nd May 1994 (The Vatican, 1994). © Libreria Editrice Vaticana. Reproduced with permission from The Vatican; Pope John Paul II: Address at the Opening of the 19th Ordinary Plenary Assembly of the Latin American Episcopal Council (CELAM), 9th March 1983, L'Osservatore Romano English edition, 18th April 1983 (The Vatican, 1983). © Libreria Editrice Vaticana. Reproduced with permission from The Vatican; Pope John Paul II: Familaris Consortio, On the Role of the Christian Family In The Modern World, November 22nd 1981 (The Vatican, 1981). © Libreria Editrice Vaticana. Reproduced with permission from The Vatican; Pope Paul VI: Dei Verbum, Dogmatic Constitution on Divine Revelation, November 18th 1965 (The Vatican, 1965). © Libreria Editrice Vaticana. Reproduced with permission from The Vatican; Pope Paul VI: Gaudium et Spes, Pastoral Constitution on the Church in the Modern World, December 7th, 1965 (The Vatican, 1965). © Libreria Editrice Vaticana. Reproduced with permission from The Vatican; Pope Paul VI: Lumen Gentium, Dogmatic Constitution on the Church, November 21st 1964 (The Vatican, 1964). © Libreria Editrice Vaticana. Reproduced with permission from The Vatican; Pope Paul VI: Sacrosanctum Concilium, Constitution on the Sacred Liturgy, December 4th 1963 (The Vatican, 1963). © Libreria Editrice Vaticana. Reproduced with permission from The Vatican; D. Stroik: quote, (D. Stroik, 2016). Reproduced with permission from Duncan, G. Stoik; UNICEF: 'A League Table of Teenage Births in Rich Nations', Innocenti Report Card No.3, July 2001. (UNICEF Innocenti Research Centre, Florence, 2001). Reproduced with permission from UNICEF.

We have made every effort to trace and contact all copyright holders before publication, but if notified of any errors or omissions, the publisher will be happy to rectify these at the earliest opportunity.